India's Living Constitution

Ideas, Practices, Controversies

Anthem South Asian Studies
Series Editor: Crispin Bates

A selection of our other titles in the series:

Mills, Jim (ed) *Subaltern Sports* (2005)

Joshi, Chitra *Lost Worlds: Indian Labour and its Forgotten Histories* (2005)

Dasgupta, Biplab, *European Trade and Colonial Conquests* (2005)

Kaur, Raminder *Performative Politics and the Cultures of Hinduism* (2005)

Rosenstein, Lucy *New Poetry in Hindi* (2004)

Shah, Ghanshyam, *Caste and Democratic Politics in India* (2004)

Van Schendel, Willem *The Bengal Borderland: Beyond State and Nation in South Asia* (2004)

India's Living Constitution

Ideas, Practices, Controversies

EDITED BY
ZOYA HASAN
E. SRIDHARAN
R. SUDARSHAN

Anthem Press
London

Anthem Press
An imprint of Wimbledon Publishing Company
75–76 Blackfriars Road,
London SE1 8HA

or

PO Box 9779, London SW19 7ZG
www.anthempress.com

This edition first published by Anthem Press 2005
First published by Permanent Black 2002

British Library Cataloguing in Publication Data
A catalogue record for this book is available from the British Library.

Library of Congress Cataloging in Publication Data
A catalog record for this book has been requested.

1 3 5 7 9 10 8 6 4 2

ISBN 1 84331 136 4 (Hbk)
ISBN 1 84331 137 2 (Pbk)

Typeset by Footprint Labs Ltd, London
www.footprintlabs.com

Printed in India

In memory of T.V. Satyamurthy, political scientist and iconoclast, who embodied much that is 'wild in human nature and warm in the human heart'.

CONTENTS

PREFACE

This volume originated in the felt need for an exploration of the terms of discourse in Indian constitutionalism and politics at the turn of the century and millennium, the completion of fifty years of the existence of the Indian constitution, and a little over half a century of Indian independence. An earlier book—the one that provided inspiration for this enterprise—though sharing points in common, is very different from our volume: T.V. Sathyamurthy's four-volume work titled *Social Change and Political Discourse in India: Structures of Power, Movements of Resistance* (Delhi: Oxford University Press). The Sathyamurthy project was conceived as a large collective at the end of the 1980s against the backdrop of four decades of Congress Party hegemony in independent India, a bipolar world order with India situated in the non-aligned space, four decades of slow growth in a state-regulated import-substitution-oriented mixed economy, and a decade and more of subaltern social movements.[1]

The political landscape a decade later, in the early years of the new century, was so different as to be almost unrecognizable. While the constitution completed fifty years on 26 January 2000 with its basic structure intact, India had five general elections from late 1989 to late 1999, all resulting in hung parliaments, leading to over a decade of mostly minority and/or coalition governments. Since 1996, India has had the largest coalition governments, in terms of the number of parties, in the world. Since 1998, the ruling coalition has been led by the Bharatiya Janata Party (BJP), which had never crossed the ten percent vote share mark until November 1989, but has since risen to almost a quarter of the vote and the status of single largest party in the lower house of parliament. This is also a party whose ideology is essentially at odds with the secular, liberal-pluralist vision and basic structure of the constitution. Indeed, the BJP-led National Democratic Alliance government set up a National Committee to Review the Working of the Constitution, as an executive decision, bypassing parliament and initiating a move opposed by the major opposition parties. This committee presented its report two years later, in early 2002.

Along with this development has been the decline of the Congress Party, still the largest in vote share, to a little over a quarter of the vote, and second in seats, and the rise of a diversity of single state-based parties. These developments have been paralleled by the rise of new social movements and currents—the Hindutva ideology of the BJP and its allied organizations; the political assertiveness of the Other Backward Classes (really castes) and Scheduled Castes, and a powerful secessionist movement in Kashmir. They have also been paralleled by over a decade of economic liberalisation since 1991 (still continuing), an associated burgeoning of the middle classes and integration with the world economy, and the growth of cable and satellite television and international cultural and ideological influences as a part of globalisation. All this has been in the context of the collapse of the bipolar world order and the rise of unchallenged Western dominance, led by the United States, the collapse of authoritarian regimes of diverse kinds, and the spread of democracy around the world.

Against this background, it was felt that fifty years of the Indian constitution and democracy—a major achievement in a developing country without the generally accepted prerequisites for stable democracy, and one that requires an explanation by social scientists—required an exploration of the terms of discourse of Indian constitutionalism and politics as well as analysis of the career of the democratic ideas, organizing concepts and vision explicitly present in, or implied in, the constitution. The idea originated with R. Sudarshan, Zoya Hasan and Satish Saberwal, later including E. Sridharan, and was hammered out over several meetings in 1999. The University of Pennsylvania Institute for the Advanced Study of India (UPIASI) took it up as a project. The Ford Foundation agreed to support the project financially, making a grant to the Center for the Advanced Study of India (CASI), University of Pennsylvania, which subcontracted the grant to UPIASI. UPIASI organized an international conference, which was held over 23–25 January 2000, on the eve of the fiftieth anniversary of the constitution, as well as follow-up work on the volume. The present book consists of revised and updated papers presented at that conference.

We are grateful to the Ford Foundation for its financial support to the project, particularly to Mark Robinson, Program Officer, Local Governance and Civil Society. We would like to thank Francine Frankel, Director, CASI, University of Pennsylvania, for facilitating UPIASI's implementation of the project; S. K. Singh, Secretary-General, UPIASI, for his enthusiastic overall support; Satish Saberwal, who has contributed the introductory essay, for his contribution to developing the project proposal; and Fali S. Nariman, M. P. and legal luminary, for delivering the keynote address. We are grateful to

Adil Tyabji for copyediting the manuscript; to Reuben Israel for technical support; and to the UPIASI staff, S. D. Gosain, Ruchika Ahuja and Supan Manjhi. And last but not least to the contributors who attended the conference and who have since rewritten the essays that comprise this volume.

End Notes

1. The four volumes edited by T. V. Sathyamurthy, collectively called, Social Change and Political Discourse in India: Structures of Power, Movements of Resistance, Volumes 1–4, are: *State and Nation in the Context of Social Change*, Delhi: Oxford University Press, 1994; *Industry and Agriculture in India Since Independence*, Delhi: Oxford University Press, 1995; *Religion, Region, Caste, Gender and Culture in Contemporary India*, Delhi: Oxford University Press, 1996; *Class Formation and Political Transformation in Post-colonial India*, Delhi: Oxford University Press, 1996.

Notes on Contributors

Javeed Alam teaches Political Philosophy at the Centre for European Studies, Central Institute of English and Foreign Languages, Hyderabad. Earlier, he taught at Himachal Pradesh University, Shimla, for twenty-five years. His most recent publication is *India: Living with Modernity* (1999).

Granville Austin has studied India through its constitutional development. He has published two major histories on the subject. The first describes the constitution's framing; the second its working from 1950 to 1985, entitled, *Working a Democratic Constitution—The Indian Experience*. He holds a D. Phil. degree from Oxford University.

Upendra Baxi, Professor of Law, Warwick University, has been vice-chancellor of the universities of Delhi and South Gujarat. His most recent publication is the *Future of Human Rights* (2002).

Rajeev Bhargava is Professor of Political Theory and Indian Political Thought at Delhi University, and Honorary Director, Programme for Advanced Social and Political Theory, Centre for the Study of Developing Societies, Delhi. He taught at Jawaharlal Nehru University for over twenty years. His publications include *Individualism in Social Science* (1992) and, as editor, *Secularism and its Critics* (1998).

Neera Chandhoke is Professor, Department of Political Science, Delhi University. She specialises in comparative politics and political theory. She is the author of *State and Civil Society: Explorations in Political Theory* (1995) and *Beyond Secularism: The Rights of Religious Minorities* (1999). She is a contributor on public affairs to newspapers and also writes on the politics of developing countries.

Peter Ronald deSouza is Professor and Head of the Department of Political Science, Goa University, and Adjunct Fellow, Centre for the Study of Developing Societies. He looks at puzzles of democratic politics, especially those concerning India, and has worked on issues such as righting historical wrongs, the banning of books, the idea of the 'political', the political responsibility of intellectuals, and the dynamics of decentralised democracy in India. He has recently edited *Contemporary India: Transitions* (2000).

Marc Galanter, John and Rhylla Bossard Professor of Law and South Asian Studies at the University of Wisconsin-Madison and LSE Centennial Professor at the London School of Economics, studies lawyers, litigation and legal culture. He is the author of *Competing Equalities: Law and the Backward Classes in India* (1984) and *Law and Society in Modern India* (1991).

Zoya Hasan is Professor of Political Science, Centre for Political Studies, and Director of the Women's Studies Programme, Jawaharlal Nehru University, New Delhi. Her books include *Quest for Power: Oppositional Movements and Post-Congress Politics in Uttar Pradesh* (1998), and, as editor, *Politics and the State in India* (2000) and *Parties and Party Politics in India* (2002). She is co-editor of *Transforming India: Social and Political Dynamics of Democracy* (2001).

Sunil Khilnani, formerly Professor of Politics at Birkbeck College, University of London, is currently Professor of Politics and Director, South Asia Studies, at the Nitze School of Advanced International Studies of the Johns Hopkins University in Washington DC. He is the author of *Arguing Revolution: The Intellectual Left in Post-War France* (1993) and *The Idea of India* (2nd edition, 1999). He is co-editor of *Civil Society: History and Possibilities* (2001).

Pratap Bhanu Mehta is Professor of Philosophy and of Law and Governance, Jawaharlal Nehru University. He was previously Associate Professor of Government and Social Studies at Harvard University. He has published numerous articles in political philosophy, the history of political thought, social theory, and constitutional law and politics in India. He is the author of *Consolations of Modernity* (forthcoming) and *Facing Democracy* (forthcoming).

Martha Nussbaum is Ernst Freund Distinguished Service Professor of Law and Ethics at the University of Chicago, and the director of its new Center for Comparative Constitutionalism and the Implementation of Constitutional Rights. Her most recent books are *Women and Human Development: The Capabilities Approach* (2000) and *Upheavals of Thought: The Intelligence of Emotions* (2001).

Satish Saberwal was Professor of Sociology at the Centre for Historical Studies, Jawaharlal Nehru University, New Delhi. He has done fieldwork among the Embu of central Kenya (1963–4) and in a Punjabi industrial town (1969, 1989), and has read about Europe, Islam, India and China.

E. Sridharan is Academic Director of the University of Pennsylvania Institute for the Advanced Study of India, New Delhi. He is a political scientist with diverse research interests, including party systems and coalition politics and the political economy of development. He is the author of *The Political Economy of Industrial Promotion: Indian, Brazilian and Korean Electronics in Comparative Perspective 1969–1994* (1996) and numerous papers and book chapters.

R. Sudarshan is Senior Governance Advisor to the UNDP in Indonesia, and has served the UNDP since 1991, heading divisions in the India Office dealing with public policy and human development. An alumus of the Delhi School of Economics, he was a Rhodes Scholar at Balliol College, Oxford, and a research fellow at St. John's College, Cambridge, where he worked on judicial review of economic legislation. He has been a Program Officer for Human Rights and Governance in the Ford Foundation's South Asia office.

A. Vaidyanathan has been with the Madras Institute of Development Studies since 1984. He has worked at the Centre for Development Studies, Trivandrum, and the Planning Commission. His research work covers agricultural development; poverty assessment and policy; employment; data base of the Indian economy; and macro aspects of development strategy. He has written extensively on these subjects.

Douglas V. Verney is Professor Emeritus of Political Science at York University, Toronto, and Adjunct Professor, South Asia Regional Studies at the University of Pennsylvania. He is the author of five books, among them *British Government and Politics: Life without a Declaration of Independence* (1976) and *Three Civilizations, Two Cultures, One State: Canada's Political Traditions* (1986). He has co-edited *Multiple Identities in a Single State: Indian Federalism in Comparative Perspective* (1995). In recent years he has published articles on comparative parliamentary and federal systems in American, British, Canadian and Indian journals and is currently working on a book titled, *Choosing a Regime: Eight Major Models*.

1

INTRODUCTION
Civilization, Constitution, Democracy

SATISH SABERWAL

This volume seeks, as the seminar that laid the groundwork for it sought, to review the working of the constitution of India during its first half century, and to look towards the future. In these appraisals, the tumbler can be seen to be both half full and half empty. The constitution was produced speedily, and it has thus far survived without major damage for two generations, yet sections of Indian society continue to have major difficulties in reconciling themselves with its core principles. What remains undone, or has gone wrong, may be pinned on particular actors—persons or categories—but some of the gaps and malfunctioning may also be tracked to long-standing features of society and history.

A society's key organizational principles evolve gradually; and this was the more so before the printing press, the communication revolutions, and all the other churning of our times. This introductory essay seeks to place India's extraordinary experience in constitution-making, and its aftermath, in relation to the long-term processes and structures, going back to the first millennium of the Common Era.[1] It begins by sketching in the civilizational setting, and then considers the implications of the colonial experience. The experience disempowered Indians, yet it was part of a much wider civilizational encounter with the West, opening out to much that Indians found in tune with their own predilections.

The experience of colonialism included encounters with arrogant

Europeans, and their sometimes racist nineteenth-century attitudes. To the Western missionaries' humiliating criticism of indigenous traditions, the responses tended to be bifurcated, separating Muslims and Hindus, corresponding to the missionaries' different points of attack. This was one element in the nineteenth-century consolidation of identities along the religious axis; the axis that has offered some of the most potent resources for political, including electoral, mobilization on the subcontinent.[2] There was 'nationalism', and its vehicle the Indian National Congress, but in a setting as segmented as India's, finding adequate space for all the fragments in a simple nationalism has not been easy, as the post-1947 history of Pakistan and India powerfully demonstrates. Given their numbers, growing wealth, and other markers of potential power, much larger fractions of Hindus than of Muslims felt comfortable within the 'nationalist' Indian National Congress. Partition, and the moment of Independence, were to punctuate the making of the constitution. All this has to be noted, indicatively, for the earlier difficulties associated with assertive religious identities have continued into later public life and political processes, posing difficult issues for the constitutional regime too.

This Introduction has three parts. Part 1 considers the wider civilizational setting, and some of its transformations during the colonial period; part 2 addresses a specific puzzle concerning the constitution: how to account for the ease and the speed with which it was drafted; its relatively steady course amidst tumultuous changes in Indian society; and the relatively orderly functioning of 'democratic' processes and civil society in India during this period; and part 3 previews the other essays in this volume.

PART 1: THE CIVILIZATIONAL SETTING

We could begin by recognizing that by the twentieth century India had an astoundingly complex society—because of its fabled capacity to absorb all manner of diversities. The secret of that capacity lay in the caste system: what was different could stay in its own niche without having to conform to what happened in other niches within the whole. Political order in this milieu rested partly on internal regulation within the countless niches, and partly on rights of conquest: which would be acknowledged not merely at an imperial level but also, simultaneously, at various levels lower down. The setting has had no parallel in history.

Complexity and diversity are not however unmixed blessings. Indic civilization has had this extraordinary social mechanism, the caste system, which, accommodating diversity, could enble the complexity to keep growing; but it had no clear routines, or institutional loci, to simplify its arrangements, to reduce that complexity. The powerful Indic tug towards cellular complexity sets it apart from other major civilizations: Chinese, Islamic, European.

A one-way journey into increasing complexity had pitched India into a cul-de-sac, a civilizational dead end. The division of labour between caste groups underlay an agrarian order producing sufficient wealth to support state structures, a learned class, wide-ranging commerce, and varied forms of creative literature and the arts, together adding up to a major civilization. The bountiful wealth it produced was also a magnet, powerful and permanent, drawing in merchants, adventurers, and conquerors from far and wide. Their presence added to the complexity of Indian society. Elsewhere I have explored the costs of its segmentation: the difficulties in political mobilization beyond a point, and the arrest of particular forms of learning and creativitiy within jati, caste, groups, or even smaller entities.[3]

The idea of the Kshatriya, the warrior, came to be embodied in the Rajput, the jati constituted out of ruling families during the first millennium; a jati that took fighting, conquering, and governing as its hereditary occupation. It gave its name to the region called Rajputana, the latter-day Rajasthan, but with its delicate blanket enveloped at least all north India. Its frameworks for mobilizing force, and for governing, relied heavily on personal bonds, principally of kinship and marriage. It was difficult to extend these bonds beyond the web of ties which their leader could personally oversee; but equally an individual's followers could switch to a rival Rajput whose bid for power could lead to an equally legitimate dynasty. Considering the size of the subcontinent, the Rajput states tended to be small or fragile or both.[4]

The theatre of state formation in north India featured another set of actors. Horse-rearing nomadic warriors from the Central Asian steppe have long supplied waves of conquerors for the settled civilizations to their south and west: China, India, Iran. The Brahmins, and the literati castes, in India were willing to serve the conquerors impartially, as were the Confucian literati in China. Difficulties arose with the Sultanate, and later the Mughals, because the new conquerors brought their own confident religious guides with them. The Brahmins' virtual exclusion from their councils had long-term consequences. Briefly, the caste order survived, and with it the Brahminical ideology. It tended, at least in large parts of northern India, to place Muslims at the margins of the caste order. There was separatism here and, as we shall see, it fed into other impulses to separatism that began to gather strength during the nineteenth century.

Men of the literati castes in medieval India were, however, willing to serve the new regimes, the late Sultanate, and more vigorously the Mughals; and some of them took to the Persian language. This introduced them to Persian literature and etiquette, and to a (limited) experience of the apparatus of governing, especially in collecting revenue. However, the 'brahmanical notion of pollution', notes Muzaffar Alam, prevented even these limited influences from entering 'the life of a Hindu beyond the threshold of the inner apartments of his house'.[5] The European encounter would cut much deeper.

The caste order, and the consequent complexity, may have led India into a civilizational dead end, yet, tucked away in its numerous social folds were two sets of resources: one set concerned the kinds of values, ideas, and attitudes that make civilizations possible. These may have seemed dormant, say, in the eighteenth century; they were not absent. The other set concerned the social bonds and the identities—and animosities—which all added up to the segmented society. These, in turn, may have seemed fixed and immutable but, given a change of scene, these became mobile and labile; the bonds, the identities, and the animosities have proved to be virtually infinitely mutable.

During the colonial period, and subseqently, both forms of resources were quickened, releasing energies of wholly unforeseen magnitudes. Within that larger framework, members of some jatis had long learned ways in which to work with men of other societies. Among them were the literati whom we just met.

The Nineteenth Century

During the colonial period, when new generations of men of literati castes—Brahmins, scribes, traders, physicians, and so forth—took to English literature, etiquette, and style of government, their ancestors' experience with Persian was in some measure repeated, but with several significant differences. In comparison, say, with Akbar, who sent his Rajput wife's nephew, Man Singh, at the head of the force that established Mughal control over eastern Bengal,[6] the British dragged their feet in inducting Indians into the highest ranks of their government.

Access to the English language did something else, something extraordinary, for the Indian literati: it gave them access to the world-views and epistemologies that had been evolving in Europe over the centuries since, and before, the Renaissance. The literati in India had, traditionally, been willing to try their hand at the language and culture of whoever happened to be the masters of the day. Now they had bumped into an alien civilzation of an exceptional cast, one that had taken to the habit of seeking conceptions of maximal generality to anchor both its social and technical arrangements. This habit had had momentous consequences in Europe: it had pushed a wide gamut of scientific activity and of technological skills; the industrial and related revolutions had generated alternative assumptions of existence; vigorous reflection had entered every nook and cranny of human experience.

However impressive the European achievement, the Indian literati saw it in its colonial visage. They found themselves up against not merely unequal power but also an arrogant, ignorant—at times racist—dismissiveness towards indigenous traditions: think of Macaulay. Embedded within this humiliation of being colonized was perceived a challenge emerging from the civilization of Europe.

In that nineteenth century colonial society arose such men as Bankim Chattopadhyay, Bhudev Mukhopadhyay, Sayyid Ahmed Khan, and Shibli Nomani[7] who were persuaded to scrutinize their own past, and also to consider the making, and the working, of European society. Bankim's novels and essays, for example, drew on the resources of thought, of authorship, and of imagination, resources both indigenous and Western, to offer a radical critique of his own tradition, of the colonial society in which he lived, and of the West. In course of this reflection on their own past, and on that of other civilizations, vitalizing urges for the future began to emerge. Values and attitudes, embedded within the several strands of their own civilization, were recovered and discussed extensively. Bankim and others went further: they visualized collective futures in terms starkly different from what they had known of their past, and they established precedents for such visualizations by later generations: 'Clearly, in [Bankim's] last novels there is a suggestion about bringing together an organized people and a directing element through their common allegiance to an ideal, a common object of political action.'[8]

By the late nineteenth century, small restless groups were active in several centres—Calcutta, Bombay, Deoband, Aligarh, Lahore, Lucknow—determined to draw upon both Western and Indian, and Islamic, traditions pragmatically in order to project for their land and their peoples ambitious visions for the future. By then, too, members of this literati were employing Western skills of scholarship to highlight the economic 'drain' and other mechanisms that, they argued, served to impoverish India and enrich Britain. A consciousness of collective Indian interests was beginning to emerge.

Something else had meanwhile been happening. The printing press, the railways, and the other new forms of communication had opened the possibility of reshaping public opinion far and wide, and doing so consciously at a pace and on a scale that had no precedent. Representations to the government, and arenas for debating issues publicly, had been emerging. All this provided impulses for restructuring Indian society—for 'social reform' if you prefer—at multiple levels: beginnings in such diverse realms as the questioning of established hierarchies, such as those in the caste order; re-thinking on gender relations; changes in how the self is defined; not to mention the arenas of power and wealth.[9]

Drifting Apart

Over the centuries, the subcontinent had seen diverse, variable patterns of relationships between Muslims and Hindus: various shared beliefs, practices, and political arrangements, as well as insolent exclusivities, especially on the part of the custodians of the respective religious traditions, each with their own absolute claims to sovereign truth. The authority, and the political interests, of the Mughal state in its heyday had prevailed over the exclusivities. With its decline in the early 1700s, the political reasons for accommodation lost some ground, allowing more room to separative stances.

Seen in the eighteenth and nineteenth centuries, there were significant differences between the internal structuring of Muslim and Hindu social spaces, an issue that can be broached here only indicatively. Even though the caste order, a scriptural tradition, pilgrimage centres, and the like covered the subcontinent, the Hindu social space through this period was, and remained, decentralized and diversified, each locality organized in its own entrenched caste order. In coping with the insecurity and the anxieties of the times, the Hindus seem to have found anchor and support within the caste order. At one level it offered the assurance of belongingness within the individual and jati, at another, it offered the possibility of drawing on networks within, and adjoining, the jati, in pursuit of a variety of purposes.

The eighteenth- and nineteenth-century Muslim social space in the subcontinent was, if anything, even more disaggregated and diversified than that of the Hindu. Urban centres like Calcutta, Hyderabad, and Madras had Urdu-speaking Muslim immigrants from the north; but most Muslims in the subcontinent—Sind, Gujarat, Punjab, Delhi and its vicinity, Bengal, Tamil Nadu, Malabar and elsewhere—were a disparate lot, speaking the local language and well integrated into their respective regional societies and their local caste orders.

Expressed differently, the social scene in early-nineteenth-century India was somewhat ambiguous. The caste-organized localities accommodated numerous groups with quite clear boundaries; and in many regions these groups partook of elements from diverse religious traditions.[10] Alongside these diffuse identities, there were the exclusivist perspectives associated with the custodians of the respective religious tradition: purist ulema at one pole; Brahmins, anxious about their own high level of purity, at the other. Each of these latter groups had its own patrons and allies.

As the nineteenth century wore on, it became increasingly clear, at least in the latter-day United Provinces, that the colonial administration would not defend the established pecking orders in many urban localities where, say, the Muslim élites had held sway in recent centuries. It proclaimed, rather, its notions of official neutrality and of 'equality'—in a society that had in fact been deeply hierarchical. Consequently, old privileges could now be challenged with impunity; hitherto quiescent Hindu groups, able now to gather crowds, became alarmingly assertive.[11]

In this milieu, the Christian challenge was thrown at both Muslims and Hindus, but the missionaries attacked them separately for their particular beliefs and practices. Their responses were correspondingly separate: Muslim and Hindu publicists found ways of stressing the glories of their respective traditions, and exchanged doctrinal barbs both with each other and with Christian missionaries.

The arrival of the new modes of communication—the printing press, post office—created channels that were to be used by several groups of visionaries, each to push its own agenda. From about the mid-nineteenth century the more potent agendas tended to be separative not integrative. Groups that did not place themselves clearly on the Muslim or the Hindu side drew special attention: on one side, the *shuddhi* campaign by the Arya Samaj, seeking to reconvert those who had earlier been converted to other faiths, including Muslims of Rajput descent in northern and western India; on the other, the campaign, centred especially in Deoband, to draw into a fuller, purer, Islamic way of life those who continued to believe in, and practice, much that came from their pre-Islamic tradition.[12]

The framework of identities and differences used to be principally local, within the caste order. Given the communications revolution, beginning to gather pace in the course of the nineteenth century, and related processes, Indians found themselves under pressure to recast their frameworks of identities and differences on larger scales. For reasons we have seen, it was the religious identities (and therefore differences) that began to be canvassed vigorously just at that time. From both poles of what had been something of a Muslim–Hindu continuum, strong, persistent pulls were being directed at those who had occupied what might be called middle ground: where an individual's principal identity would have been defined in terms of his jati, caste, not a great religious tradition. The new campaigns sought to recast these identities and differences in exclusive, religious terms, with global space–time references. By the late nineteenth century, I have argued elsewhere, a palpable bar of separation between Muslims and Hindus was beginning to form, especially in northern and eastern India.[13] By 1925, the Rashtriya Swayamsevak Sangh (RSS) would begin to add its own, sometimes violent, plans to a process that was already well under way.[14]

Only with the emergence of Gandhi did the great importance of the political reasons for mutual accommodation come to be recognized in full measure; but the social cleavage was meanwhile getting entrenched. The social base for the 'Two Nation Theory' had been laid, perhaps inadvertently, by the competing, yet convergent, labours of such institutions as the Arya Samaj, Deoband, and RSS. Significant elements in Muslim political leadership were beginning to be persuaded to distance themselves from what they saw as a Hindu-dominated national movement.

PART 2: THE CONSTITUTION AND CIVIL SOCIETY

In the event, there was Partition, and the constitution of India was framed. In an era of numerous, rather fragile, post-colonial constitutions, that in India has not done badly in underwriting both civil society and democratic politics. How did it happen? The following pages argue that this Indian achievement has been largely fortuitous. I shall discuss three key elements going into this somewhat surprising achievement: the strength of India's literati and its role in the national movement; Gandhi; and the legendary segmentation of Indian society. Resting on an accident of circumstances, I shall argue, the achievement of India's constitution, and the strength of her democracy and civil society, remain somewhat unstable.

The Literati, the National Movement, the Constitution

In the beginnings of the national movement, led by the Indian National Congress, the literati stood at the centre. The Congress was an open association, it was committed to reasoned deliberation (and not, say, to scriptural authority), non-coercively.[15] Among the domains of Western learning to which the Indian literati had been drawn was that of law. Learning Western law proved to be a dual-use, indeed a triple-use, resource: (1) Given the colonial laws of property and contract, backed by the courts and their enforceable decrees, legal skills opened the doors to a profession which, at the higher levels, could be very lucrative. (2) The (Western) language of law, it transpired, also provided an effective medium with which to engage the colonial rulers; and therefore men trained in law were drawn into salient roles in public life—and then into whatever elective bodies came to be established.

Through the 1920s and the 1930s they were also involved, as Neera Chandhoke shows in this volume, in devising constitutional schemes, anticipating the moment when the real thing would have to be done. New in India's long historical experience, they prepared for a democratic polity, taking a civil society space for granted. (3) Consequently, influential men, grounded in, and committed to, the principles underlying Western law, happened to be members of the Central Legislature when it doubled up as the Constituent Assembly in 1946, and as parliament during the decade following. Of the twenty 'most influential members of the Constituent Assembly' identified by Austin, twelve 'were lawyers or had taken law degrees'.[16] A group of votaries of Western law, elected democratically (though indirectly, on a limited franchise), came thus to dominate the process of constitution-making in India.[17] The social assumptions, and the legal techniques, that shaped the constitution were drawn from the West, almost entirely from outside India, even though the underlying purposes were emphatically Indian. This had consequences.

In different societies, there is a variable gap between the legal arrangements and the social norms and practices prevalent in society. Where the legal prescriptions pull away from the prevailing social norms and practices, the greater the gap between them, the higher the 'costs' of giving effect to legal prescriptions. The costs arise partly because the functionaries who have to apply and enforce the legal and constitutional prescriptions may not themselves believe in them. Prevailing social norms may authorize ways of acting that run counter to, ways not authorized by, the letter and the spirit of the constitution; and these alternative norms may persuade even constitutional functionaries and others to sabotage constitutional and legal prescriptions and principles.

The constitution wrote the assumptions of civil society into the foundations of the law of the land. Scraping beneath the million struggles and mutinies, one sees the contrasts between the kind of social assumptions that led to democratic constitutions, in Europe and the United States, on the one hand, and on the other the assumptions operative in the Indian social fabric as it struggles with a similar framework. Repetition may have made the terms trite, but the sharp disjunctions between the constitutional and the social designs remain to exact their daily tributes—even as these tensions generate the energies for much that changes in society.

The constitutional design assumes certain patterns of social arrangements and of individual motivations: an open society whose members would engage in dialogues over issues of common concern, relating to and appraising, one another as individuals: willing to regard one another as equals, in however restricted a sense; individuals who would devote themselves to the collective purposes of institutions, including governments, in which they were located.

Against these assumptions have been the societal realities: in countless places, mutual perceptions are heavily stereotyped; ingrained ideologies and practices are inegalitarian and hierarchical; politicians, bureaucrats, and others pursue their personal and familial advantages heedless of formally accepted collective agendas (Austin); and, as vehicles of communication, words give way, all too easily, to bullets. This gap between constitutional norms and societal realities runs like a red tape through the past fifty years, and through the chapters of this volume.

In the long view of Indian history, the cast of the Indian constitution was a surprise: not an unhappy surprise, but a surprise nonetheless. Nothing like this had happened in the past; and if a new Constituent Assembly were to be elected today, its commitment to Western legal principles would probably be weaker (though independent legal minds might be invited to advise). There is nothing automatic about the drafting of such a document, or about the kind of career it has subsequently had.[18]

Gandhi

Gandhi emerged from the literati's ranks. His father had been the chief administrator of a princely state in Kathiawad and, in the late nineteenth century, sending a talented young man to England to study law was a family's investment in its own future. His personal style drew on the forms of piety, and modes for engaging in conflict familiar in Gujarat. When he returned from South Africa in 1915, he rose to become, in less than a decade, the virtually undisputed leader of the national movement, able to challenge the Raj on a scale not seen before. The man brought to his work a quite extraordinary sense of purpose and dedication.

The Mahatma was a complex man: a man with a vigorous inner life, given to spells of silence, as he waited for his 'inner voice' to show him the way forward; a modern man willing to employ such techniques as prolonged fasting on key issues; one of the most successful public men of his century who communicated a good deal in a religious idiom, but in a manner widely seen as benign; a man steeped in his tradition, yet committed to individual responsibility—and to a personal obligation to act. He dominated Indian public life for over a quarter of a century, but always stood outside the apparatus of state. As a public man of reasoned deliberation, he led numerous mass movements, but insisted on their remaining non-violent; and he promoted, too, numerous voluntary initiatives, in a prototypic civil society for engaging in 'constructive' work among the lowest castes, among hill or tribal peoples, in the area of cottage industries, and so forth.

I see Gandhi as another surprise, an historic 'accident': his personality was the fortuitous product of very personal responses to a range of experiences in India, England, and South Africa—and to numerous other stimuli, including Tolstoy. Surely he was not internally shaped in any detail by Indian institutions. No one even remotely comparable with his mix of renunciation, public activity, and charisma has appeared on the Indian scene during several centuries preceding him, nor during the half century since the day he was assassinated.[19]

One momentous consequence of Gandhi was that his example introduced the idea of the renouncer into public life. The role model he provided built on that of the sadhu, yet one who would engage fully in public activity.[20] I do not deny the damage done to our Republic by the rampant corruption of recent decades; this has to be set against the continuing resistance to this corruption in, and of, public life, and the continuing examples of integrity and idealim. Much of this latter has been inspired by Gandhi's legacy.

Throughout the nineteenth century, the possibility of mobilizing around caste and religious identities was becoming clear all over the subcontinent. As Gandhi cast about for axes along which to draw people into the national movement, he tried religion, most explicitly during the Khilafat movement, and also the jati groups, through his choice of key lieutenants. While Gandhi worked with the structure of society as it was then, he also worked actively both against communal divisiveness and against untouchability, and therefore against caste ideology as a whole, even though his earlier writings had suggested a wish to salvage *varnashramadharma*, the traditional ordering of society, including the caste system.

The Segmented Society

A third factor in the shaping of India's constitutional democracy has been the country's legendary segmentation. I shall argue, on the positive side, that the presence of thousands of groups, some small some large, held together in the caste order, has been a key resource in making electoral politics work in India; and, on the negative, that this segmented society has always carried a load of inter-group animosities, and these have continued to be released into public life through the politicization of caste and religious groups or, as E. Sridharan says, through the politicization of social cleavages. Segmentation as a political resource is essentially ambiguous.

Everyone knows of the availability of caste and religious groups for political mobilization. These social entities emerged historically within social frameworks which had been oriented towards anything but democratic processes. That these entities became a key resource in the working of India's democracy is assuredly one of the great surprises of modern Indian history. Nevertheless, groups based on caste (and religion) have been major entities in the political spaces created by the constitution: elections, legislatures, etc. These have enabled such figures as Jagjivan Ram, Mayawati, and Mulayam Singh Yadav, and parties like the Muslim League, Akali Dal, and Bharatiya Janata Party (BJP) to make their mark on the Indian political scene. We may go further and say that the possibility of mobilizing such segmental entities, at relatively low costs, has been crucial in keeping the constitutional order going. 'This is messy,' Austin notes, 'but it is democracy and the social revolution in action.'

On the positive side, caste and religious groups and the like have constituted a field for learning. There is much social traffic along such networks; and this kind of milieu also carries a measure of trust: such groups have provided useful settings within which we can learn about the possibilities of the day from trusted sources. Consequently, these settings have been major social fields for political (as well as other forms of) learning. These have provided cost effective fields in which to learn about politicking as well as to mobilize at elections at relatively low costs. Yet the learning in this kind of milieu tends to be contextual and commonly rather limited, not the open, inter-culturally valid learning of our ideal scholar and the ideal university. This difference is crucial. The kind of learning possible within these segmental spaces is not the kind of resource that would enable an informed citizenry to work through diverse, open associations. Quite the contrary. Much of what is learned in these spaces are matters either of parochial loyalties or what are believed to be sacred, sovereign truths: truths of the kind that you may examine critically only at your own peril.

However, a segment—a caste, a religious category—carries not only social bonds on which to build political support; our segments also carry animosities and antagonisms directed at other social segments; these animosities too have been powerful resources in political arenas. Yet these animosities are not a fixed quantity: interested parties can work on arousing the hostile feelings, hoping to enlarge, and strengthen their hold on, what they see as a support base. Segmental identities then can generate acute ethnic conflicts, leading to such phenomena as thousands getting killed, as during the anti-Sikh riots of 1984, or tens of thousands driven out of their homes, as with Kashmiri Pandits during the 1990s.

Where identities which lay claim to sovereign truth are caught in antagonistic relations, the ensuing conflicts can be remarkably destructive. Assured of bountiful rewards in the afterlife, as in jehad, one may forgo the reasoned consideration of the likely consequences of one's actions, for oneself and for others, in this life. Somewhat more circumspect than the jehadis have been the votaries of Hindutva in India's polity, as the millennium turns over. They are a little more circumspect because the rewards they seek are not in the afterlife, but here and now, in terms of power and all that flows from power. The consequent calculation—of having to optimize their electoral base and, in the year 2002, of their continuing dependence on their coalition partners in the central government—restrains them somewhat. Even so, this calculation works with narrow horizons, being anchored to a particular religious identity, and to the balance of advantage at the next election. It does not take much to tip the calculation towards recklessness, as happened on 6 December 1992, during the assault on Babri Masjid.

Passions similar to those associated with religious identities may also be aroused on territorial, linguistic, and other similar grounds. Where a particular identity has come to dominate a region, with an exclusionary agenda, the others may be defined socially and politically as outsiders and, de facto if not de jure, their access to their citizenship rights may at best be partial. Sundry liberation forces, and other forms of militancy, in north-eastern India illustrate this active abridgement of citizenship—and a more general confrontation of local identities—phenomena which are much more widespread. The general principles at work here are conceived in terms of small-scale identities and small-group interests; their implications, for their victims, can be anomic, marked with normlessness.

*

In the argument above, several disparate resources are seen to converge in favour of constitutional democracy and civil society. Given such convergence, considerations of cognitive economy impel us to look for forces—which may include intentions and teleologies—that funnelled the convergence. In large societies, this requires an examination of the course taken by events through history; and the earlier section on the nineteenth century noticed a nurturing of ambitions to harness whatever resources were at hand for shaping the future.

A variety of visions was in fact forming in the late nineteenth century, arising in the memories and dispositions of particular persons and groups and social categories, and spreading far and wide. Some of these visions influenced, or grated against, one another. The implications of leaning on religious identities in the political domain were expressed in the phenomenon of Partition.

The vision that informs the constitution, sometimes called the Nehruvian vision, rested on secular European streams of thought more than on Indian ones. As some, exclusionary, versions of the latter have gained ascendancy in recent years, it has become clear that the triad of elements we have considered does not add up to a stable model. On the contrary, some of the pressures, arising in impulses inherent in the politicization of caste and religious identities, place democratic processes and civil society—indeed the whole constitutional and legal order—in difficulty. Recognizing this, contributors to this volume address the general question: what must be done to make them a durable achievement?

PART 3: THE CONTRIBUTIONS

We open our consideration of this formidable set of contributions with those concerning the constitution itself, as a text, and the experience of working with it on the larger scene. Then we look at the subaltern angles, social justice for the poor, reservations in various domains, pressures on minorities, and women's concerns. Finally, a series of moves, or possible moves, towards renewing the republic: women's electoral representation, electoral alternatives for improving the representativeness of the legislative bodies, reversing the fragmentation of the political party system, and finally the ongoing experience with panchayati raj institutions.

The Constitution

The first of our chapters, by Upendra Baxi, opens with two sets of reflections, namely the on-going transformation of constitutional theory itself: from a stance that the 'higher order rules' of constitutions can ensure only formal, not substantive, justice, to one that is beginning to define the criteria for judging the justness of constitutions themselves: overlapping consensus, legitimate law, enhancement of human capability; and a tension inherent in all constitutions between the apparatus of governance, on the one hand, with reasons of state authorizing the construction and use of the instruments of power and force, and securing immunity for those who use this force; and, on the other, citizenship rights, including the right to justice. India's experience over the past half century illustrates the tension between these two poles in abundant measure.

Over the decades, a vast range of scathing critiques has been directed at the Indian constitution, and Baxi reviews these under several rubrics: the Left, Gandhian, neo-Gandhian, Hindutva, the indigenous peoples', and the several subaltern perspectives. That this vast range of attitudes and agendas has flourished in India's polity is a tribute to its open society. The making of the constitution in mid-century set new benchmarks for placing a transformative vision for an ancient society into its directive document. Its working has generated in full measure both 'fairy tales and ... horror stories'; yet 'fifty years down the road, this vibrancy of vision survives'.

The founding text meets a different order of concerns in Sunil

Khilnani. There is a possible, seldom recognized, opposition between the logic of constitutionalism and the pressures of democracy.[21] A constitution, embodying higher order, more durable, principles for defending the citizens' sovereign liberties, is intended to offer a bulwark against the sometimes turbulent, passing passions of the crowd—or of a parliamentary majority, thereby serving to discipline the polity, to hold it to the Republic's foundational vision. This doctrine surfaces also in relation to the constitution's basic structure which the Supreme Court has sought to place beyond amendment even by a large parliamentary majority.

Khilnani comments at length on another aspect of the constitution: numerous concepts entered it without much reflection over their underlying premises. Khilnani concentrates on the terms *representation*, *rights*, and *equality* employed in the constitution without thought to the range of their meanings or to their likely fortunes in a society that had not hosted the historic evolution of the conceptions underlying them elsewhere. The constitution, it so happens, was drafted principally by lawyers and practising politicians, not by political philosophers. There may be opportunity now for much greater critical self-consciousness with words and concepts than prevailed half a century ago.

These tensions receive attention in their historical contexts from Granville Austin, whose chapter continues where his account of the making of the constitution left off some four decades ago. Austin's appraisal is grounded in years of archival research and interviews for his new book. What he calls the 'seamless web' in the constitution, spun from three principles—unity and integrity of the country, democracy, and the imperative for a social revolution—has proved resilient. It has drawn the country back to its core logic whenever passing impulses pushed things too far off this central course, and this has occurred repeatedly. Indira Gandhi's drive to consolidate her personal power by imposing the Emergency was the gravest of the threats, yet the system recovered.

The seminar organizers' initial hunch about a culturally rooted gap between words and deeds found echoes in Austin's analysis: 'the empty promise syndrome ... A declaration of intent imposes no need to ascertain that the action has actually been carried out.' The rhetoric might come from ideological impulses, or from considerations of electoral strategy, but pulling against it are the politicians and bureaucrats who relentlessly use the government to advance their own, their children's, and their allies' careers, interests, and wealth. 'Government by majority, "democratic" though it may be, will produce and perpetuate society's inequities until a sense of civic responsibility causes it to ameliorate them. Government in India will regain credibility only when there are no longer forgotten Indians.'

Accountability is the key issue; and the Nehruvian vision may have taken it for granted. Reflecting the then anxieties about territorial integrity, especially in the wake of Partition, it sought to forge a strong, dominant, centre, as Javeed Alam, Douglas Verney, and others note; but, given India's vastness and complexities, monitoring the exercise of the consequently concentrated power was difficult. National integrity was sustained despite all odds; but the centralization drove into revolt many who would have been comfortable in a more relaxed arrangement.

The half century since has seen the centre loosening somewhat, through (1) the linguistic reorganization of states, which has aided the rise of state parties, building on specific linguistic (and related) identities, (2) their consequent assertiveness in national politics in the era of coalitions, (3) judicial activism, including the effect of the Supreme Court's Bommai judgment (1994), restraining the centre from dismissing state governments too easily, (4) the 'liberalized' economy, which takes major economic controls out of the hands of the centre—while leaving a good many in the hands of the state and local governments, and (5) panchayati raj. We shall return to this last with de Souza's chapter towards the end. This level of governance has by far the greatest potential for making public life, and the agencies of the state, more accountable to the ordinary citizen—where the other processes may be seen as a mere shuffling of powers and privileges between different layers of dominant élites.

India is more, not less, of a federation than it was fifty years ago, Verney believes, and none the worse for it. Austin welcomes the coming of coalition governments, for these have enlarged the space for political participation. Hung parliaments and shaky coalition governments cause anxiety, yet in Austin's judgement, it is 'likely the new political flexibility is for the better.'

The constitution necessarily sought to advance multiple values, national integrity versus accountability among them; and this has generated inevitable, and welcome, tensions. Other sources of tension have included the pursuit of a 'social revolutionary' agenda, which promoted compensatory discrimination in favour of certain categories, and land reform legislation; it ran against the value of equal treatment in law and the right to property. Austin sees the basic structure doctrine, enunciated by the Supreme Court, as following from this tension; but the doctrine marked a watershed in India's constitutional history, and two of our chapters give it detailed attention.

Defined cautiously and used consistently, Pratap Mehta notes, the basic structure doctrine would protect the core, higher order values in the constitution, on behalf of the present and future generations of citizens, against parliament's pressures arising from the moods of the day. What the Supreme Court has called basic structure, in Mehta's reading, does no more than patch together assorted phrases from the constitution; it does not embody a critically conceived *general principle*. Consequently, its application of the doctrine appears to be inconsistent and wayward, seeking to reconcile shifting pressures, changing from one case to another, and seeming 'to replace the whim of transient legislators by equally indiscriminate whims of its own'.

For R. Sudarshan, the doctrine at issue has a rather different thrust: it concerns the idea of the state as 'embodying a rational commitment to a substantive notion of the public interest', as embodying public power and authority in an impersonal mode, rather than the highly personalised forms of authority characteristic of the political traditions in India. This idea of stateness permeates the entire constitution; it is not amenable to summary statement in a few sentences. It has evolved in the European—German and French—experience, not in the Anglo–American tradition; and therefore the Supreme Court could not advance 'the idea of state ... with confidence and doctrinal authority as the judges were not sufficiently schooled in European civil law traditions.' Yet the indigenous political ideas, current political practices, and some of the constitutional amendments were so at odds with coherent governance that the Supreme Court was pushed into formulating the 'basic structure' defence against the all too real prospects of parliamentary irresponsibility.

Subaltern Perspectives

Several contributors review India's republican experience in relation to the numerous categories that see themselves as marginalized; deprived of much that ought to be part of citizenship. Javeed Alam considers the scene overall. Central to the Indic civilization had been the caste order within which much of 'the daily routine activity' in thousands of jatis 'was left to evolve on its own'. The consequent diversity had made it difficult to construct large, durable states in the subcontinent. The British created a subcontinental state ('an iron-fisted bureaucracy', law and courts, a pan-Indian market) linked together by 'a large ... middle class educated in English but bilingual in nature'. At Independence, the constitution did embody an emancipatory and egalitarian vision; but the state, anxious over its own integrity, chose to deploy the full force of the coercive apparatus, inherited from the colonial order, to suppress popular movements. To the Assamese, the Bodos, and numerous other groups, India presents today the visage of a colonial power. In order to redeem our society it is imperative that the process of democratization be made more real.

Reverse Discrimination

Among the constitution's concerns with subaltern groups, none was more salient than with the Scheduled Castes and the Scheduled Tribes. In compensation for their historic deprivations, a framework for reservations in legislatures, government employment, and the like followed. Provisions made for ten years have now endured for fifty years; and the principle has taken hold as a mantra to address all manner of inequity, despite the 'creamy layer' syndrome. Marc Galanter finds the Mandal framework particularly egregious, a scheme whereby 'resources would be redistributed from the least advantaged members of the most advantaged groups to the most advantaged members of less advantaged groups.' The time may have come to subject the whole mindset about compensatory discrimination to critical scrutiny: 'A serious programme of compensatory preference must include measures for self-assessment and a design for dismantling itself.' Looking into the future,

> one could imagine a future renewal based on a critical assessment of the working of the policy, its accomplishments and shortcomings. One could imagine a

well articulated scheme that included, for example, a short-term enhancement of reservations to be followed by a graduated phasing out over, say, fifty years, racheting down as specific performance goals are achieved. Measures for inclusion in élites should be complemented with more broadly based measures to enlarge opportunities. For all its failures in implementation, India's policy of compensatory discrimination has been remarkable in its scope and generosity. It is time to upgrade its effectiveness while acknowledging the limits of what can be accomplished with it.

Social Justice

Beyond compensatory discrimination, several essays note that the polity's centre of gravity has been moving downwards, and consider the implications of this. A. Vaidyanathan's wide-ranging survey of 'social justice' notes that the levels of poverty in India have, over the decades, declined somewhat. While land reforms, as such, made headway in only a few states, the large cultivating castes' political clout rose sharply, persuading upper-caste landowners to sell out and move to urban areas, thus anyway shifting the pattern of agrarian landownership towards the middle and lower castes.

Further down the line, it is the electoral weight of the poor that secured the substantial poverty alleviation programmes (PAPs); but the allocations have tended to stay with those manning the pipelines: politicians, bureaucrats, and contractors, with their greater socio–political weight. Frustration with this persistent situation led to the constitutional changes presaging panchayati raj institutions (PRIs). If these institutions control the PAPs, if the poor can find adequate representation in these local institutions, and, one may add, if the movement for administrative transparency continues to bite, the PAPs may deliver to better effect.

Vaidyanathan is apprehensive about pressure on PAPs arising from globalization, amidst growing élite apathy, indifference and hostility. On one hand, the élite's orientation outwards, to careers in multinational corporations and to going abroad, the stoking of consumerist passions, and the rich countries' pressure on poor countries' bargaining capacities; on the other, a budgetery squeeze, especially on PAPs, and developmental expenditure generally. This squeeze becomes all the harsher because groups with a stronger political presence can defend budgetary allocations for themselves: government staff salaries have risen sharply; and major subsidies continue on a range of goods and services, leaving the really poor virtually untouched. The consequences of globalization worry Sudarshan too. He sees a potential antidote in decentralized governments, though it is a moot point whether the Goans telling DuPont to pack up and go is an adequate pointer to how most other localities would behave.

Secularism

Several esaays deal with a different set of subaltern questions in the Indian setting: those concerning secularism, minorities, group rights, and political representation. The state–religion relationship may take several forms, Rajeev Bhargava argues; but the secular state has two defining features: (1) it keeps religion apart from the state for the sake of religious liberty, and (2) it ensures equality of free citizenship.

It accords respect, not mere tolerance, to all religions. By these criteria, India's constitution made it a secular state. There is the well-known criticism that the Indian state had in fact engaged with bearers of the Hindu religious tradition much more than with others. Bhargava rebuts it with reference to 'equality of free citizenship'. Hindu society has been too unorganized to have attempted thorough social reform from within. Given the entrenched hierarchies within the Hindu socio–religious tradition, the state's intervention to secure this equality in this space may be defended as still maintaining 'principled distance' from religion. The secular state may intervene in a particular religious space in advancing an overriding value.

Similar considerations would, of course, have obliged the state to intervene, for example, in Muslim personal law, which ends up defending, in Zoya Hasan's view, principally 'multiple marriages and easy divorce'; but Bhargava skirts that aspect. On this count, has the state failed in its duty to India's Muslims? Rightly or wrongly, influential Muslim public men make support for, or at least neutrality towards, Muslim personal law the touchstone for the state's, and the civil society actors', attitudes. To press the issue is commonly interpreted as baiting India's largest minority.

Minorities' Anxieties

There was concern rather over the varied sources of anxiety among Muslims today. One element is in what Austin sees as a dangerous confusion, trying to promote national *integrity* with an agenda for national *integration*, through enforcement of social and cultural (and, at times, religious) homogeneity: '50 years have shown that the compartments cohabit successfully with only very partial integration.' There are however other reasons for anxiety: severe underrepresentation in parliament and state legislatures and in government employment, inequitous implementation of laws, negative stereotyping, targeting for violence during riots, sometimes cold-blooded violence by agencies of state, and so forth (Hasan, Chandhoke).[22] The political rise of Hindutva has heightened these pressures. Muslims particularly carry the burdens of Partition, even though most of them were not even born in 1947, of Indo–Pak hostility, and of the continuing struggle in Kashmir. We have a mass of hard attitudes here: attitudes of apathy, indifference, and worse.

What then can be done? Granting the menacing shadows of Kashmir and of the relationship with Pakistan, the ideology directing governments at the several levels is crucial. Beyond that, much would be gained by making citizenship rights effective; these cover the minorities equally. Also to reassure minorities, Sridharan proposes the extension of citizenship rights to 'derivative group rights':

> religion, places of worship, cultural heritage sites and structures, place names, language, script, educational rights, particularly medium of instruction and optional language facilities, second official language status in the states, and the like. ... This would qualify majoritarianism by limiting the range and extent of basic policies and institutions which can be altered by legislative majorities or by executive fiat.

Neera Chandhoke, however, proposes a larger agenda, for 'the individual right to culture'. In her complex argument: 'cultures and communities are a good for the individual, and ... access to this good is of such overriding importance, that we should secure this access through the grant of a right'. The formulation raises many questions. Here we can indicate them only briefly:

- A slippage between two levels of culture: C1, one's total repertoire of meanings, and C2, the numerous smaller complexes associated with one or another of one's multiple identities. C2 elements are often more important for one's identity than as being 'the resources that enhance and deepen our personal faculties of reflection and judgement, even as we appropriate and pattern the world in the sense of making it comprehensible', and so forth. These latter pertain to C1, not C2.

- As India has historically had both overlapping C1s and an intricate mosaic of C2s, what exactly is involved in securing 'access [to C1/C2] through the grant of a right'? Beyond citizenship rights, should there be some blanket right more comprehensive than, say, Sridharan's proposals? Should this right apply to the entire mosaic of C2s, or only to select ones?
- Both C1s and C2s are plastic, malleable, changing. As we have seen, the nineteenth and twentieth centuries were thick with projects aimed at redrawing the subcontinent's sociocultural map, consolidating diffuse identities into exclusionary religious ones; in the cafeteria of cultures and identities, Indian as well as global,[23] persons try a variety for their individual tastes, making the custodians of received identities jittery; and there is always a Luther or a Gandhi out to recast the assumptions of his or her culture. If the 'grant' of such a right is to mean more than Austin's 'empty promise syndrome', we have to ask: Who does the granting, to whom, and against whom?

That said, there remains the hostility towards religious and other minorities, stoked by Hindutva zealots. Yet, given past experience, can we reasonably expect civil society, the judiciary, and the like to be able to do much more than strive for the effective availability of citizenship rights?

Women and Privacy

While the minorities' question worries our contributors the most, issues concerning women also show up repeatedly. The American legal philosopher, Martha Nussbaum, focuses on the idea of 'privacy', primarily in relation to women's rights in law but really more comprehensively. Citing a wealth of case law in the United States and India, she uncovers the traps hidden in this notion. Whatever purposes the 'privacy' rubric may be thought to advance are better served, she argues, in terms of the equality of genders, of liberty, and of a range of rights appropriate for the realization of an array of human capabilities. She would expel privacy from judicial discourse completely: it is 'too diffuse and unclear', serves 'as protection of male bad behaviour' within the home and, especially, the bedroom, and is invoked needlessly for interests better defended on other grounds. Implicitly, Nussbaum makes a vital case for a close examination of our terms, decluttering our conceptual spaces, for clarity in thought, including that in law.

Women in Legislative Bodies

Zoya Hasan carries the women's issue into the political domain, especially women's representation in legislatures. She reviews the debates on such representation since the early 1900s, and its brief reality under the Government of India Act, 1935. The current proposal before parliament for reservation of a third of the seats has been thwarted, as of mid-2002, apparently by a cluster of small parties, but with wider connivance. In the proclaimed 'fears' that women's seats would be won by the more sophisticated upper-caste women, undercutting the overall lower caste elective representation, Hasan sees a mere fig leaf for anxieties over men's own political careers. Insofar as caste identities remain vital in voters' choices, and therefore in the nomination of candidates by political parties, reservations for women will not disturb the caste composition of legislatures. Political mobilization along the caste axis will work for women no less than for men: impressive numbers of women of 'backward classes' and the like are emerging in panchayati raj institutions without the necessity of any caste-based reservations.

Reservations for women in parliament and legislatures would have great significance. Clearly, nothing has subverted the caste order in modern India more powerfully than the sizable presence of Scheduled Castes in our legislative bodies—and their consequent ability to monitor both legislation and the executive. Strictly parallel, nothing can subvert the patriarchal order more powerfully than a strong presence of women in the legislative chambers—and what will flow from it. Patriarchy will feel the heat in every home in the land.

Renewing the Republic

Enhanced presence of women in legislative bodies, and the consequent pressure on patriarchy, will have momentous implications for renewing the republic. Several other proposals look to the polity of the future similarly; and some of these have implications for the constitution itself because, E. Sridharan reminds us, the constitution is a device for sharing power, and the political community may well choose to modify that device if that will help secure a more equitable sharing of power.

Mitigating Political Alienation

We owe Sridharan an extensive consideration of India's electoral rules, their evolution, their implications, and a wide range of alternatives and supplements now available. The prevailing 'first-past-the-post' (FPTP) system of elections, adopted from the UK with its two parties, has belied its two traditional justifications, namely that it would foster political stability by reducing the role of small players, and would inhibit the channelling of the party system along 'ethnic' cleavages. Indeed, numerous 'ethnic' parties have flourished, and the consequent fragmentation has undermined political stability. Furthermore, FPTP has worked for gross, persistent, under-representation of various kinds of dispersed, or subordinated, groups: religious minorities, women, political groups—say socialists, categories of non-heterosexual persons, environmentalists, or whatever. That is to say, significant groups in India in the past have felt, now feel, or may do so in future, that the nature of the electoral system prevents them from pressing their concerns and interests upon the polity. No society mindful of its future can afford this kind of alienation.

To mitigate the situation, Sridharan considers a wide swathe of possible responses.

(a) reservations in legislatures (and in other institutions);
(b) enlargement of fundamental rights;
(c) umbrella political parties, like the Congress of yore;
(d) the idea of proportional representation; and
(e) multi-member constituencies.

For more equitable ways for sharing power, then, a wide menu is available. Choices in this direction are vitally important for enlargement of a sense of belongingness, and, therefore, for the future of the republic. In organizing this sharing of power, however, there are other considerations, among them the sheer number of discrete political parties.

Proliferation of Political Parties

India has sought to discipline its polity through the Anti-defection Act and through the sharply increased deposits required of candidates at elections. Douglas Verney calls now for restraining also the runaway growth in the number of political parties:

	1980	*1999*
National parties	6	7
State parties	19	40
Registered parties	11	122

To make political competition less disorderly, Verney proposes that, for national elections, the 'state' and 'registered' parties be persuaded to club together in 'federal parties', a new category suggested for the family of political parties in India. To be recognized in this category, a party could be required, say, 'to win five per cent of the vote in at least three states'. This kind of institutionalization could counter the mushrooming of discrete, tiny parties—and help stabilize the polity.

Panchayati Raj Institutions (PRIs)

The sheaf of proposals for the renewal of the republic in the future apart, several participants, led by Peter deSouza, highlight the PRIs as a recent, ongoing process that is expanding local politics, giving people somewhat greater control over their own lives. We may speak of the 'total power' in a society in terms of how much 'say' the different members and categories feel that they have in shaping the course of events. In this view, alternative political arrangements may generate more total power or less. The PRI regime may help to sharply enlarge the sense of 'total power' within Indian society—and this could be translated into a capacity to get things done at the ground level.

Some two and a half million, a third of them women, are now active in panchayati raj institutions, giving democracy in India its 'second wind' (deSouza). Within the overall framework of the Seventy-third Constitutional Amendment Act (1992), it is state-level legislation, and government orders shape much of the PRI operative framework and provisions. Most states began as reluctant de-centralizers but, given the increased national-level political competitiveness of the 1990s, deSouza now sees the states beginning to compete with one another in making their respective PRIs more effective.

With relatively small constituencies, this level draws into the political arena persons of social categories which tend to get swamped in the larger state and national-level constituencies. A new generation of political leadership rises here; some of tomorrow's national leaders are cutting their teeth in panchayati raj. To start the process of planning from the *gaon sabha*, and then build up to the state level, Kerala style, is hugely cumbersome, but also a learning experience of unparalleled power: the experience of learning to manage public affairs openly. Local politics is about face-to-face relationships, and Sudarshan sees in this churning room for greater mutual understanding, reaching across our diversities.

*

'A more generous politics' is Zoya Hasan's phrase for what we need. To that one may add the need for a more generous society: one that is generous to those rendered defenceless for reasons of history, gender, age, or whatever.

Notes and References

1. Parts of this essay draw substantially on my 'Democracy and Civil Society in India: Integral or Accidental?' *Sociological Bulletin*, in press, and 'Integration and Separation of Traditions: Muslims and Hindus in Colonial India', in Supriya Verma and Satish Saberwal (eds), volume on Traditions in Honour of Professor Shireen Ratnagar, forthcoming. I thank Zoya Hasan and E. Sridharan for their advice.
2. For one discussion of nineteenth-century Bengali Hindu authors' perceptions of the past, see Ch. 5 in Partha Chatterjee, *The Nation and its Fragments: Colonial and Postcolonial Histories*, Princeton University Press, Princeton, 1993, Oxford University Press, Delhi, 1994.
4. Satish Saberwal, *Wages of Segmentation: Comparative Historical Studies on Europe and India*, Orient Longman, New Delhi, 1995.
4. Ibid., Ch. 2 reviewed the evidence.
5. Muzaffar Alam, 'Competition and Co-existence: Indo-Islamic Interaction in Medieval North India,' *Itinerario*, 1989, 13: 56.
6. R. Eaton, *The Rise of Islam and the Bengal Frontier, 1204–1760*, Oxford University Press, Delhi, 1994, p. 148; Ishtiaq Husain Qureshi, *The Administration of the Mughal empire*, N. V. Publications, Patna, n. d., p. 102.
7. Tapan Raychaudhuri, *Europe Reconsidered: Perceptions of the West in Nineteenth Century Bengal*, Oxford University Press. Delhi, 1988; Barbara

Daly Metcalf, *Islamic Revival in British India: Deoband, 1860–1900*, Princeton University Press, Princeton, 1982, pp. 320–5, 339–41.

8. Sudipta Kaviraj, *The Unhappy Consciousness: Bankimchandra Chattopadhyay and the Formation of Nationalist Discourse in India*, Oxford University Press, Delhi, 1995, p. 147.
9. Kenneth W. Jones, *Socio-Religious Reform Movements in British India*, Cambridge University Press, Cambridge, 1989 [*The New Cambridge History of India III:1*] offers a recent survey.
10. On the Meo, south-west of Delhi, Shail Mayaram, *Resisting Regimes: Myth, Memory and the Shaping of a Muslim Identity*, Oxford University Press, Delhi, 1997, pp. 36–48 and elsewhere; on eastern Bengal, Rafiuddin Ahmed, *The Bengal Muslims 1871–1906*, Oxford University Press, Delhi, 1983, pp. 53–6, 63–7; on south India, Susan Bayly, *Saints, Goddesses and Kings: Muslims and Christians in South Indian Society 1700–1900*, Cambridge University Press, Cambridge, 1989, p. 1.
11. C. A. Bayly, *Rulers, Townsmen and Bazaars: North Indian Society in the Age of British Expansion, 1770–1870*, Cambridge University Press, Cambridge, 1983, pp. 336f. See also Sandria B. Freitag, *Collective Action and Community: Public Arenas and the Emergence of Communalism in North India*, University of California Press, Berkeley, 1989.
12. Kenneth W. Jones, *Arya Dharm*, Manohar, New Delhi, 1976, pp. 303f; Metcalf, op. cit., pp. 87–260, *passim.*
13. 'Integration and Separation of Traditions', see n. 1 above.
14. David Baker, 'The Muslim Concern for Security: The Central Provinces and Berar, 1919–1947', in Mushirul Hasan (ed.), *Communal and Pan-Islamic Trends in Colonial India*, Manohar, New Delhi, 1981, pp. 237–42; see also Walter K. Andersen and Shridhar D. Damle, *The Brotherhood in Saffron: The Rashtriya Swayamsevak Sangh and Hindu Revivalism*, Vistaar/ Sage, New Delhi, 1987.
15. Non-coercive? Subhas Bose forced out of the presidentship of Indian National Congress in 1939, Purushottam Das Tandon in 1951: such events were indeed coercive, though these may be seen as relatively mild examples of power play. Khilnani's essay castigates Gandhi as an 'autocrat'; yet on any general scale of autocratic behaviour, Gandhi's coercive capacities would be seen as very modest indeed.
16. Granville Austin, *The Indian Constitution: Cornerstone of a Nation*, Oxford University Press, Bombay, 1966, p. 19.
17. At the seminar leading to this volume, a strong view expressed was that constitution-making cannot be a mass activity: no more so than designing a skyscraper. When a participant from Indonesia said that everyone in

his country today has an idea or two about what his country's constitution ought to have, Granville Austin saw that as a dangerous situation!

18. We may note in passing that Pakistan, arising in roughly comparable circumstances, has had, and continues to have, difficulties in the matter of working a constitution grounded in Western law. Why Pakistan and India have taken such divergent courses in this domain is a question that cannot be addressed here.
19. When this argument was first presented publicly (29 Dec. 2000 at Indian Sociological Conference, Thiruvananthapuram, Kerala), Professor Surendra Munshi asked: 'If Gandhi was an "accident" in India, where else would he have been "normal"?' In one way, of course, Gandhi would have been normal anywhere, insofar as he did no more than realize something of what are universal human potentials, however extraordinary the manner and the magnitude of his effort. In another way, however, he has to be seen as a once-off quantum leap which did not get routinized: it was in a class by itself, non-replicable, and therefore it could not be seen as 'normal' anywhere. It is my conflation of these two angles on Gandhi that had Munshi baffled.
20. Rajni Bakshi, *Bapu Kuti: Journeys in Rediscovery of Gandhi*, Penguin, New Delhi, 1998, has a recent report on the wide, if thin, but vitalizing spread of Gandhi's influence.
21. On 21 Sept. 2001, the Constitution Bench of the Supreme Court unseated Ms Jayalalitha as Chief Minister of Tamil Nadu on grounds of conviction in criminal cases of corruption, despite strong endorsement at the polls. 'The "will" of the people prevails', the Bench said, 'if it is in accordance with the Constitution.' *The Hindu*, 22 Sept. 2001.
22. In the seminar preparatory to this volume, Imtiaz Ahmad, 'The Constitution and Minorities,' focused on these issues too.
23. Ulf Hannerz, *Transnational Connections: Culture, People, Places*, Routledge, London, 1996, discusses a 'global ecumene' where all cultures have to learn to cope with powerful influences of diverse provenance.

2

THE (IM)POSSIBILITY OF CONSTITUTIONAL JUSTICE
Seismographic Notes on Indian Constitutionalism

UPENDRA BAXI

1. Constitutions: The Will to Stateness

This contribution to a volume marking fifty years of the Indian republic addresses the triumphs and tragedies of Indian constitutionalism. The central problem I wish to explore is one of the 'justness' of the Indian constitution. Much here depends on how the very notion of 'constitution' is constructed and from whose point of view and for whose benefit. The imagery of constitution/constitutionalism[1] varies from the perspectives of those who rule and those who are ruled and of the epistemic communities which develop empirical and normative theories/images of constitutions. However, as we all know, the 'ruled' and the 'rulers' do not constitute homogeneous classes of beings, with a singular essence (that is, the property or attribute of ruling and being ruled, or people with and without power). We also know that constitutional theorists also constitute a heterogeneous range of reflexive beings, marked by their distinctive class, race, gender, social origins, experience, and imagination (that is, the capacity to negotiate/transcend these.) At the outset, then, we ought to acknowledge that the conceptions of constitutions, and their relation to tasks of justice, far from being settled, vary enormously. That acknowledgement is however in short supply in the dominant discourse for a variety of reasons.

Juridical conceptions, for example, assign to constitutions the prime, even sole, function of providing criteria of validity for all legal norms. The tradition of analytical jurisprudence, from John Austin and Hans Kelsen onwards, highlights, in all its complexity, the basic notion that constitutions constitute a 'higher law' governing all forms of authoritative legal enunciations and performances. However, the high ground thus occupied has no relation to 'justice' values; Kelsen exemplified this by his famous assertion that the Basic Norm may have any content whatsoever, so long as it performs the core analytical function enabling us to draw bright lines between realms of 'law' and 'non-law'. Understanding constitutions entails legalization of notions about legitimacy: that which is legal is legitimate and that which is legitimate is legal. 'Legitimacy' is here conceived in terms of the production of belief systems that makes the life of state law both *analytically* legible and possible.

Another mode conceives constitutions as a will to stateness. Constitutions, typically, are thought of as collective volitional performances through which the collective political life of a territorially enclosed totality of individuals and groups become possible.[2] The will to stateness is a complex historical formation. It is also a totalizing formation, in that it seeks to personify/embody in a single entity diverse peoples and generations into a 'imagined community' of a nation-state[3] from whom some real obligations of loyalty are expected. It is a will that catalyses both the notion of sovereignty and of constitutionalism. That is, the will to stateness manifests a state as a sovereign entity in an external sense (that is, within communities of states) and as a constitution in an internal sense (that is, the framework for legitimacy of apparatuses and performances of governance). As concerns other states, a sovereign state is defined by conditions of autonomy and self-determination: namely, in the articulation of power to construct its own imaginative forms of constitutional life. As concerns its peoples, sovereignty assumes forms of orderings that determine the boundaries of collective political life/living, outside which one is condemned to a Hobbesian state of nature in which human life is 'poor, nasty, solitary, brutish and short'.

Both in the external and internal dimensions, then, the will to stateness consists of *the right of autonomous, self-determining peoples to have a constitution*, unburdened by the exercise of a similar right by other states. These latter may not impose any universal, cross-cultural prerequisites upon the making of a nation's constitution. Nor may peoples once constituted into a state, founded on a constitution, raise questions regarding the 'justice' of a constitution *as such*. These questions remain appropriate, even justified, to the workings of a constitution; they remain inappropriate, even unjustified, in relation to the constitution as promulgated. 'Treason' is sensible only within the boundaries of (to borrow a phrase from Habermas) 'constitutional patriotism'. Sovereignty then is the place of inscription for bright lines between 'dissent' and 'treason'. The question of the justice of constitutions addresses, in vital ways, the task of how, with what labours of justification, these bright lines may be drawn. In an ideal–typical sense (the sense that Max Weber gave to it), Gulag constitutionalism necessarily manifests a will to stateness that represents dissent as treason; the 'open society' constitutionalism incarnates this will by a dispersal of the distinction into various domains of criminal law and administration of justice.

The post-metaphysical/post-foundational discourse, however, raises the possibility of the emergence of justness *of* constitutions as such. It conceives contingent universals of justice variously, whether in terms of 'constitutional essentials',[4] wrapped into regimes of 'overlapping consensus',[5] or the production of 'legitimate law',[6] or of human capability. This genre of discourse subjects constitutions to tasks of negotiated normativity of human rights norms and standards, as ordaining meaningful forms of individual, associational, and collective life. Of necessity, then, this form of theoretical discourse rejects the notion that the will to stateness may extend to an external (based on international law) positivist right to have *any* form of constitution.[7] The Kelsenite thesis that the Basic Norm may have any content is thus repudiated at the very threshold by the discourse of contemporary normative constitutional theory. It is also now possible to articulate the notion of a 'just' constitution without the trappings of 'old iusnaturalist' metaphysical baggage.

In an era of global digital capitalism one may, further, conceptualize constitutions in terms of hardware and software programming of codes of justice and of injustice. On this view, notions of justice are programmed into the constitutional hardware as well as software, which determine the (im)possibility of justice under constitutions. The 'hardware' is the stuff that constitutes the materiality of state power, the institutions and apparatuses of governance, the 'webs of coercion',[8] and the state as a 'war machine'.[9] The constitutional hardware then is designed to combat challenges to the life of the sovereign state, discursively described, in earlier languages, as the doctrine of the Reason of State. No normative constitutional theory, as far as I know, addresses the hardware issues: the architecture of the armed forces, security and police establishments, methods and means of organizing levels of delivery of violence when the life of state is stated or seen to be threatened. Normative constitutional theorizing occurs under discursive conditions that concede the will to stateness (the hardware). It concedes the practices of writing and reading constitutions that entail many forms of epistemological and collective political violence. The founding act (the act of making a constitution) is usually preceded, even accompanied, by collective political violence and the foundational violence this inaugurated is reiterated in constitutional unfolding/development.[10] Programming constitutional software is meaningful only within this boundary.

Within this, constitutions also programme 'cultural software'[11] which provide relatively free access to divergent experiences and enunciations of 'justice' in ways that do not permit interrogation of the validity of the constitution as such. It is this 'software' that opens up dialogue boxes of rights, justice, and development.

Most constitutions design their distinctive interactive software. Constitutions contain programmes designing both rights and governance encoded in the texts of the Preamble, and related aspirational enunciations (such as the Directive Principles of State Policy or Fundamental Duties of Citizens) and constitutional rights. These programmes allow for meaningful 'surfing' that almost always expands the life of the constitution beyond the 'original intention'. The possibility of surfing depends on how a constitutional corpus is constructed and how open it is to revision. As to the first, almost all constitutional designs structure asymmetry between governance and rights and justice; the unwieldy corpus of the Indian constitution[12] illustrates this hiatus quite distinctively. The corpus of the constitution is crowded with governance texts. Rights and justice texts remain slender in comparison to the governance texts. As to the second, amending articles are software programmes that facilitate 'live updates', as it were, by providing for changes *in*, though never *of*, the text of the constitution. Constitutional engineering devises 'rigid' or 'flexible' types of constitutional design; the Indian programming is unusual, even unique, in the ways in which it provides for its 'live updates'. A prime task of normative constitutional theory is to evaluate these programmes and to design ideal ones.

Constitutional software does not always relate to high tasks of justice. Forms of constitutional engineering often produce software which, prima facie, remains indifferent to normative considerations, including those of 'justice'. These typically address the difficult design of institutions of governance, raising issues concerning efficiency (programming outcomes that produce the belief: 'Whatever is efficient is always just') rather than those of justice (that is, concerns about the justness of ordering regimes of public policy efficiency). Constitutional software that designs governance formats (for example unitary rather than federal, constitutional–monarchical rather than republican, presidential rather than cabinet, rigid rather than flexible constitutional arrangements) do not readily invite consideration on the grounds of justice, at least in terms of extant justice theorizing. In contrast, constitutional software that programmes rights remains eminently suitable to the discourse on justice. Much contemporary normative constitutional theorizing remains preoccupied with the nature and scope of rights, justified modes of resolving conflicts of rights, and the place of rights in polity, economy, and society. It furnishes forms of narrative risk-taking. Its message, expressed in a sentence, is: Constitutional orderings, structures, and processes are just when they affirm the equal human worth of all human beings, advance 'human capabilities', ensure 'human rights', promote 'authentic public participation in governance', and 'diversity' and 'pluralism' by acts of articulate abstention from promulgation of a state-sponsored vision of the good life. The heaviness of this shorthand camouflages many a conceptual minefield!

2. Governance and Justice in the Design of the Indian Constitution

I proceed, within this context, to imagine the ways in which the theory and practice, the origins and development, of Indian constitutionalism may be said to relate to tasks of justice. These tasks have been defined distinctively in the corpus of the Indian constitution, through the articulate divide between the governance and rights/justice texts.[13] This divide can be summarized, roughly, by saying that the governance institutions have almost exclusive constitutional power to define meanings and paths of development, while the judiciary (especially the Supreme Court of India) retains almost exclusive power to interpret and implement constitutional rights. This broad divide continues even in these halcyon days of Indian judicial activism (indeed, the tenth wonder of the world!), which recognizes the imperative of adjudicatory deference to the executive supremacy in the realm of instituting macroeconomic policies of 'development', even when it may properly review and rectify microeconomic practices that may be construed to impinge on fundamental rights.

From its inception, then, the Indian parliament, and the union executive (really the prime minister of India till the 1980s) bore the singular burdens of identifying the tasks of development as justice. I cannot pursue here in any significant detail the history of executive-sponsored notions of justice. It remains necessary though, for the present purpose, to highlight three overarching contexts within which this discourse has been framed. Tasks of justice have been presented as integral to peace and security, development, and 'globalization'.

(a) National Integrity and Unity as 'Justice'

The tasks of constitutional (in)justice have always been conceived within the discourse of state security. The integrity of India defined minimally as the security of its post-colonial borders has always been privileged and valued by the constitutional classes. The argument here is, and has always been, that failure to preserve the sovereign integrity and unity of the Indian nation is a form of collective injustice to Indian people. 'India' must exist and survive if tasks of justice for Indians are to be fully addressed. This existence may be threatened by other sovereign states through war or warlike actions as well as by internal subversion. Citizens have little role to play in the formulation of foreign and national defence policies; policies that often distort developmental priorities.[14] Nor does contemporary normative constitutional theory go so far as to provide for dialogical rights or participatory democracy in such matters; even Jürgen Habermas[15] is of no assistance on this count.

The constitution, as initially framed, and in its subsequent development, elaborates precise ways that uphold the belief that almost all practices of power directed to maintaining the unity and integrity of the nation are inherently justice enhancing. Both external aggression and internal subversion are portrayed as inimical to Indian development, and constructions of what forms the latter forever succumb to definitions by constitutionally insincere classes. Any form of popular (mass) action/movement that expose illegality and illegitimacy of the ruling 'development' paradigms invite legal, even constitutionally justified, repression. As threats, both internal and external, to India's 'integrity' remain perennial, the dominant discourse maintains, so must Draconian security legislation. Not merely must the colonial security legislation continue to operate with full vigour in independent India,[16] but preventive detention based on jurisdiction of suspicion, is authorized by Article 22 as a just order of exception to the precious fundamental rights to life and liberty. The Fifty-ninth Amendment to the constitution provided, for a while, that situations of armed insurrection or rebellion might justly trigger a declaration of 'partial emergency' during which even the right to life might be suspended.

Security forces (the army, paramilitary forces, and police) acting under these and allied conditions (like those provided under the regime of Disturbed Areas Act) remain, in almost all respects, beyond the pale of constitutional and legal accountability.[17] Indicative of the identification of national 'unity' and 'integrity' with development as justice is the recent, and altogether outrageous, proposal of the Indian Law Commission commending the enshrinement of preventive detention powers in the Criminal Procedure Code.

This identification of the 'unity' and 'integrity' of the nation with justice complicates, in many ways, the discourse concerning the possibility of the (in)justice of Indian constitutionalism. At the same time, as we see later, it has been a constant source for reflexive critiques as well as for people's struggles for democratic rights.

(b) Development as Justice

At first sight, the rights and justice texts provide authoritative starting points for the articulation of notions of development as justice. The Directive Principles of State Policy, read as a whole, define and prescribe minimal indices for development. Some Directives even mandate time periods for their realization. Thus, for example, provision of free and compulsory education for children less than fourteen years of age had to be accomplished within ten years of the adoption of the constitution. Fundamental rights provisions creating a right against exploitation (Articles 23, 24, and 35) specifically required expeditious and effective constitutional and legal action ensuring immunity from forced and bonded labour, trafficking in human beings, agrestic serfdom, and child labour. Overall, the constitution defines development as a series of governance obligations: the progressive implementation of policies, programmes, and measures that disproportionately benefit and empower the impoverished masses of India.[18]

The executive-sponsored regimes of development have not always been consistent with the constitutional vision. These programmes articulate development policies through various acts of deferral, dispersal, and even denial of rights/justice texts. I do not propose to revisit the admirable narratives of the histories of hegemonic constructions of 'development',[19] but it remains necessary for the present purpose to offer a capsule account of how 'justice' and rights have been negotiated through various enunciations of development. I highlight, very summarily, certain trends.

First, development planning has since its inception been heavily concerned with a sustained rate of economic *growth*. While the Five Year Plan documents remain suffused with the rhetoric of equitable social development, there has been very little actual progress towards the fulfilment of the minimal obligations of the directive principles, and the fundamental rights enshrined in Articles 17, 23 and 24.

Second, development design moves back and forth between the model of *land* reforms and *agrarian* reforms. Land reforms aim at enhancing expansion of agricultural productivity, necessary both for self-reliance in the production of foodgrains and for global markets for agricultural produce. Development here is conceived of in terms of efficient management of agricultural production. The agrarian reform model, by contrast, is primarily directed at state-sponsored equitable land distribution, debt relief, protection of the rights of agricultural workers, and elimination of practices of agrestic serfdom.

Third, the planned economy casts the state in the role of inventor of forms of state regulated capitalism. This implicates the state and law heavily in tasks of quite comprehensively monitoring economic enterprise. Markets for political power are increasingly determined by claims to ability to produce forms of compliant market activity. The management of development processes and programmes was cast in the mode of command and control,[20] leading to extraordinary formations of bureaucratic and political power, with resulting corruption, waste, and an ethos of unaccountable executive power.[21]

Fourth, development planning unfolds the role of the state, requiring it not just to function as an allocator and regulator but also as the producer of economically valued resources. The commanding heights of the economy thus remained captured by state industrial monopolies. The constitution is invoked (especially Article 39) to justify nationalization of key sectors of production. A network public enterprises (statutory corporations, government companies, holding companies) putting people before profits is represented as signifying the enhancement of state capacity to perform tasks of justice.

Fifth, the 1970s simultaneously mark the discovery/reinvention of mass impoverishment; it is indeed an awkward fact that Dadabhai Naoroji's classic *Poverty and Un-British Rule in India* should find, at very long last, a resonance in the Indira Gandhi led 'Garibi Hatao' programmes of the early 1970s. Whatever may be said to be the impact of this revival on the Indian impoverished, it certainly led to the 'greening' of Indian economic theory. Anti-poverty programmes begin to fashion the vocabulary of development economics. This latter then exposed the multifarious human, and human rights, violative impacts of the unleashing of the Green Revolution, and also led to a renewal of social science concern with insurgent violence (especially the Naxalite movements).

Sixth, this period also witnesses the growth of state finance capitalism with the nationalization of banks and insurance industries,[22] marking a very significant transformation of rural economy, at least in terms of access to credit.

Seventh, with disparities in regional development, economic federalism begins to emerge, in terms of demands for greater regulatory autonomy for states and equitable allocation of federal revenues through the renovation of normative approaches by the Indian Finance Commission. The governance formats for development begin to undergo significant transformations. New conceptions of economic federalism emerge, where the states (Assam, Gujarat) now contest before the courts the arrangement of royalty-sharing for natural-resource exploitation, and the discourse of the constitutionally ordained Finance Commission undergoes dramatic shifts in approaches to federal revenue sharing.

Eighth, 'New social movements begin to contest hegemonic notions of development. The Total Revolution of the 1970s seeks to redefine development in terms of greater peoples' participation in governance and a peoples' war against corruption in high places. The authoritarian 'politics' of the Emergency Rule (1975–6) marks a crucial response: for the first time, the fundamental right against exploitation and related Directive Principles guide the reformation of notions of development and renovation by a constitutional amendment of the Directive Principles (the Forty-second Amendment tainted by the Emergency also enunciates a concern for environment in development planning; so do the Fundamental Duties of Citizens). Movements for social empowerment of the educational and social backward classes redirected development, in the early 1990s, towards more explicit commitment to egalitarianism. Feminization of development definitions and paradigms begins to occur with the rise of women's movements. Environmental movements begin to orient (even if in terms of 'sustainable development') the logic of practices of planned development.

Ninth, the 1990s also mark a much-deferred decentralization and devolution of power to panchayati raj processes and structures in ways that eventually foster the flow of redefinitions of development as justice from the grassroots to national levels.

These processes mark the history of consolidation of the hegemonic practices of planned development. However, constitutional losers (the 'weaker sections of society') begin to contest reigning notions of development; their 'million mutinies' seek to supplant these by more people-oriented, participatory development. Insurgent social violence seeks to direct the benefits of development to the constitutional have-nots. Even as violent protest de-legitimates the ruling paradigms of development as justice, its 'management' by constitutionally insincere and insecure classes leads to militarization of the Indian state.

(c) Globalization

The onset of the contemporary politics of economic 'globalization', however, introduces a just order of anxiety concerning the future of constitutional justice. The software of rights and justice texts is steadily being overlaid with programmes of globalization in ways that generate insoluble hardware conflicts. The global economic situation and diplomacy have always affected the course of Indian constitutional development. What is new, however, about contemporary economic globalization is that it encases the Indian constitution within the emergent paradigm of global economic constitutionalism.[23] This paradigm creates many-sided impacts, principal among which is the transformation of notions of accountability/responsibility. The Indian state (like many other South states) is placed in a situation where internationally assumed (or imposed) obligations to facilitate the flows of global capital, trade, and investment command a degree of priority over the order of constitutional obligations owed to Indian citizens and peoples. The three Ds of economic rationalism (deregulation, disinventment, and denationalization), for example, favour many development policies that threaten, and at times nullify, achievements of rights and justice discourse.[24] On the other hand, there is room for the argument that the politics of economic globalization remains human rights friendly, especially in terms of empowering networks of global civil society solidarity. Indian NGO communities deploy these in various deeply conflicted ways.[25] The future of normative Indian constitutional theory at least, then, lies in those dialectic progressive and regressive discursive profiles of contemporary global economic constitutionalism. I do not essay this task here.

In what follows, I trace the itineraries of illocution to the theory and practice of Indian constitutionalism, and the moves that shape the contingent careers of many conceptions of rights and justice. Constitutional discourse has been subject not merely to people's illocution; those who thrive under it also count as constitutional 'malcontents'. The multitudinous constitution-talk in India combines celebration as well as mourning: the *shehnai* (the celebratory note) as well as the *matam* (the voice of lamentation), true to the classical Hindi film song refrain: *Jahan bajti hey shahnai, wahan matam bhi hoti haye* (where the trumpets blow, the voice of lamentation also finds its power).

3. The Shehnai

The celebratory discourse remains integral to the nationalist project. From the debris of colonialism, India, that is at the same time also named Bharat, is born as a union of states. The quest for identity of a post-colonial nation is a performative act of political imagery: the invention of 'India', with the dangerous supplement of 'Bharat'; a register of continuity with a colonial past laced with the revivalist potential for the foundational bases for a 'Hindu' notion of an imperial India, reinventing its mythic pasts. Even so, the constitution facilitates forms of enduring nationhood, in the midst of astonishing civilizational and cultural multinational diversity. It is, in this vital sense, inaugural of the creativity of the postcolonial. The shehnai seeks to overcome the matam.

Much before the times of post-liberal churnings, the Indian constitution dares to innovate notions of governance, rights, justice, and development. Summarily expressed, the triumphal register celebrates institutionalization of an order of constitutional facts that:

- Establishes and implements universal adult suffrage, without a trace of gender-based discrimination, in ways that reproduces astonishingly vibrant forms of constitutional élites. This amidst electoral practices violative of fair and free elections, not at all redeemed by the comparable, recent developments in the United States: 'perforated chads' discourse sacrificing the integrity of right to vote.[26]
- Recognizes rights of political participation by her First Nations peoples and millennially deprived Dalit populations (those beyond the pale of the caste system) on the basis of a system of affirmative action through legislative reservations.
- Provides for constitutional platforms/anchorages for affirmative action for social, educational, and 'other' backward classes.
- Structures relatively autonomous adjudication, with all its complex and contradictory entailments, endowing it with the potential for activist adjudication.
- Establishes a free press and creates contradictory spaces for vigorous political and social dissensus.
- Puts to work the dynamic of growth for a progressively authentic federal polity that provides spaces for the realization of autonomy movements charting changing forms of cartography of the Indian federation.
- Enables deepening of grass-roots democracy.

Notably, the Indian constitution innovates the liberal model of rights.

Rights are not just conceived of as a corpus of restrictions on the power of the state. Civil society is also identified as a source of human rights violation. The constitution thus ushers in the notion of a progressive constitutional state.

Also, well ahead of the International Bill of Rights, the constitution-makers enact a distinction between civil and political rights, on the one hand, and, on the other, social/economic rights. The Directive Principles of State Policy define the constitutional essentials of good governance; they provide constitutional criteria or bases, even languages, for evaluating political practices and performance. The fundamental rights (basically civil and political) enable, by processes of judicial enforcement, changing forms of authoritative discourse on governmental arbitrariness or abuse of power. [27]

What is more, the Indian constitutional experience is unique for its reflexive character. Not merely did the Constituent Assembly consider a whole variety of divergent approaches to the constructions of 'constitutional essentials'[28] but also a half-century functioning of the constitution has been characterized by an ongoing critique emanating from constitutional winners as well as losers. Political actors, including India's apex adjudicators, have always put the legitimacy of the Indian constitution to test;[29] and so have people within the dominant classes who feel aggrieved by its workings.

In what follows, I briefly outline the modes of the ongoing 'critique' of the Indian constitution, both in its foundational and reiterative moments. I recognize that the summary presentation does not as fully attend to major analytic distinctions[30] or the complexity of the practises of politics that are entailed in each genre of 'critique'. Even when the hybridity of the narrative may prove irritating for the dominant practitioners of Indian constitutional movement and theory, I persevere in the hope that it may prove constitution-reinforcing/regenerative in its present and profound moment of crisis.

4. The Left 'Critique'

This extremely fluid and heterogeneous discourse permits no easy summation. At a meta-level, we find articulations of parliamentary communism as well of Naxalite, and neo-Naxalite, formations. At the micro-levels, we encounter many situated, cadre-based critiques of both the regimes of Left governance and insurrection.

Both parliamentary and extra-parliamentary theory and practice characterize the foundational constitutional choices of rights and justice as embodying bourgeois conceptions.[31] E.M.S. Namboodripad, on pain of contempt, characterized the Indian judiciary as an agency of class domination and rule, rendered somewhat ahistorical by Justice Hidayatullah's judicial gloss on Marxist texts.[32] The gist of this denunciation is that the making and the working of the Indian constitution celebrate the rights of the propertied classes over the proletariat. The rights and justice discourse thus generated by the dominant institutions of the Indian state and law, with all its apparently complex differentiation, is distinctly neo-colonial. While promoting regimes of civil and political rights of citizens, this discourse denies most or all democratic rights of the Indian peoples. The unfolding of the Indian constitution, on this view, occurs in predictable ways of reproduction of dominant legality, which remains complicit, overall, with continuing immiserization of the working classes, the rural impoverished, and is marked by accentuation of the anti-people consolidation of the class character of Indian state agents and managers.

Beyond this, the Left critique suffers a loss of ideological coherence. Of necessity, the very possibility of the emergence and growth of the radical (Maoist/post-Maoist) critique entails critical moments of constitutional collaboration. At the same time, it is confronted with the need for the *invention of politics* that does not altogether undermine the logic of revolutionary cadre-based movements that vigorously challenge the bourgeois character of Indian constitutionalism. Parliamentary communism is thus deeply conflicted. It can accommodate its Other—modes of extra-parliamentary communist critique of Indian state and law—only up to a point. That point it provides is a shifting horizon of unstable constitutional compromises: the cadres may reign but also the governments must rule in ways that return them at the polls. The West Bengal communist regime vivifies an institutionalized critique of the Indian constitution, and of the dominant regime styles of the non-socialist ways of the Indian state. It harnesses the constitutional space for enactment of the Left programme, especially agrarian reform and literacy. Howsoever bourgeois the federal principle and detail may appear in theory, the Left governments in India have actually revitalized Indian federalism.[33]

In contrast, the forms of extra-parliamentary communism (whether Maoist or post-Maoist) offer more sustained Left critiques of Indian constitutionalism. In this genre, the bourgeois–landlord comprador capitalist state is prefigured as an order of violence, even permanent war, against the Indian masses. The constitutional practices of the rule of law emerge variously as masks for the reign of terror. Forms of constitutional practices of liberal democracy signify, at the end of the day, what the Ghanian thinker C. Ake[34] terms 'the democratization of disempowerment'. The Naxalite, neo-Naxalite, and post-Naxalite movements remain committed to the destruction of the enemies of the Indian people; in particular, people's war groups position themselves in a state of permanent armed hostility to constitutional norms, standards, apparatuses, and functionaries.[35] Extra-parliamentary communist critique directs attention to the anti-people subversive ways of parliamentary communism. Occasional harvesting of available civil rights spaces by these formations is regarded as non-threatening to militant ideological 'purity'.

These militant forms of critique reproduce self-fulfilling prophecies concerning the violence of the Indian state, constitution, and legality. Organized armed insurrection reinforces unconstitutional, and profoundly, human rights violative, even catastrophic, practices of power; these, in turn, signal the plenitude of a lawless 'dual' state which protects and rewards ideologically compliant (and complicit) citizenry and penalizes, even terrorizes, the practitioners of alternative constitutive visions of a radical democratic India that is not Bharat. The governance prose of Indian states regards some of its dissentient active citizens as vermin (the prose of 'Naxalite-infested' areas) destined to face acts of extermination. In Mahasweta Devi's *Draupadi* metaphor, the constitutional rule of law itself is (en)countered. The reiteration of state illegality, and terror, reproduces, dialectically, violent popular illegalities. In all this, the death of Indian constitutionalism is born. The beginning of the end of Indian constitutionalism is heralded when practices of violence in the pursuit of politics of equality are considered as a threat to the underlying values of Indian constitutionalism, as defined by schizoid–paranoid élite constitutional formations. 'Constitutional' violence that consigns citizens to a permanent state of rightlessness extravagantly, and often with fierce practices of cruelty, surrenders the strength of the original intent as well as the power, and potential, of future imaginings for juster Indian democratic ordering.

5. The Gandhian Critique

The Indian constitution, in the act of its making and in many subsequent developments, appears Westoxifying in Gandhian and Neo-Gandhian thought. Readers of Mohandas Gandhi's *Hind Swaraj* (1911)[36] will recall the continuity of his critique of Western parliamentary institutions and industrial society with his proposals concerning the new constitution of India, based on a network of self-determining people's institutions of village republics. For Mohandas[37] Gandhi, the very notion of democracy conceived solely as a system of management of distribution of power was in itself undemocratic. For him, competitive democratic politics carried with it the manifold potency of denial of a true Swaraj. Viewed in relation to colonial rule as a signifier of political self-determination for India, Swaraj, once freed from colonial yoke, becomes an arena for individual and collective moral, even spiritual, self-determination. Mohandas Gandhi did not regard institutionalized party politics as having the potential for the achievement of true Swaraj, which emerged only with communities and individuals learning to practice their freedoms as an order of responsibility to the Other. In a sense, Mohandas Gandhi was a more committed republican than all the members of the Constituent Assembly put together.

An unusual combination of colonial (Nehruvian) legal liberalism[38] and the creatively modified subaltern legal liberalism of Dr B.R. Ambedkar defeated, for better or worse, Mohandasian aspiration. For the former, Mohandasian notions had outlived their utility once Independence had been achieved;[39] for the latter communitarian self-determination appeared only to revive the spectre of the millennially entrenched forms of casteism.[40] As a result, Mohandas's conception normatively survives only in enfeebled forms in the constitutional text: principally through the Directive Principles of State Policy urging the state to move towards prohibition of intoxicant drinks and a ban on cow slaughter.[41]

6. The Neo-Gandhian Critique

Acharya Vinoba Bhave and Jayaprakash Narayan revitalized the Gandhian tradition. Each sought in distinctive ways to approximate Mohandas Gandhi's Swaraj within the contexts of Indian parliamentary democracy. Each deployed the notion of fundamental rights to create forms of mass politics to attract Indian democratic development to the Gandhian vision. Each had a moment of constitutional triumph and tragedy.

Vinoba Bhave translated Gandhian notions of Swaraj into a series of ideas rolled up in the coinage of conceptions of Sarvodaya, signifying equitable and equal empowerment of all. Against the unedifying backdrop of constitutional wrangles on the right to private property, Bhave revived the Gandhian notion of dialogical amity through which landowners were persuaded to relinquish 'surplus land' in favour of the landless. The Bhoodan and Gramdan (*lit.* gift of land and of villages) movements urged the super-rich to educate themselves to be compassionate to the super-impoverished, in frameworks that transcended the terms of the constitutional discourse.[42] In this way, Bhave (and later Narayan) struggled to reintroduce the Gandhian notion of 'trusteeship' against the constitutional canon of *the right to property*, with results that have been variously evaluated.[43]

Bhave, and then Narayan, Indianized the liberal notion of the right to free movement throughout the territory of India into a right to *padyatra*, walking through 'Bharat' in ways that repudiated 'India', Through a decade or more of padyatra, Bhave sought to achieve a transformation of agrarian relations in India by the production/cultivation of social trust and cooperation. The Bhoodan and Gramdan movements provided alternatives to violent and coercive state/insurrectionary modes of land redistribution; the movement sought to provide the constitutional state with a communitarian base. For Acharya Vinoba Bhave, the constitutional state can become related to tasks of justice; only a tradition of community/social trust are reinvented or reinforced, rendering citizenship into an ethical, not merely, legal notion. A constitutional order that placed citizens and the state in adversarial roles, or which made classes of citizens complicit with or indifferent to the regimes of state/insurgent terrorism, did not provide the prospect of authentic civic cooperation necessary for a just social transformation.

In contrast, the later Jayaprakash Narayan, somewhat ambivalently, sought to transform constitutional politics through forms of mass politics that frontally challenged the decadent bourgeois politics of parliamentary democracy and its notions of 'development' as justice. Accentuating the legitimation crises of the early 1970s, his 'Total Revolution' movement was directed against the increasing corruption in governance and visions of participatory democracy.[44] The 'Total Revolution' movement, in so many senses bigger and bolder than the events of May 1968 in Paris, revitalized Indian democracy in ways yet to be adequately recounted, let alone adequately theorized. The Emergency Rule of Indira Gandhi has almost permanently erased it in constitutional and public memory. Indeed the 'Total Revolution' proved to have a short constitutional shelf-life, unless we attribute the panchayati raj amendments to that democracy-deepening stream of neo-Gandhian thought.

The poverty of Indian liberal social/constitutional theory is manifest in its near-total lack of narrative interest in neo-Gandhian development of regimes of trusteeship and people's power pitted against the logic of 'possessive individualism' through the languages and logics of the right to property and élitist conceptions of development as justice. The golden jubilee of the republic came and the Indian had no word of remembrance for the great neo-Gandhian moments.

Nonetheless, as and when the history of Indian constitutionalism is adequately written, the Total Revolution movement will be perceived as laying the true foundations of a new Indian constitutionalism, reverberating now in the adjudicatory crusade against corruption in high public places. Each and every Indian judge who today inveighs against corruption in public life is an unacknowledged lineal descendent of Mohandas Gandhi, Vinoba Bhave and Jayaprakash Narayan. It is another matter altogether that judicial beings remain wholly narcissistic, wallowing in unacknowledged histories of social movements that serve as midwives to judicial activism.

7. The Hindutva Critique

The 'Hindutva' critique inverts the Gandhian vision and means. It transforms the notion of multi-religious Indian society and polity into the prose of a politically reconstructed 'Hinduism.'[45] An ideology long in the making, Hindutva begins to explicitly address the failings of the Indian constitution only in the 1980s.[46] The 'Hindutva' critique grounds itself on the notion that the constitution, as originally enacted and in its subsequent development, remains hostile to the majority of its citizens, who are born as, and choose to remain, 'Hindus'. It thrives on empirical instances of discrimination against 'Hindus', which it insists are generated by the working and interpretations of the text and context of the Indian constitution.[47] It insists that constitutional secularism is deeply flawed for the following principal reasons.

First, while the Constitution mandates reform of Hindu religious beliefs and practices that manifestly violate human rights (practices of 'untouchability'), non-Hindu religious traditions are allowed constitutional impunity principally through the perpetuation of the 'personal law' rights-violative formations. Second, the near-absolute protection, under Article 30, of the rights of minority communities to establish and administer educational institutions of their own choice is said to favour non-Hindu religious traditions. Third, affirmative action programmes disadvantage 'Hindu' citizens by favouring quotas that blight the future of the non-complicit present generation, despite demonstration of manifest 'merit' for righting past millennial wrongs. Fourth, the interpretive ways in which the Representation of People's Act rendered appeals to religion as 'corrupt practices', at least till the so-called Supreme Court Hindutva judgment,[48] denied construction of 'Hinduism' as a political ideology articulating legitimate visions of a future polity, readily available to secular, even godless, political parties. Fifth, constitutional protection of religious practice and belief is said to foster practices of conversion which are said to disadvantage non-missionary religious traditions (like Hinduism) and favour 'minority' religions.[49] Sixth, provisions for special constitutional status for the state of Jammu & Kashmir enabled hostile discrimination against the Hindu minority, resulting in the enforced diaspora of Kashmiri Pandits, rendered altogether rightless. Hindutva critics decry Indian constitutionalism, for all these and related reasons, as 'pseudo-secular'.

The future of Indian constitutionalism then, on this perspective, lies in redirection of constitutional secularism. Secularism that affirms the religious tradition of a dominant community is presented as the very best hope there is for a multi-religious society and nation. The Hindutva platform advocates that the future of the 'children of the lesser Gods' will be more secure with an affirmation of the dominant religious tradition. An insecure majority religious-cultural tradition scripts a death warrant for 'minority' rights; it points to the exemplary flourishing of these rights where the secularist constitutional balance is struck in ways that do not reduce the dominant tradition to a minority syndrome.[50] As of the time of writing, calls are frequently made for Indianization of Islam or Christianity, presumably a process through which these traditions will be relocated within the 'Hindu nationalist', rather than 'pan-Indian', religious traditions.

The politics of Hindutva systematically seeks to *enforce* the notion of a Hindu Rashtra, in which 'Hinduism' shall be the de facto state religion. It deploys a variety of strategies and tactics designed to prepare the ground for what may eventually be presented as a compelling national consensus for constitutional change.[51] It transforms forms of padyatra into those of *rathyatras.* If the former were oriented to new forms of production of communitarian trust, the latter remain directed to the destruction of all forms of social trust and cooperation. The rathyatras (lit. 'national' leaders leading a procession in a van decked out as a chariot) constitute, at one level of understanding, legitimate exercises in the fundamental right to movement throughout the territory of India and the right to free speech and expression. At the same time, they innovate forms of hate speech against minorities, especially Indian Muslims.

Freedom of speech in the Hindutva understanding is a near-absolute right to be, and remain, articulately intolerant of minority religious communities. Bal Thackeray is a virtuoso exponent of hate speech. Open advocacy of mass violence against targeted minority groups is presented as constitutionally justifiable. Practices of collective political violence are presented as a constitutional mode of righting past wrongs done to the majority community. Thus, history is reinvented in relation to places of religious worship; a large number of mosques are discovered to have been built by Muslim rulers, centuries ago, on the sites of Hindu temples or sacred shrines, and their removal by the Hindutva forces is presented as an act of constitutional redemption. Popular action to 'reconvert' the lower castes to 'Hinduism', as well as the movement of legislative restriction on conversion by 'force' and 'fraud', is presented as a necessary reworking of conceptions of constitutional secularism. Equally so are the militant practices of Hindutva hooligans who arrogate to themselves the right to enforce some version of 'Hindu' critique of taste and beauty, and to act as violent surrogate state censors.[52] It is also urged that all performers of such sacred, historic deeds—demolishers of the Babri Masjid, fomenters of hate speech, church-burners, commanders-in-chief and all subalterns engaged in acts of sponsored 'communal' violence, supporters of sati, and the self-styled enforcers of pseudo-Hindu aesthetics (Bajrang Dal activists)—should be spared even a semblance of rigorous law enforcement. At the time of writing, they possess sovereign immunity, as befits plenipotentiaries of a resurgent Hindu India, currently constituting a state within a state.[53]

8. The 'Matam' of First Nations

The making of 'modern' constitutions always constitutes a narrative of violent appropriation of the peoples of the First Nations, which the dominant discourse on constitutionalism can scarcely privilege. The theme, however, was prominent in the making of the Indian constitution. Even as Nehru complained, in tabling the First Amendment, about the theft of the Indian constitution (this magnificent edifice, he said, is already being purloined by lawyers and judges), Jaipal Singh said, memorably, on the very first day of the Constituent Assembly that the making of the Indian constitution was itself an act of theft, taking away the forms of nationhood from the indigenous peoples of India. The Nehruvian lamentation is, after all, a triumphal narration of the grieving charismatic constitutional élites at judicial incursions on their sovereignty. Jaipal Singh's matam represents, in contrast, the epic of sorrow of the millennially deprived peoples. I have elsewhere described (in an article in the *Delhi Law Review, circa* 1987, and an unpublished theme paper presented at the international conference on the rights of subordinated peoples at the University of La Trobe), the significance of the contrast between self-serving and historically irredeemable forms of constitutional grief.

Unsurprisingly, the constitutional response is to deny any and all claims for continuing to exercise the right to self-determination. Not unexpectedly, the result has been a long state of civil war, though not thus described, in the north-east. The impact of this civil war upon the formative practices of Indian constitutionalism has yet to be written, but this much is clear: radical claims to self-determination (secession) have been delgitimated. All that remains permissible is the translation of residual autonomy aspirations into federal adjustment (that is, the creation of new states status within the Indian Union). This, too, has been achieved at great human rights cost—as the history of the transformation of the north-east into so many states, and the recent creation of three new states, from the belly of the Indian beast (Uttar Pradesh, Madhya Pradesh, and Bihar) records. Proliferation of cultural and political identities remains sensible only within the parameters of federal cartography.

The fact that redrawing the federal map rarely signals the beginning of the end of internal colonialism within the nation has left very little impress on Indian constitutional theory and practice. Nor has, as far as one can tell, the highly innovative device of legislative reservations in the Indian parliament for the 'scheduled tribes' achieved any significant reversal of an extractive, neo-colonialist pattern of devolution of power. The most natural resource-rich areas of federal India are also the areas in which, for the past half century, the highest rate of mass impoverishment is sustained and it is no coincidence that these are also the areas where indigenous peoples live.[54] Unfortunately, leading constitutional law, and even political theory, treatises have little space for this subject. The inaugural constitutional sigh of Jaipal Singh hovers across many a vaunted constitutional development during the past fifty years.

9. Subaltern Critiques: Cornerstones as Tombstones

One overarching way of describing this genre, this conglomeration of critiques, is to say that it articulates the voices of constitutionally dispossessed and disenfranchised peoples. Their voices emerge with poignant authenticity outside the dominant narratology of Indian constitutionalism. The extent of alienation may be measured when we juxtapose dominant discourse concerning constitutional development with the realistic fiction of a Sadat Hasan Manto, Mahasweta Devi, Rohinton Mistry, and Shivaram Karanth. These bring to us lived collective histories of hurt in ways that even the most rights-imbued prose of constitutional discourse rarely achieves. Indian constitutional theory and practice needs to ground itself, if it is ever to maintain a modicum of conversation with the constitutional underclasses, in the narratives of *Draupadi*, *A Fine Balance*, or *Chomu's Drum: One Day in the Life of a Bonded Labourer*.

The interiority of orders of constitutional violence is also mirrored in the gifted, and anguished, social theory scholarship. I have here in mind the corpus of Veena Das, and the agonizing labours of feminist historiography[55] relating the histories of the partition of India as sites upon which the practices of building the Indian nation stood, and are still heavily inscribed. These marked the birth, and growth of the constitution as providing inaugural, and still fecund sites, for the production and reproduction of citizen-monsters. Thus, writes Veena Das, 'if men emerged from colonial subjugation as autonomous citizens of an independent nation, they emerged simultaneously as monsters'.[56] From a suffering feminist perspective, the foundational violence against women enacted during the moment of constitution-making, iterates itself, over and over again, through fifty long years of unfoldment of its vicious patriarchal logic.

In a different vein, ecological historians (like Ramachandra Guha), de-globalizing reflexive environmental activists (like Vandana Shiva), and the pre-Arundhati Roy-overlaid history of Narmada struggles, embodied by Medha Patkar and Baba Amte, offer many insights into the 'heart of darkness' of the Indian practices of development as justice, proselytised as 'development' by the peddlers of Indian constitutionalism. Equally so is the germinal discourse in *Twenty-Eight Report of the Commissioner of Scheduled Castes and Tribes*, which I regard as historically as important as the Constituent Assembly Debates.

In comparison to all these genres, the dominant discourse does recognize the constitution as a site for struggle of Indian *atisudras* (social and economic proletariat, as Babasaheb Ambedkar designates the disenfranchised); a site where numerous battles, symbolic and real, are waged against the myriad forms of violent social exclusion leading to the development of the 'pre-Mandal' and 'post-Mandal' constitutionalism. In the process, new practices of social violence and hate speech become constitutionally legitimate, marking an end to the residue of civility in public life. In the process, too, C2 (adjudicatory hermeneutic) emerges, more or less, as a therapeutic form of state power, seeking to restore constitutional justice to a beleaguered, though not entirely fragile, place of its own amidst the practices of violence *for* 'equality' and violence *of* equality.

For the dominant raconteurs, the constitution is the 'cornerstone' of the nation, a site for welding several 'nations' into a 'modern' state ('unity in diversity') and for progressive state formation, oriented to visions of Indian prowess and development ('India's place in the world'). For the subaltern critics, the cornerstone is also a tombstone for justice. The 'strong' state makes itself possible by lawless and unconstitutional exertions and endeavours. It fosters practices of national integration that remain deeply and pervasively human rights violative; it emerges for the minorities as an 'institutionalized riot system';[57] it remains a 'state in search of a nation'[58] and embodies a resilient rape culture.

It is on this register that cultural postmodern critics complicate subaltern critiques, in that they denounce the constitution, including its notions of secularism, as exemplifying the 'demonology' of the spirit of modernity. For Ashis Nandy, for example, constitutional secularism is as detestable an aspect of 'modernization' as the techno-scientific model of Indian development (1985.) However, this form of constitutional nihilism, responsible as well as irresponsible, portraying the constitution as a liability, renders it liable to dire labours of *kar seva*; the missionary social work aimed at its swift and thoroughgoing demolition. The new form of kar seva was inaugurated on 26 January 2000 when the present national, globalizing regime dedicated itself to the celebration of its golden jubilee, ironically, by announcing a committee for its rewriting.[59]

10. The 'Inconcludable'

This essay provides a *suffering* exploration of what Jean François Lyotard describes as the differend, clashes of phrase regimes that must forever remain incommensurable.[60] The fairy tales and the horror stories pose numerous challenges to any 'master' narrative of Indian constitutionalism. None may be wholly privileged. Each destroys hegemonic narrative monopolies. Both profile a distinctive dynamic of the (im)possibility of constitutional justice.

True, in a comparative perspective, the Indian constitution marks a historic break with 'modern' constitutionalism, of the colonial and Cold War genres, and its impact on the constitutionalism of the South is indeed striking, even pervasive. The normative discontinuities are, indeed, astonishingly inaugural.[61] Whatever be the point of arrival, the point of departure is, indeed, startling. No previous constitutional model envisaged such an explicit and comprehensive transformation of a 'traditional' society and installed a description of a constitutionally desired social order and good life, and ways of deep contention regarding these. Even fifty years down the road, this vibrancy of vision survives.

This having been said, each of the critiques here explored raise sufficient ground for anxiety concerning the potential for justice in Indian constitutionalism. The work of celebration must then remain perforce the work of matam, a work of mourning. Should that labour of sorrowing necessarily be a clone of the postmodern matam?[62] To say in response that I do not know would perhaps be politically correct but also to say so would also be a form of 'cop out'; a form that renders epistemic communities complicit with the constitutional order of 'things'; which assimilates the suffering masses of humans to the order of nonhuman.

What needs *saying* matters because of the audacity of enunciation that complicates, at each beginning of the Indian constitutionalism day, that well-touted 'progressive Eurocentrism' which, shorn of its claims to empathetic trappings, remains a wolf in sheep's clothing. Even when the shehnai remains globally orchestrated, shouldn't our matam at least be irreducibly our own?

Notes and References

1. To understand this variation, I enunciate three categories: C1 (the text), C2 (interpretation), and C3 (ideology/theory). C1 stands for the word as the world, a site of initially formulated, or the founding historic, texts. C2 signifies the site of constitutional hermeneutic, the site of formative practices of constitutional interpretation, normally called 'constitutional law'. C3 represents discursive sites for justification (or mystification/demystification/re-mystification) of practices and performances of

governance. (See U. Baxi, 'Constitutionalism as a Site of State Formative Practices', *21 Cardozo L, Rev.* 1183, 2000a.) These three forming practices (cf. G. Simmel, 25 *The Sociology of Georg Simmel*, ed. Kurt. H. Wolff Free Press, New York, 1950) constitute the complex and contradictory practices of formations of power and reflection that we in a shorthand way call the 'constitution'. Ever present in this formation is the issue of the production of 'legitimate law' (Jürgen Habermas, *Between Facts and Norms: Contributions Towards a Theory of Discourse Ethics,* trans. W. Rehg, MIT Press, Cambridge, 1995) or the question of authority (J.M. Bernstein, *The Philosophy of the Novel: Lukacs, Marxism and the Dialectics of Form,* Harvester Press, Sussex, 1984).

2. Ulrich K. Preuss, *Constitutional Revolution: The Link Between Constitutionalism and Progress*, trans. D.L. Schneider, Humanities Press, N.J., 1995, pp. 18–22.
3. B. Anderson, *Imagined Communities: Reflections on the Origins and Spread of Nationalism,* Verso, London, 1983.
4. John Rawls, *Political Liberalism,* Columbia University Press, New York, 1993.
5. See Jürgen Habermas, *Between Facts and Norms.* See Note 1.
6. A. Sen, *Development as Freedom*, Oxford University Press, Oxford, 1999.
7. John Rawls, *The Law of the Peoples,* Harvard University Press, Cambridge, Mass., 1999.
8. J. Braithwaite and P. Drahos, *Global Business Regulation,* Cambridge University Press, Cambridge, 2000.
9. G. Deleuze and F. Guattari, *A Thousand Plateaus: Capitalism and Schizophrenia,* University of Minnesota Press, Minneapolis, 1987, pp. 351–423.
10. 'The Force of Law: The Mystical Foundations of Authority', in *Deconstruction and the Possibility of Justice,* ed. D. Cornell, *et al.*, New York, Routledge, pp. 3–67.
11. J.M. Balkin, *Cultural Software,* Yale University Press, New Haven, 1998.
12. Probably, the most over-written constitution in human history, the text of the original constitution contained close to 400 articles (with a whole variety of sub-articles) and Eleven Schedules. The constitution has undergone over eighty amendments.
13. For the distinction between these two kinds of texts, see U. Baxi, 'Constitutionalism as a Site of State Formative Practices', *21 Cardozo L, Rev.* 1183, 2000a.
14. A national budget that since Independence inflates defence expenditure

to about 40 per cent of national resources and remains impervious to questioning on the grounds of rights and justice.

15. Jürgen Habermas, *Between Facts and Norms*. His notions of 'public sphere' and deliberative justice take no account of the state as a war machine.
16. Like the Official Secrets Act, which converts acts of free movement within a territory designated as prohibited places, into treasonous activity, liable to military trial of citizens as spies. The initial site of protest in South Gujarat against the Sardar Sarovar (Narmada Dam) project was thus notified, empowering the local state to arrest innocent tribal peoples moving across these notified places who had no access to legal understanding of the state law!
17. Of course, the Supreme Court, and now the National Human Rights Commission, has moved towards providing compensation for excesses committed by the army and paramilitary forces (see, for the jurisprudence of constitutional compensation for violation of human rights, S.P. Sathe, *Judicial Activism in India*, OUP, Delhi, 2001. S.P. Sathe, 'Judicial Activism', *Journal of Indian School of Political Economy*, 10, pp. 400–41, 604–39; 11, pp. 1–37, 219–58, 1998–9). The present chair of the national Human Rights Commission has recently bemoaned indifference of the union executive to the suggestion that such operations be brought within the purview of the Human Rights Act.
18. U. Baxi, 'Taking Suffering Seriously: Social Action Litigation before the Supreme Court of India', in U. Baxi (ed.), *Law & Poverty: Critical Essays*, N.M. Tripathi, Bombay, 1989, pp. 387–415.
19. L. and S. Rudolph, *In Pursuit of Lakshmi: The Political Economy of the Indian State*, Chicago University Press, Chicago, 1987; F. Frankel, *India's Political Economy 1947–1977: The Gradual Revolution*, Princeton University Press, Princeton, N.J., 1978.
20. L. and S. Rudolph, *In Pursuit of Lakshmi*.
21. The fantastic growth of administrative law in India [U. Baxi, 'Postcolonial Constitutionalism', in H. Schwartz & S. Ray (eds), *Blackwell Companion to Postcolonial Studies*, Blackwell, Oxford, 2000b, and the materials there cited] attests the various forms of pathologies of state power.
22. U. Baxi, 'Taking Suffering Seriously: Social Action Litigation before the Supreme Court of India'.
23. D. Schneiderman, 'Investment Rules and the New Constitutionalism', *Law and Social Enquiry*, 25, 2000, pp. 757–86; E. Sridharan, 'Economic Liberalization and India's Political Economy: Towards a Paradigm

Synthesis', *The Journal of Commonwealth & Comparative Politics*, XXXI, 1993, pp. 1–31.

24. The principal casualties remain—
    - The shrinking horizons for affirmative action programmes for employment, as the state ceases to be a principal constitution-bound employer
    - The constitutional obligation to protect unorganized labour and the 'weaker sections of society'
    - The state capability to fulfil the right to health, arising out of recognition of the intellectual property rights of a transnational pharmaceutical industry
    - The state regulatory capacity to combat hazardous transnational corporate power to create environmental and industrial catastrophes, of which the suffering of Bhopal remains the archetypal symbol
    - Systemic development policies aimed at elimination of slave, and slave-like, labouring conditions under which masses of rural and urban impoverished eke out their 'livelihood'

    The list can be further enlarged in terms of description of the emergence of a trade-related, market-friendly human rights paradigm threatening, and at times supplanting, the paradigm of universal human rights. See Baxi, *The Future of Human Rights,* Oxford University Press, Delhi, 2001.
25. Swami Agnivesh is thus constrained to internationalize, through the United Nations, the issues of bonded and attached labour; Gail Omvedt is moved to resort to the World Bank and IMF as agencies that may redress the Indian state's failure to do justice to landless labourers; and in relation to the Narmada movement, the World Bank finds momentary solace in the withdrawal of resourcing for the dam. None of these, and related initiatives, surrender people's power to critique the agendum of global capitalism embodied in the international financial institutions. Even when 'driven' to use these fora, these forms of strategic recourse also recognize the varied potential of judicial activism through social action litigation.
26. One hopes that the Indian judiciary will never go so far as the American Supreme Court's recent assertion that people have *no* constitutional right to elect their president and vice president outside legislative bounty—that determines how the electoral college votes may be constituted but it remains important to note that the right to adult suffrage in India is not a fundamental but merely a constitutional right, subject to parliament's plenary power of the amendment of the Indian constitution. One hopes that any misguided amendments will be restrained by the fecund doctrine of the un-amendability of the Basic Structure of the constitution.

27. These two inaugural features realize their full potency for extraordinary forms of activist adjudication in the working of the constitution, especially since 1973.
28. See, for this notion, Rawls, Note 4 above.
29. U. Baxi, 'The Little Done, the Vast Undone: Reflections on Reading Granville Austin's *The Indian Constitution*', *Journal of the Indian Law Institute*, 9, 1967, p. 323.
30. Distinctions, for example, between:
    - *Criticism* and *critique.*
    - *Constitutional patriotism* (that is, fidelity to forms of constitutionalism to legitimate power) and *commitment* (that is the will to achieve the ideals of liberty, equality, dignity, of all Indian citizens)
    - Constitutional and extra-constitutional forms of politics
    - Hierarchies of citizenship: *super-citizens* (beyond the law), *negotiating citizens* (typically upper middle class, who, through their capabilities to negotiate the law, often remain immune from the law, but have the power to represent law enforcement as regime persecution); *subject-citizens* (the vast majority of the Indian impoverished to whom the law applies relentlessly, and for whom the presumption of innocence stands inverted); *insurgent citizens*, often *encountered* or exposed to vicious torture, whose bodies construct the expedient truths of the security of the state; *gendered citizens* (women, lesbi-gay, and transgender people, recipients, and often receptacles, of inhuman societal and state violence and discrimination) and finally (without being exhaustive) the *PAPs—citizens*, the project affected peoples who remain subjects of state practices of lawless development
31. Sobhanlal Datta Gupta, *Justice and Political Order in India,* Firma K.L. Mukhopadhyaya, Calcutta, 1979.
32. U. Baxi, *Marx, Law and Justice: Indian Perspectives,* N. M. Tripathi, Bombay, 1993.
33. Especially by leading the opposition to the device of imposition of President's Rule on states, and effectively critiquing arbitrary interference with autonomous governance, well archived by the Sarkaria Commission: *Report of the Commission on Centre–State Relations* (2 vols.), Govt. of India Press, Nasik, 1988.
34. C. Ake, 'The Democratization of Disempowerment', in Jochen Hippler (ed.), *Democratization of Disempowerment,* Pluto Press, London, 1995, pp. 70–89.
35. But see the extraordinary churning reflected in the documentation prepared by the Committee of Concerned Citizens, *In Search of Democratic Space: Documentation of the Efforts by the Committee of Concerned Citizens*

(CCC) to bring peoples aspirations and right to live with dignity on the agenda of Naxalite movements and Governments, Hyderabad, August 1998, especially pp. 18–28, 45–55, 84, 96.

36. A.J. Parel, *Gandhi: Hind Swaraj and Other Writings*, Cambridge, Cambridge University Press, 1997.
37. The insistence of the first name is essential, given that his last name is more familiar to contemporary generations through many leaders of the Indian National Congress. I do not use the word 'Mahatma' to distinguish him from other Gandhis (and not just in the light of Ananda Coomarasawamy's critique of that notion).
38. Ganesh Prasad, *Nehru: A Study in Colonial Liberalism,* Sterling Publishers, New Delhi, 1976.
39. P. Chatterjee, *Nationalist Thought in the Colonial World: A Derivative Discourse?*, Zed, London, 1986.
40. U. Baxi, 'Justice as Emancipation: Babasaheb Ambedkar's Legacy and Vision', in U. Baxi & B. Parekh (eds), *Crisis and Change in Contemporary India,* Sage, Delhi, 1995, pp. 122–49.
41. U. Baxi, 'The Little Done, the Vast Undone', p.323.
42. T.K. Oommen, *Charisma, Stability, and Change: An Analysis of Bhoodan–Gramdan Movement in India,* Thompson Press, New Delhi, 1972.
43. J.D. Sethi, *Trusteeship: The Gandhian Alternative*, Gandhi Peace Foundation, New Delhi, 1986.
44. U. Baxi, *The Crisis of the Indian Legal System,* Vikas, New Delhi, 1982.
45. See T. Blom Hansen, *The Saffron Wave: Democracy and Hindu Nationalism in Modern India,* OUP, Delhi, 1999; C. Bhatt and P. Mukta, 'Hindutva in the West: Mapping the Antinomies of Diaspora Nationalism', *Ethnic and Racial Studies,* 23, 2000, pp. 407–41.
46. P. Mukta, 'The Public Face of Hindu Nationalism', *Ethnic and Racial Studies,* 23, 2000, pp. 407–41.
47. The triggers being provided by a whole series of critical events: the legislative reversal of the Shah Bano judgment, the opening of locks at the Ram Mandir in Ayodhya, the Deorala discourse concerning the right to perform sati, and the implementation of the Mandal Report. See Brenda Cossman and Ratna Kapur, *Secularism's Last Sigh?: Hindutva and the Rule of Law,* Oxford University Press, New Delhi, 1999.
48. S.P. Sathe, *Judicial Activism In India,* Oxford Univesity Press, New Delhi, 2001. I say the so-called 'Hindutva' judgment because the issue of constitutionality of Hindutva was never before the Supreme Court, which had to deal with the rather more specific question of whether freedom of speech and expression during election campaigns appealing to utopian alternatives to present policy (whether of the Left or the Right

genre) amounted to a 'corrupt practice.' Quite rightly, the Supreme Court decline to so rule. Unfortunately, Brother J.S. Verma unduly extolled 'Hindutva' as a way of life in a couple of paragraphs, which grew larger than life in the public outcry that followed.

49. This type of propaganda overlooks the fact that the Supreme Court of India has upheld the constitutionality of Orissa and Madhya Pradesh legislations as prohibiting the use of 'force' and 'fraud' in such practices.
50. U. Baxi, 'The Constitutional Discourse on Secularism', in U. Baxi, A. Jacob and T. Singh (eds.), *Reconstructing the Republic*, Indian Association of Social Science Institutions and Har-Anand Publications, Delhi, 1999, pp. 211–33.
51. U. Baxi, 'The Kar Seva of the Indian Constitution? Reflections on Proposals for Review of the Constitution', *Economic and Political Weekly*, XXXV (11 March 2000), pp. 891–5, 2000c.
52. As the incidents concerning the making of *Water*, a film on Indian widows at Varanasi, or the film *Fire*, or systematic defacement of F.M. Hussain's paintings, demonstrate.
53. The most recent example of sovereign immunity enjoyed by Thackeray occurred when he was indicted on rather minor charges of hate speech last year. When a warrant for his arrest was issued , he and his supporters issued dire threats of retaliatory violence. Hindutva ideologues do not of course critique such open defiance of the law. Rather, they provide fuel to the fire by foregrounding the claim that all other religions, and cultural politics associated with them, have been repressive and retrograde and the best, even only, reassurance for a 'democratic' Indian future lies in the hegemony of reconstructed Hinduism. See Arun Shourie, *World of Fatwas, or Shariah in Action,* ASA Publications, New Delhi, 1995; and *Harvesting Our Souls: Missionaries, their Design, their Claim,* ASA Publications, New Delhi, 2000.
54. 28th Report of the Commissioner of the Scheduled Castes and Tribes, Government of India, New Delhi, n.d.
55. Urvashi Butalia, 'Community, State and Gender: On Women's Agency During Partition', *Economic and Political Weekly*, 28, 24 April 1993, WS 12–14; R. Menon and K. Bhasin, 'Recovery, Rupture and Resistance: Indian State and the Abduction of Women during Partition', *Economic and Political Weekly,* 28, 24 April 1993, pp. WS 2–11.
56. Veena Das, 'Language and Body: Transactions in the Construction of Pain', in Arthur Kleinman, Veena Das, and Margaret Lock (eds), *Social Suffering*, California University Press, Berkeley, 1997, p. 67.
57. Paul R. Brass, *The Theft of an Idol: Text and Context in the Representation of Collective Violence,* Princeton University Press, NJ, 1997.

58. G. Aloysius, *Nationalism Without a Nation,* Oxford University Press, New Delhi, 1999.
59. U. Baxi, 'The Kar Seva of the Indian Constitution?'
60. Jean-François Lyotard, *The Different: Phrases in Dispute*, 1992, New Haven, Yale University Press: Georges van den Abbeele, trans.
61. Indeed, from that point of view, the imaginative features of the Indian constitution are constituted by its salient departures from the paradigm of 'modern' constitutionalism. It constructs, first, the ordering principles of legitimation of state power, such that make legitimation wholly problematic, creating practices of public opinion and 'democratic will formative practices' (*cf.* Jürgen Habermas, *Between Facts and Norms*) that enable contestation concerning political practices of cruelty as well as imposition of the law and the constitution as *political fate*. Second, it marks the practice (and the continuing possibility) of naming orders of radical evil in the Indian state and civil society. In a creative departure from the classical liberal–modern notions of human rights, the Indian constitution addresses not just the state as a violator of human rights but also formations of power in civil society as millennially originary sites. Articles 17 (constitutional abolition of untouchability) and 23 (providing forced labour, trafficking in human beings, *begar*) are monumentally addressed to civil society. Third (thanks to Ambedkar) the constitution also innovates participatory rights: rights of the underclasses (the Dalits, the *atisudras*, the millennially dispossessed, disadvantaged, and deprived masses of India—U. Baxi, 'Justice as Emancipation: Babasaheb Ambedkar's Legacy and Vision', pp. 122–49; Marc Galanter, *Competing Equalities: Law and the Backward Classes in India,* Oxford University Press, New Delhi, 1984—to representation in the civil services of the states and legislatures. Fourth, the constitution, through its distinction between fundamental rights and directive principles of state policy, also innovates the international regime of human rights. It presages the distinction between the Covenant on Civil and Political Rights (rights entitled, as it were, to here-and-now judicial enforcement) and the Covenant on Social, Economic and Cultural Rights (subject to a regime of 'progressive realization'). Assurances of 'minority' rights are spectacularly enshrined. Fifth, the constitution, defines *development* as those governance policies which accomplish a *disproportionate* flow of rights and beneficence to the *atisudras* or the Dalits. The regime of representation in the Indian constitution is thus inherently, and innovatively, people-friendly. Sixth, contrary to the 'original intent' (if such phrase-regimes are meaningful!), the Supreme Court of India becomes the Supreme Court

for Indians. This happens initially, through the logics and paralogics of *Kesavananda Bharati*, by an unprecedented assertion of judicial power to review and annul, on the grounds of basic structure, amendments duly made by parliament, and then by the explosive invention of social action litigation, democratizing judicial access and redefining the mission of activist adjudicatory power and policy.

62. See Jacques Derrida, *The Spectres of Marx: The State of Debt, the Work of Mourning and the New International*, Routledge, London, 1994.

3

The Indian Constitution and Democracy

SUNIL KHILNANI

'I know that most MPs see the Constitution for the first time when they take an oath on it. They hardly know the history of their own political party, leave alone that of the competing party.'—Pramod Mahajan, Union Minister for Information and Technology, speaking while inaugurating a school for RSS/BJP politicians.[1]

Fifty years after its inauguration as a republic, India is passing through the toils of what might be called 'pure politics'. By this I mean that struggles over the access, capture, and holding of power have intensified sharply in ways that appear to show little concern for the procedures that regulate power's exercise, let alone any interest in publicly reflecting on the uses of political power and the ends to which it may be used. Raw competition for power has weakened the organizing frameworks initially set up to regulate such competition, and has set up alternative, informal, and often opaque patterns that preside over political life. Familiarity with the constitution, always pretty thin beyond a few restricted circles, is today stretched to virtual invisibility. Those who do claim for themselves some knowledge of the constitution have expressed in increasingly strident terms the view that it is a relic and hindrance; a document that has been superseded by history and whose only function today is to serve as a block to the will and interest of a putative majority.

Unfamiliarity with and neglect of the constitution goes further. In the national parliament, as in state assemblies, we have become accustomed to hearing about and now to seeing (thanks to TV) episodes of political carnival: the dismantling of public furniture, the hurling of footwear, 'rushing the well' (a fine Indian contribution to the terminology of international parliamentary practice), regular uproar, and chronic stalling of business. These parliamentary mutinies are an established and regular feature of our democratic life: like the kerfuffle surrounding elections, they have achieved the status of a public spectacle, staged for effect, which we have come to expect. There is of course a facile and prime reaction to this: one that simply expresses shock and outrage at such impropriety. This however is not a very revealing response. After all, the elected politicians in question are sufficiently professional to learn the rules they wish to; and their actions are, in their own way, themselves rule-bound. It would be more useful to ask: what does this mean? What can it tell us about the changing character of our democracy, of our constitution, and of the relationship between the two?

What is the nature of the constitutional voice in Indian public life? More specifically, who speaks in the constitution, from where, and to whom? Such questions are properly prompted by the fact that the weighty presence of the constitution within India's formal political system belies its actual externality in relation to the society as a whole. It is helpful to begin with the question of what exactly is a constitution—and what, therefore, is the nature of its presence in a society. It is quite difficult to give a clear answer as to what a constitution actually is. Lawyers, and those fond of jurisprudential and political theory, tend to see constitutions as precise and determinate mechanisms which specify, regulate and coordinate political powers and rights, and which possess identifiable and predictable causal properties. They see constitutions as texts, the legal specification of political principles and commitments, which are to be observed and enacted by those whose public duty it is to so do. Politicians, and most of the rest of us, however, tend to think of constitutions considerably more vaguely. Rather than seeing them as strict regulatory documents, in this view constitutions represent a 'system of intentions'; intentions that are modified over time, as new generations of interpreters (elected politicians, judges, and lawyers, citizens) bring their own intentions to it. From this perspective, constitutions are severely circumscribed in their practical effects by the causal powers that are available to the state at any given moment, just as they are circumscribed by the fact that they are understood only within limited circles.

The nature of a constitution's presence in a society is difficult to focus upon. When, as is often the case, we speak of the 'spirit' of the constitution or that of its framers, what exactly are we talking about? Does this 'spirit' have some kind of objective presence, external to us; are we referring to the intentions of specific dead individuals (the original members of the Constituent Assembly), to the presumed intentions of a historically stable collectivity known as India, or to a system of meanings that exist in the minds of individual present-day Indians (which can be identified through some conception of a 'majority')?

Something important does turn on what sorts of responses we choose to give to such apparently innocent questions. How we answer will specify, in particular, how we understand the nature of the relationship between a set of ideal and formal rules and actual social practices: between, on the one hand, 'law' and, on the other, 'culture'. One might see a constitution as expressive of the customs and habits of a society: in the way that Montesquieu described the English constitution as an (unwritten) embodiment of the 'laws of spirit' of that society, a set of beliefs that held together and coursed through the veins of English life. Or, quite contrastingly, one might see a constitution as a set of laws whose function is to be corrective of that society and its practices: in the way in which Jeremy Bentham thought of a constitution as a clear statement of rational ideals, that could be used to reform and remake the society. Each perspective bears differently on how one sees a constitution's relation to its society. In the former view, the constitution is simply an articulation of principles that are latent in the practices of the society, and as such it functions as a kind of aide-mèmoire: it gives voice to what is already immanently present. In the latter case, it has necessarily a more external relation, and it functions as an authority to which both government and people, rulers and ruled, must turn for adjudication and guidance; it voices things not yet available to the society question. The Indian constitution is today the subject of a disagreement between these two views of what a constitution is, and what its role might be.

The idea of founding a new political order by drawing up a legible document specifying the current future goals of that order, as well as specifying limits and constraints on the pursuit of these goals, was an entirely novel one in Indian history, and marked a distinct break with the past. Previous large-scale regimes—the Cholas, the Mughals—had not had recourse to such an idea. The British, initially through company charters, and then most fully through the 1935 Government of India Act, had implanted this idea in India. The Indian constitution of 1950 broke with the belief that a polity or society could be founded upon or sanctioned by a religious or divine order, by inherited social practice, or simply by forcible conquest. It installed for the first time in India the idea of humanly created law as the basis and foundation of all public activity in society.

It is difficult, therefore, to accept a view of the 1950 constitution as the capstone of a long story of constitutional and democratic development in India: a view which sees a slow entrenchment of a democratic ethos and principles among Indians, an expansion of the rights and forms of representation, of the rule of law, and of the separation of powers. This story, with differing inflections, sustains both imperial and nationalist views of India's political development. I'd like to address this issue here by way of a gloss on one particular sentence in my book, *The Idea of India*, which has proved particularly troublesome, both to readers of the book and to myself. I wrote there that, '[l]ike the British empire it supplanted, India's constitutional democracy was established in a fit of absentmindedness.' I went on to explain that I did not mean that it was unintended, nor that it was set up without deliberation: what I did mean to do was to draw attention to a certain blitheness, not to say blindness about the potential implications of introducing political equality into a society of great economic and social inequality, as well as a neglect of questions surrounding the nature of political representation, the status of rights, and of how each of these—and their relationship with one another—might change over time.

My remark has drawn ire: as an unfair exaggeration, as a restatement of 'the cultural inadaptability thesis', and as representing a 'biased view of the history of liberal democracy in India'. I have been reminded that: democracy arrives in India in the form of nationalism; that this democracy was necessarily liberal in its inclinations, because of commitment to civil liberties and its vision of social justice and equality; and that the cultural character of nationalism forced the constitution-makers to move beyond individualist liberalism, and to balance it against collective attachments (Bhargava, 2000).

I am not so certain. The national movement certainly had a pragmatic attachment to forms of consensual decision-making. The two decades preceding the setting up of the Constituent Assembly in 1946 were thick with debates and plans about the appropriate future political order, and there was a shared sense that this order had to be explicitly specified, and agreement about it reached between the parties to it: between Indians and the British, and between Indians themselves. It is possible, too, to point to a series of declarations that expressed a commitment to democratic procedures: The Motilal Nehru Report of 1928, the 1931 Karachi resolution on fundamental rights, and Nehru's address to the Faizpur Congress of 1936 which called for a Constituent Assembly elected by universal suffrage, each gives clear expression of this. It is also true that the elections of 1946, although based on a restricted franchise, still encompassed vast absolute numbers. Beyond this, one might also notice the demand of autonomy for the multiple groupings of India; a long-standing demand that goes back at least to the late nineteenth century.

However, neither this nor the fact that there existed a developed debate about social reform stretching back into the nineteenth century should lead us to accept the view, advanced by some and accepted by others, that liberalism had deep social roots in India; roots that were struck well before the introduction of democratic principles and practices (Pannikar, 1962, Bhargava, 2000). To suggest that one could find in India's past precursors or embryonic forms of constitutional and democratic politics is, it seems to me, a case of faith triumphing over evidence. It was precisely the absence of a broader liberal climate that has, in the decades since Independence, made for a fraught and uneasy relationship between the constitution and democratic politics.

There was, in pre-Independence India, a restricted and partial familiarity with forms of representative politics, as well as an acquaintance with the operation of the legal systems installed by the British Raj. However, pre-independence political currents were not much taken by democratic principles. The Hindu Right, in the form of the Hindu Mahasabha and the RSS, took a vehemently anti-democratic position, preferring organicist conceptions that lent themselves to authoritarianism (Jaffrelot, 1996). Indeed, even the principal school for political learning in India, the Congress movement itself, could not be described as an organization wedded to practices of internal democracy. It was always a rule-following organization and, after Gandhi's rise to power, more observant of the need to base decision-making on consensual forms; and, beginning in 1937, it showed a capacity to develop impressive skills in campaigning for and winning elections. Nonetheless, these practices and skills do not exhaust even a narrow definition of democracy, or of liberalism. Gandhi himself operated as a benign autocrat: through a medley of fasts, silences, and abstinences he bent opponents or dissidents to his will. He was also quite prepared, whenever necessary, simply to overturn elected outcomes, as he did in the case of Subhas Chandra Bose's election to the presidentship of the Congress in 1939.

Gandhi's own embrace of universal suffrage, in the wake of the Karachi resolution of 1931, was in a quite particular context. It was a claim directed not only against the limited representation offered to Indians by the British, but it was directed also against the demands of the minorities: Muslims, Sikhs, Europeans, and Depressed Classes, the 'so-called Untouchables', for separate electorates. To press for universal suffrage within a joint or common electorate was, Gandhi saw, the best way of shutting down the demand for separate electorates (see Gandhi's Memo: 'The Congress Scheme for a Communal Settlement', 28 October 1931, Round Table Conference; and his Speech at the RTC, 13 November 1931). His endorsement of democracy might therefore be seen as a pragmatic manoeuvre rather than a principled commitment—as a way of trying to secure unity within the Congress rather than driven by a recognition of democracy as principle for registering differences.

The Congress Left, meanwhile, also had little regard for democracy, at least in its actually existing liberal (or 'bourgeois') forms. Bose himself, jackbooted and be-medalled, could hardly be portrayed as a democrat; and socialists within Congress tended to see democracy as a superannuated political form. Internationally, the 1930s and '40s were not high days for democracy: crumbling in Europe, to those outside its

European hinterlands it seemed little more than the trademark ideology of the imperial states of the West. Nehru spoke repeatedly of its limits, and in the decades immediately before Independence, the terms which appeared more commonly in Congress talk were those such as 'self-government', 'independence', 'swaraj', 'self-rule', 'the will of the people'. From a purely lexical point of view, therefore, 'democracy' did not make frequent appearances.

Nehru, in his 'Objectives' speech, explained the resolve that India should aim to be an 'independent sovereign republic'. The absence of the word democracy should not, he insisted, discomfort people: it was obvious that India would choose this form, since 'the whole of our past', he said a little disingenuously, 'is witness to this fact that we stand for democratic institutions' (13.1.46, SW2nd:1:247). However, the institutional forms and procedures of democracy would not be copied from Europe. India would finds its own way to improve on existing models, and thereby would establish the 'fullest democracy'. By this he meant to suggest that it would achieve economic democracy, or 'socialism'—also a word missing from the Objectives Resolution, a word he claimed to avoid in order to cut short controversy. 'Therefore', he declared, 'we have laid down no theoretical words', words like democracy or socialism, in the statement of aims placed before the Constituent Assembly as it meets for the first time for fear that such terms might raise unnecessary disputes.

The unwillingness to enter into the controversies surrounding 'theoretical words' had its costs, curtailing argument over some of the fundamental elements of democracy: the nature of representation, the status of rights, and the claims of equality. It retracted attention from how these elements might interact with one another over time, producing mutations in the forms of democracy, while also changing the internal character of the nature of representation, rights, and equality. To put the point differently, faced with the impressive sophistication of the Constituent Assembly debates, it is striking to find relatively little reflection on the historical character of political concepts: the sense that their meanings, and therefore the range of practical activities which they may be used to sanction and to legitimate, would alter over time.

Representation

Take the issue of representation. The constitution installed a specific view of representation, derived from a notion that imbued the thinking of all members of the Constituent Assembly: that of acting on behalf of the society taken as a whole. This is not surprising, given that when it was convened in 1946, the Assembly was not elected by universal suffrage and was in fact a strikingly narrow body in terms of its social composition: it consisted of around 300 men (the numbers increased after the princely states joined the Union), elected on the restricted franchises and divided electorates of the provincial legislatures that had been set in place by the 1935 Government of India Act. The Assembly was dominated by the upper caste and Brahminic élites within Congress: it is worth recalling that there was no organized representation of India's Muslims, no presence of Hindu communal groups (although Congress itself harboured many Hindu conservatives), and, after 1948, no Socialist interest. Within the Assembly itself, the drafting of the constitution was left to around two dozen lawyers.

The conception of representation that emerged was based on what might be called a philanthropic politics, in the sense that it sanctioned a politics by an élite self-consciously acting on behalf of a larger group of whom they were not part, to whom they did not belong, and with whom they could claim to share neither identity nor interests. As with the intellectuals and members of the upper classes who joined the British labour movement in the late nineteenth and early twentieth centuries, there was a sense that the only way to make an honourable career in politics was to militate in favour of interests that were not directly or immediately one's own (Furbank, 1999). One might call this view of representation an incarnational rather than a numerical one, and it was given clear expression by Gandhi when he wrote, for example, in his *Autobiography* of his experience of drawing up a new constitution for the Congress:

> I hold it to be an utter delusion to believe that a large number of delegates is in any way a help to the better conduct of the business, or that it safeguards the principle of democracy. Fifteen hundred delegates, jealous of the interests of the people, broad-minded and truthful, would any day be a better safeguard

for democracy than six thousand irresponsible chosen anyhow. To safeguard democracy the people must have a keen sense of independence, self-respect and their oneness, and should insist upon choosing as their representatives only such persons as are good and true.

Dismissing those 'obsessed with the idea of numbers', Gandhi's view of representation bore an oblique relation to the idea of democracy understood in terms of elections.

Clearly, the political psychology as well as the public legitimacy of an actor who sees his or her representative role in this way is different from that of a politician who claims to act on behalf of a group of which they are themselves a member, with whom they share an identity or interests. The former, when speaking against injustice, can draw a special force, precisely because they are disinterested. However, this distance from those on whose behalf they claim to speak also necessarily leaves them open to two serious charges: that of betrayal, and to the accusation that they wish merely to create others in their own image. Of all Indian politicians, Gandhi was one who embodied this view of representation:

> I claim myself in my own person to represent the vast mass of the Untouchables. Here I speak not merely on behalf of the Congress, but I speak on my own behalf, and I claim that I would get, if there was a referendum of the Untouchables, their vote, and I would top their poll.

It was a conception that was widely shared by the Congress leadership, and certainly chimed with Nehru's views. It allowed virtually no space for forms of self-representation, as Jinnah and his colleagues in the Muslim League were to learn. Jinnah, of course, refused this view of philanthropic representation, insisting that only a Muslim leadership could rightfully represent the subcontinent's Muslims.

Men like Ambedkar and Maulana Azad were located in a more ambiguous space in the field of political representation. These were men who sometimes spoke, or who were seen to be speaking, on behalf of their own kind, but they were also able to claim to stand for a larger and less particular conception of collectivity and interests. Azad's presence as a member of the Congress High Command, for instance, was seen as an indication of Muslim participation in Congress leadership circles, but he was also seen as a representative of all nationalist Indians, not simply those Muslims who supported the Congress. Ambedkar, while acknowledged as leader of the Scheduled castes, was also seen more generally as a representative of the exploited and oppressed.

The spread of democratic politics, in particular through means of regular elections over the past fifty years, has given rise to a third form of representation, distinct from the models associated with Gandhi and Nehru or with Ambedkar and Azad. This is sometimes referred to by phrases such as the 'politics of identity', or of 'presence'. In this understanding of representation, the political actor claims to act on behalf not simply of his own kind—caste, religion, racial or linguistic group—but actually, at the limit, to act simply on behalf of his or her own self. This can generate a politics of immediacy, which bridles at what it sees as the delaying tactics of policy-formation, or of legislation as the outcome of discussion and deliberation. It can, if taken up widely and used persistently, induce a critical condition in the form of representative government, and can force its collapse. It is the presence of this third understanding of representation that helps to comprehend the neglect among contemporary politicians of constitutional rules and procedures.

As far as those who operate with this understanding of representation see it, their duty as elected politicians is not to act on behalf of anyone else but themselves and their own supporters linked by kin, caste, or religion. Previously, a representative (operating with the earlier conception) had to be seen ostentatiously to follow rules and procedures properly on behalf of others, precisely to absolve himself of the charge of not acting correctly on behalf of others, or of acting in his own interests. Now, to follow such etiquette under the new conditions of representation is to lay oneself open to the charge of assimilation with an alien élite and of betrayal of one's supporters. Political representatives under these conditions wish above all to leave a literal, physical trace and impress of their presence in the space of public power—in the assembly parliament. They literally wish to fill the space of these chambers with their physical presence. This, it seems to me, is a clue to the current codes of parliamentary practice.

These conditions of representation have yielded up a politics that is hard to contain within the conventional rules of constitutional observance. Here one might remark that the original framers of the Indian constitution were either very optimistic or perhaps insufficiently imaginative when it came to reflecting on the consequences and effects which the extension of democracy would bring with it. In particular, the effects of the entry of new classes into politics, and of the issue of what motivations these groups might themselves have to respect the motivations of the original constitution-makers, were unaddressed. As compared with India, in Europe the slow process of democratic extension helped to give popular focus to the idea of a constitution as a fundamental way of structuring public power, and it helped to extend this focus to widening bands of the citizen body and to slowly implant motives and reasons to act in certain ways rather than others. In India, however, no effective way of self-consciously achieving this outcome was invented; nor was there sufficient historical lag which might have allowed such understandings to become part of the everyday practice of sufficient numbers of citizens so as to ensure its social reproducibility. Instead, the constitution came to be perceived not as something that was constitutive of public life, but rather as akin to club house rules: a set of complicated procedures for regulating etiquette in a very narrow sphere of life, and which could be dispensed with.

When the meaning of representation is transformed to signify a politics on behalf of oneself, this is quite unlikely to sustain a larger sense of a *polis*; of a constitutional social and political order. Such a view proposes no alternative image of the social order, other than that the social order exists simply as a vehicle for serving particular claims; claims made by some groups against other groups within the order. It is a politics that seeks to derive power from winning acceptance for a particular claim about who one is, and therefore what privileges one might claim, rather than for what one might propose to do with political power. Such a politics of 'identity' or 'presence' is of a radically different kind from the politics that the constitution envisaged. Its character is captured by P.N. Furbank: 'It [such a politics] retains within it relics of traditional politics, but not of the domestic but of the international or "balance of power" kind. Its habit is to create around itself an aura of diplomatic relations, frontier incidents, chauvinism and irredentism' (Furbank 1999:114). This is all played out within the frames and structures of domestic politics

Each of these three models today informs the character of political representation in India. Their complicated interplay has created a situation in which the constitution, while it has enabled the emergence of each of these models, now appears as a document little prepared to deal with their effects.

Rights

The shifts in the character of representation are related to the peculiar form taken in India by the language and what some have called the 'culture' of rights. The link between representation and rights has been sustained by the notion of reservation. In the pre-Independence discussions of the future political order, a set of fundamental issues of principle was left unresolved, given only a pragmatic gloss: this centred on the character of political community, on the issue of whether or not it did offer full and equal membership to all, and if it did not, what sorts of remedy could it offer? Religion and caste position were correctly seen as distributing power and possibilities asymetrically, and thus as bars to full membership and to the exercise of rights that went with this, and as a remedy to these fears, the principle of reservation gained currency. Reservation was a way of securing representation on behalf of groups which might otherwise have no presence in the political process, and no share in the opportunities which the political power had the capacity to distribute.

There were at least three possible ways that reservations could be given practical form. The first, the method devised and deployed by the British Raj, was to establish separate or reserved electorates, thus ensuring that numerically minor groups would still have a political presence. The issue of joint, as opposed to separate, electorates, was to become a topic of fierce dispute among Indians during the 1930s and '40s, with the Congress ranged against the Muslim League, against Ambedkar and his supporters, and also against the Raj. The nub of the issue turned on how the substance of the political community was specified, on the membership it provided, and on how that was to be represented in the arenas of political decision-making. For Jinnah, the fear was that the political equality promised by universal franchise within a unitary state eventually would be undermined by the numerical inequality of being a religious minority; Ambedkar, sensitive to Muslim fears of social discrimination, believed such discrimination would be applied with even more force against India's outcastes. Indeed, in his 'Memorandum and Draft Articles on the Rights of States and Minorities', Ambedkar himself shifted away from the method of separate electorates, to call more drastically for separate geographical territories for India's 'untouchables'. This makes clear the second method: by what was effectively the reservation of territory of specified geographical areas, in which numerically minor communities could decide and manage their own affairs. This logic was pushed to its terminus by Jinnah and the Muslim League, and resulted in Partition.

The third method rejected both separate electorates and territorial reservation, seeing each as threatening the idea of a single community of common membership. It was the method of law and legal redress, established and dispensed within the framework of a single state. The latter was the chosen method of Congress and of the Constituent Assembly. This view established citizenship (and the membership of political community that it implied) as primary, yet it also recognized citizenship as one identity alongside others: for example, those of religion and caste community. It assumed that the latter were transient, and would yield finally to the more permanent claims of citizenship; but in the interim, both transient and permanent forms had to be acknowledged. These presumptively permanent and transient identities were allocated rights with different scopes of operation: the permanent rights of citizenship were (temporarily) restricted, while the transient claims of religious and caste belonging were (temporarily) extended.[2]

Rights came by such means to be seen as plastic in relation to the state's interpretation of the character of the political community at any given time, and therefore of how it was appropriate to treat its members. This entrenched a heavily paternalist view of rights, and downplayed the understanding of rights as a form of agency. The position was well captured in the remark by a member of the Constituent Assembly, Somnath Lahiri, that in the constitution rights had been framed 'from the point of view of a police constable' (CAD III, 2, 384, cited in Austin, 1965: 72). Freedoms and rights were limited and constrained from two directions: they were curbed in the name of social reform and change, as well as in the name of stability and order. Indeed, what Granville Austin had represented in terms of the image of a 'seamless web'—the smooth intertwining of the three foundational strands of democracy, social reform and unity—might be seen otherwise: as resembling more a cat's cradle, in which democracy was a fragile pattern, easily overturned by the claims made in the name of the other two. Also, when it came to the injunctions of stability and order, the emergency powers of the constitution were of course able to provide the firmest limits to democratic freedoms. Within the Constituent Assembly, as Ambedkar, Jagjivan Ram, and Hansa Mehta had pointed out, there was significant resistance to the prospect of making universal suffrage a basic right (cf. Sarkar, pp. 28–31). Sardar Patel, for instance, when presenting the Rights to Freedom to the assembly, had excluded clauses on rights to peaceful assembly and on formation of associations and unions (which had been part of the subcommittee draft (see CAD I, 30.4.1947, p. 132).

The character of rights was thus shaped by the mode of their introduction into Indian politics. Rights were seen as conditional on the state's purposes, and this attitude persisted in the inaugural years of the Republic (consider the logic underlying the Ninth Schedule of the constitution, and the 'anti-judiciary sentiment' which pervaded the Congress Working Committee throughout the 1950s: see Austin, 1999). There is an important historical question about how democracy, and its attendant concepts and practices, emerges in a society like India's, and about how the particular history of its emergence affects and shapes the kind of democratic politics that results. In the Indian case it cannot be claimed that democracy emerged as the cumulative outcome of popular pressure for rights, representation, and equality of treatment (although it is of course part of the nationalist story to insist that this was how democracy emerged). In fact the periods of mass politics in India have been brief—sporadically in the 1920s and 1930s, from 1942 to the late '40s, and then again from the early and mid-1970s, and in the late 1980s and early 1990s. The acquisition of mass democratic rights (the franchise) was not the product of popular action, and it therefore could not embody in any secure way the learning and memory that results through such action.

Equality

The constitution's problematic relation to the idea of equality was stated most trenchantly by Ambedkar in his grand, uneasy, closing rumination on the debates of the Constituent Assembly:

We must begin by acknowledging the fact that there is complete absence of two things in Indian society. One of them is equality. On the social plane, we have in India a society based on the principle of graded inequality which means elevation for some and degradation for others. On the economic plane we have a society in which there are some who have immense wealth as against many who live in abject poverty. On the 26th of January 1950 we are going to enter a life of contradictions.

An underlying puzzle about India's democracy is that of why a political system based on the distribution of equal formal political powers across the citizenry, and one which has functioned as such over time, still should have failed to favour economic redistribution. (This is not quite true: in fact professional politicians in India have found ways of making democratic politics function effectively as a redistributive mechanism. They just happen to have done so in ways that polite political opinion finds offensive, by means, usually, of corruption, a pretty effective form of redistribution in India.) The fear that all democratic regimes would tend to redistribute towards the poor, and that ultimately democracy would dispossess the rich, was always the classic fear about democracy—and it has been given expression in a line of thinkers from Plato onwards, via Macaulay, and on to Hayek.

One might put the issue differently: what happens when political equality is introduced into a society specifically designed to perpetuate social and economic inequality? Clearly it doesn't follow that social and economic equality is attained as a necessary consequence. Nehru and many of his colleagues shared a hope—a hope they had in common with the advocates of social democracy in Europe, politicians who had chosen the parliamentary route to socialism—that universal suffrage would shift the balance of governmental power towards the poor, and would encourage policies that in time would deliver real benefits to the poor. Explanations as to why this has not happened have been various. They range from intricate general arguments about the inherent game—theoretic problems that preclude any shift, by parliamentary means, from a capitalist economy towards one based on public ownership (Przeworski, 1985), to, in the Indian context, claims about the bad faith of the original framers, or explanations that focus on the obstacles posed by social hierarchies and the failure of the state to break these (an unwillingness, for instance, to challenge the right to private property). To all these, one important explanation should be added: the unavailability of any feasible strategy for running an economy based on the public ownership of wealth—the failure, over the past half century, of socialist economics.

In the early 1950s, and again for a time in the 1970s, the issue of equality in India was focused around the right to private property. Constitutions generally wish to pre-guarantee the right to property, and usually do so by making it a natural or fundamental right. However, no constitution operating within a democracy can ever provide such a guarantee with any finality. Such rights will remain open to potential political challenges and pressure. Indira Gandhi in the 1970s invoked a popular mandate and claimed to speak for democracy when she threatened the rich with dispossession by appealing to the rights of the poor majority. That particular line of rhetorical argument seems now to have faded, at least for the time being. The project of radical redistribution, of constructing the 'order of equality', seems not to be on the agenda of the participants in what has been called India's 'second democratic upsurge': their interests are focused more on the smaller and relative gains afforded by reservations or regional allocations. Their politics are not based on universalist claims to justice, but on a desire for compensation for injuries committed by past generations. Further, the history of socialism over the past fifty years seems to have forced a recognition that the private ownership of capital is a public good (which is not to say that particular individual beneficiaries of a system based on private capital can themselves hope to be considered as a public good).

Since the brief episodes of radicalism in the early 1950s and the 1970s, which claimed to try to alter the property order, the issue of equality has been translated into a different arena, and has been primarily addressed through the concept of reservation and its attendant policies. The persistence and extension of policies of reservations has helped to redefine the vocabulary of merit and distinction, by linking them to, and locating them as effects of, sequences of very long historical and moral causality. It is always a nice question as to where exactly the beginning of such a sequence might be most appropriately located (are you, or my forefathers, responsible for the fact that you hold the job you do?). How far back ought one to delve in order to account for the current distribution of inequalities? Who can claim the authority to judge what Nehru called 'the justice of yesterday' (*Parliamentary Debates*, 16.5.1951, cited in Austin 1999:87)? These are not and cannot ever be questions to which there could conceivably be settled or technical answers: they will always be subjects of intense political and moral contest, in which symbolic victories and defeats can play an unpredictably important role. Merit and distinction have in many fields in contemporary India come to be seen as an effect of historic privilege and discrimination. It is a nice question as to who exactly has the force of justice behind them: the spokespersons of the disprivileged or the appointed guardians of standards. The rhetorical energies of democracy have sometimes been turned towards effacing the fact that democracy does not affirm or imply that we are all, in practice and in fact, equal in all respects: it merely distributes an equal share in political power to equals and unequals alike.

There is always and necessarily an intrinsic tension in the cord connecting the idea of democracy to that of the idea of a constitution: as Plato had long ago seen and as Roberto Unger, from a very different perspective, reminds us today. Constitutions place immense, even their entire, faith in institutional causality and structures. They wish, by means of institutions designed to stabilize beliefs and filter out passing enthusiasms, to restrict and mitigate the role of contingency, of historical time, in the life of a human collectivity. A democracy, on the other hand, is of all political regimes least susceptible to understanding in terms of institutional causalities. This is because of its intensely historical character. A democracy is, at its ineliminable core, simply a stream of human intentions and judgements, which are themselves likely to be shaped by the full spectrum of factors that shape human motivations. Because it gives centrality to agency, a democracy is best understood through careful historical analysis, not through the grid of constitutional mechanisms and structures. As such, and in a practical sense, a constitutional regime stands opposed to a democracy.

This tension is reaching acute levels in India today. The growing historical character of democracy in India, the fact that democratic politics here are increasingly registering the myriad content of those who make up the society, is in some ways making it more purely representative, and in ways that disrupt the formal structures of the constitutional order. Yet the remedy does not lie in seeking to remove this tension, by for instance trying to do away with certain filtering and restraining mechanisms in the name of making the political order more representative—as those who call for proportional representation, or for a presidential form of government, would have us believe. The tension between democracy and the constitution is a fertile one: each must check and moderate the other.

Notes

1. *Outlook,* 23 Dec. 2000.
2. This raises a larger issue of how timing and sequence were understood in the disputes of the mid-twentieth century. In the argument between Jinnah and the Congress, for example, the Congress wanted Independence and a unitary state with a single constitution first, before settling the communal problem. Jinnah, however, wanted two Constituent Assemblies, two constitutions, beneath a higher executive power—and any such union must be preceded by 'grouping'. The Congress meanwhile insisted on a strong centre, with significant powers bestowed on provincial units; but such powers and such units to be determined by the centre itself.

References

Ambedkar, B.R., 'Memorandum and Draft Articles on the Rights of States and Minorities', in M. Gwyer and A. Appadorai (eds), *Speeches and Documents on the Indian Constitution, 1921–1947,* Oxford University Press, Bombay and London, 1957.

Austin, G., *The Indian Constitution: Cornerstone of a Nation,* Oxford University Press, 1965.

———, *Working the Constitution: The Indian Experience,* Oxford University Press, Delhi, 1999.

Bhargava, R., 'Democratic Vision of a New Republic: India 1950', in F.R. Frankel, Z. Hasan, R. Bhargava, and B. Arora (eds), *Transforming India: Social and Political Dynamics of Democracy,* Oxford University Press, New Delhi, 2000. 1946–1950.

Constituent Assembly Debates, 1946–1950, 12 vols, Lok Sabha Secretariat, New Delhi.

Gandhi, M.K. (a), 'The Congress Scheme for a Communal Settlement', 28 Oct. 1931, Round Table Conference (Memo), in M. Gwyer and A. Appadorai, *Speeches and Documents on the Indian Constitution, 1921–1947,* op.cit.

Gandhi, M.K. (b), 'Speech by Gandhiji at a Meeting of the Minorities Committee, 13 Nov. 1931', in Gwyer and Appadorai, op.cit.

Gandhi, M.K., *An Autobiography or The Story of My Experiments with Truth*, Penguin, Harmondswoth, 2001.

Furbank, P.N., *Behalf*, Nebraska University Press, Lincoln and London, 1999.

Jaffrelot, C., *The Hindu Nationalist Movement and Indian Politics 1925 to the 1990s*, Hurst, London, 1996.

Kaviraj, S., 'The Culture of Representative Democracy' in P. Chatterjee (ed.), *Wages of Freedom: Fifty Years of the Indian Nation-State*, Oxford University Press, New Delhi.

Khilnani, S., *The Idea of India*, 2nd edn, Penguin India, New Delhi, 1999.

Nehru, J., 'Aims and Objectives of the Constituent Assembly' (1946) in S. Gopal (ed.), *Selected Works of Jawaharlal Nehru*, second series, vol. 1, Oxford University Press, New Delhi, 1985, pp. 240–51

Noorani, A. G., *Constitutional Questions in India: The President, Parliament, and the States*, New Delhi: Oxford University Press, 2000.

Panikkar, K.N., *In Defence of Liberalism*, Asia Publishing House, Bombay, 1968.

Prezworski, A., *Capitalism and Social Democracy*, Cambridge University Press, Cambridge, 1985.

Sarkar, S., 'Indian Democracy: The Historical Inheritance', unpublished, 1998.

4

THE NATION AND THE STATE IN INDIA
A Difficult Bond*

JAVEED ALAM

'... A nation is happy that has no history.'[1]

It may not be the best strategy to look at the journey of India as a nation-state as a single entity born of constitutional consent; a hyphenated unity. It would perhaps be preferable to drop the hyphen which makes it a single entity and to see it as two separate objects for purposes of analysis. The two have evolved, over the course of Indian history, following different itineraries. These two routes came together at the time of Independence and were then given a certain shape in the constitution adopted in 1950. Since then, though their paths are intertwined, the nation and the state in India have developed in distinct ways in terms of their historically created inner dynamics. There is a complexity to the nature of national formation in India which is not the case with the emergence and development of the modern state. This state in India is much more a result of colonial experimentation with the needs of administering a vast and diverse society that was gradually captured by the British.

In the course of the argument I intend to bring out the central role of cultural and social forces in the emergence of those preconditions necessary to the making of a modern nation. This also emphasizes the distinct nature of the historical process in India where a certain pattern of unification of diversities came about without the pressures exerted by a centralized state or a hegemonic institution—as has been the case in other instances of nation-state formation. Section 2 deals with the path of the evolution of the nation, and section 3 takes the discussions into a substantiation of the central issue that emerged earlier. To seek a link with history, I start with some commonly observable features of contemporary politics in India in section 1. The state and its trajectory is taken up in section 4 and its implication for the Indian nation and society is the subject of section 5.

We are all witness to the development of a pattern in Indian politics since 1996 in which the government of the nation-state called India has been made up largely by political forces and parties which have a base in only one or the other of the various linguistic–cultural regions or 'nationalities' that make up India. No all-India party, or what in India are called 'national parties', has been successful in providing a government to the country. Conventionally speaking, it is, by the European example, a coalitional pattern. However, given the multi-ethnic or linguistic–cultural specificity of India, it is, on a deeper analysis, more than a coalition. It is much more a case of *co-governance* of the country by the nation and the regions that make up the nation; a coalition is just a combination of any two or more parties in the government, but what we have is the specific manner of the ascendance of regions into the government of the Union. What constitutes the centre at the level of the nation-state is made up as much as those who speak on behalf of and claim to represent the nation as those who do so for the various regions or nationalities. Indeed, this configuration has been a result of long contestation, going back to the early years of Independence, between various forces, as to how and by whom the 'nation' would be represented. What will characterize the cultural identity of the nation (-state). The result has been a gradual process towards congealing the respective claims of the diverse forces representing the nation-state and those of different regional formations. One cannot do without the other. I term it co-governance in that sense, not denying that it is a coalition. The sense of this will become clear if we compare it, as we soon will, with an earlier period in the history of governance in India in the 1960s.

It is quite clear from the foregoing that this period in the 1990s has been marked by a pronounced ascendance of regional parties. In the short term (there is no long term trend that can be analytically discerned in Indian politics), there appears to be no possibility of this trend being reversed. However, what marks the ascendance of the regional parties is the absence of any fear of a threat to 'national unity'. This trend crystallized during the period of the two United Front ministries in 1996-7. Even the BJP, despite its chauvinistic nationalism, rabid communalism, and centralizing ideology, has been forced to accept this framework and pay lip service to the code of behaviour entailed by it, notwithstanding its efforts to push its hidden agenda. Barring the stray region on the borders, the national unity of India appears to be taking deeper roots. It will be my effort here to look for reasons and some causal chains in the making of this phenomenon.

The first time when the regionally based political parties representing the various linguistic–cultural regions of India emerged as a force was the period 1967-72. The contrast between that period and the present one is revealing. The former was marked by an intense (and shrill) struggle between the centre and the states; backbiting and mutual accusations. The central government charged the regional governments with being opposed to the nation-state; in Indian phraseology, of posing a threat to national unity. The state governments accused the centre of being authoritarian, posing a threat both to democratic aspirations and the federal arrangement. Most of the parties ruling in states, such as Tamil Nadu, Kerala, Punjab, West Bengal, Tripura, Kashmir, went on to produce documents enumerating measures for the protection of the rights of the states, detailing how the centre had gone on encroaching into their sphere of jurisdiction and had thereby violated the rights of the states.[2] Each of these governments represented diverse ideological views, class preferences, social bases, and the like. It was of slight concern to them how the various states would utilize these additional powers; all that mattered was to acquire them for their own ends. What brought them together against the centre, as the nation-state, was an *objective complementarity* notwithstanding the very divergent ideological and class moorings of the governments concerned.[3]

Today there is no sharp contradiction between the centre (the nation-state) and the states (regional governments), though there may be many differences of opinion or even conflicts of interest centred around economic and fiscal or monetary policies and on questions of cultural and language policies. In the earlier period, the dominant class forces in most of the states—the regionally based, non-big bourgeoisie both in industry and agriculture—also seized the opportunity to use the power of state governments to better bargain with the centre for resources and get a better deal in the pan-Indian market. The national market with its price mechanisms and terms of trade was, and still is to a relatively lesser extent, controlled by the big capitalist; it has lessened only to the extent of investment choices too being determined by the process of globalization. This made the entry of the smaller, regionally based bourgeoisie into the pan-Indian market that much more difficult, through controls on the grant of licences, input–output prices, restrictive trade practices, and the like. This indeed was a factor that intensified the tussle between the centre and the states.

As an aside it needs to be said that within this general pattern there was one marked exception. The Left forces in general and those states in which they were in power were also in the forefront of the struggle against the 'centralizing' and the 'authoritarian' tendencies of the centre, but they sought the autonomy of the states to curb the power of the ruling classes and to use the autonomy of the state to further the interests of the working classes and the peasantry. Nonetheless overall the struggle for greater power to the states cut across all ideological and class barriers.

At the present time there seem to be no such contradictions; at least not decisive ones. Both the centre and the states are competing to attract transnational capital in the form of foreign direct investments (FDIs). All are votaries of globalization, barring the Left-Front ruled states of West Bengal, Tripura, and Kerala, though these too, given the policy imperatives of the Indian nation-state, are keen to attract as much foreign capital as possible. The difference is a greater emphasis on public investment and a sharper focus on other components of social democracy such as democratization of agrarian relations, local self-government, all round decentralization, and the like. In short, there is general competition for investible resources soon to be ensured by FDI in industry and the services.

The upshot of this has been that the enormous diversity of India is getting mobilized in the shaping of a united India, rather than being a threat to unity as was earlier feared. This is an important stage in the democratization of centre–state relations in India, and one that the

Left as well as the various regionally based democratic forces have been fighting for. The crucial point is however that this has come about not as a result of any alteration in the constitutional scheme due to the pressure exerted by these forces but as a result of a politically emergent constraint on the power of the centre; the unintended consequence of co-governance. The danger to governance remains the BJP, a party committed to centralization, becoming strong enough to form a government on its own.

How did this situation come about? Is there an inner logic to it? What is the substance of this logic? I would like to speculate here, and in the course of doing so make a postulate. To come to the postulate, let us go back a little into history. In the making of present-day Indian diversity, two pre-colonial legacies are of central importance. As an extension of this, in the making of the modern political unity or the 'nation' out of this diversity, one legacy out of the many colonial inheritances is of great consequence. The postulate that emerges out of the interplay of these three long-term forces is: a centralized state in any form is inimical to the natural growth of political unification in Indian society.

One important legacy from history has been that what are now the linguistic–cultural communities (evolving as distinct linguistic regions from the time of the Sangam period in the south roughly during the tenth century and from the period of Bhakti movements in the rest of India in the sixteenth) could never have been held together in a single state through conquest. This is of considerable consequence and in great contrast to China, where a centralized state could oversee the play of socio–cultural forces and maintain civilizational unity. The relatively high degree of *civilizational uniformity* across the regions in India that we find and varying degree of *cultural unity* within the different regions achieved prior to colonialism has not been the result of a coercive state, imposed mores, and restraints, as was the case in China. That said, such an assertion does not negate the play and intermingling of various other factors in Chinese civilization; or, alternatively, forced incorporation of outlying regions, as in Czarist Russia. The civilizational uniformity came about imperceptibly, and the regions formed patterns of affinity with this uniformity, drawn into a framework based principally on the varna order: ideology and prescriptions or rituals and the slow dissemination of a set of philosophical presuppositions like, for example, notions such as karma and moksha (which are common both to the high tradition and local religious beliefs). Both these features, the framework of social action as well as the philosophical presuppositions, had acquired a deep-rooted social acceptance, even in the face of the jati-order keeping various jatis apart from one another, before the British came. The coming of the Muslims and their variable large-scale presence in different parts of India only added a diversity to the cultural unity of the various linguistic–cultural regions; a diversity quite unlike the others in the sense that it could not be assimilated into the Hindu worldview, and this subsequently became problematic with the rise of the national movement.

Suffice it to note here that there was neither an enduring presence of a centralized state (as in China) where the bureaucracy with its Confucian outlook was an important presence; its 'competitive' make-up also made the family a site of piety; an institution open to influences from the state. Nor was there an organized Church (as the Roman Church in Western Europe), a hegemonic institution with enormous power, to enforce centrally conceived compliance with a belief system and social or ritual norms. Such institutions have not been unimportant historically in facilitating the creation of civilizational belts. Hundreds of locally based, traditionally inherited modes of enforcing compliance do not induce a sense of being forced by an external power; local chieftains must surely have played a role, but these cannot be considered to be the key elements in the system of compliance which was the dominant, enduring form in India.

The state as a centralized institution, though not absent, was an episodic presence, with very long periods intervening without any such institution. This mode of creation of common or similar cultural complexes and the conceptions and practices embedded in them is very much an Indian inheritance. This inheritance, in multiple reconfigurations and constructions, became an important ingredient in the making of modern India, India as a nation state, as we will soon see.

All this came about through a peculiar pattern, and this is the second pre-colonial legacy, of brahminical expansion, an important feature in the evolution of the principles of statecraft. In this mode of social formation and cultural incorporation, the brahminical or high culture confronted proto-state or insulated sections of society whose world-view was very different from the brahminic, taking various forms and levels, variations notwithstanding, of tribal existence. The brahminical culture entered into a process of give and take, accommodation, or, to use a more current term, compromise. Leaving aside the essential features of the social structure—the highly hierarchical caste system (with brahminical supremacy at one end and at the other untouchability) and the core philosophical beliefs of Sanatan Dharam—everything else was allowed to remain as it was, or was left to itself.[4] This provided for an inherent, non-definable plurality of practice in the daily life of the people. This insulated plurality[5] was to remain the basis of a great deal of autonomous cultural innovation in the different regions of India. Thus, the pre-colonial hegemonic system—civilizational uniformity across the regions and cultural unity within them—in India was built around core definitions about the world by the literati, but ordinary day-to-day activities were left to evolve on their own. This has given birth to a 'unique' entity called India with a high degree of unification in the social formation as well as bewildering diversity.

It is in such a context that the British entered and became the paramount power. I do not want to pursue the story of colonialism in India. For the purposes of the present argument I wish to point to three things very briefly. First, the many-faceted and immense diversity of India dumbfounded them. To get a grasp over it, they went about codifying customs and practices and from this sought to create what has come to be called the 'Indian tradition' as some kind of singularity, hitherto nonexistent. Secondly, they questioned the very notion of India being or capable of ever becoming a 'nation'. Finally, they went about creating a centralized state centred around an iron-fisted bureaucracy, a common jurisprudence, and a court system built around it, and gave a major impetus to the emergence of a pan-Indian market within which capital acquired a high, cross-regional mobility under the control of a trans-regional bourgeoisie.[6] To manage all this there also emerged a very large, and growing, middle class educated in English but bilingual in nature. It became instrumental, together with expanding capitalism, in the transformation of the diverse linguistic–cultural communities into self-reflecting entities demanding recognition that we find today. There was also in parallel a national consciousness of India being a nation; a nation comprising a number of distinct linguistitic–cultural belts with their specific make up.[7]

This national consciousness in its early phase in the nineteenth century was spontaneous, in the sense that it was not directed from any one centre or by any one dominant class. It was besides an amalgam or a blend of two related but autonomous developments discussed below. It was a gradual development but decisive in its growth as a self-conscious force, or alternatively, its subjective basis was the freedom movement and especially the period that witnessed mass popular upsurges starting with the Rowlatt satyagraha of 1919. The creation of a uniform bureaucracy, the development of railways, etc. did lay the physical basis of unity, but this in itself was an insufficient basis. It is therefore erroneous to believe that the unity of India was a creation of British rule; the British, on the contrary, did everything to create as many dissensions as possible along all the fault lines in society. There was, on the one hand, the growth in awareness within various linguistic-cultural communities of being distinct entities with the emergence of prose literature in the nineteenth century, and on the other hand a growing awareness that they all belonged to a common country called India. Both these processes have been slow and in an important respect are still in progress. As has been noted above, India has been one of the very few large civilizational areas that developed into a nation in spite of a multiplicity of linguistic–cultural belts. In Europe the process took quite the reverse direction. There was a dismantling of larger empires into nations largely constructed around linguistic communities; and this process continues in regions that escaped it due to the socialist revolutions. Even in the 'third world' two large civilizational belts, with the added advantage of a single language, namely the Arab world and Spanish Latin America, went in the direction of the formation of separate sovereign states.[8] Thus, the transformation of the civilizational uniformity of India into national consciousness and then into a nation(-state) is an uncommon phenomenon.

Apart from this process British views on India also became a source of a nationalist counter-reaction in which everything asserted was in admiration of India as a nation, culture, and civilization. There were numerous attempts to contest British notions of India as not being a nation. This led to many competing, monolithic definitions of tradition, sought to be imposed on society top downwards.[9] The second form of discursive counter-attack from the nationalist élite, important for the argument here, was to insist that India had always been a nation from time immemorial. A model of a nation on the pattern of those in Western Europe was soon to be propagated and became widely held, becoming an intrinsic part of Indian nationalism.[10] Both these discursive counter-moves had a deeper unity, in that these were deeply informed, barring exceptions like the Communists or the socialist strain in Congress represented by Nehru, by Hindu religious content and idiom. This became one of the many sources of a Muslim reaction and a subsequent refusal to be part of the national platform, contributing eventually to the creation of Pakistan.

When India became independent this second feature of the nationalist counter-offensive got embodied in the constitution adopted in 1950 and was sought to be actualized by the nation-state. It took the form of an undiscussed consensus across the ideological spectrum; the question of the criteria that were to make it a nation different from Germany and Portugal in Europe or Egypt and Malaysia in the decolonized world were never even raised. If one were to examine the debates in the Constituent Assembly on what become Article 1 of the constitution ('India is a Union of states') one scarcely finds any discussion worth mention.[11] The only organized political group to raise the question of the nature of India as a 'nation', of its specific features, and so on, were the Communists, and for this they were and are accused of being anti-national.[12]

What needs to be noted and emphasized in the end is a serious disjunction that emerged at this point between the process and the discourse. The process by which India was emerging as a political unity out of civilizational uniformity had two features simultaneously constituting it. On the one hand, there was the slow emergence of a self-reflective awareness of being different within the linguistic–cultural regions out of the earlier cultural unity, but this was happening, on the other hand, within the context of the emergence of a sense of nation of a varied kind out of the earlier civilizational uniformity. The nationalist discursive counter-reaction completely ignored this and superimposed a simplistic, European-like, notion of a nation on a very complex process. What the constitution embodies is this monolithic notion, and this monolithic character, as we will soon see, cuts across the ideological spectrum, whatever be the important differences in the content of conceptualization. This has ever since remained a source of tension.

At this point two clarifications are necessary. One has to do with the fact that the Constituent Assembly spent a considerable amount of time debating the rights and powers of the provinces or the states and those of the Union. It arrived at a delicate balance. That is the basis of the implicit federation, even if the constitution does not use the term. I presume that this can be a ground to argue that no such thing as a monolithic notion of nation can be inferred. The problem in reading the debates in this manner is to miss the difference between federation and the idea of a nation called India. Such debates and contentions can also be part of a federation like that in Australia or Germany. Nothing in the debates suggests that India is any different from these countries. My point is that India is a nation different from any in Western Europe with a specificity all its own. The second clarification has to do with the creation of linguistic states in India beginning in 1956. The central élites remained strongly opposed to it and what came about was reluctantly conceded in the face of mass movements that were getting out of control, starting with that in Andhra. As far as the élite was concerned, India could well have been a federation akin to that in Germany or Australia.

What I want to do in the next section is to attempt to substantiate my assertion that what informed the national élite was a monolithic conception of India as an immemorial nation. I do so through Nehru's writings.

Nehru never explicitly asserts that the Indian nation has always existed. On the contrary, he says that 'In ancient and medieval times, the idea of the modern nation was non-existent, and feudal, religious or racial or cultural bonds had more importance'.[13] Having said this he immediately adds: 'Yet I think that at almost *any time* in recorded history an Indian would have felt more or less at home in any part of India.'[14] There is a sense implicit here that in the case of India other 'bonds' mentioned above may have been transcended in some sense. This implicit sense becomes more marked when, writing on 'The Variety and Unity of India', he says:

The Pathan and the Tamil are two extreme examples; the others lie somewhere in between. All of them have their distinctive features, all of them have still more the distinguishing mark of India. It is fascinating to find how the Bangalees, the Marathas, the Gujeraties, the Tamils, the Andhras, the Oriyas, the Assamese, the Malayalis, the Sindhis, the Panjabis, the Pathans, the Kashmiris, the Rajputs, and the great central Indian block comprising the Hindustani people, have retained their peculiar characteristics for *hundreds of years,* have still more or less the virtues and failings of which old tradition or record tell us, and yet have been *throughout these ages* distinctively Indian, with the same *national heritage* and the same set of moral and mental qualities.[15]

The key words in looking at the immemorialness of the Indian nation is not simply that the people here are marked by an imprint that is characteristically Indian but that this has been characterized *throughout the ages*, as an overarching *national heritage* over the individual, linguistic features of the various people who have been living in India. What is observed today as the intersection of the regional–national and pan-Indian features is not a modern phenomenon but has always existed. It is being clearly suggested that this Indian nation is immemorial in the sense that what has unified the innumerable , distinct, linguistic–cultural groups in India has been a *national heritage* for hundred of years.

At another place Nehru says: 'Though outwardly there was diversity and infinite variety among the people, everywhere there was that *tremendous impress of oneness*, which had held all of us together *for ages past*, whatever political fate or misfortune had befallen us.'[16] Immediately adding: 'The unity of India was no longer merely an intellectual conception for me, it was an emotional experience which overpowered me.'[17] The underlying notion of oneness is spoken almost in the sense in which it is nowadays used for a nation.

This sense of oneness or national heritage existing for ages comes through to Nehru not through a rational mode of appropriation of social reality, as is the case when Nehru talks of other social phenomena like secularism, socialism, democracy, but by an overpowering emotional perception; a kind of a mystic vision of India's uniqueness as a nation. This is Nehru in his nationalist mould: non-rational in the way he seeks to understand reality. Nehru in all other respects is the child of the Enlightenment who searches for the specificity of the process of becoming social phenomena.

This aspect of Nehru's nationalist thought, I would like to argue, is indicative of a deeper continuity across all shades of nationalist thought. The immemorialness of India, the unique nation, is the pole that unifies the distinct streams that make up nationalist discourse and give a specific imprint to conceptions of the Indian nation. Nehru however remains blissfully immune to any chauvinistic influence in his nationalism—unlike the militant Hindu right wing.

There is in this an unexamined equation of the 'national' with the 'civilisational'. The Arab world, Spanish America, Western Europe can be taken as classic examples of the inappropriateness of such an equation, even if China can be cited as an exception. What many in India do not realize is that the logic of cultural diffusion and political integration have separate trajectories and very rarely come together. No historically based reasoning can permit one to infer that one form of unity (civilizational) can necessarily lead to the other (national). Nehru would have been on sound ground had he limited his assertions to India's civilizational uniformity.

I have discussed Nehru for one reason. Nehru the radical liberal is so much out of step, when reflecting on the nation, with his own intellectual pedigree. It is undoubtedly true that he encapsulates his idea of the nation with future oriented goals like industrialization and economic development, science and scientific temper, democratized social relations, secularized society, socialist social system, democratic polity, and other such things. That is precisely why the Nehruvian sense of nationalism does not get loaded with any narrow notion of nation. His nationalism remains expansive and inclusive, and therefore anti-imperialist and emancipatory. In spite of all this, we also find that his core sense of the Indian nation is so different from that of nations in general. It is in this we find that Nehru is in tune with his peers and predecessors: the chain that began with cultural reassertions in the 1880s. The core sense of the Indian nation has a surprisingly high degree of agreement without, happily, creating a corresponding sense of nationalism. Such a position implied a pre-reflective link to culture and tradition of a somewhat restrictive kind.

I wish to suggest here that whenever the nation is faced with a crisis or there are felt to be serious threats to 'national unity', the immemorialness of the nation becomes the central plank of its defence. Who then can best defend this immemorialness located in the cultural antiquity of India? It is precisely here that claims on behalf of Hindutva—'let people decide what Indian nationalism is all about'—become important and gain credence. It is, I believe, important to recognize that Hindutva is not only seeking legitimacy by locating itself in the religiously based cultural foundations of the Indian nation but also seeking legitimacy as spokesman of the dominant nationalist tradition, even if it finds it inconvenient to mention Nehru's name.

The extent to which this conceptualization of the nation has refracted in Indian society and seeped down into the consciousness of the political class is not simply because of the earlier religio-cultural reassertions but also due to its contemporary legitimacy as it has also been the plank of secular, radical nationalist thought in India. It is really this deeper continuity of nationalist thought or the way in which the nation has become an object of knowledge within it that has become a source of strength for Hindutva or national chauvinism, and a ground that places secular opinion in India in a quandary. This is a source of distinct advantage to Hindutva. The secular trends in India will continue to fight the battle for national solidarity—but like soldiers under duress who are unfamiliar with the terrain on which they are fighting.

When India gained Independence it was this processual complexity of the making of the nation, unnaturally simplified conceptually, that was to be embodied in the state and represented by it. The state ought to be looked at from two angles. There is the normative aspect in terms of the values it wants to actualize, emancipatory goals it seeks to pursue, socio-egalitarian transformations it aims at, and the like. Let us call it, in the Aristotelian sense, the polity. There is, on the other side, the organization of power and the institutions through which it is exercised and this, in modern usage, is what the state is actually taken to be. I will primarily concentrate on the second aspect, trying to show that the way in which it got institutionally constituted has not best served the realization of its normative side, nor has it been able to deepen the national bonds that were growing during the freedom struggle.

I will start with an inadequately analysed feature of Indian politics at the time of Independence in 1947. Mahatma Gandhi, the father of the nation, turned against the newly constituted state in independent India. This state too became highly suspicious of his moves. At the end of the long journey to Independence he could see no light; indeed, there was darkness all around. Gandhi refused to acknowledge the legitimacy of the power of this state, and took up cudgels on behalf of society against the state. He went on protest padyatras, undertook a 'fast unto death', and demonstrated his dismay in many other ways. It is easy to interpret all this as a result of his 'anarchist' tendencies. This manner of looking at Gandhian moves does not allow us to see the significant questions that Gandhi was raising. I will come to these questions after dispelling a persistent misconception about Gandhi. It is generally believed that Gandhi was reluctant to exercise power. On the contrary, a little before India's Independence Gandhi made a very revealing remark:

> Whatever the Congress decided will be done; nothing will be according to what I say. *My writ runs no more.* If it did the tragedies in Punjab, Bihar, and Noakhali would not have happened. *No one listens to me any more.* I am a small man. True there was a time when mine was a big voice. Then everybody obeyed what I said; now neither the Congress nor the Hindus nor the Muslims listen to me. Where is the Congress going today? It is disintegrating. *I am crying in the wilderness.*[18]

This, it seems to me, very clearly shows that Gandhi would have greatly liked to influence the course of events. We have wrongly read his refusal to have anything to do with power at the level of state institutions. In doing so he was raising a fundamental question: where should the final authority to determine the destiny of society reside? Can the state, a coercive institution, take over the voice of society?

Here I would like to suggest that the Gandhian refusal to be part of state power and his protests were a defiant move on the part of society to be taken over and wholly represented by the state. The defiance was to keep the voice of society above the legal claims of the state. The state in India, immediately in the wake of Independence, was making moves to take over and wholly represent society and nation.

This was, logically considered, a case of inversion. Prior to Independence, the society and the awakened nation were to give birth to the state. After Independence, in a reversal of roles, the state was to absorb the nation and assimilate society. Much of the leadership which made the society such a vibrant site of activity moved over to the state. What remained outside the state was the oppositional leadership, but that became state oriented. The reconstitution under the state of the social forces released during the anti-colonial movement and the anti-feudal struggles took place under the leadership of capitalists and substantial landowners. This reconstituted state power managed within a parliamentary system the justification to elevate itself, assume democratic credentials.

To see the consequences of this ascendance of the state over the nation or of the governmental power over the autonomy of society, let us now examine how the newly created state in independent India was taking shape and how it was going to prop itself in face of the initial upheavals. Finally how, theoretically, it was going to relate to Indian society in its transformative project. All of these questions are going to impinge on how the conceptualization as it works itself out is going to become problematic.

In face of the communal carnage or the problem of integrating princely states like Hyderabad and Junagadh and, in a different way in the case of Kashmir and the war with Pakistan, the emergent state had no choice but to rely overwhelmingly on its coercive apparatus. However, so far as popular upheavals were concerned, whether in Bengal or Tranvancore–Cochin or Hyderabad or with workers and employees and ordinary people, it had, theoretically, two choices. It could, if it had so wished here, have used the popular upsurge to initiate reorientation of state institutions in a popular direction by bringing about a realignment of the class and social forces then contending for supremacy. It could, alternatively, have relied on inherited colonial coercive institutions to subdue popular movements. Given the alignment of forces in the Congress party, the first option would have entailed a destabilization of political initiatives. These may have had beneficial consequences in the long run; the leadership would have succeeded in making the institutional set-up of the state relatively more responsive: the risk of loss of control cannot be discounted, but the politics of radical transformation has to take calculated risks. The leadership chose not to do so. It was not simply a case of ruling class pressure. That would be too deterministic a way of understanding the problem; if the configuration of forces foreclosed all options we can do nothing other than weep at the reality of class domination. It seems to me that the moral and psychological predilections of the leadership were also decisive in structuring the choices. The fear of uncertainty and of disorder, however temporary, was too galling a prospect for the middle class sensibilities of the leadership, including, those of Nehru.

The choice made then was to rely entirely on the inherited bureaucracy and police and armed forces to contain upheavals and beat back popular movements/agitations. This was to have long-term consequences both on the immediate exercise of power as well as on the nature of the state in India. It allowed these structures of power so constructed to insulate themselves from popular pressure or accountability, to acquire a certain degree of permanence by making the state dependent on them in maintaining societal control. This had one immediate repercussion for state power in India. The state in India was unable to become the vehicle/inheritor of the values and aspirations of the national movement. The political leadership of the newly independent state simply stepped into all the institutional and administrative apparatus left by colonial power; most of it still remains intact.

We thus have state institutions whose character has continued to be of a derivative nature. The popular transformative impulses carried within the anti-imperialist struggles together with the goals of emancipation or empowerment of the underprivileged and disenfranchised sections of society which were so often talked about were to become dependent for their realization on these derivative state institutions. Inherent in this lay underlying contradictions. One is the consistent failure of the state to translate what it speaks to the people as their minimum due into anything meaningfully concrete; here it is not simply the question of the class nature of the state, as is often averred, but also the failure to attempt whatever is permissible within the constraints of bourgeois–landlord state power. It is simplistic to say that these forces can subvert plans or projected legislation because they have the political clout. What we have in fact is a much more reciprocal reinforcing of the iniquitous claims to power and entitlements, and the Indian bureaucracy is one such institutional network that sustains the power of the privileged. Partial exceptions to this were the states where the Communist party could consolidate itself.

The consolidation of the colonially derivative state so soon in the life of a new nation had some far-reaching repercussions on the articulation of the traditional bases of the Indian polity. In pre-colonial India, the norm-setting functions, the compliance mechanisms, and the reprisal instrumentalities were never directly under the charge of the state. We all know about the high incidence of infant mortality in the central states in India. In spite of their sporadic nature, we also know the more or less rigid nature of enforcement of caste and ritual norms in Indian society. The power for these was diffused in the local village communities; the severity of enforcement was such that few would escape punishment for deviant behaviour. The equation between tolerance–intolerance has been an unanalysed feature of the traditional Indian social order: unanalysed because the protagonists of tradition as a popular resource have emphasized only the tolerance aspect of Indian tradition. What we need in order to apprehend the contemporary situation is a much more differentiated analysis of these features in Indian society. While it is true that the Indian tradition displayed an extraordinary tolerance towards those beyond its purview, such as those belonging to other religious persuasions, it was also characterized by an extreme degree of intolerance *vis-à-vis* those within its normative set-up. Muslims or Christians or whoever could get away with anything; those who belonged to any of the core traditions of Hinduism faced severe retaliation for transgression. This *internally directed intolerance* has slowly spilled over, under the strains caused by the encounter with the 'modern' under colonial tutelage.

The persistence of colonial modes of governance and the reliance of derivative state institutions on the coercive apparatus also had the (un)intended consequence of bringing closer together the modern state and traditional modes of enforcement. The inability or unpreparedness of the state to alter the institutional set-up in a popular direction also meant that the more intransigent popular demands had to be curbed or repressed, depending upon their militancy. This functional need was also allowed by the state to slip into the hands of those who had always been responsible for class dominance. The state could in such situations assume an attitude of sweet reasonableness and allow the buck to pass on to 'irresponsible' elements. In earlier times, people had not normally held the state responsible for repression due to deviance. The state could even now play upon the survival of this uncritical faculty in people's thinking. This was a way of cushioning its legitimacy. This (un)intended consequence is not a result of culture invading the sphere of politics or tradition impinging on the modern, as a great deal of mainstream analysis has innocently assumed. This innocence is itself a form of ideological blinker permitting the viewer to erase the ugly from his sight.

This development, as the ruling classes came to realize, became a handy instrument to protect the security of big property and its dominance in the life processes of society. The state, as an instrument of the ruling classes, need not carry out all the repressive functions required to protect the class interests of the dominant. This function is carried out directly by agents of the ruling classes. Hirelings of all kinds abound as a part of the productive sector and perpetrate the most abominable outrages on working people. The state can intervene and act as the minimizer of the worst kinds of repression; of all our political leaders this art was perfected by Indira Gandhi. Today it has become a part of managing political defiance, particularly in rural areas. Here, the state takes recourse to surviving caste bonds among the people; the ruling classes also drive a bonus from this: the poor are pitted against one another and rendered even weaker.

This is no simple aberration. It is causally linked by innumerable chains in the structure of power fashioned by the ruling classes immediately after Independence. The political leadership is hedged all around by reasonably well-functioning democratic–electoral practices which support its claims to rule. In a way this is a tenable claim. The problem arises when it refuses to treat popular agitations too as forms of democratic articulation. The state does not see any contradiction in relying on one democratic mandate to crush another form of democratic expression through its coercive instruments. Its long-term interest is to let the dominant sections or the ruling classes handle the situation on their own, yet it can restrain these same forces when they cross certain limits. It acts to minimize terror. Thus it ensures goodwill for itself, a negative form of 'legitimacy'. In this sense non-institutional coercion is not an aberration.

The electoral democracy operating within such a non-institutional coercive framework does not require of the state to have much legitimacy, as understood in political theory, to extract democratic electoral consent. All it needs to do is to act as a buffer between the people and the predatory ruling classes in situations of the 'third world': social discriminations, inherited forms of oppressions, and the like, over and above modern forms of exploitation. It often succeeds in transferring consent from one ruling class formation to another in terms of such minimal functions. Therefore, exercises seeking to increase or decrease the legitimacy of the Indian state in terms of certain presuppositions in theory become suspect academic exercises.

On such a conceptual foundation the state sought to build itself. It justified the claims in terms of its transformative projects. It sought time and demanded stability. In varying degrees people waited, hoping for a better future. Little was realized; far less than was possible within the constraints of bourgeois–landlord rule. We have already seen how the state was forced to beat a retreat and the consequent withdrawal of people into their communities, and with that the erosion of the secular and progressive foundations of politics. Within the larger failure of the secular–transformative programme, the inability to solve the peasant question and handle the nationality aspirations gave rise to two further consequences. The failure of all major land reform initiatives after the abolition of the zamindaris and other large landed estates recreated the rupture between the peasant masses and the politics represented by the state; a rupture which was an enduring feature of pre-Gandhian politics. Its reappearance after Independence has been steadily widening as the state, in consolidating itself, has leant heavily on the propertied classes. This has knocked out the one important cushion that permitted a great deal of stability in spite of the other failures of the state. A free-wheeling politics between all kinds of unstable political formations with a propensity for unprincipled alliances has become a regular feature of the political life of the country.

The assimilative attitude of the state towards the 'nation' (as also society) has resulted in a monolithic definition of nation, nationalism, and national unity being imposed on diversity. This monolithic definition is not a recent creation of Hindutva as is assumed but with a different set of meanings and content has also been the basis of secular politics. From pre-Independence times the secularist–nationalist leadership has refused to even countenance the possibility that different people with varying 'national compositions' could have different notions of what it means to be an Indian. It has thoughtlessly insisted on treating India as a nation in the sense in which Portugal or Sweden or Germany are nations. This kind of transferred a priori understanding of what it means to be a nation is obviously out of tune with the specificities of India. It has come to be met with varying degrees of resistance in different parts of the country. The Nagas or the Tamils or the Malayalees or the Punjabis, and the different communities within the various linguistic–cultural belts, may have very different notions of what it means to be an Indian. India is too vast and diverse a country to be able to live with a single, imposed conception of nation or nationalism. It is clear on a careful reading of the nationalist history of India that many regions, or the communities within these regions, had unstable or shifting relations with all-India nationalism. All this may become a cause of new forms of tensions within the Indian 'union'.

The normal types of federal tensions can be understood and explained in terms of political economy—uneven development, lopsided economic transformations, disjunction between industry and agriculture, etc.—but secessionism is not easily explicable *only* in terms of economic criteria; something more is required. What seems to me to be crucial is the previous history of the relations of the regions or of the communities within them with pan-Indian nationalism. This hypothesis can in fact be tested. To the extent this can be validated, it also forces on us the need to reassess the way the Indian state built itself up on a particular conception of the relation of the state to the society or the nation over which it presides. In the face of problems faced by society and the crises of the 'nation', the only direction suggested by this analysis is a democratization of this relationship.

A propitious circumstance led to some kind of a resolution or a partial mitigation of these strains and confrontations. Since 1989 no political party has been able to win a clear majority at the centre. India entered an era of coalitional politics. It is not my argument here that coalitions are a solution. Rather, that in the short run, the government at the centre cannot be constituted without the participation of political parties representing the various ('sub') nationalities. This has led to a situation that has put a brake on the articulation of any one variety of monolithic claim (as well as the centralizing tendency) on behalf of the nation by the state. From the opposite perspective, it also happens that the distinct regions can now insist on being heard as regards what in their conception it means to be Indian; there are multiple voices now seeking to define India as a nation(-state). To understand how this has become a compulsion built into the present political conjuncture, we have merely to watch the BJP, with its 'Hindi–Hindu–Hindustani' notion of India forced to work through a triple agenda: one, agreed upon with the partners known as the National Agenda; two, the deferred agenda around the Ram Mandir and such assorted issues; and three, the hidden agenda of surreptitiously using state power to saffronize society. This forced withdrawal of the government at the level of the nation-state as the *only* or dominant voice has created a condition for the contest between the regions and the nation-state to assume a form which is symbiotic in a way it never could be since the colonial state came to India. This has also brought about an *alignment*, of a rough sort between what I have called the *long duration* and the *trend* delineated above. The conjuncture needs to be provided with constitutional cushions so that it acquires the features of a structure.

Notes and References

* I am deeply grateful to Niraja Gopal Jayal, Satish Saberwal and E. Sridharan for detailed, critical observation on an earlier draft. I am also thankful to the participants in the seminar for their questions and comments.

1. Raghavan Iyer (ed.), *The Moral and Political Writings of Mahatma Gandhi*, vol. 1, Oxford University Press, New Delhi, rpt, 1996, p. 187.
2. The better known of these are the 'Rajmanar Committee Report' of the DMK-led government in Tamil Nadu, the 'Document on Centre–State Relations' by the Left Front, and the 'Anandpur Sahib Resolution' of the Akali Dal.
3. See Javeed Alam, 'State Autonomy Movements in India', *Social Scientist*, no. 111, 1983.
4. See Romila Thapar, *From Lineage to State: Social Formations in the Mid-First Millenium* BC *in the Ganga Valley*, Oxford Paperbacks, New Delhi, 1990, and *Ancient Indian Social History*, Orient Longman, New

Delhi, 1978, concluding chapter, for exceptions to this pattern; see also R.S. Sharma, *The State and Varna Formation in the Mid-Ganga Plains: An Ethnoarchaeological View*, Manohar Paperback, Delhi, 1996.

5. I am indebted to Satish Saberwal for this term.
6. Amiya Bagchi, 'Reflection on Patterns of Regional Growth in India During the Period of British Rule', *Bengal Past and Present*, XCV, pt. 1, p. 180, Jan. 1976.
7. See Javeed Alam, 'Dialectics of Capitalist Development and National Crystallization: Notes on the Past and Present of National Question in India', *Economic and Political Weekly*, 29 Jan. 1983.
8. See Benedict Anderson, *Imagined Communities: Reflections on the Origin and Spread of Nationalism*, Verso, London, 1983, for a fascinating account of how differently the Spanish and Portuguese Latin empires developed into nations.
9. See Javeed Alam, 'Tradition in India Under Interpretative Stress', in *Thesis Eleven* no. 39, 1994; also Amartya Sen, 'Indian Tradition and the Western Imagination', *Daedalus*, vol.126, no. 2, 1997.
10. I have examined, among others, Nehru, because he was the most historically sensitive of all the nationalist leaders and was also deeply informed on the patterns of historical evolution worldwide and was keenly tuned to the anti-imperialist radical debates, and yet was surprisingly immune to debates on nationalism and the national question. Here is a small sample from one of his works.
11. See *Constituent Assembly Debates*, vol. 7, for details.
12. See Javeed Alam, 'Nation: Discourse and Intervention by the Communists in India', in T.V. Sathyamurthy (ed.), *State and Nation in the Context of Social Change*, Oxford University Press, New Delhi, 1994.
13. See Jawaharlal Nehru, *Discovery of India*, Signet Press, Calcutta, 1948, p. 41.
14. Ibid.
15. Ibid., p. 40, emphasis added.
16. Ibid., p. 38.
17. Ibid.
18. Gandhi, *Collected Works*, vol. 87, p. 187, emphasis added.

5

India's Secular Constitution

Rajeev Bhargava

Secularism is a beleaguered doctrine in India. Today, only someone with a blinkered vision can deny its crisis. An ideal could be threatened by two broad categories of factors. The crisis may be caused because its core values, or the interpretations of them, are themselves flawed. Alternatively, because the form of the doctrine is such that it cannot fit into conceptual spaces available within the culture where it is meant to work. Such reasons are *internal* to the doctrine. *External* causes of the crisis need not question the doctrine's internal coherence or validity but seek explanation in the political, economic, or socio–psychological domain. Here are some examples from recent literature on the subject: (a) the demise of the one party, Congress dominated, system opens up a fresh struggle for power among the new and the older élites. In this ensuing conflict, traditional élites find a handy resource in communalism with which to reassert hegemony. As secularism and communalism are believed to be antithetical, the rise of one necessarily entails the decline of the other. (b) The sustained political manipulations of symbols of group identity to bolster the centralizing and homogenizing tendency within Hinduism and, through simultaneous stigmatization and emulation of the other, the attempt to gain massive comparative advantage for a modern, centralized Hindu community has negatively affected secularism.[1] (c) The availability of new bargaining strategies and opportunities to directly undermine political opponents and of techniques of open manipulation of symbols in the political field has helped the growth of militant Hindu nationalism and undermined secularism.[2]

Inclined as I am to believe that the current crisis of secularism is due largely to external factors, I know that this view is not shared by most contemporary writers on secularism.[3] My principal objective in this essay is to show that internalist explanations of the crisis of secularism are mistaken. Elsewhere, I have argued that such explanations mis-identify the background cultural conditions of modern secularism and mis-recognize the model of secularism embedded in the best practice of the secular state in India. Here, I contend that such critics misunderstand the form secularism takes in the Indian constitution. In addition, I show that the best judicial practice of the Indian state is consistent with my interpretation of secularism.

Theocracy, Establishment, Multiple Establishment

I wish to begin with some crucial ideal–typical distinctions. First, the distinction between a state that establishes religion and a theocratic state. A theocratic state is governed by divine laws directly administered by a priestly order claiming a divine commission. Major historical examples of theocracies are ancient Israel, some Buddhist regimes of Japan and China, the Geneva of John Calvin, and the Papal states.[4] In our times, the Islamic republic of Iran run by Ayatollahs and the Taliban-led Afghanistan come closest to being theocracies. On the other hand, a state that establishes religion grants it official, legal recognition. Here, religion benefits from a formal alliance with government. The sacerdotal order need not *govern* a state where religion is established.

The establishment of religion takes two forms. In the classical European view, it means that 'a *single* Church or religion enjoys formal, legal, official monopolistic privilege through a union with the government of the state.'[5] The principal motivation behind monopolistic establishment is obvious: to privilege one religious group over all others.[6] Historical examples of established churches are the unreformed Anglican Church in England, the Anglican church in the state of Virginia prior to disestablishment, and the established Roman Catholic churches of Italy and Spain. Typically, where religion is strongly established, the state recognizes a particular religion as the official religion, compels individuals to congregate for only one religion, punishes them for failing to profess a particular set of religious beliefs, levies taxes in support of one particular religion or makes instruction in one religion mandatory in educational institutions. Where a particular religion is established, equality among religions is non-existent, and while members of the established religion may enjoy a modicum of religious liberty, those belonging to un-established religions are unlikely to enjoy legally guaranteed freedoms.

This classical European view of establishment is to be distinguished from one where the state respects more than one religion, recognises and perhaps nurtures all religions without preferring one over another. This might be termed 'multiple establishment' or 'establishment without a name'.[7] Such a state may levy a religious tax on everyone and yet grant the freedom to remit the tax money to a church or religious organization of their choice. It may financially aid schools run by religious institutions, but on a non-discriminatory basis. It may punish people for disavowing or disrespecting religion, though not compel them to profess the beliefs of a particular religion. A state that respects multiple establishment treats all religions non-preferentially. It gives liberty to each group to conduct its religious affairs but is likely to be indifferent to the freedom of members within the group. The state of New York in the mid-seventeenth century permitted every church of the Protestant faith to be established and furnishes perhaps the earliest example of 'multiple establishment'. The colonies of Massachusetts, Connecticut, and New Hampshire show a similar pattern.[8] Related examples are also to be found in India: the fourteenth-century Vijayanagar kingdom appears to have granted official recognition to the Shaivites, the Vaishnavites, and perhaps even the Jains. Arguably, the British empire gave de facto legitimacy to something akin to multiple establishment in India.

Secular State: Disestablishment

A secular state is to be distinguished not only from a theocracy but also from a state where religion is established. It is a state in which religion has been disestablished. The disestablishment of religion means the separation of the state not merely from one but from all religions (I shall call it feature-a). A secular state is not anti-religious but exists and survives only when religion is no longer hegemonic. It admits a more general equality between believers and unbelievers. It secures peace not only between different kinds of religious believers but between believers and non-believers. It legally sanctions freedoms for all religions but also freedom from religion itself. (All these aspects make it different from a state with multiple establishment.) Thus, in a secular state, a formal or legal union between state and religion is impermissible. Official status is not given to religion. persons are as free to disavow religion as they are to profess one. No one is compelled to pay tax for religious purposes or to receive religious instruction. No automatic grants to religious institutions are available. The state of Virginia, after the disestablishment of the Anglican church (1786), the US, particularly after the first amendment to its constitution (1791), and France, especially after the separation law of 1905, provide the clearest examples of a secular state. Despite the formal establishment of churches in England and Scotland, the UK too is in many respects a secular state.[9] As Donald Smith points out, 'any modern state within the liberal democratic tradition will have many of the characteristics of a secular state.'[10]

Values of a Secular State

A secular state is therefore constitutively tied to the value of religious liberty that has three dimensions. The first refers to the liberty of members of any one religious group (feature-b). It is a harsh truth that in most religious communities, one or two interpretations of its core beliefs and practices come to dominate. Given this dominance, it is important that every individual or sect within the group be given the right to criticize, revise, or challenge these dominant interpretations. The second aspect of this important liberty in a secular state (feature-c) is that it is granted non-preferentially to all members of every religious community. It is entirely possible that non-preferential treatment by the state of groups that accord religious liberty to its members is also found in states respecting multiple establishment. However, religious liberty is not part of the core principles of multiple establishment but is a constitutive feature of the secular state. The third dimension of religious liberty (feature-d), quite unthinkable in states with multiple establishment, is that individuals are free not only to criticize the religion into which they are born, but at the very extreme, given ideal conditions of deliberation, to reject it and to remain without one. There is a huge difference between merely tolerating atheists, which may happen in states with multiple establishment, and granting them full legal rights to be what they are, a feature of modern, secular states.[11]

Religious liberty, broadly understood, is one feature of a secular state. To understand its second crucial ingredient, it is necessary to grasp the point that liberty and equality in the religious sphere are all of a piece with liberty and equality in other spheres. It is not a coincidence that the disestablishment clause in the first amendment to the American constitution institutes not only religious freedom but also the more general freedom of speech, of peaceful assembly, and political dissent. It is entirely possible that a state respecting multiple establishment permits *religious* liberty and equality but forbids other forms of freedom and equality. For instance, it may be that a person freely defies the authority of the religious head of his own denomination but is not free to challenge the authority of the state, or that the undisturbed conduct of religious worship is guaranteed to religious dissenters or minorities though they continue to suffer the statutory disabilities that had accumulated against them in the past. A degree of religious liberty may easily go hand in hand with second-class citizenship.[12] This is impermissible in a secular state, which is committed to more general freedom and equality. Thus, the second value to which a secular state is constitutively linked is the equality of free citizenship.

The value of equal citizenship has two dimensions that require elaboration, one active and the other passive. To be a passive citizen is to be entitled to physical security, a minimum of material well-being, and a sphere of one's own in which others ought not to interfere. Although a part of this idea of passive citizenship goes back to ancient Rome, the radical emphasis on material well-being and on privacy is a result of a profound trans-valuation of values that has taken place under conditions of modernity.[13] This lies at the root of the idea of the right to life, liberty, material welfare, and perhaps, education. A citizen is entitled to these benefits. This is partly an extension of the argument implicit in the defence of religious liberty but in part it adds something substantial of its own. The benefits of citizenship must be available to everyone and there is no room here for discrimination on grounds of religion (feature-e). This equal treatment is entailed by equal (passive) citizenship. State agencies and the entire system of law must not work in favour of one religious group. If the state works to protect the security and well-being of some individuals or groups but fails to secure these meagre but important benefits to others, then the principle of equal (passive) citizenship is violated.[14] Likewise, as citizenship is conditional upon education, no one must be denied admission to educational institutions solely on grounds of religion (feature-f).

The active dimension of citizenship entails the recognition of citizens as equal participants in the public domain. Such active citizenship rights can be denied in two ways.[15] This may occur when they are brutally excluded from the political domain or when their recognition in the public domain betrays the social acceptance of a belief in the intrinsic superiority of one group, as when there is communally weighted voting or efforts to dilute the votes of religious minorities through the employment of gerrymandering techniques.[16] Groups singled out as less worthy are demeaned and insulted; encouraged to feel that patterns of disrespect existing in society at large enjoy official sanction. In contrast to this, equality of citizenship to which secularism is tied conveys a community-wide acknowledgement of equal respect for everyone in the political domain (feature-g).

Misconceptions of Secularism

The core idea of secularism is then the separation of religion and the state for the sake of civic peace, religious liberty, and equality of free citizenship. From what I have said above, some alleged conceptions of secularism are ruled out as conceptions of secularism. First, the point about the constitutive links between a secular state and the values of peace, liberty, and equality removes a widespread misunderstanding that the only thing required for a state to be secular is its separation from religions. On this, the purely instrumentalist view of secularism (whether or not any substantive value is realized, and even when some key values are undermined), a state is secular if religious and political institutions of the society are separated, and the neater and stricter the separation, the more secular it is. I have however claimed, if not exactly argued, that mere separation of religion and politics does not create a secular state.[17] Second, a non-instrumental view that overburdens secularism is equally mistaken. This view identifies secularism with rationalism, individualism, disenchantment, scientization, indeed with a particular, extremely partial, prejudiced understanding of the whole process of modernization.[18] Secularism is not a comprehensive doctrine laden with every single substantive value in the empire of modernity nor merely a strategy with instrumental significance. Rather, it seeks separation, for the sake of specific values. Third, secularism is not a single value doctrine. Suppose therefore that we have a state that prevents religious conflict, then this feature alone does not make it secular. Although every secular state must prevent the onset of barbarism, not every state that manages to prevent it is secular. For example, a state that installs religious peace by undermining religious liberty cannot be deemed secular. Moreover, a state that permits, even promotes, religious liberty but violates the principle of equal citizenship, either in its passive or its active dimension, is not secular. Even a 'tolerant' state is not necessarily secular. Recall that to tolerate is to refrain from interfering in the affairs of any individual or group, however disagreeable or morally repugnant, even though one has the power to do so. Given this definition of tolerance, a tolerant state can be at ease with social and political inequalities between religious communities. However, in the view outlined above, a state that does not grant equal citizenship rights is not a secular state. It follows that tolerance and secularism are two quite different, and sometimes incompatible, ideals.

State in the Indian Constitution: Is it Secular?

The state in the Indian constitution appears to possess all the features (features a to g) of a secular state. Feature-a is specified in Article 27 which rules out the public funding of religion and Article 28(1) under which 'no religious instruction is to be provided in any educational institution wholly maintained out of state funds'.

Articles 25, 27 and 28 guarantee religious liberty and meet the conditions specified by features b, c, and d. Under Article 25(1), 'all persons are equally entitled to freedom of conscience and the right freely to profess, practice and propagate religion' (features b and c). The phrase 'freedom of conscience' is meant to cover the liberty of persons without a religion (feature-d). Under Article 27, 'no person is compelled to pay any taxes, the proceeds of which are specifically appropriated in payment of expenses for the promotion or maintenance of any particular religion or religious denomination'. Finally, under Article 28(3), 'no person attending any educational institution ... shall be required to take part in any religious instruction or to attend any religious worship that may be conducted in such institution.'

Equality of citizenship is guaranteed by Articles 14, 15(1) and 29(2) of the Indian constitution. Article 15(1) states that the state shall not discriminate against any citizen on grounds only of religion, race, caste, sex, place of birth, or any of them (feature-e). Article 29(2) declares that no citizen shall be denied admission into any educational institution maintained by the state on grounds only of religion, race, etc. (feature-f). Article 16(1) & (2) of the Indian constitution affirm an equal opportunity for all citizens in matters relating to employment or appointment of any office under the state. It further affirms that no citizen, on grounds of religion or race, be eligible for or discriminated against in respect of any employment or office under the state. The clause on universal franchise as well as Article 325—that declares a general electoral roll for all constituencies and states that no one shall be ineligible for inclusion in this roll or claim to be included in it on grounds only of religion, etc.—embody the value of equal active citizenship. Thus feature-g is specified in the articles on equality of active citizenship.

Accepting that the state in the Indian constitution is meant to possess features a to g has some implications that are not always spelt out. First, the constitution rules out theocracy and the establishment of religion. The term 'secular state' is usually contrasted simply with theocracy. This is misleading, if not false, because the absence of theocracy is compatible with the establishment of religion. The secular credentials of the state cannot be derived from the mere absence of theocracy. Second, the secularism of the Indian constitution is neither purely procedural nor hyper-substantive, but a complex, multi-value doctrine. Third, the Indian state is not merely a tolerant state (in the sense specified above). Indian secularism must not be confused with a generally professed Hindu tolerance. It is frequently claimed that Indians have a natural, traditional affinity with secularism. In view of our traditional obsession with subtle and not-so-subtle hierarchies, this claim must be taken with a pinch of salt if not also pepper. It is of course true that tolerance, even within a hierarchical framework, forms an important background condition for the development of modern secularism, and elements of this background condition can certainly be found within India.

Forms of Secularism: The Individualist, Wall of Separation Thesis

A further point to note concerns the precise form of secularism to be found in the constitution. Broadly, secularism is the view that religion must be separated from the state for the sake of extensive religious liberty and equality of citizenship. This view can be differently interpreted. For Donald Smith, the secular state involves three distinct but interrelated relations concerning the state, religion, and the individual.[19] The first relation concerns individuals and their religion, from which the state is excluded. Individuals are thereby free to decide the merits of the respective claims of different religions without any coercive interference by the state: the libertarian ingredient in secularism. The second concerns the relation between individuals and the state, from which religion is excluded. Thus, all individuals are entitled to the same citizenship rights irrespective of the religious beliefs held by them: the egalitarian component in secularism. Finally, for Smith, the integrity of both these relations is dependent on the third relation, between the state and different religions. Here he argues that secularism entails the mutual exclusion of state and religion. Just as political power is beyond the scope of religion's legitimate objectives, equally it is not the function of the state to promote, regulate, direct, or interfere in religion. This interpretation is in line with the dominant American interpretation of secularism as erecting 'a wall of separation' between religion and the state. In the classical American view of disestablishment, there can be no support for religion even on a non-preferential basis. Even partial aid to educational institutions run by religious organizations will constitute some form of establishment. Moreover, a state that disestablishes all religions is one that has no power to interfere in the affairs of religious institutions. For better or for worse, the state is powerless to bring about changes in religion. Therefore, for Smith, secularism means the strict exclusion of religion from the state for the sake of the religious liberty and equal citizenship of individuals.

Does Indian secularism erect a similar 'wall of separation' for the sake of individualistically construed values? Articles 15, 16, 25, 29(2), and 325 support the 'wall of separation' interpretation. Though there is no direct reference to disestablishment, Articles 27 and 28(1) imply strict separation. By giving the president of the republic the option of not taking an oath in the name of God, Article 60 confirms the strictly neutral character of the Indian constitution. Thus far it appears that the state in India is constitutionally bound to follow Smith's model of secularism. However, further examination of the constitution reveals this impression to be mistaken. To begin with, Article 30(1) recognizes the rights of religious minorities which, unlike other articles applicable to citizens qua individuals, are group-specific. Indeed, another group-specific right granting political representation to all religious minorities was almost granted and was removed from the constitution only at the last minute. Second, Article 30(2) commits the state to give aid to educational institutions established and administered by religious communities. Also permitted is religious instruction in educational institutions partly funded by the state. These are significant departures from the 'wall of separation' view of the secular state. Even more significant are Articles 17 and 25(2) that require the state to intervene in religious affairs. Article 25(2)(b) states that 'nothing in Article 25(1) prevents the state from making a law providing for social welfare and reform or the throwing open of Hindu religious institutions of a public character to all classes and sections of Hindus.' Article 17 is an uninhibited, robust attack on the caste system, arguably the central feature of Hinduism, by abolishing untouchability and by making the enforcement of any disability arising out of it an offence punishable by law. Both appear to contravene Article 26 and take away the individual freedom of religion granted under Section 1 of Article 25.

These features of the Indian constitution depart from the strict separation view in two ways. First, unlike the strict separation view that renders the state powerless in religious matters, they enjoin the state to interfere in religion. Second, more importantly, by giving powers to the state in the affairs of one religion, they necessitate a departure from strict neutrality or equidistance. This power of interference may be interpreted to undermine or promote Hinduism. Either way it appears to strike a powerful blow to the idea of non-preferential treatment.

In short, some articles in the Indian constitution support an individualist interpretation and others a non-individualist one. Some conceive separation as exclusion, others as non-preferential treatment and, finally, some depart altogether from separation understood as exclusion or neutrality. At the end of the day, a confusing, somewhat contradictory, picture on secularism emerges from a reading of the constitution.

Critics could hardly fail to notice this and, therefore, for many, Articles 17, 25(2), 30(1 & 2) compromise the secularity of the Indian state. For Donald Smith, any intervention in Hinduism, for example the legal ban on the prohibition of Dalit entry into temples, or any protection of the rights of communities, seriously compromises secularism. For others, like Madan and Chatterjee, the presence of these features in the Indian constitution shows why the Indian state cannot be really secular. The Indian constitution does not give unambiguous criteria for maintaining the secularity of the state and, quite simply, given Indian conditions, it could never have.

In the rest of the essay, I oppose this view and argue that the core principles of secularism do not dictate the particular model of secularism advocated by Smith and implicitly accepted, though not endorsed, by Madan and Chatterjee. I argue that the conception of secularism embodied in the Indian constitution is not as ambiguous or contradictory as is made out by these critics. Though different from the standard, individualistically grounded 'wall of separation' model, the conception of secularism in the Indian constitution is a defensible version of secularism because it does not depart from the appropriately interpreted, core principles of secularism. Most critiques of secularism, on the ground that it is conceptually unsound or culturally inadaptable in India, appear to me to be unsuccessful. Therefore, an internalist rather than an externalist explanation for its crisis must be pursued. In what follows, I try to defend my claim by discussing two issues integral to the critique of Indian secularism: (a)intervention by the state in the affairs of Hindus, (b) group-specific minority rights.[20]

MODERN INDIAN SECULARISM

State Interference in Religion: The Idea of Principled Distance

The constitution sanctions interference in Hinduism by the state. Do Articles 25(2) and 17 violate Articles 15(1) and 26 of the constitution? Take for instance the Hindu Bigamous Marriages Act (1946) and the Hindu Marriage Act (1955). Does the fact that monogamy is enforced on Hindus and not on Muslims constitute discrimination against Hindus? Or for that matter against Muslims? More importantly, does it not breach the wall of separation, and by implication, secularism? Such interference violates secularism only if separation is taken to mean exclusion or a poorly understood neutrality. It does not compromise secularism if separation is taken to mean what elsewhere I call 'principled distance'.[21]

It is important to understand that the idea of separation within a value-based secularism cannot only mean exclusion. Recall the ties of secularism with the value of equal citizenship. Equal citizenship rights easily challenge hierarchical religions which are particularly insensitive to the vital interest of some of its members: those at the bottom of a sanctioned hierarchy. To ensure equal treatment, to uphold the value of equal citizenship, and therefore secularism, the state must interfere in hierarchically organized religions.

It is equally important to grasp the point that principled distance is not mere equidistance. In the strategy of principled distance, whether or not the state intervenes or refrains from action depends on what really strengthens religious liberty and equality of citizenship for all. If this is so, the state may not relate to every religion in exactly the same way; intervene to the same degree or in the same manner. All it must ensure is that the relation between religious and political institutions be guided by non-sectarian principles that remain consistent with a set of values constitutive of a life of equal dignity for all—in other words, principled distance.[22] Principled distance builds upon two ideas, at least one of which derives from a distinction drawn by the American philosopher Ronald Dworkin[23] between equal treatment and treating everyone as an equal. The principle of equal treatment, in the relevant political sense, requires that the state treat all its citizens equally in the relevant respect, for example in the distribution of a resource of opportunity. The principle of treating people as equals entails that every person is treated with equal concern and respect. This second principle may sometimes require equal treatment, say equal distribution of resources, but it may also occasionally dictate unequal treatment. Differential treatment is entirely consistent with treating people as equals. To take a familiar example, permitting Sikhs to wear turbans in the armed forces does violate the principle of equality. This idea is the second ingredient in the idea of principled distance. To say that a state maintains a principled distance from religion is to claim that it intervenes or refrains from interfering in religion, depending entirely upon whether or not some values (liberty and equality) are protected or advanced. Moreover, it is to admit that a state may interfere in one religion more than in others, depending once again on the historical and social condition of all relevant religions. For the promotion of a particular value constitutive of secularism, some religion, relative to other religions, may require greater interference from the state. In this interpretation of separation, a secular state neither mindlessly excludes all religions nor is blindly neutral towards them.

Consider once again laws that constitute an interference within Hinduism. The relevant consideration in their evaluation is not whether they immediately encompass all groups but whether or not they are just and consistent with the values undergirding secularism. There are reasons why all social groups need not be covered by these laws. First, they may be relevant only to Hindus. Take the abolition of child marriage and devadasi dedication or the introduction of the right to divorce. Here, before deciding whether it was necessary to enact a special provision for Hindus, the legislature took into account their social customs and beliefs. Similar laws for Muslims were simply redundant. Second, laws in liberal democracies require legitimacy; the consent of at least the representatives of communities is vital. If consent has indeed been obtained from the representatives of only one community, it is sometimes prudent to enact community-specific laws. It is wise to apply the general principle in stages, rather than not have it at all. Finally, 'it is perfectly within the competence of the legislature to take account of the degree of evil which is prevalent under various circumstances and the legislature is not bound to legislate for all evils at the same time. Therefore, an act passed by the legislature cannot be attacked merely because it tackles only some of the evils in society and does not tackle other evils of the same or worse kind which may be prevalent.' Thus, if the legislature acting on these considerations, wanted to enact a special provision in regard to, say, bigamous marriages among Hindus, it cannot be said that the legislature was discriminating against Hindus only on the ground of religion.[24] A state interfering in one religion more than in others does not automatically depart from secularism. Secularism requires principled distance, not exclusion or equidistance.

Secularism and Minority Rights

Does the recognition of rights for religious minorities violate the core principles of secularism? A cursory reading of the Constituent Assembly debates might yield the impression that some members at least found the recognition of *any* community-specific rights morally and politically disturbing. The grant of community-specific rights was seen to encourage a spiralling estrangement between social groups, which elsewhere I have called the minority–majority syndrome.[25] For these members of the Constituent Assembly, the very words 'minority' or 'minority-interest' were anathema. P.S. Deshmukh, a member from C.P and Berar, found 'no more monstrous word in the history of Indian politics than the word "minority"'. He claimed it to be 'a demon that hampered the progress of the country'.[26] Sidhwa, a Parsi from C.P and Berar, wanted 'the phrase "minorities" to be wiped out from history'.[27] A closer reading of the debates reveal that this venom is directed not against the idea of minorities per se but specifically against the notion of *religious* minorities. They claimed that to grant religious minorities a *social* right to establish their own educational institutions 'will block the way to national unity, promote communalism and a narrow anti-national outlook'. It was further contended that 'in a secular state, minorities based on religion or community should not be recognized. Recognition of minorities based on religion is the very negation of secularism. Only minorities based on language deserve recognition.'[28] A more detailed examination of the debates shows that even this objection to religious minorities was limited to a few members. Most members justified the grant of social rights not only to linguistic but also to minority religious communities. In other words, they willingly endorsed what might, in contrast to the syndrome, be called a majority–minority framework. Their principal objection was directed at *community-specific political rights*, in particular against the demand for separate electorates. For them, separate electorates were outside the acceptable framework and could not but help generate a syndrome. Their quarrel was not with religious minorities per se but with the specific *political* form of their demands. The demand for separate electorates was seen to be inherently anti-secular.

Why did they think so? And what was the argument favouring separate electorates? The debate in the assembly over separate electorates is illuminating. Pocker Sahib Bahadur, an advocate of separate electorates, began his argument with the premise that human beings identify themselves with particular communities, and since such communities cannot be numerically equal, there are bound to be minorities in every land.[29] For him, there was little use regretting or wishing away this fact. Minorities could not be 'erased out of existence'. Coming to terms with them, therefore, entails reconciling with the fact that complete unity or harmony between communities or the total eradication of differences among them is impossible. On the other hand, the minimization of difference is, and this can occur only if minorities are satisfied with the overall political framework within which they reside. A condition of such satisfaction, Bahadur argued, was that their views and grievances be given an effective voice in the deliberations of the legislature. As all members of the minority community cannot bring their own voices in the deliberative assembly, attempts must be made to induct their authentic representatives, and 'to lay down a procedure by which the best man who can represent that community and voice forth the feelings of that community is elected to the legislature'.[30]

Many premises of this argument were acceptable to opponents of separate electorates. For example, Govind Ballabh Pant began by agreeing that in a free and democratic state citizens would satisfy not only their material wants but also 'a spiritual sense of self-respect'. This self-respect, he assumed, was linked to their community-based identity. It was linked also with their recognition as equals by other communities. This requirement entailed that the majority be 'informed and inspired by genuine feelings of regard for the minorities and for all its decisions to be actuated by a real sense of understanding and sympathy.' Therefore, he thought it incumbent upon the majority to examine the issue of separate electorates from the point of view of the minorities. Implicit in much of what he said was a deep understanding of the active dimension of citizenship. Active participation does not mean a mere presence in the political domain or the possession of the right to vote but more importantly a right to participate in public deliberation. Citizens are not treated as equals in the public domain if, despite a formal right to vote, they are excluded from public deliberations by informal mechanisms. As a result, they begin to have a persistent feeling that they are inadequately heard, that their views are not properly taken into deliberation, that they have no real say in public matters. They then begin to assume a 'shrill and discordant voice'. For Pant, the Muslim voice in the legislatures must be 'powerful', not shrill or discordant.[31]

Bahadur conceded that these premises were shared by some of the best Congressmen. Differences arose over the procedure to effect them; over how adequate representation for Muslims could be achieved. For the Congress, initially, the best procedure for this was a system of community-based reservations of a certain number of seats based on joint electorate. This was consistent with the view that Muslims have a better practical knowledge of the needs of their own community. Bahadur however saw defects in this procedure because it could elect a person favoured solely by the majority; one who fails to represent the real views and interests of Muslims. He insisted that the true real interests of Muslims can be understood *only* by Muslims themselves. Furthermore, even the fact of belonging to a community was not a sufficient precondition for proper representation. The elected person must be the right sort of man from the community and this, he argued, could be ensured only by separate electorates.[32] To elect the best man, only Muslims must choose their Muslim representative. For this requirement to be met, separate electorates were essential.

Separate electorates were fiercely opposed by all members except those who belonged to the League. Four arguments were advanced against separate electorates, all quite convincing but only two of which addressed the issues raised by Bahadur. First, inherent in the logic of distributing political rights on a purely religious basis was the installation of a theocratic state, which in the Indian context could only be a Hindu state. This was clearly against the interests of the minorities. Second, under separate electorates, religion was mixed freely with the desire for profit, for office, and for the encroachment on others' properties, and this led directly to communal crimes and massacres. More important were arguments that accepted the initial premises of Bahadur's argument but rejected his conclusion. The argument from democratic accountability advanced by Pant appealed to the best interests of Muslims themselves. Pant argued that under a system of separate electorates both majority and minority representatives would be chosen separately by their respective communities. When this happens, representatives of the majority will not be accountable to the minority community. In the absence of general accountability, and despite the formal presence of minority representatives in the deliberative assembly, they could easily take decisions against the interests of the minority. If this were to occur, the chosen representatives of the minority will have been reduced in the legislature to playing the role of mere advocates, with little power to affect decision-making. The price of guaranteed representation in the legislature might be reduced representation in the most effective decision-making body, the cabinet, and that, Pant insightfully argued, was a heavy price indeed. Pant concluded that it was dangerous for the minorities to be segregated from the rest of the community, to keep aloof in an air-tight compartment 'where they would have to rely on others even for the air they breathed'. To have a powerful, rather than a shrill and discordant voice, the Muslims must, he pleaded, reject separate electorates. In short, Pant agreed that if people are excluded from or discriminated against within the deliberative assembly solely on the ground that they belonged to a particular religion, then the principle of equal citizenship and a core value of secularism is violated. He however argued that separate not joint electorates force this exclusion and, by implication, breach the core principles of secularism.

A related argument was made by Ayyangar who distinguished between religious difference and communal division, arguing that though religious difference was inevitable, communal division was not. By making cross-communal political representation impossible, separate electorates congealed communal divisions. Here, Ayyangar was alluding to the very real possibility, opened up by communal political representation, of a future society in which citizens remain permanently alienated from one another, never addressing mutual needs or sharing a common destiny. This is a mockery of the very idea of citizenship that presupposes shared membership in a political community. It is clear from this discussion that it was not community-based difference that was unacceptable to the best Congressmen. Nor, going by their initial acceptance of reservations for Muslims based on joint electorates, did they entirely reject what is frequently called 'mirror representation', namely the view that a legislature is representative only if it mirrors the ethnic, religious, or gender characteristics of the public. Rather, they unequivocally rejected the sufficiency of mirror representation. For them, separate electorates embodied a generalized mirror representation. Muslims could represent members of their own community but, it was argued, they need not, by law, have monopoly over such representation.[33]

It is also important to note that separate electorates were rejected not because they fostered communal difference as such or because they endangered a simple, undifferentiated notion of immediate national unity but because, as Patel put it, 'they had in the past sharpened communal difference *to a dangerous extent* and had proved one of the main stumbling blocks to the development of a *healthy* national life.' (Emphasis mine) I wish to stay with this point because, by stressing the compatibility of communal difference and a healthy national life, it shows the anti-assimilationist streak even in Patel. It also indicates what form of assimilation is required by nation-states and why.

Liah Greenfeld has recently drawn attention to a change in the semantics of the term 'nation'.[34] In the late thirteenth century, the term 'nation' meant a community of opinion where the constituents of the said community were representatives of cultural and political authority. In short, a nation was a group of social élites. In the sixteenth century, however, the reference of 'nation' changed; it began to be applied to the entire population of a country and became synonymous with the word 'people'. This change in meaning signalled the symbolic elevation of the rabble into an élite, its move from irrelevance to relevance, from the wings on to centre stage. Henceforth, every member of the population could partake of this superior, élite quality.[35]

This effected yet another change: in their self-understanding, the nation exists prior to and independent of the political organization of society, which has the power to give itself a constitution. This idea that the basic rules of society stem from the common action of a people, of a nation, is coterminous with the democratic idea that sovereignty is located within a people with a fundamentally equal status. As Greenfeld puts it, 'nationalism was the form in which democracy appeared in the world, contained in the idea of the nation as a butterfly in a cocoon.'[36] Now, I wish to argue that underlying the anxious talk of national unity and the almost obsessive attack on communal division lay the very real need to create and sustain what one assembly member called 'the unadulterated identity of people, a democracy'.[37] This is of a piece with a point recently made by the political philosopher Charles Taylor that, unlike other political systems, democratic states need cohesion, a common identity, a common personality, and a common agency. In other words, democracy is not just a procedural but also an identity-related communitarian issue. It allows for differences but it cannot stomach divisions that are 'sharpened to a dangerous extent'. It was precisely for this reason that a 'suffrage based on religious affiliation was ridiculous'[38] and why in the end religion in India had to be separated from a democratic state. This explains why eventually community-differentiated political rights were not granted in the constitution. This of course is an entirely contextual issue. The exclusion of religion from politics was necessary in India because religion-based divisions had here become too dangerous, and not because such exclusion is necessarily required by every form of secularism.

Indeed, the rejection of community-specific political rights was entirely consistent with the acceptance of community-specific social rights. The rights granted under Article 30 were as necessary for a democratic state as the rejection of separate electorates under Article 325. The reason for their inclusion is also found in the debates. Members believed that even if the majority–minority framework was subject to the 'historical process of assimilation', 'the minorities must be dissolved into the majority by *justice*'. As Hridaya Nath Kunzru put it, 'if this elementary justice is not given to minorities, we may open up the dangerous path of fanatical nationalism.' The principle of elementary justice, and the very same principles of liberty and equality that ruled community-differentiated political rights out, necessitated community-differentiated social rights. Ambedkar's riposte to Mahavir Tyagi is very telling on this issue. Tyagi asked him if the grant of cultural and educational rights to minorities in India should not wait till the fate of minorities residing in Pakistan was more clearly known. Ambedkar replied firmly that the rights of minorities are not relative or conditional upon the decision of other states but were absolute: 'No matter what others do', he urged, 'we ought to do what is right in our own judgement and, therefore, every minority, irrespective of any other consideration, is entitled to the right to use their language, script and culture and the right not to be precluded from establishing any educational institution that they wish to establish.'[39]

Forms of Secularism: Group-sensitivity and Principled Distance

It is time I addressed the issue I promised to tackle head on at the end of part I: by accepting community-specific rights for religious minorities and endorsing state-intervention in Hinduism, did the constitution depart from secular principles? I do not think it did. Rather, it developed its own modern variant. This distinctiveness of Indian secularism can be understood only when the cultural background and social context in India is properly grasped. At least four such features of this sociocultural context call for attention. First, there exists the mind-boggling diversity of religious communities in India. Such diversity may coexist harmoniously but it invariably generates conflicts, the most intractable of which, I believe, are deep conflicts over values. Second, within Hinduism in particular and in South Asian religions more generally, a greater emphasis is placed on practice rather than belief. A person's religious identity and affiliation are defined more by what she or he does with and in relation to others, than by the content of beliefs individually held by them. As practices are intrinsically social, any significance placed on them brings about a concomitant valorization of communities. Together, these two features entail inter-community conflicts which are further exacerbated if fuelled by competing conceptions of democracy and nationalism. Third, many religiously sanctioned social practices are oppressive by virtue of their illiberal and inegalitarian character, and deny a life of dignity and self-respect. Therefore, from a liberal and egalitarian standpoint, they desperately need to be reformed. Such practices frequently have a life of their own, independent of consciously held beliefs, and possess a causal efficacy that remains unaffected by the presence of conscious beliefs. Furthermore, a tendency to fortify and insulate themselves from reflective critique makes them resistant to easy change and reform. It follows that an institution vested with enormous social power is needed to transform their character. Fourth, in Hinduism, the absence of an organized institution such as the Church has meant that the impetus for effective reform cannot come exclusively from within. Reform within Hinduism can hardly be initiated without help from powerful external institutions such as the state.

In such a context, India needed a coherent set of intellectual resources to tackle inter-religious conflict, and to struggle against oppressive communities not by disaggregating them into a collection of individuals or by derecognizing them but by somehow making them more liberal and egalitarian. A political movement for a united, liberal, democratic India had to struggle against hierarchical and communal conceptions of community, but without abandoning a reasonable communitarianism. Besides, the state had an important contribution to make in the transformation of these communities, which is why a perennial dilemma was imposed on it. The state in India walked a tightrope between the requirement of religious liberty that frequently entails non-interference in the affairs of religious communities, and the demand for equality and justice which necessitates intervention in religiously sanctioned social customs. Secularism in India simply had to be different from the classical, liberal model that does not recognize groups, and dictates strict separation between religious and political institutions.

If we abandon the view, such as Donald Smith's, that political secularism entails a unique set of state policies valid under all conditions which provide the yardstick by which the secularity of any state is to be judged, then we can better understand why despite 'deviation' from the ideal, the state in India continues to embody a model of *secularism.*[40] This can be shown even if we adhere to Smith's working definition of secularism as consisting of three relations. Smith's first relation embodies the principle of religious liberty construed individualistically, i.e. pertaining to the religious beliefs of individuals. However, it is possible to make a non-individualistic construal of religious liberty by speaking not of the beliefs of the individual but rather of the practices of groups. Here religious liberty would mean distancing the state from the practices of religious groups. The first principle of secularism can then be seen also to grant the right to a religious community to its own practices. Smith's second relation embodies the value of equal citizenship, but this entails, and I cannot substantiate my claim, that we tolerate the attempt of radically differing groups to determine the nature and direction of society as they best see it. In this view, then, the public presence of the religious practices of groups is guaranteed and entailed by the recognition of community-differentiated citizenship rights. Smith's version of secularism entails a charter of uniform rights. It is however clear that the commitment of secularism to equal citizenship can dictate community-specific rights and therefore differentiated citizenship.

In principle, this could easily accommodate a reasonable demand for community-specific political rights. In India, for reasons outlined above, it meant community-specific social rights, such as the right to administer and maintain educational institutions. Smith's third principle pertains to non-establishment and therefore to a strict separation of religion from the state, under which religion and the state both have the freedom to develop without interfering with each other. Separation, however, need not mean strict non-interference, mutual exclusion, or equidistance, as in Smith's view. Instead, it could be a policy of principled distance, which entails a flexible approach to the question of intervention or abstention, combining both, depending on the context, nature or current state of the relevant religions.

It was largely this group-sensitive conception of secularism of the principled distance variety that legitimized the practices of the state in which religion was alternatingly excluded and included as an object of state policy. By its refusal to allow (a) separate electorates, (b) reserved constituencies for religious communities, reservations for jobs on the basis of religious classification, and (c) the organization of states on a religious basis, the Indian state excluded religion from its purview on the grounds that its inclusion would inflame religious and communal conflict and produce another Partition-like scenario. However, the very principles that excluded religion from state institutions also influenced its inclusion in policy matters of cultural import. For example, a uniform charter of rights was not considered absolutely essential for national integration. Separate rights were granted to minority religious communities to enable them to live with dignity. Integration was not seen as coterminous with complete assimilation. Similar liberal and egalitarian motives compelled the state to undertake reforms within Hinduism. By making polygamy illegal, introducing the right to divorce, abolishing child marriage, legally recognizing inter-caste marriages, regulating the activities of criminals masquerading as holy men, introducing temple entry rights for Dalits and reforming temple administration, the state intervened in religious matters to protect the ordinary but dignified life of its citizens.

To sum up: (a) modern secularism is fully compatible with, indeed sometimes even dictates a defence of, differentiated citizenship; and (b) the secularity of the state does not necessitate strict intervention, non-interference, or equidistance but rather any or all of these, as the case may be. If this is so, the criticism that the constitution envisages a state that cannot be secular because it explicitly abandons equidistance is mistaken. A secular state need not be equidistant from all religious communities and may interfere in one religion more than another. A critique of constitutional secularism on the grounds that it acknowledges group rights, or that it gives up on neutrality, simply does not wash.

POSTSCRIPT: THE PRACTICE OF SECULARISM

How successful has the Indian state been in implementing the principles of the secular state? Which principles has it implemented anyway? It is obvious to any observer that the practice of secularism by the Indian state has at best been inconsistent. However, to show this is beyond the scope of this essay. To assess the performance of all the institutions of the Indian state over the past fifty years is hardly easy. To make my task manageable, I focus on one moment in the life of one institution of the Indian state, namely, the Supreme Court. Under special scrutiny, in what follows, is the important Supreme Court judgement of 1995 on *Prabhoo* vs *Kunte*. By looking at this judgement, I hope to show that the judiciary has understood the principles of secularism in much the same way as I have interpreted them here. Expressed differently, the best practice of the Indian state conforms to my interpretation of constitutional secularism.

The judgement I examine pertains to the inflammatory speeches by Shiv Sena supremo Bal Thackeray during the election campaign of Ramesh Prabhoo, a candidate for the Maharashtra State Legislative Assembly. A sample of the speeches cited in the judgement are given below:

> 'We are fighting this election for the protection of Hinduism. Therefore, we do not care for the votes of the Muslims. This country belongs to Hindus and will remain so.' [Again]: 'You will find Hindu temples underneath if all the Mosques are dug out. Anybody who stands against the Hindus should be showed [*sic*] or worshipped with shoes. Prabhoo should be led to victory in the name of Hindu. Though this country belongs to Hindus, Ram and Krishna are insulted. We do not want Muslim votes. A snake like Shahabuddin is sitting in the Janata Party. So, the voters should bury this party.'

The election of Prabhoo, an independent candidate supported by Shiv Sena, was declared void by the Bombay High Court on the grounds that he and his agent Bal Thackeray had appealed for votes on the basis of the returned candidate's religion and also that Thackeray's election speeches promoted feelings of enmity and hatred among citizens of India on grounds of religion and community. Both Thackeray and Prabhoo contested this judgement and appealed to the Supreme Court, claiming that their acts did not constitute a violation of the Representation of the Peoples Act, 1951, that prohibits *only* a *direct* appeal for votes on the ground of the religion of the candidate. (They also argued that their public speeches did not amount to appeal for votes on the basis of their religion because Hindutva implies Indian culture as a whole and not merely the Hindu religion. Shockingly, the court accepted this view. Thus we have a judgement that exemplifies a combination of the best and worst practice of the Indian judiciary.) Their counsel argued that, because they violate the fundamental right to free speech given by Article 19(I)(a) of the Constitution, sub-sections 3 and 3A of Section 123 of the act are unconstitutional.

The Supreme Court rejected the arguments of the appellants, particularly their contention that sub-section 3 of Section 123 is violated only when an election speech makes a direct appeal for votes on the basis of the candidate's religion. In the view of the court, the nature of the speech is determined by its substance as well as by the manner in which it is meant to be understood by the audience within a particular social setting and, if a reasonable interpretation of the speech leads to the same conclusion as a direct appeal, then the speech violates the relevant sub-section of the act. The purpose of enacting the provision, the court argued, was to ensure that no candidate at an election gets or is denied votes only because of his religion.

Is this judgement of the court consistent with secularism? More specifically, which version of secularism does it endorse? As one goes through the judgement, one arrives at the unambiguous conclusion that the court ratifies the conception of secularism outlined above. For example, it contends that it is part of the meaning of secularism that the state has no religion (feature-a). The judgement claims that a secular state guarantees to all its citizens the right to follow their religion according to their own convictions. It further clarifies that secularism is one facet of the right to equality, for it means equality in matters of religion to all individuals and groups (features b and c). In several passages, the court also endorses equality of citizenship (features f and g). However, in the opinion of the court, secularism cannot allow the mixing of religion and politics. Its professed goal is violated when a candidate appeals for votes on the grounds of his religion. Does it mean that the court understands separation to mean the exclusion of religion from politics? If so, its understanding of secularism is very different indeed from the one outlined above.

Fortunately, the court clarifies that this secular principle must not be understood simplistically. The mere mention of religion in an election speech is not forbidden by the act. Religion may figure in an election speech so long as its introduction does not amount to an appeal to vote on the grounds of the candidate's religion or an appeal not to vote for the opponent on the grounds of his religion. For example, an election speech made in conformity with the fundamental right to freedom of religion guaranteed under Articles 25–30 of the constitution cannot be treated as anti-secular. Similarly, if a speech refers to discriminatory acts against any particular religion and promises removal of this imbalance, then, because its objective is the promotion rather than the denial of equality and justice, the speech is entirely consistent with secularism. This means that the court endorses Articles 25–30 where every group is protected from discrimination on grounds of religion and is granted the right to obtain funds from the state for educational purposes on a non-preferential basis. Only when an electoral or political speech promotes enmity between religious communities, thereby seeking to alienate the electorate from a candidate on the grounds of his religion or when the candidate wants to gain political mileage for himself simply on the grounds of his own religion, that mixing religion with politics is inappropriate and anti-secular. Thus, only when the use of religion in political or electoral speeches creates alienation among citizens instead of encouraging solidarity, when it violates the principle of equal citizenship, is secularism violated. It was to uphold the principle of equal citizenship, and to prevent political alienation among citizens that, according to the court, the makers of the constitution rejected separate electorates. Forbidding the use of religion for gaining votes is of a piece with the rejection of separate electorates. Both mix religion and politics in an inappropriate manner. This distinction between appropriate and inappropriate mixing of religion and politics is at the heart of the idea of principled distance. As this distinction is accepted or presupposed by the judgement, it follows unambiguously that separation is understood not as the exclusion of religion but in terms of the idea of principled distance.

Notes and References

1. See Christophe Jaffrelot, *The Hindu Nationalist Movement and Indian Politics*, Penguin India, 1999, Ch. 1.
2. See Thomas Blom Hansen, *The Saffron Wave: Democracy and Hindu Nationalism in Modern India*, Princeton, Princeton University Press, 1999.
3. I have in mind the writings of T.N. Madan, Ashis Nandy, and Partha Chatterjee, available in R. Bhargava (ed.), *Secularism and Its Critics*, Oxford University Press, New Delhi, 1998.
4. These historical examples are taken from the *New Catholic Encyclopaedia* which defines theocracy as a form of political government in which the deity directly rules the people, or as the rule of a priestly caste. (Catholic University of America, Washington, vol. 14, p. 13). Theocracy in India would mean the rule of Brahmins in accordance with the Dharma Shastras.
5. Leonard W. Levy, *The Establishment Clause*, University of North Carolina Press, 1994, p. 7.
6. This is perhaps an obvious point but may be obscured by the present, benign form of established states. However, it comes out sharply when nineteenth-century debates on church–state systems are examined. Consider the following powerful statement in the House of Commons in 1871 by Edward Mial, Congregational minister and MP from Bradford: 'Take a survey of the operation of this State–Church policy ... what does it show? It shows you a nation sharply divided by law in regard to their religion into two great sections—the ones privileged, the other tolerated. It shows you one half, or thereabouts, of the people of this kingdom condemned by law to occupy before the law an inferior position as compared to the other half—to be tolerated, endured, humiliated in what they regard as their most incontestable right and in the discharge of their most sacred obligations.' See David Nicholas, *Church and State in Britain since 1920*, Routledge & Kegan Paul. London and New York, 1967, pp. 85–6.
7. Ibid., p. 12.

8. Ibid., p. 11.
9. The de facto disestablishment in England (the relaxation of Anglican monopoly) began with the Toleration Act of 1689 that granted limited, hitherto unavailable freedom to non-Anglican but Trinitarian Protestants; was continued first by the repeal of the Test and Corporation Act (1828), then by a series of acts relating to the emancipation of Roman Catholics (1829) and Jews (The Jewish relief act of 1858). The secular nature of the state of the UK is likely to be tested by the presence of Hindus, Muslims, and Sikhs.
10. See Donald Smith, *India as a Secular State*, Princeton and Oxford, 1963, p. 21. My discussion confirms that the terms 'theocracy', 'monopolistic and multiple establishment', and 'secular' are all ideal–typical. No actual state has been unambiguously theocratic or established or purely secular. Most really existing states, as T.M. Scanlon points out, are likely to reflect a mixed strategy. See T.M. Scanlon, *The Difficulty of Tolerance*, in Bhargava (ed.), op. cit., pp. 54–70.
11. On this, see for example, John Semonche, *Religion and Constitutional Government in the United States*, Signal Books, North Carolina, 1986, pp. 22–5. He writes: 'establishment in the United States meant a linkage of the state with religion in the sense of using the force of the state, primarily through the use of its taxing power and its enforcement of other laws, to aid the religious cause.' He continues: 'often this basic faith was labelled Protestantism which excluded, among other groups, Roman Catholics and Jews, or to Christianity which included Catholics but still excluded Jews and others.' Semonche notes that 'When requirements were changed to a simple belief in God, the reformers concluded that they had achieved true religious freedom.' Clearly, as he acknowledges, they saw 'no infringement of liberty in a discrimination between believers and non-believers.'
12. On these points, see the excellent discussion of religious toleration in England by U. Henriques, *Religious Toleration in England, 1787–1833*, Routledge & Kegan Paul, London, 1961.
13. See Charles Taylor, *Sources of the Self*, Cambridge University Press, Cambridge, 1989.
14. As briefly discussed above, these civic disabilities were commonplace in states with a religious establishment. For instance, 'Protestants in France were outlawed, their marriages illegitimatized, their children bastardized, their inheritance and even their lives insecure.' See, Henriques, op. cit., p. 13.
15. Once again, such political disabilities were common in established states.

For example, the Test and Corporation Acts in England disqualified dissenters from office by requiring communion in the Anglican Church. Before 1858, Jews were not even qualified to vote in England. Similar test oaths were used, prior to disestablishment, in Maryland, North Carolina, New York. Indeed, oaths requiring a belief in God survived in a number of states well into the twentieth century. See Semonche, op. cit., p. 23.

16. Charles Beitz, *Political Equality: An Essay in Democratic Theory*, Princeton University Press, New Jersey, 1990, p. 110.
17. This rules out communist states as being properly secular. Though controversial, this point has been made by others. For example, Donald Smith claims: 'Church–state separation can exist simultaneously with flagrant violations of freedom of religion, as in Soviet Russia; this is *not* a secular state.' Smith, op. cit., p. 20. On morally indefensible versions of secularism, see the discussion of hyper-substantive secularism in Bhargava, 'What is Secularism For', op. cit., pp. 511–31.
18. See Ashis Nandy in Bhargava, op. cit.
19. See Donald Smith, op. cit.
20. Shortage of space prevents me from dealing here with a third, fascinating issue concerning religious instruction in state-aided educational institutions.
21. Rajeev Bhargava, 'What is Secularism For?' in Bhargava (ed.), *Secularism and Its Critics*, op. cit., pp. 5–15.
22. Ibid.
23. Ronald Dworkin, 'Liberalism', *in* Stuart Hampshire (ed.), *Public and Private Morality*, CUP, Cambridge, 1978, p. 125.
24. AIR, 1952, Bom. 84, *The State of Bombay* vs. *Narasu Appa.*
25. 'Should We Abandon the Majority-minority Framework?', in D.L. Sheth and Gurpreet Mahajan (eds), *Nation State and Minorities*, Oxford University Press, New Delhi, 1999.
26. The *Constituent Assembly Debates* (*CAD*), 27 Aug 1947, p. 201.
27. Ibid., p. 209.
28. Ibid., 8 Dec., 1948, p. 899. Therefore, it was argued, only minorities based on language should be recognized.
29. Ibid., 27 Aug. 1947, p. 211.
30. Ibid., p. 212.
31. Ibid.
32. The casteist overtones of Bahadur's demand could hardly have gone unnoticed. He was anxious that hegemonic considerations might compel members of the majority community to strategically vote for a lower

caste Muslim candidate, 'some illiterate sweeper or scavenger', who may not be capable of understanding the real needs of the community and whose selection, therefore, could be detrimental to its long-term interests!

33. Farzana Sheikh, who claims that the Congress categorically assumed that the unit of representation simply had to be the individual, is mistaken, for the Congress did not completely rule out community-based political representation. See Farzana Sheikh, 'Muslims and Political Representation in Colonial India: The Making of Pakistan', in Mushirul Hasan (ed.), *India's Partition: Process, Strategy and Mobilisation*, OUP, New Delhi, 1993, pp. 81–101.
34. Liah Greenfield, *Nationalism: Five Roads to Modernity*, Harvard University Press, Cambridge and London, 1992, introduction.
35. The transformation of a rabble into a people and of the people into an élite presupposes a profound change in the way societies are imagined, i.e. from hierarchical communities, to networks consisting of free and equal individuals. On this, see Taylor, 'Modes of Secularism', in Bhargava (ed.), *Secularism and Its Critics*.
36. Ibid., p. 10.
37. *CAD*, 27 Aug. 1947, p. 219.
38. Ibid., p. 218.
39. Ibid., 1 May 1947, pp. 507–8.
40. For an interesting critique of Smith's interpretation of Indian secularism as derived from the American model with an 'extra dose of separation', see Marc Galanter, 'Secularism, East and West' in Rajeev Bhargava (ed.), *Secularism and its Critics*, pp. 234–67.

6

How Has the Proliferation of Parties Affected the Indian Federation? A Comparative Approach*

DOUGLAS V. VERNEY

1. Introduction

This essay explores what has been happening to one of the organizing principles of the constitutional framework, India as a federation.[1] Far from federalism 'beginning to look worn out', India today is not less but more of a federation than it was in 1950. Certainly there has not been a movement away from federation towards greater centralization (with India moving in the direction of a unitary state or union). Rather, there have been fears in some quarters of too much decentralization. The truth appears to be that India is still a federation, and is still quite centralized in some of its features. However, in some respects, notably in the proliferation of state parties, it has a political system very different from the days when Rajni Kothari could describe India as a 'one-party dominant' state.[2]

In the 1950s India's political system was described as 'parliamentary', today it is described as 'federal'. A conflict between the two is rarely contemplated.[3] As we shall however see, the nature of India's federation owes much to its Westminster-inspired parliamentary form of government.

2. Federalism, Federations and Confederacy: How they Differ

It is important to distinguish between two terms, 'federalism' and 'federation'. Until recently there was considerable disagreement over just what federalism meant. In the Constituent Assembly debates, T.T. Krishnamachari said: 'It is not a definite concept, it has not got any stable meaning. It is a concept the definition of which has been changing from time to time.'[4]

Nowadays many scholars distinguish between federalism, which they assume is a concept, and federation, which they regard as a system of governance.[5] What has changed has been not so much the concept of federalism (an important 'ism' like liberalism), as the nature of federations, some of which have been more centralized than others.[6] In describing the Indian constitution the Sarkaria Commission sensibly concluded that it was neither federal in the classical (or American) sense nor unitary: 'It envisages a diversified political system of a special type. Some authorities have classified it as a "quasi-federal" Constitution.'[7]

The term 'quasi-federal' refers to the many centralized federations, Canada and India among them, which began with constitutions that provided the national government with a number of important powers not granted to the US in its 1787 constitution. Because they had several unitary elements, K.C. Wheare described these constitutions as 'quasi-federal'. He did not mean that they in any way had an inferior constitutional structure, but simply that the constitutions of these countries had elements not only of federation but also of union.[8]

Formal constitutions are not the same as the practice of government. Wheare distinguished between constitutional law and political practice. Yet he still concluded that in practice, as well as in law, India in its early days was quasi-federal. He went on to add: 'To say this is not, of course, to suggest a criticism of the constitution or the government. A quasi-federal system may well be most appropriate for India.'[9]

In addition to union and federation, there is a third major form of governance: confederacy. A distinguishing feature of a confederacy is that the national government does not have direct dealings with the citizens of the constituent states. For example, George Washington and the Continental Congress had to ask the states for money and troops. For a long time confederacy was denounced. It was associated with the Articles of Confederation that preceded the American constitution and with the defence of slavery by the American Confederacy in the Civil War. But times have changed. Thanks to the work of American scholars like Daniel Elazar, who concluded that segregation and Southern sectionalism were history and the position of the Federal Government secure, confederacies have recently come back into favour.[10]

The European Union is often described as a form of confederacy, but it is a confederacy with some federative features.[11] In Canada, the *Parti Québecois* has examined the European Union and favours something approaching quasi-confederacy, in which Quebec would have more powers. In the US there is growing interest in the contribution that the aboriginal peoples, the American Indians, made long ago to confederate governance. After all, the Iroquois Confederation dates back to 1570.[12]

In recent years there have been few proponents of confederate government in India. However, in addition to dealing with federalism and federations, it is necessary to ask whether the proliferation of state political parties is introducing an element of confederacy into the political system. India's present federation appears to combine both centralization and confederacy.

3. Recent Changes in the Study of Federalism and Federations

The study of federalism and federations is much broader than it used to be. The modern study of federations dates from 1946 when K.C. Wheare published the first edition of his classic *Federal Government*. He classified only four systems as genuine federations: the US, Switzerland, Canada, and Australia. (It was in later editions that Wheare made some references to the new Indian constitution.) He stressed the coordinate relationship of general and regional governments under federal constitutions. As an Australian-born Oxford don writing for British readers, Wheare was familiar with the Westminster system of unitary government, one in which parliament was supreme and local government subordinate to the central government. The British then had no conception of the very different *co-ordinate* relationship between governments in federations. At the time they were somewhat sceptical about the value of federation, having been influenced by Harold Laski's famous observation in 1939 that federalism was obsolescent.[13]

The second phase saw the emergence of a number of American scholars, such as W.H. Riker, Ivo Duchacek, Vincent Ostrom and Daniel J. Elazar, who were much more familiar than Wheare with American federalism. Elazar contributed the entry 'Federalism' to the International Encyclopedia of the Social Sciences, published in 1967, and included in his survey a larger number of political systems as federations, including India. He drew an important distinction between decentralization, which a unitary state can practice, and the constitutional 'non-centralization' that characterizes federations.[14] This important distinction is still not always understood, particularly by economists. The British decentralized government to Northern Ireland in 1922. But as they showed in 1972, what they decentralized could be recentralized. In a federation power is *constitutionally* distributed between two orders of government, not simply decentralized.

The third and present phase has witnessed a growing interest in federations among scholars in a large number of countries.[15] Most notable are Australia, Germany, India and Canada, where Ronald Watts (who studied under Wheare in the 1960s) has recently published a book comparing federations, which he suggests now number 24.[16] Whereas for Wheare the model was American federalism, it has now become common to describe American federalism as unique and to draw a distinction between the American presidential-congressional federation and the parliamentary federations of countries such as Canada, India, Australia and Germany.[17] For one thing, the US has weak national political parties. Each state has its own election laws and party organization. The reason that presidential nominating conventions are held every four years is to bring the fifty state organizations of each party together to select a nominee for president. No other country has this form of governance, one in which the electoral apparatus is based on the constituent states. In the US, the Federal Election Commission is primarily concerned with campaign contributions: it does not organize elections.

4. Assessing India's Centralized Federation: A Comparative Perspective

If, then, we can assume that American federalism is unique and concentrate on parliamentary federations, how do we assess India's system of government? There is general agreement that the 1950 constitution provided for a centralized (or quasi-federal) federation. This was in marked contrast to the Objectives Resolution moved by Jawaharlal Nehru in the Constituent Assembly in 1946. This envisaged a decentralized federation in which the states would retain residuary powers.[18] Partition, and the fear that India might suffer further division, convinced the Constituent Assembly that there needed to be much tighter control from Delhi. There was no reference to federalism or federation in the 1950 constitution.[19] The Government of India was called the 'Union' government, a term reminiscent of the American Civil War when the Union forces opposed the Confederacy.[20] The Government of India was also commonly referred to as 'the centre'.

In describing India's federal structure, one legal authority has stressed its centralizing tendency as follows:

> ... the Indian Constitution exhibits a centralizing tendency in several of its provisions, e.g. the adoption of a lengthy Concurrent List, the power of Parliament to re-organize the political structure of the country, supremacy of Parliament over State Legislatures if there is a direct conflict between their respective jurisdictions, vesting of the residuary legislative power in Parliament, and powers of Governors to reserve Bills for the consideration of the President of the Republic. Fourthly, in certain circumstances, the Union is empowered to supersede the authority of the State, or to exercise powers otherwise vested in the States.[21]

There are many other ways in which the constitution exhibited a centralizing tendency. It retained the national civil service and police service of the Raj. State governors were still appointed by the centre, not elected. A Planning Commission and a Finance Commission controlled by the centre were established to develop the economy. Yet despite all this centralization, making India a quasi-federation, the country was by no means a unitary state.

For some concessions to non-centralization were inevitable in such a vast, heterogeneous society.[22] The Rajya Sabha, which replaced the House of the Princes, was a body elected in large measure by the states. More important, in the Seventh Schedule of the constitution the states were given sixty-six constitutional responsibilities. Eighteen of the Schedule's sections dealt with taxes for which the states were responsible.

Strictly speaking, India, like Canada, remains legally in some respects a quasi-federation. In practice, both countries today are federations, and each has its unique qualities.[23] Canada is often said to be a much looser federation than India. But in both instances, the basic institution of government was originally the Westminster parliamentary system.[24] Federation was added on.

The adoption of parliamentary government on the British model has made them very different from the first federation, the United States. The Americans based their 1787 constitution on federal principles. The phrase 'based on federal principles' is important. It means that the Americans wanted above all a limited role for government at all levels. To ensure this they adopted a number of basic principles of governance. Among them were the separation of the executive and legislative powers; bicameralism to protect territorial minorities; checks and balances; the distribution of power between two levels of government; and in due course judicial review. It was to implement these principles that the framers established a presidential-congressional form of government. This notion of federalism as limited government sustained by basic principles played no role in the Canadian or Indian constitutions.

India and Canada also differ considerably from the second federation, that of Switzerland. In 1848 the Swiss too based their constitution on federal principles. In implementing them they also introduced a variety of novel institutions, notably a separate collegial executive. Like the United States, Switzerland rejected Britain's parliamentary government with its strong cabinet based on majority rule.

India and Canada did not, then, follow the American and Swiss examples and did not base their system on government federal principles. Instead they adopted the Westminster form of parliamentary government with a strong cabinet: a system that some of the framers had already experienced as chief ministers at the provincial level. Today these countries are therefore classified as *parliamentary* federations. Their national governments, to a greater or lesser extent, still appear reluctant to modify their parliamentarism in order to become more federative.[25] For example, the cabinet remains responsible to the lower house alone, the house elected on the principle of majority rule.[26]

A fourth important parliamentary federation is Germany, but that country has developed differently from the three that have been influenced by the Anglo-American political tradition. Before 1870 Germany was a collection of states that developed into a quasi-federation under

Prussian leadership. Parliamentary government did not come into operation until the Weimar Republic (1919–33). Only since 1949 has Germany been both parliamentary and federative, and with a distinctive federative tradition that makes it different from the other parliamentary federations, but one that is worth exploring.[27]

The framers of the Indian constitution intended to provide the country with strong government. Indeed, all the Westminster parliamentary federations appear to have shared this concern. That is why they were based on parliamentarism, *not* on federal principles. 'Federation' was understood to mean not the set of principles underlying American government but mainly a constitutional distribution of powers between the national government and the various states or provinces.[28] To repeat, instead of being based on federalism as a concept, they added a federation on to their parliamentary systems.

5. Changes in India's Federation: The Federalization of the Party System

While there is general agreement that India is not as centralized a federation as it used to be, there is some disagreement about the degree to which it has become more federative. A number of changes in the fields of law, economics and culture, and particularly in the field of party politics, offer clues.

In law, there have been many changes in the constitution, some by amendment and others by judicial interpretation. An indication that India is a federation has been the use of an American-style judicial review by the Supreme Court that has challenged the Westminster doctrine of parliamentary supremacy. The centre used to exercise extraordinary power over the states through the emergency power in Article 356. In 1994, in the Bommai case, the Supreme Court drew attention to its frequent abuse and restricted the power of the Union government to use Article 356 to dismiss state governments. [29] President's Rule is not as useful an instrument to the centre as it was.[30]

In the economic sphere, the centre was able to direct economic policy under the constitution through the Finance Commission and its power of the purse. In addition there was the Planning Commission set up by Jawaharlal Nehru, and central control over the economy supported by successive Industrial Policy Resolutions (1948 and 1956). However, with the adoption by the Congress government of a policy of liberalization after the 1991 election, central control over the economy began to decline. It was not only the activities of business corporations that were affected, but also the policies of the state governments, for many of these corporations were located in the states. 'It is now state level politicians who are the gatekeepers of private investment by national enterprises and multinational corporations, with control over sanctions to acquire land, building, power connections, telephones and other services.'[31] In the economy too, the centre's ability to direct policy has diminished.

One of the first important changes in the federation occurred in the cultural sphere. As early as 1956 a new policy was adopted whereby states were created on the basis of the predominant language. The creation of linguistic states did not appear to have immediate political consequences. The Indian National Congress remained in power at both the national and the state level, and Jawaharlal Nehru (who opposed the creation of linguistic states) remained prime minister until his death in 1964. Eventually there *were* consequences, one being the proliferation of state parties.

It is now clear that there have been modifications to the centralized federation of 1950 not only in party politics but also in the linguistic, legal, and economic spheres.

Linguistic states encouraged a sense of regional identity in those states that adopted a language other than Hindi as their regional language. Gradually the Congress party began to face serious and permanent challenges to its control over a number of important states. An early example was West Bengal, where the new Communist Party of India-Marxist (CPI-M) participated in the government in 1967. In Tamil Nadu, where the DMK fought its first national election in 1962, a rival state party, the AIDMK, entered the national arena in 1977. In 1983 the Telugu Desam Party (TDP) was formed. Mrs Gandhi took note of what was happening in the south and that year established the Commission on Centre-State Relations (the Sarkaria Commission). In the 1984 elections, when the TDP contested the national elections for the first time, it won 30 of the state's 42 seats. In the 1984 elections, the number of MPs representing state parties more than doubled, from 35 to 75.

In the legal sphere, the Supreme Court's judgments, especially its 1994 restriction on the use of the emergency powers under Article

356 has limited the centre's interference in state politics.[32] In January 2000 no states were being governed under President's Rule.

Turning to the economic sphere we can see that the government's decision in 1991 to encourage a market economy, and ultimately to abolish the 'permit, licence, quota Raj', also came to have widespread political repercussions. Not only did it reduce the control of the national bureaucracy over the economy but it also encouraged the states to become more competitive. The relaxation of controls provided new opportunities for private business, much of it located in the various states. Business companies found it to their advantage to support state parties.[33]

These developments, the evolution of linguistic states, the restriction on the use of President's Rule, the liberalization of the economy, and above all the growth of permanent and significant state-based parties, helped to transform India's federation in the 1990s. In the 1996 elections the state parties were able to challenge the hegemony of the national parties generally and the INC in particular. By 1999 the number of state parties had doubled the number in 1989.

TABLE 1: NUMBER OF NATIONAL, STATE AND REGISTERED PARTIES

Category	1980	1984	1989	1991	1996	1998	1999
National Parties	6	7	8	8	8	7	7
State Parties	19	17	20	13	30	30	40
Registered Parties	11	9	89	190	171	139	122

The Election Commission has distinguished between the three types of parties. Its most elaborate definition is of State Parties. This may be summarized as follows. These parties must have been engaged in political activity for at least five years and must have won either four per cent of the seats in a general election or three per cent in a state election. In addition they must have had the support of six per cent of the votes cast. A national party is a political party that is recognized as a state party in four or more states. The Election Commission concludes its explanation of the three types of parties by stating that 'A political party which is registered with the Election Commission of India, but is not a State or National Party, is known as a Registered (Unrecognised) party.'[34]

In the analysis of federations, it used to be assumed that, as in unitary states, there could be two-party or multiparty systems (or in India after independence a 'one-party dominant' system), but they were all primarily national parties. Occasionally, as in the American southern states, in Quebec, or in parts of India, there might for a time be parties whose goal was a looser federation, but these parties always had minority status.

Today, however, we are witnessing in India and elsewhere (for example in Belgium, Spain and Canada) the emergence of parties that confine their appeal to a particular province or state and yet are able to exert considerable influence in national politics. In Canada, the Bloc Quebecois replaced the Conservative Party as the Official Opposition in 1993, to be replaced by the Reform Party after the 1997 election. In India, the government was brought down as a result of a tussle between rival state parties that had no appeal beyond the borders of Tamil Nadu.

While India itself is very much a federation, it is possible that something approaching confederacy is developing in Indian party politics. Instead of majority government by a national party there have been 'Fronts' and now an 'Alliance'. These bring state parties into the government and provide one of the national parties with a majority. It is necessary to ask whether these ad hoc arrangements are adequate. In the 1999 election 169 parties participated. As Table 1 showed, the Election Commission classified them into three types: National parties (7), State parties (40) and Registered (Unrecognised) parties (122).

Previous challenges to governmental stability have resulted in firm action. Legislation has been passed to limit party defections in parliament and also to limit the number of independent candidates. But so far there have been few changes in the rules governing the types of party that may take part in national elections. The national party system has not been modified to classify as national parties only those parties that are truly nationwide in their appeal. Neither is there any requirement that only those state parties able and willing to reach out beyond one or two states will be recognized as having the right to contest general elections. So far there has been little concern in Delhi about the proliferation of parties. Indeed it appears to be welcomed by some.

6. The Decline of the National Parties?

Until a short while ago it was taken for granted that India was governed by National Parties. The third edition of *India Decides*, published in 1995, paid most attention to the national parties and gave the results for each of them in separate columns. Interestingly, there has been no decline in the actual *number* of national parties apart from 1957, when there were only four parties. Since 1952 the number has varied between five and eight.

What *has* declined is the percentage of Indians who vote for one or other of the national parties. From 1977 to 1991 they received about 85 per cent of the votes cast. After 1991 there was a drop in support. The percentage voting for one of the national parties declined from 85 per cent in 1991 to 69 per cent in 1996, 68 per cent in 1998, and 67 per cent in 1999.

It is tempting to conclude that these figures merely report a decline in the support for the INC. This may be an inadequate explanation. As the Table below indicates, there have been previous occasions when the support extended to the Congress Party has declined, but without a change in the support to national parties as a whole. The 1996 elections were a watershed:

TABLE 2: VOTE FOR THE INC AND NATIONAL PARTIES

Percentage vote	Vote for the INC and National Parties					
	1971	1977	1991	1996	1998	1999
for INC	44	35	37	29	26	28
for National Parties	77	85	81	69	68	67

What has happened is interesting. In the elections since 1991 the other national parties have not taken up the slack. In 1989 the Janata Dal had showed promise as a new national party with 142 seats, but after that election it split into fragments. As for the BJP, which saw its support rise from 2 in 1984 (when it first contested a national election) to 86 in 1989 and 120 in 1991, it has so far failed to obtain a majority. Despite increasing to 161 in 1996 and 179 in 1998, it was in 1999 still 90 seats short of the elusive 272 seats needed to form a majority government. It may well be that barring some catastrophe neither the INC nor the BJP, the only truly nationwide parties, will in the foreseeable future win a majority of the seats. Coalition politics may become the norm.

Apart from the INC and BJP, none of the other national parties has much hope of becoming nationwide in its appeal. Though they would like to be nationwide in their representation, the Communist parties together have never polled more than 10 per cent of the votes, and their success has been confined to a small number of states. The other fourteen or so parties that have contested as national parties since 1952 have been ephemeral. Except in their aspirations, none of the parties other than the INC and BJP are truly 'national' in the sense of having nationwide appeal.

Most of the so-called national parties have been small ephemeral groups that have rarely reached double digits in their percentage of voter support. While not ephemeral, the Communists have had a low level of support year after year. Even so, the rules governing national parties still allow these parties to contest in as few as three states provided their candidates have been elected from at least two per cent of the total number of parliamentary constituencies (i.e. eleven).

Were the term 'national' to be confined to parties that had nationwide appeal, stricter rules might be helpful. For example, it could be stated that:

1. A national party is a party that contests elections in at least half the constituencies.
2. To retain its status, a national party must win at least five per cent of the total vote and five per cent of all the seats in a national election.

Rule (1) would restrict the term 'national party' to parties that made a serious attempt to be nationwide. The five per cent requirement under rule (2) is fairly common in other liberal democracies. Under these two rules, the INC and BJP alone would at present qualify as nationwide national parties. As we shall see in Section 7, a reclassification of the other national parties would be necessary.

7. The Rise of State Parties

There have always been state parties contesting national elections, but until recently their role was not regarded as very significant. We have already noted that *India Decides: Elections 1952–1995* listed them until 1980 as 'Others' followed by 'Independents'. By contrast, it had separate columns for each of the national parties, however small.

Following Mrs. Gandhi's assassination and the 1984 elections, which favoured her son, Rajiv, it became apparent that some state parties were becoming important in national politics. The 'Others' column was therefore divided into two columns: 'Major state parties' and 'Others'. The number of successful state party candidates reached an all-time high in that year.

The term 'major' is a bit vague. *India Decides* listed five 'major' parties, among them the TDP, which won over half the seats in this column. The 'Others' column included nine parties, one of them the DMK, which did badly in 1984. With hindsight it appears that a better division would have been between State Parties and Registered Parties, following the classification of the Election Commission.

While the change in classification from 1984 onwards, and the rather vague nature of the division between 'Major state parties' and 'Others,' makes it difficult to draw comparisons between all thirteen general elections, certain things are clear. One is that until 1996 the total number of seats won by non-national parties did not change much. Their number varied between a low of 31 (1957) and a high of 75 (1984). There were 46 MPs representing state or registered parties in 1989 and 54 in 1991. The important role of 'major state parties' first noted in 1984 did not become apparent until the 1996 election, after Rajiv Gandhi too was assassinated.

It is with the 1996 election that a great change occurs. The seats won by the non-national parties are as follows:

TABLE 3: SEATS WON BY STATE AND REGISTERED PARTIES

Category	1991	1996	1998	1999
State Parties	54	127	100	158
Registered Parties	0	4	49*	10

*The year 1998 appears to have been an anomaly. Following the break-up of the Janata Dal, a number of splinter parties put forward candidates, and had to do so under the rubric of registered parties.

After the 1996 election a national survey was conducted to find out what the voters of different ages, religions, class, etc. knew about politics. One of the most interesting findings was that the percentage of respondents able to name the chief minister of their state had almost doubled in twenty-five years. In 1971, 29 per cent of those interviewed were able to name their chief minister. In 1996 the percentage was 54.[35]

The major state parties are of various types.[36] In one group are parties that are confined to one state. For example, the Shiromani Akali Dal (SAD) caters to the needs of the Sikhs in Punjab, and the Telugu Desam Party (TDP) to the Telugu-speaking people in Andhra Pradesh. In Tamil Nadu there are various parties that function only in that state (and tiny Pondicherry). These are the DMK, AIDMK and various small parties.

Another group includes parties like the Shiv Sena and BSP. These have hoped that by expanding to other states they may ultimately become national parties. So far the Shiv Sena has failed to expand outside Maharashtra, but the BSP has succeeded in being classified as a national party.

All the state parties, whether ambitious to be national parties or not, appear to want to contest national elections. The 158 seats won by the state parties in 1999 was a record. Most of the parties supporting the BJP were successful in only one state. Of course all MPs have to reflect local concerns, and we do not know whether single-state parties have a more parochial outlook.

8. A Reappraisal of the Parties: A Place for New Federal Parties?

Although a fluid situation has persisted since 1996, so far there have been few changes in the party system, despite the proliferation of parties. There is still a division into national and state parties, with nothing in between. It is nonetheless clear that there are a number of parties that are not nationwide in their appeal and yet are not confined to a particular state. Parties like the CPI-M, SP and BSP that reach out beyond a particular state might be better classified as 'federal parties' different not only from national parties like the INC and BJP but also from state parties like the TDP, SAD and DMK.

As for the state parties themselves, they might qualify for participation as federal parties in general elections in two ways. The smaller ones might be persuaded to join with other state and registered parties to form new and larger federal parties, with a minimum number of seats in the Lok Sabha. Larger state parties might be classified as federal parties when they take part in national elections.

At some point there may have to be the institutionalization of the emerging party system. Successful attempts have been made to obtain a majority of seats in parliament by a number of private ad hoc arrangements, such as the 1989 National Front and the 1996 United Front (with its post-election Common Minimum Programme). In 1999, the 24-member National Democratic Alliance was able to reach a pre-poll agreement. It may be time to take these arrangements a stage further. One way of doing this would be to review the classification of political parties, and to encourage the development of new federal parties. This is because although the rules governing party participation in national elections have been modified, nothing has been introduced comparable to the 1985 Anti-Defection amendment to the constitution or to the 1996 law curbing independent candidates.[37]

It is tempting to suggest that federal parties should be required to win five per cent of the vote in at least three states. This would be difficult to achieve. At present no state party fulfills these conditions. In 1998 not one of the 30 state parties won five per cent of the votes in any state but its own. (Ten did not even receive five per cent even in their own state.) However, the creation of federal parties to contest national elections would encourage the formation of pre-poll federative parties and so reduce the number of parties in parliament. In due course the requirement of five per cent of the votes in three states might not be unreasonable. For example, by these criteria the CPI (M) would have qualified as a federal party in 1996, 1998 and 1999, because it won over five per cent of the vote, and seats, in three states. (The CPI (M) also won over five per cent of the national vote.) The JD would have qualified as a federal party in 1996, but not in 1998. Neither the CPI nor the BSP would have qualified even as a federal party in either election. (The BSP won over five per cent of the vote in five states, but seats in only two.)

9. Registered Parties and Independents

No one wants to dampen the exuberance of Indian elections, but just how many parties is enough? The increase in the number of registered parties contesting national elections is nowadays well over 100, most with very few candidates.

For example, in 1996 there were 171 registered parties, but they put up only 1048 candidates between them, less than six apiece.[38] Of these 1048, 1020 lost their deposits. Only four candidates from these 171 parties and 1048 candidates actually won. Registered parties, which no doubt have a place in state and local elections, still swamp the ballots in a national election.

Independent candidates no longer present much of a problem. In 1996 there were no fewer than 10,635 independent candidates, of which as many as 10,603 lost their deposits. Faced by such a large increase in the number of what the British would call 'frivolous' candidates, parliament increased the number of nominees required by candidates and raised the deposit from Rs.500 to Rs. 10,000. This had an immediate effect. In the elections of 1998 and 1999 the number of independents was less than 2000.

Parliament acted to bring order to its proceedings by passing the Anti-Defection Act of 1985. It limited the proliferation of independent candidates in 1996 by amending the Representation of the People Act. However it has not so far amended the rules governing the status of political parties.

Tightening the rules would not eliminate any of the parties seriously interested in contesting elections. It would merely require that small parties in one or two states wishing to be represented in parliament should have a broader appeal. As participants with other parties in national campaigns they would be classified as federal parties.

Problems may soon arise if there is further proliferation of parties whose appeal is confined to one state. Until 1996, the existence of state parties did not threaten the stability of the political system. The main parties were still national parties, with state parties forming the tail, so to speak. Since 1996 there have been indications that the tail is sometimes able to wag the dog.

The trend towards regionalism in party politics, with the growth in the number of state parties and registered parties, is often viewed favourably, as an indication that India is now less centralized and more federal. Things may, however, one day go too far, with other states following the example of Tamil Nadu, the first state to have its own party (the DMK), able to form a single party government. In recent years the party has splintered into several parties. It should not be assumed that Andhra Pradesh, Uttar Pradesh, and Bihar will not go the same way. Failure to attend to the problem of the proliferation of non-national political parties could ultimately result in undermining India as a federation.

The present practice of parties joining together in a loose alliance on the basis of a 'common minimum programme' has resulted in a new type of coalition politics, based on informal and ad hoc alliances and fronts. At some point it may be worth considering an institutionalization of the best features acquired from this experience.

In the 1999 election, when there were 169 parties, 40 of them were state parties. Some of these now play an important role in the determination of national policy. Nine of the minor parties hold 24 seats in the ministry, with the BJP having the remaining 50. At the same time, national parties are showing themselves less able to dominate the national scene. Decisions that used to be made within an umbrella national party, the Indian National Congress (INC), are now hammered out between the governing national party, whether the INC or BJP, and its numerous supporting parties. A new style of governing, which some think is more 'federative' but which may be in danger of becoming confederate, appears to be emerging.

10. Is Canada also Witnessing a Shift from National to Regional Parties?

The trend away from national parties is not confined to India. Something similar appears to have happened in Canada, where traditionally there have been two national parties, the Liberals and Conservatives, and a third party, usually the New Democrats. In 1993 the Conservatives, who had won 211 out of 282 seats as recently as 1984, were reduced to two seats, and the New Democrats to nine. Two regional parties emerged, the Bloc Quebecois in Quebec and the Reform Party in the four western provinces. Fortunately for the stability of government in Canada, the remaining national party, the Liberal Party, was able to win a majority of the seats and form a majority government. However, in 1993 it was the separatist Bloc Quebecois, with 54 seats, that became the Official Opposition. Reform won 52 seats. Both were regional parties.

In 1997, the Conservative and New Democrats did a little better, managing to win 41 seats. However they did so largely at the expense of the Liberals, who were reduced from 177 seats to 155. The regional parties continued to attract support, and with the decline of the Bloc Quebcois from 54 to 44 seats, it was the western Reform Party that with 60 seats became the official opposition.

The elections of 2000 confirmed the growing regional schism in support for the parties. Only the Liberal Party won seats in all ten provinces. The Reform Party had changed its name to the Canadian Alliance Party, hoping to replace the Conservatives as the second national party. It failed to do so, winning 64 of its 66 seats in the four western provinces (the other two being in Ontario). The Liberals won 100 of the 103 Ontario seats. In Quebec the Liberals won 36 seats compared to the Bloc Quebecois.

The demise of the Conservative Party has no counterpart in Canadian history. In the past both national parties have on occasion done badly, but they have recovered. One or other has always managed to win more seats than the third parties and independents combined.[39] Now, two regional parties have replaced the second national party.

Table 4 makes the transformation clear:

TABLE 4: SEATS WON BY CANADA'S NATIONAL AND REGIONAL PARTIES

Parties	1988	1993	1997	2000*
Bloc Québecois and Reform	0	106	104	104
The three national parties (Liberals, Conservatives and New Democrats)	295	188	196	197
Other	0	1	1	0
Total	295	295	301	301

*In 2000 the Reform Party changed its name to the Canadian Alliance.

The emergence of regional parties at the expense of the traditional national parties in both India and Canada, two heterogeneous federations, should give us pause. Are they moving away from a national party system? Canadians long thought that the American state-based party system was cumbersome, requiring presidential nominating conventions every four years. The American system has however managed to curb the growth of regional parties and to preserve the two-party system. Third parties periodically emerge in the United States, and occasionally influence the outcome of the next presidential election, but they ultimately disappear. They have not (so far) replaced the two major parties. In the United States, the Republicans and Democrats have been the only major parties for over 150 years.

Elsewhere, however, and in countries as different as Sweden and

Russia, a multiparty system is common. Where this occurs, coalitions are necessary, together with willingness on the part of the various leaders to compromise. What seems to be different about Canada and India is that regional parties are seriously challenging the national parties.

11. Conclusion

The constitution established a centralized federation. It was a document framed against the background of Partition, with the fear that India might be further divided unless there was strong government at the centre. It was also a time when China was about to follow the Russian example of becoming a communist regime. There were fears of communist rebellion in parts of India.

Over the past fifty years the hold of Delhi on the polity has weakened in a number of respects. First, the Indian National Congress has been unable to hold on to power, and to ensure that the centralized federation would be preserved. Second, the BJP has so far been unable to take the place of the INC as a majority party. India is no longer a state with one-party dominance. Thirdly, the number and importance of state and state-based parties has gradually increased. Some of these, such as the SP, no doubt hope to become truly national parties, but it seems unlikely that in the foreseeable future any such party on its own will be able to win even a hundred seats. Other state-based parties, for example the TDP and DMK, remain confined to a particular state. India's multiparty system seems destined to continue for some time. Whether an attempt will be made to limit the impact of the proliferation of so many small state and registered parties remains to be seen.

There is no simple answer to the question posed in this chapter. If by 'federation' is meant the centralized federation of the constitution, then the proliferation of parties has helped to make it less centralized. It is true that in some ways the states are still subordinate to the centre, but they are less subordinate than they were. An Indian government may still replace recalcitrant chief ministers of its own party. But it is less likely to remove an Opposition government through the use of President's Rule.

It is arguable that the Indian states still have some way to go before they enjoy anything like the autonomy of states in long-established federations. But this is not to suggest that further proliferation of parties would pose no danger to the Indian polity.

12. Epilogue: Liberal Principles, Conservative Tradition and Socialist Ideology

Finally, it may be helpful to question the assumptions underlying what have been described as 'Organizing Principles', among which federalism is assumed to be one However, 'federalism' as a concept has to be distinguished from 'federation' as an actual system of governance. Federalism as a concept has been fundamental to the American liberal ethos.[40] But is it an organizing principle of India's federation? The very notion of organizing principles or fundamental concepts reflects a liberal view of governance. It is one taken for granted by most Americans. Elsewhere, however, in countries such as Canada, Sweden and the United Kingdom, there is more to governance than principles; there has also been conservative tradition and socialist ideology.

Conservative tradition explains why in the UK a hereditary House of Lords, in Canada an appointed senate, and a monarchy in Canada as well as in the UK and Sweden, have survived for so long.[41] Conservative tradition also explains much of the Indian constitution, including its appointed state governors with reserve powers, and the presidential appointment of twelve members of the Rajya Sabha.

There has also been tolerance of socialist ideology. This explains why social democratic parties have been able to form governments in Sweden, the UK, and in a number of Canadian provinces. And as we all know, it was in India that the first Communist government to be democratically elected took office in Kerala in 1957.

Neither conservatives nor socialists are overly enamoured of liberal principles, and this goes for their view of federalism too because of its close connection with liberalism. Socialist federal governments, for example, have not relished the prospect of dealing with provincial or state governments that opposed a planned economy. For both conservatives and socialists, federalism, with its separation and distribution of powers, is considered not only to be limited government but weak government, and government that gives pride of place to (liberal) individualism.

Living in the US I tend towards the liberal persuasion, but I cannot forget the roots I have in the UK, Sweden, Canada and even India. Therefore I cannot dismiss the conservative and socialist alternatives as unacceptable. Unlike the US and France, none of these four countries has had a revolution. Consequently, liberal principles have had to co-exist with conservative tradition and socialist ideology. The Indian constitution contained much that was liberal, notably Fundamental Rights and Directive Principles. However the discretionary powers it preserved for the government at the centre and for the governors in the states were reminders of its conservative tradition. When, in 1976, the Indian government altered the Preamble to make India socialist as well as secular, socialist ideology too was given the nod.

India, therefore, did not start out in 1950 with a commitment to federalism as an organizing principle. Unlike Canada's Constitution Act of 1867 the Preamble did not even pay lip service to federation. The centre often treated the states as subordinate, not coordinate. Yet in many ways India has always been a federation, and will continue to develop its unique brand of federalism for the foreseeable future. In the fifty-two years since January 1950 there has been no hiatus, and certainly no fall from grace. Rather, in its federative aspects, India in its gradual revolution has shown a remarkable capacity to adjust to changing times.

Notes and References

* I am grateful to Balveer Arora, Francine Frankel, Eswaran Sridharan, and Ronald Watts for their comments on an earlier draft of this chapter and to Dr M.S. Gill and Mr S.K. Mehendiratta for answering questions about elections and parties.

1. 'The project's objective is to examine the hiatus between certain ideas underpinning India's governance, largely rooted in the Constitution of India, and political practices in India as these have evolved over the past fifty years. ... Therefore, this project is much more sharply focussed on ideas having their roots in the Constitution and the hiatus between these and political practices as these have evolved in India.' (Extracts from the statements sent to the author from University of Pennsylvania Institute for the Advanced Study of India [UPIASI].
2. '... many of the institutions of liberal democracy are beginning to look worn out.' (Extract from the statements sent to the author from UPIASI.)

3. For a discussion of possible conflict, see Douglas V. Verney, 'Parliamentary Sovereignty versus Judicial Review: Is a Compromise Possible?' *Journal of Commonwealth and Comparative Politics*, 27, 2, 1989, 29–44.
4. *Constituent Assembly Debates (CAD)*, vol. XI, 1949, London, p. 950.
5. Preston King, *Federalism and Federation*, Croom Helm, 1982; W.H. Stewart, *Concepts of Federalism*, University Press of America, New York, 1984.
6. For a further development of this theme, see Douglas V. Verney, 'Federalism, Federative Systems and Federations: The United States, Canada and India', *Publius: The Journal of Federalism*, 25, 2, 1995, pp. 81–97.
7. Commission on Centre-State Relations, *Report, Part I,* 8. This appears to be a paraphrase of what Khandubhai K. Desai said in the closing debates on the constitution (*CAD,* 11, 1949), p. 679.
8. K.C. Wheare, *Federal Government*, Oxford University Press, London, 1960, p. 27.
9. Wheare, *Federal Government*, 1963, p. 28.
10. Daniel J. Elazar, *Constitutionalizing Globalization: The Postmodern Revival of Confederal Arrangements*, Rowman and Littlefield, Lanham MD, 1998. See also his *Federal Systems of the World: A Handbook of Federal Confederal and Autonomy Arrangements,* 2nd edn, Longman, Harlow (UK), 1994. Professor Elazar died on 2 December 1999, just after a first draft of this chapter was completed.
11. F.W. Lister, *The European Union, the United Nations and the Revival of Confederal Governance,* Greenwood, Westport, CT, 1996.
12. 'The complete, unabridged version of the Great Binding Law, or Great Law of Peace as it is also known, probably exists only in the Iroquois oral tradition, still maintained and recited by tribal traditionalists in Canada and the United States. It takes seven or eight days to recite fully.' Donald S. Lutz, 'The Iroquois Confederation Constitution: An Analysis', *Publius: The Journal of Federalism*, 28, 2, 1998, 99.
13. Harold J. Laski, 'The Obsolescence of Federalism', *New Republic*, 3 May 1939, 367–9. There still appears to be little interest in federalism in the UK.
14. Elazar developed his ideas in a number of books and articles. See, for example, Daniel J. Elazar, *Exploring Federalism*, University of Alabama Press, Tuscaloosa, Alabama, 1987. There is a brief survey of the field in 'International and Comparative Federalism', published by the American Political Science Association in *PS: Political Science and Politics,* June 1993, 190–5. He also edited 'New Trends in Federalism', *International Political Science Review*, Special Issue, 17:4, 1996.

15. Michael Burgess and Alain-G. Gagnon, *Comparative Federalism and Federation: Competing Trends and Future Directions*, Harvester Wheatsheaf, Hemel Hempstead, UK, 1993; Brian Galligan, *A Federal Republic: Australia's Constitutional System of Government*, Cambridge University Press, Oakleigh, Melbourne, 1995; Campbell Sharman, *Parties and Federalism in Canada and Australia*, Federalism Research Centre, Australian National University, Canberra, 1994. J.F. Zimmerman, *Contemporary American Federalism: The Growth of National Power*, Leicester University Press, Leicester, UK, 1992. According to Elazar, who co-edited with John Kincaid, *Publius: The Journal of Federalism,* the American journal had more subscribers abroad than in the US itself.
16. Ronald L. Watts, *Comparing Federal Systems*, 2nd edn, McGill–Queens University Press, Montreal, 1999, p. 10.
17. An example of the international study of federalism is Michael Burgess and Alain-G. Gagnon (eds), *Comparative Federalism and Federation*, noted above. In October 1999, the Government of Canada agreed to establish a secretariat for an international Forum of Federations. Ronald Watts was appointed a member of the board.
18. For a brief discussion of the original proposals see R. Sudarshan, 'The Political Consequences of Constitutional Discourse,' in T.V. Sathyamurthy (ed.), *State and Nation in the Context of Social Change* , Oxford University Press, New Delhi, 1994, p. 75.
19. There is no reference to federation in the subject index of such volumes as P.M. Bakshi's *The Constitution of India,* 3rd rev. edn, Universal Law, Delhi, 1999. However, see footnote below for his note to Article 1 on India as a federation.
20. Article I, Section 1 states: 'India, that is Bharat, shall be a Union of States.'
21. P.M. Bakshi, *The Constitution of India*, p. 4.
22. Students of federations now accept Daniel J. Elazar's term 'non-centralization' instead of 'decentralization'. What is decentralized (e.g. Northern Ireland's devolution of government) can be centralized again. Non-centralization involves a *constitutional* distribution of powers.
23. Although P.M. Bakshi has no reference in his subject index to 'federation' he has a note on Article 1: 'The Union of India is a federal Union, with a distribution of powers, of which the judiciary is the interpreter. Although there has been considerable controversy whether India is or is not a federation, and although some writers have called it 'quasi-federal,' it would seem that essentially the Indian Constitution is a federal one.' *The Constitution of India,* p. 4.
24. See for example Sandeep Shastri, 'Parliamentarism vs. Presidentialism',

in D.D. Khanna and Gert W. Kueck, *Principles, Power and Politics*, Macmillan, Delhi, 1999, pp. 291–316.

25. When a proposal to give the Lok Sabha a fixed five-year term was debated in the Rajya Sabha in October 1999, 'senior Congress member Pranab Mukherjee said the parliamentary system in the country was based on the Westminster pattern and therefore the proposal was not feasible.' *Indian Express*, 27 Oct. 1999.
26. A fourth important parliamentary federation is Germany, but that country has developed differently from the three that have been influenced by the Anglo-American political tradition. Before 1870 Germany was a collection of separate states that were developing into a sort of federation under Prussian leadership. Parliamentary government did not come into operation until the Weimar Republic (1919–33). Only since 1949 has Germany been both parliamentary and federative, and with distinctive features that makes it different from the other parliamentary federations.
27. For a comparison of the German and Indian federations, see Gert W. Kueck *et al.*, *Federalism and Decentralisation: Centre-State Relations in India and Germany*, Mudrit, New Delhi, 1998.
28. In the famous joke about how people from different countries would begin an essay on 'The Elephant', the Canadian response is said to begin with: 'The elephant: is it a matter of federal or provincial jurisdiction?' According to Ronald Watts, Canada is the only country where it is possible to buy a book on federalism at an airport bookstore.
29. For a brief discussion of the *Bommai* case, see Ajit Mozoomdar, 'The Supreme Court and President's Rule', in Balveer Arora and Douglas V. Verney (eds), *Multiple Identities in a Single State: Indian Federalism in Comparative Perspective*, Konark, Delhi, 1995, pp. 160–8.
30. For a recent assessment of the use of Article 356 see Balveer Arora, 'Political Parties and the Party System: The Emergence of New Coalitions', mimeo., Dec. 1999, Section III.
31. See Francine R. Frankel, 'Symposium on Emerging Issues in Center–State Relations: The Problem,' *Seminar*, 459, November 1997, 13–4.
32. *S.R. Bommai vs Union of India*. JT 1994 (2) SC 215
33. See Sanjaya Baru, 'Economic Policy and the Development of Capitalism in India: The Role of Regional Capitalists and Political Parties,' in Francine R. Frankel, Zoya Hasan, Rajeev Bhargava and Balveer Arora, *Transforming India*, Oxford University Press, New Delhi, 2001.
34. *Statistical Report on General Elections, 1996 to the Eleventh Lok Sabha*, Election Commission of India, New Delhi, 1996, vol. I, final page. Since this report the Union Territories (except for Delhi and Pondicherry) are

excluded from the classification of state parties, and the votes required have increased from four to six per cent.

35. Subrata K. Mitra and V.B. Singh, *Democracy and Social Change in India: A Cross-Sectional Analysis of the Indian Electorate*, Sage, Delhi, 1999, Table 3.12, p. 105.
36. For a classification see Douglas Verney, 'Improving Coalition Government in India: A Third Reform', *Denouement*, Delhi, vol. 9, Jan.–Feb. 1999, 17–22.
37. This may change, following the report of the National Commission to Review the Working of the Constitution.
38. It is not always clear whether all the registered parties actually nominate candidates. '... once registered, a political party would stay registered in perpetuity, even if it does not contest any election over decades of its existence. This is because there is no specific provision to de-register a party.' Election Commission of India: *Electoral Reforms (Views and Proposals)*, New Delhi, n.d., but probably 1997–8, p. 8.
39. The Conservatives' previous low point was 39 seats in 1935 and 1940. In those elections other parties and independents won a total of 35 and 28. The Liberals' low point was 1958, when other parties and independents won nine seats.
40. See for example Louis Hartz's provocative *The Liberal Tradition in America*, Harcourt Brace, New York, 1955, the title of which would seem to be an oxymoron.
41. David E. Smith, *The Republican Option in Canada, Past and Present*, University of Toronto Press, Toronto, 1999.

7

'Stateness' and Democracy in India's Constitution

R. SUDARSHAN*

Introduction

This chapter attempts to set the importance given in Indian politics to the *form* of the constitution against the *substance* of politics.[1] It focuses on the concept of 'stateness' to account for the importance of the *form* of the constitution. It argues that only by deepening democracy at the local level in India will it be possible to diminish the dissonance between the form of the constitution and the substance of politics. However, as it cannot be wholly eliminated, cynicism about the seamier side of politics is unwarranted.[2]

Consequences of Conceptual Eclecticism

The constitution prescribes the shape and form of governance, and sets down the rules by which the right to rule can be conferred upon rulers. It protects a set of individual and group rights. It has checks and balances to restrain a majority from adopting policies that could hurt the interests of minorities, and it regulates relations between the central government and the states that constitute the Union of India. Most constitutions are intended to serve these purposes, and many of them place limits on majoritarian rule. The multiple purposes of constitutions need not be inconsistent and necessarily create dissonance between form and substance. However, in the case of the Indian constitution, there *is* a source of inherent dissonance between form and substance, theory and practice. It originates in the eclecticism with which the framers of the constitution borrowed different elements from diverse political traditions. Conceptual incommensurabilities have consequently bedevilled constitutional interpretation. It is this dissonance that judicial politics has attempted to dispel.

The constitution incorporates many provisions of the Westminster *Government of India Act of 1935*, continuing the colonial and conceptual legacy of Britain. 'Due process of law' and 'police power of the state', concepts originating in the US, were discussed extensively in the Constituent Assembly. They were deliberately excluded from the provisions on the right to life (Article 21), and the right to property (Article 31), respectively. Nevertheless, judges deciding cases involving these provisions made detailed references to the proceedings of the Constituent Assembly. That is how 'due process' and 'police power' came to influence Indian constitutional law.

There is a long line of cases in which the Supreme Court came full circle, from initial rejection of 'due process of law', because the framers had rejected it, to enthusiastic endorsement. In *A.K. Gopalan*,[3] the court began by affirming that the only test of legality of executive action should be its conformity with 'procedure established by law'. Nearly thirty years later, in *Maneka Gandhi*,[4] the Supreme Court ruled that 'procedure established by law' must be fair and reasonable. It could not be just about any kind of procedure. 'Due process of law' thus made a comeback into the constitution. The constitution's draftsmen had worried about incorporating 'due process' explicitly in the constitution because progressive New Deal legislation, of the kind that India would need, had fallen foul of it in the US. Restrictions on the freedom of contract, according to the US Supreme Court, violated 'substantive due process'. The procedural part of 'due process of law', according to the Supreme Court, is unobjectionable and fit to be incorporated into Indian constitutional law.

'Police power' is a concept that featured prominently in cases dealing with the government's power to compulsorily acquire property for public purposes. Another long and complex line of cases witnessed a shift in the Supreme Court's views on the right to property. In the early cases, in which zamindars contested land reform laws, the court was firm in its insistence that 'compensation' must not be 'illusory', and must necessarily be fair, just, and equivalent to market value of what was acquired. Litigation and want of political will eventually put paid to the possibility of serious implementation of land reforms in India. Parliament expended considerable energy and ingenuity in devising constitutional amendments that would permit expropriation of large landlords while protecting the property rights of small tenants.[5]

Administrators, typically, tend to use discretionary powers to draw distinctions on the basis of categories such as 'more or less'. Judicial course, on the other hand, is more rigorous. It does not easily admit such distinctions. Judicial decisions tend to follow a binary logic of 'all or none'. Either everyone has the right to property or no one does. Repeated attempts to bring judicial logic in line with the logic of bureaucrats was abandoned in 1979 when the Forty-fourth Amendment deleted the right to property from the list of fundamental rights. The right to property (with compensation at 'market value') has not disappeared, but it is no longer a *fundamental* right. The Supreme Court did not object to the deletion of the fundamental right to property when it reviewed the constitutionality of the Forty-fourth Amendment.

The class background and ideological inclinations of judges in India are no different from those of most politicians and public servants who exercise greater power. 'Overtly, covertly, and subtly' (as Justice D.A. Desai was fond of saying), class, caste, and communal biases often creep into the decisions of public officials. Critics focused on the class bias of the judiciary failed to appreciate that the Supreme Court was attempting to establish the authority of the constitution in order to ensure a proper form of political rule that is the hallmark of the modern state.

The *Privy Purses*[6] case is a good example of this. The court struck down a 'midnight executive order' that 'derecognized' the former rulers of princely states after a constitutional amendment to terminate their privileges fell short of the required majority by one vote. The judges struck down the order, but not because their class bias inclined them to think that maharajas should continue to have anachronistic privileges. They did so because the commitments made to rulers in the constitution, whose territories had been merged with the Union of India, could not be reneged by executive fiat. Political rule in a proper form required that the abolition of the privileges of the former rulers be done properly through a proper amendment of the constitution.

The Supreme Court has creatively coped with features of the constitution that originate in Anglo–American jurisprudence. The judges however faltered when it came to grasping some distinctively European features in India's constitution that instil and seek to enhance the degree of 'stateness' in Indian political life. The Supreme Court grasped the idea of state, but could not do so with confidence and doctrinal authority as the judges were not sufficiently schooled in European civil law traditions.

'Stateness' in the Indian Constitution

J.P. Nettl first demonstrated the usefulness of 'stateness' as a conceptual variable in comparative politics.[7] He surveyed the evidence from developing countries facing the problem of establishing the legitimacy of new regimes while simultaneously dissociating themselves from their colonial past. Nettl noted that 'stateness' could be developed if a politically supported regime is able to transpose its own norms across the high threshold of time. The Indian National Congress, through a long phase of nationalist struggle, succeeded in gaining widespread recognition and legitimacy as the Swadeshi alternative to the British Raj. The Congress was able to transpose its own norms and ideological goals into the constitution, thereby giving India a higher degree of 'stateness' than most other newly independent countries.

However, the idea of state was not clearly articulated by the framers as they were still in quest of it, and had nearly grasped it. They were aware of Indian elements of statecraft, but they did not Indianize the constitution. Mahatma Gandhi's appeal to make directly elected village panchayats, not parliamentary democracy, the foundation of the Republic was not heeded by the Constituent Assembly. Gandhi was a radical insider who believed (as did J.D.M. Derrett, an eminent authority on Hindu Law) that only those elements in the constitution that are firmly rooted in Indian traditions would work effectively, and all others would be subverted and negated.[8]

Traditional Indian political theory emphasized personal qualities, powers, and the dharma of the ruler, and the duties, not rights, of subjects. Nothing could be further from traditional Indian ideas of statecraft than the European idea of state. Indian traditions did not emphasize the impersonality of public power, and could not clearly differentiate public interest from a wide array of ascriptive attributes based on caste and status. Hierarchy and social segmentation were inherent in Indian forms of rulership. That is why the egalitarian aspirations of the constitution are revolutionary. Even in Western Europe it took a long period of revolutionary change to develop a strong disposition to recognize the state as an integrating and legitimizing concept, and political authority as impersonal.

The idea of state also identifies the basic values of the political community with reference to which power and authority is to be exercised. It encompasses institutions whose purposes and actions have a prestigious character, embodying a rational commitment to a substantive notion of the public interest. The state's purpose, in the European tradition, is to give society a sense of direction, and transcend partisan politicking through proper forms of political rule that establish values thought to be good for the community.[9] Although abstract, the idea of state has become part of the common sensibility of citizens in Western Europe. It is this idea of state, not *rajadharma*, that gives life to the Indian constitution.

The framers of India's constitution opted for the European idea of state because they were not certain that political parties could be trusted to give the newly independent nation the proper ideological orientation necessary for state and nation building. They decided to prescribe principles and substantive goals of the state in the constitution itself. They placed them above the sway of everyday politics, denying in the process the norm-setting role of political parties in parliamentary democracies. The Directive Principles of State Policy in Part IV (borrowed from the Irish constitution that has a lineage to Europe through the Roman Catholic church) are part of the idea of state. They are described as 'fundamental in the governance of the country and it shall be the duty of the State to apply these principles in making laws.' They are not an assortment of second-class rights that cannot be enforced in a court of law. These principles were meant to represent basic values of the political community with reference to which power and authority should be exercised. The idea of having constitutional norms and teleology to the constitution is important. Some of those norms have a long-term validity and are absolutely essential for proper forms of political rule. Other norms could however be changed as warranted by circumstances and the preferences of people, and constitutional norms are not numbered into particular provisions. They are to be grasped by an understanding of the entire constitution, not some particular provision that contingently comes up for judicial scrutiny.

Mahboob Ali Baig, a Muslim League member from Madras, pointed out the depoliticizing implications of granting constitutional status to a particular set of ideological norms that the Congress party favoured. He argued that a set of principles 'to bind and tie down political parties was contrary to the principles of parliamentary democracy'.[10] The chairman of the drafting committee, Ambedkar, and its constitutional adviser, Sir B.N. Rau, 'one of the more Europeanized intellectuals', overruled these objections.[11]

Ambedkar was firm about incorporating principles and goals that ought to be fundamental in the governance of India. Their fulfilment could not be left to ordinary legislation that 'simple majorities (whose political fortunes are never determined by rational causes) have a right to make and unmake.[12] However, Ambedkar could not persuade the Constituent Assembly to incorporate his preferred principles, i.e. 'state socialism' and 'economic democracy'. The principles eventually adopted were part of the contradictory ideology of the Congress, combining conservative protection of the right to property with egalitarian aspirations of socialists in the party.[13] The constitution prescribes a set of substantive aims, and commands the state to take steps to achieve those. This command is universal, applying to all functionaries of the state, and also applies to citizens, as it is their will that these aims be realized. The constitution positively empowers governments to take affirmative action, envisaging a state with sufficient 'steering' power to transform traditional Indian society.

'Stateness' is more than the sum of particular constitutional provisions. It is primarily an idea that permeates the entire constitution. It is intended to capture the imagination of citizens, and supply what is in fact a missing tradition in India. The idea of state was difficult to articulate clearly when the constitution was framed because it was new and was not part of the more familiar traditional and colonial forms of rule. As it is also more abstract, in comparison to concepts from Anglo–American sources, most commentators on the Indian constitution prefer to avoid it. Conceptual untouchability is the sin of commentators. A concept cannot become unimportant because it is abstract and not easy to grasp[14] It is more understandable that 'stateness' has not been sufficiently emphasized and elaborated because the concept does not have historical and sociocultural moorings in Indian society. It is gradually becoming part of the common sensibility of a people who are more accustomed to the habits of the colonial sarkar.

India's colonial past has not been helpful in firmly instilling the idea of state, or 'stateness', in the constitution. Political thought and tradition in the UK (and in the US), unlike that in continental Europe, is empirical and pragmatic. It has a distinct preference for avoidance of holistic concepts like 'state' in favour of more accessible, albeit partial, concepts. The Common Law (derided by Bentham for its want of a rational structure, not because it was abstract) lacks a clear distinction between *jus*, regulating transactions among citizens, and *lex*, regulating relations between the state and citizens. English judges did not view themselves as servants of the state. They had no calling to develop the idea of state as a legal institution, or enunciate principles that should govern the framing of legislation by the parliament in Westminster. Similarly, the Bill of Rights in the American constitution, despite its revolutionary roots in France, has the practical character of operative provisions. The Anglo–American intellectual legacy came in the way of the principal draftsmen of the constitution being able to articulate more clearly their quest for 'stateness'.

Antecedents of the Basic Structure Doctrine

The idea of state lies at the root of the *basic structure* doctrine enunciated by the Supreme Court in *Kesavananda Bharati* vs *State of Kerala*.[15] The doctrine states that any provision in the constitution may be modified or deleted provided it does not alter the constitution's *basic structure and framework*. The *Kesavananda* case is undoubtedly problematic from the standpoint of Anglo–American modes of constitutional interpretation. However, to French and German jurists the basic structure doctrine would appear to have a strong basis in the idea of state. The French Declaration of Rights was conceived as being outside and above the constitution, providing overarching principles to which all laws, including constitutional provisions, must conform. The Federal Court in Germany has held that the German Basic Law contains 'super-constitutional' norms that have precedence not only over ordinary legislation, but also over specific provisions of the Basic Law itself.[16]

It is noteworthy that some scholarship on the European origins of the idea of state, and its eventual embodiment in the basic structure doctrine, did have some influence in the *Golaknath* case, and subsequently also in *Kesavananda*. The source of that inspiration was a sensitive, unassuming German scholar, Dieter Conrad.[17] Conrad was concerned that what happened with the Weimar constitution in Germany could just as well happen in India. In 1965 he delivered a lecture titled 'Implied Limitations of the Amending Power'.[18] At a time when the settled law on constitutional amendments was that parliament had plenary powers to amend the constitution, with no limitations whatever, Conrad made the following observations:

> Perhaps the position of the Supreme Court is influenced by the fact that it has not so far been confronted with any extreme type of constitutional amendments. It is the duty of the jurist, though, to anticipate extreme cases of conflict, and sometimes only extreme tests reveal the true nature of a legal concept. So, if for the purpose of legal discussion, I may propose some fictive amendment laws to you, could it still be considered a valid exercise of the amendment power conferred by Article 368 if a two-thirds majority changed Article 1 by dividing India into two States of Tamilnad and Hind proper?
>
> Could a constitutional amendment abolish Article 21, to the effect that forthwith a person could be deprived of his life or personal liberty without authorization by law? Could the ruling party, if it sees its majority shrinking, amend Article 368 to the effect that the amending power rests with the President acting on the advice of Prime Minister? Could the amending power be used to abolish the Constitution and reintroduce, let us say, the rule of a moghul emperor or of the Crown of England? I do not want, by posing such questions, to provoke easy answers. But I should like to acquaint you with the discussion which took place on such questions among constitutional lawyers in Germany in the Weimar period—discussion, seeming academic at first, but suddenly illustrated by history in a drastic and terrible manner.[19]

The doctrine of implied limitations on the power of amendment would not appear strange to jurists familiar with the European idea of state. It is however unfamiliar, and therefore unacceptable, to jurists nurtured in Anglo–American legal traditions. Article 79(3) of the Basic Law of the Federal Republic of Germany explicitly forbids amendments to provisions concerning the federal structure, and to the basic principles laid down in Articles 1 and 20 dealing with human rights and the democratic and social characteristics of the German state. Even if the German Basic Law did not contain such an explicit provision, it would not be unthinkable for German jurists to uphold the integrity and supremacy of those basic principles of the German constitution.

The organic relationship between Parts III and IV of the constitution has for the most part been overlooked by most Indian jurists.[20] The result of that has been an unfortunate controversy that has pitted Fundamental Rights against Directive Principles. One set of jurists accords primacy to Fundamental Rights, because they can be judicially enforced, and tends to dismiss as 'pious wishes' the Directive Principles, denying them equal standing in the constitutional scheme. Others have argued that there was merit in the constitutional amendment (Article 31C following the Forty-second Amendment) that sought to make Fundamental Rights subservient to Directive Principles. They believe that the egalitarian goals in the Directive Principles ought to have precedence 'in a poor society with massive maldistribution of property, income and wealth'.[21]

In the *Golaknath*[22] case the Supreme Court declared that Fundamental Rights could not be amended. It however did so in a way that appeared to privilege Part III of the constitution over Part IV. In trying to resist authoritarian incursions on individual liberties, Chief Justice Subba Rao succeeded in unleashing an authoritarian populism that claimed to give precedence to the Directive Principles over Fundamental Rights.

Text versus Teleology

Had the Supreme Court paid more attention to *idea of state* inherent in India's constitutional scheme it might have been able to offer a more persuasive basis for judicial review of constitutional amendments. The Supreme Court has been criticized for not specifying a definite set of elements as constituting the basic structure of India's constitution. Again, this criticism is misplaced because the idea of state, signifying proper forms of political rule, cannot be reduced to a particular set of provisions. It is more reasonable to blame the court for not explicitly adopting a teleological approach to constitutional interpretation to escape from the web of words that ensnared judges.

Justice Subba Rao based the *Golaknath* decision on his own understanding of the meaning of the word 'law' in Article 13. That article states that any 'law' that contravenes the fundamental rights in Part III of the Constitution would be null and void. Justice Subba Rao asserted that the word 'law' referred not only to ordinary legislation, as the context of its use implied, but also to constitutional amendments. The first chief justice of the Federal Court of India had cautioned that judges are 'not free to stretch or pervert the language of the enactment in the interest of any legal or constitutional theory or even for the purpose of supplying omissions or of correcting supposed errors.[23] Justice Subba Rao made a mistake from the standpoint of strict statutory interpretation of constitutional provisions. His judgement was subsequently overruled. However, even those judges in the *Kesavananda*[24] case who overruled *Golaknath* could not transcend the hold of traditional approaches of statutory interpretation. Eleven opinions of the full bench of thirteen judges devote several pages to the meaning of the word 'amendment'.

Had the Supreme Court adopted a teleological approach to constitutional interpretation rather than a textual approach, it might then have been able to more clearly elaborate the purposive rationality of the idea of the state that accommodates supra-constitutional principles. It could then have demonstrated that basic structure is a concept that is holistic, encompassing all that is necessary to serve constitutional ends, and, therefore, cannot be reduced to a particular set of provisions taken from the text of the constitution.

Six of the judges in the *Kesavananda* case accepted the doctrine of implied limitations on the power of amendment. Another six held that there were no limitations to the power of constitutional amendment in Article 368, other than those that are explicit. Justice Beg tilted the balance in favour of limiting the power of amendment. Had Justice Beg been more familiar with European civil law traditions, he would not have found it necessary to resort to the *Oxford English Dictionary*, and base his views on textual analysis. However, that is exactly what he did and offered a new meaning to the word 'amendment', in much the same way that Chief Justice Subba Rao gave a new meaning to the word 'law' in Article 13 of the constitution. Nevertheless, Justice Beg in *Kesavananda* reached the same conclusion that a jurist in the continental European tradition would have done with more doctrinal certainty and greater clarity. Another unfortunate consequence of the emphasis on words has led some critics of the Supreme Court to overlook the fact that the basic structure doctrine cannot be undemocratic because the idea of democracy animates all parts of the constitution. The *Kesavananda* case could not possibly have been perceived as negating democracy had the court's reasoning been more teleological and less textual.

The basic structure doctrine acquired real teeth in November 1975 when the Supreme Court relied upon it to strike down Clause 4 of the Thirty-ninth Amendment.[25] This amendment was passed by a parliament that had become subservient to a prime minister who had suspended the fundamental rights, having declared a state of internal emergency in June that year. The Allahabad High Court had set Prime Minister Indira Gandhi's election to the Lok Sabha aside. She feared that the 'total revolution' call of Jayaprakash Narayan would remove her from office even before the Supreme Court could hear an appeal against that judgement.

The Thirty-ninth Amendment inserted a new, Article 329A, into the constitution. It removed the jurisdiction of the Supreme Court over election disputes involving the prime minister, the speaker of the Lok Sabha, as well as the president and vice-president. It vested that jurisdiction in an 'authority or body' yet to be established by parliament for that purpose. The amendment was intended to set aside the Allahabad High Court's decision, and furthermore, rule out the possibility that the Supreme Court could reject her appeal against that decision.

Each of the five judges constituting the majority in the *Indira Nehru* case cited a different element of the basic structure violated by the constitutional amendment: rule of law, principle of free and fair elections, judicial review, and equality. The court missed another valuable opportunity to enunciate the point that the idea of impersonal rule is inherent in the idea of state. The constitutional amendment attempted to legitimize the highly personalized regime of the prime minister ('Indira is India, India is Indira'). The amendment was the very antithesis of the idea of state, and, therefore, it was a transgression of the basic structure of the constitution.

The Supreme Court reached the correct conclusion on an amendment that is a blemish on India's parliamentary democracy. However, the court ought to have grasped and elucidated upon the idea of state as a holistic concept. Had it done so it have would become apparent that it is illogical to limit the application of the basic structure doctrine only to cases involving review of constitutional amendments. Ordinary laws, as well as executive orders that do not violate any particular provisions of the constitution could, nonetheless, have the consequence of undermining an organic unit mong the basic principles and norms in the constitution as a whole.

The Supreme Court subsequently moved some distance towards recognizing this point. The case of *S.R. Bommai* vs *Union of India*[26] did not involve any constitutional amendment. It was about the permissibility of judicial review of the 'subjective' satisfaction of the executive that the constitutional machinery had broken down in a state, warranting dismissal of a state government under Article 356. Article 356 has been notoriously abused in the past. State governments controlled by parties in opposition to those ruling at the centre have been frequently dismissed on dubious grounds. Many national and regional political parties have repeatedly called for the abolition of the central government's power to dismiss a state government.

The Supreme Court used the *S.R. Bommai* case to strengthen democracy by affirming that the president's order under Article 356, although 'subjective', is subject to judicial review. The court said that if a state government's actions militated against the principle of secularism, that would be tantamount to violating the basic structure of the constitution. Violating a basic tenet of the constitution could be construed as creating a situation in which it could be reasonably held that the government of that state could not be carried on in accordance with the constitution.

In 1980 the Supreme Court relied on the basic structure doctrine for the second time and struck down some provisions of the Forty-second Amendment.[27] These clauses had been passed during the Emergency, but they could not be revoked by the Forty-fourth Amendment which meant to undo the damage done by Emergency rule to India's constitution. Although it had been routed in the 1977 elections to the Lok Sabha, the Congress majority in the Rajya Sabha had not been diminished by then. Whether out of conviction, or just to save face, the Congress insisted on the retention of some provisions of the notorious Forty-second Amendment. The Supreme Court struck down the amended provision in Article 368 that 'there shall be no limitation whatever on the constituent power of parliament' to amend the constitution. It also struck down another provision of Article 368 that held that no amendment made before or after the Forty-second Amendment could be questioned in court. These two provisions, the court held, are bad because they enable parliament to amend the constitution 'so as to damage or destroy its basic or essential features or its basic structure'.[28]

The question whether Part III or Part IV of the constitution should be regarded as part of the basic structure is misplaced because basic structure ought to refer to the coherence, conceptual connectedness, and organic unity of the entire constitution. Unfortunately, it is this question that repeatedly raises its head in most cases and much of the literature on the constitution. The majority in *Minerva Mills*[29] took the view that a provision that barred judicial review of legislation intended to give effect to Directive Principles, on the grounds of violation of the right to equality and the rights to freedoms in Part III, violates the basic structure. Justice Bhagwati dissented on this point. He held that the amendment to Article 31-C did not violate the basic structure because a law enacted to give genuine effect to the social and economic goals of the constitution should not be invalidated because of its infringement of a fundamental right. Justice Bhagwati was on the side of those jurists who believed that many of the fundamental rights could be meaningful to the masses only if some of the socio–economic goals in Part IV of the constitution are first realized.

Constitutional Form and Democratic Substance

Fifty years of constitutional interpretation by the Supreme Court has led to a better understanding of the relationship between the form of the constitution and the substance of politics. The basic structure doctrine has taken root. The roots of that doctrine lie in the idea of state that imbues the entire framework of the constitution. It is now better understood not only in Indian constitutional law but also in the international law of human rights, that fundamental rights are as indivisible as the idea of state is holistic.

Although all the inconsistencies and confusion stemming from conceptual eclecticism have not been resolved, there is sufficient conceptual clarity to be confident that the constitution is protected against subversive transformation. The constitution anticipates the transformation of India, not of itself. Its form undoubtedly influences the substance of politics, though only to a limited degree, but that limited influence of constitutional form over the substance of politics is critical. Without the force of form over substance the constitution could not have lasted until now, animating, as it has done, a great deal of debate and discourse. However, at the end of the day the form of the constitution cannot guarantee the durability of the state as conceived of by the founders of the republic.

The first two Directive Principles of State Policy have been prominent in the misplaced controversy about their superiority or inferiority to fundamental rights. The first principle is that the ownership and control of the material resources of the community should be so distributed as best to subserve the common good (Article 39(b)). The second is that the operation of the economic system should not result in the concentration of wealth and means of production to the common detriment (Article 39(c)). State control over 'commanding heights' of the economy, expansion of the public sector, controls over production and distributions, and protection behind high tariff walls were all justified by reference to these two Directive Principles. However, a good deal of legislation that purported to give effect to these principles have had, in their actual outcomes, the opposite consequence of increasing the concentration of wealth and inequalities. The economic crisis of 1991 brought about a volte-face in economic policies that had been assiduously justified on the basis of these principles. Widening inequalities and loss of livelihoods are hurting large sections of the population.[30]

The substance and outcomes of policies prior to the liberalization of the economy, and after the liberalization, have been largely negative from the point of view of the poor. Globalization has undermined the 'sovereignty' of the nation-state. The 'steering capacity' of the state has diminished because the degrees of freedom to defy global trends have diminished. In these circumstances, could the Supreme Court be called upon to strike down legislation that liberalizes the economy and removes restrictions on the freedom of contract? Such policies would seem to be, prima facie, inconsistent with these Directive Principles, and are not 'socialist' as India is meant to be according to the amended (Forty-second Amendment) Preamble of the constitution.

If the basic structure of the constitution had merely been an aggregation of particular constitutional provisions, then there could be a basis for entertaining the hope (futile, in all likelihood) that the judiciary might intervene to review liberalization laws and policies, but the basic structure is not the sum of a set of particular constitutional provisions. To think that it is would be to fundamentally miss out the idea of state that lies at its root. The basic structure doctrine does not protect particular provisions, nor extol a particular ideology. The programmatic nature of the constitution and the ideological norms it currently sets out do no more than signify the desirability of enhancing the degree of 'stateness' in India, and the right of the people, who 'have given unto themselves' the constitution, to be governed in a proper way. The Directive Principles currently set out in the constitution happen to be those that the Congress, at the time of Independence, favoured. The form of the constitution requires that governance should be norm-based, and ensure that political rule is informed by values and time-tested good principles. The constitution does not require that a set of particular norms, found in specific provisions, should be immutable.

The form of the constitution is often at odds with the substance of Indian politics, as Sathyamurthy noted. As explained above, that is only so because India is still in the process of developing the idea of state. 'Statenesss' was introduced into the Indian polity by the emphasis given in the constitution to certain ideological principles that all governments, regardless of their political orientation and preferences, ought to respect. This way of supplying a missing but desirable tradition has the consequence of *displacing* politics as an activity that should properly contend over such norms, ideologies, and viewpoints, and seek to legitimize their choices by reference to an informed electorate. The distrust of politics and politicians that was predominant in the Constituent Assembly must now give way to a more mature realization that democratic politics is essentially Janus-faced. Wheeling and dealing, pettiness and chicanery, are the obverse of the currency of statesmanship and vision. We cannot hope to create space for the latter without being tolerant of the former.

Globalization and Deepening Democracy

Deepening democracy (in ways that the makers of the constitution did not think of doing) is the only way of resisting or coping with the negative consequences of current global trends. When people begin to realize they have little power over large forces responsible for the movements of huge amounts of capital across the globe, they become more interested in issues closest to them.[31] They demand more say over what kinds of schools their children should go to, what systems of medicine they should have access to, and the like. Institutions of local self-government offer people the opportunity to assert these local priorities in the face of global forces over which national governments have little control.

Dispersing sovereignty downwards is the only viable option. Attempts to create supra-national political institutions to check global economic forces and the monopoly power of multinational corporations are unlikely to succeed. However, local democratic institutions can enable the participation of people, and give them a say in matters that matter to them. Local democracy is the best means of channelling potentially disruptive energies unleashed by the assertion of particular identities. Political impulses triggered by globalization must be given meaningful local channels to flow through, otherwise fundamentalism could become more assertive, and prove to be a real threat to democracy at all levels. Fundamentalism fosters intolerance. Frequent face-to-face gatherings of people belonging to different religions and social groups could generate a gradual process of tolerance for difference, culminating in an admiration of that difference as a political virtue.

Democratic decentralization in India, ushered in by the Seventy-third and Seventy-fourth Constitutional Amendments, is far from satisfactory. In terms of the professed objectives of local democratic institutions—designing and delivering basic services to people, and implementing development programmes—it is not likely to be spectacularly successful. Democracy, generally, is not very good at doing anything very well, but it cannot be bettered for getting a lot of things done.

The basic structure doctrine, grounded in the idea of state, remains a shield against predatory subversion of constitutionalism of the kind that was attempted during the Emergency. As 'stateness' and concomitant constitutional morality begin to be internalized in the sensibility of India's rulers and citizens, it should be possible to change particular set ideological norms, while respecting the reasons for which they were chosen in the first place. Democratic politics must be allowed to do what it is meant to do, i.e. establish ideological goals and policies based on the preferences of people at any particular point in time. This need not give rise to anxieties that the constitution will be subverted. The judiciary has played its part, attempting to inculcate the importance of the impersonality of public office, and separation of the public interest from the private interest of rulers.[32] The realization of the transformative *telos* of the constitution depends upon the shapes and substance of democratic politics.

Notes and References

* The views expressed by the author must not be attributed to his employer, the United Nations Development Programme, New Delhi.

1. T.V. Sathyamurthi, *Social Change and Political Discourse in India*, vol. 1, *State and Nation in the Context of Social Change*, Oxford University Press, New Delhi, 1994, p. 27.
2. Related material on concepts and categories in the constitution may be found in R. Sudarshan:
   (i) 'The Supreme Court as an Arena of Class Conflict: Colonial Antecedents and Contemporary Crisis in an Immobilized State', in *The State in South Asia*, Development Studies Occasional Paper no. 22, School of Development Studies, University of East Anglia, 1983.
   (ii) 'In Quest of State: Politics and Judiciary in India', *Journal of Commonwealth and Comparative Politics*, vol. XXVIII, March 1990.
   (iii) 'The Political Consequences of Constitutional Discourse', in T.V. Sathyamurthy (ed.), vol. 1 and op. cit., 1994.
   (iv) 'Law and Democracy in India', *International Social Science Journal*, July 1997.
   (v) 'Governance of Multicultural Polities: Limits of the Rule of Law', in R. Bhargava, A.K. Bagchi, and R. Sudarshan (eds), *Multiculturalism, Liberalism and Democracy*, Oxford University Press, Delhi, 1999.
3. A.K. Gopalan vs State of Madras, 1950, *Supreme Court Report* (SCR), 98.

4. *Maneka Gandhi* vs *Union of India, 1978*, SCR, 624.
5. See Granville Austin, *Working A Democratic Constitution: The Indian Experience*, Oxford University Press, 1999, especially chapters 3, 4, 10, for a narrative on the controversies over the right to property that resulted in convoluted amendments to the constitution.
6. *H.H. Maharajadhiraja Madhav Raso Jiwaji Rao* v *Union of India*, SCR, 1971 (3) 530.
7. 'Stateness' refers to the *idea* of state, and must not be confused with 'state', as it is used to refer to institutions with public authority, or as defined in Article 12 of the constitution. See J.P. Nettl, 'The State as a Conceptual Variable', *World Politics*, 20 (July) 4, 559–92.

   This confusion is evident in the reference to Nettl in L. and S.H. Rudolph, *In Pursuit of Lakshmi:Political Economy of the Indian State*, University of Chicago Press, 1987, pp. 61,73,103, where they claim that the 'Indian state is the residual legatee of a long tradition of high stateness that reaches back to India's ancient subcontinental empires of medieval regional kingdoms.' The point that Nettl makes is the very opposite, i.e., developing countries like India do not have a historical and sociocultural tradition of 'stateness'.

   When Gunnar Myrdal described India as a 'weak state', he implied the *idea* of state was weak in India, resulting in the inability of the state to enforce its laws, and proclivity among influential people to ignore rules and laws with impunity. He did not mean that India was a state that was incapable of coming down hard on people, or of being a 'hard state' in that sense. Indeed, it is want of the required degree of 'stateness' that results in 'state lawlessness', as Upendra Baxi has often described it.
8. Rajeev Dhavan has noted in his Law and Society Trust Lecture in Colombo ('A Constitution for a Civilisation: India—1950–2000', July 1998), that the real focus of a Gandhian critique of liberal constitutional theory is 'the surrender of governance to politicians'. This fundamental dilemma posed by *Swaraj* to theories of governance got reduced in the Constituent Asembly to 'a discussion about villages, local government and panchayats.' He adds: 'Taken to its conclusion [self-governance] had dramatic implications which would have (i) undermined the daunting distinction between civil and political society; (ii) challenged the monopoly of politicians to wholly control governmental processes, by eschewing control by the people other than through periodic elections; and (iii) made contemporary constitutionalism re-think the basis of governance, by moving away from dominant Western approaches towards more creative exploratory pastures.'

9. For a very lucid account of the idea of state, see K. Dyson, *The State Tradition in Western Europe: A Study of Idea and Institution*, Martin Robertson, Oxford, 1980.
10. *Constituent Assembly Debates*, vol. VII, pp. 488–9.
11. Granville Austin, *The Indian Constitution: Cornerstone of a. Nation*, Clarendon Press, 1966, p. 20.
12. Ambedkar in Rao, vol. 2, pp. 101–2.
13. For more details, see R. Sudarshan, 1999, op. cit.
14. In his authoritative account of the framing of the constitution, Austin, 1966 (op. cit.) ignores 'stateness' altogether. In his sequel volume on the working of the constitution, he picks up, once again, three strands of the 'seamless web' in the constitution: unity–integrity, democracy, and social revolution. Austin candidly confesses that the 'terms "state" and "élites" do not appear in the book because I find them more misleading than enlightening' (Austin, 1999, p. 3, op. cit.)
15. 1973 (4) SCR 225.
16. See P. Blair, 'Law and Politics in Germany', *Political Studies* (3) 1978, 348–62.
17. Dieter Conrad passed away on 1 June 2001. He deserves to be commemorated in a volume that should be devoted to his contributions and to his influence on Indian jurisprudence.
18. See A.G. Noorani, 'The Supreme Court and Constitutional Amendments', in A.G. Noorani (ed.), *Public Law in India*, Vikas Publishing House, New Delhi, 1982, pp. 278–9, and more recently, A.G. Noorani, 'Behind the "Basic Structure" Doctrine: On India's Debt to a German Jurist, Professor Dietrich Conrad', in *Frontline*, vol. 18, Issue 9, 28 Apr.–11 May 2001.
19. Conrad, quoted in Noorani, 2001, *supra.*
20. Among the exceptions to this statement is M.P. Singh, who is among the few jurists who have specialized knowledge of the civil law traditions of constitutional discourse in Europe. See M.P. Singh, 'Bridging Legal Traditions', obituary on Dieter Conrad, *Frontline*, vol. 18, Issue 18, 1–14 Sep. 2001.
21. Upendra Baxi's commentary on the *Report of the Swaran Singh Committee on Constitutional Amendments*, Supreme Court Cases: Journal Section (2) 1976, 17–28.
22. *I.C. Golaknath* vs *State of Punjab*, 1967 (2) SCR 762.
23. See judgement of Sir Maurice Gwyer on the C.P. and Berar Act, 1939, *Federal Court Reporter*, vol. 18, 1939, p. 37.
24. *His Holiness Kesavananda Bharati Sripadagalvaru* vs *State of Kerala*, 1973 Supp. SCR 1.

25. *Indira Nehru Gandhi* vs *Raj Narain*, 1975 Supp. SCC.
26. (3) SCC 1
27. *Minerva Mills Ltd* vs *Union of India*, AIR 1980 SC 1789.
28. Order read out by the Chief Justice Chandrachud before delivering the full judgement, 1981, SCR 263–4.
29. *Minerva Mills Ltd* vs *Union of India* 1981 (1) SCR 206.
30. For an elaboration of this point, see Kirit S. Parikh and R. Sudarshan (eds), *Human Development and Structural Adjustment: Papers and Proceedings of UNDP Symposium on Economic Growth, Sustainable Human Development, and Poverty*, Bombay, January 1992, Macmillan India, Madras, 1993; also Muchkund Dubey, R. Sudarshan, *et al.* (eds), *India Under Siege—Challenges Within and Without*, Wiley Eastern Ltd., New Delhi, 1995.
31. A good illustration of this point was the decision of village panchayats in Goa to deny the statutory 'no objection certificate' to a large multinational chemical factory that was to be established in their backyard. Du Pont had secured clearances from the central and state governments. It assumed that the statutory requirement of consent of panchayats in municipal law would be no more than an idle formality. It therefore fenced off the land it had acquired and commenced the construction of the plant. The panchayats of the surrounding villages opted not to have the factory, resisting offers of employment and easy enrichment. This was *swaraj* in action.
32. Among the judges whose opinions have helped in articulating the teleology of India's constitution, Justice V.R. Krishna Iyer stands out. See the essays in honour of Justice V.R. Krishna Iyer in R. Dhavan, S. Khurshid, R. Sudarshan, (eds), *Judicial Power*, Sweet and Maxwell, London, 1981. See also B.N. Kirpal, Ashok H. Desai, Gopal Subramanium, Rajeev Dhavan and Raju Ramachandran (eds), *Supreme But Not Infallible: Essays in Honour of the Supreme Court of India*, Oxford University Press, Delhi 2000, especially Raju Ramachandran, 'The Supreme Court and the Basic Structure Doctrine' (pp. 107–33), where he concludes that the doctrine should be buried now in order to enable the democratic process to 'to put half a century of politics and economics into the constitution.'

8

THE INNER CONFLICT OF CONSTITUTIONALISM
Judicial Review and the 'Basic Structure'

PRATAP BHANU MEHTA

Kesavananda Bharati vs *State of Kerala*[1] was a landmark case with profound implications for constitutionalism in India. While the case was itself complex, and the judgment it produced uncertain, no one doubted its momentous significance in at least one respect. The Supreme Court of India, in this case, took the view that any constitutional amendment, even if enacted under procedures laid down under article 368 of the constitution, could be declared invalid if it violated the basic structure of the constitution. Article 368, on this view, did not give parliament unlimited powers to amend the constitution and the court reserved the right to review even amendments to the constitution. Although the doctrine of 'basic structure' has been invoked in no more than a couple of dozen or so significant cases since *Kesavananda*, the debate over what constitutionalism means in India now largely revolves around the interpretation and validity of the doctrine that parliament cannot amend the constitution if it violates the basic structure. The 'basic structure' doctrine is important for a number of reasons. The range of issues that might be protected under the basic structure doctrine is vast. In subsequent judgments the doctrine has been invoked in cases on as diverse issues as election law, secularism, property rights, federalism, freedom of expression, equality, and so forth. Through its expositions on the doctrine of the basic structure the court has, to the mind of many observers, fundamentally altered the meaning of the

Indian constitution. The judgment seemed to reallocate power between various branches of government. The basic structure doctrine, in the minds of many observers, appears to have replaced parliamentary sovereignty and the separation of powers with judicial supremacy. In the course of elaborating on the content of the basic structure in subsequent cases, the Supreme Court seems to have taken the view that, contrary to the claims of the framers, the Directive Principles of State Policy are as equally basic to Indian constitutionalism as fundamental rights. This claim is made despite the fact that the framers of the constitution had explicitly made fundamental rights justiciable in a way in which Directive Principles are not. Both supporters and detractors of the basic structure doctrine are fiercely divided over whether this interpretation or transformation, depending on one's point of view, of the constitution can be justified. Critics of the basic structure doctrine see it as judicial usurpation of democratic sovereignty and an illegitimate attempt to place policy directives on par with fundamental rights. Supporters of the 'basic structure' doctrine present it as a necessary check on parliamentary majorities bent on jeopardizing democratic freedoms; and as a legitimate form of pressure on the state to accomplish policy goals to ameliorate the conditions of vulnerable groups within society by insisting that directive principles be thought of as being on par with fundamental rights.

Much of the debate over the basic structure doctrine, both within the Supreme Court and outside, has often been at cross-purposes for a number of reasons. The court has itself compounded the confusion by refusing to be clear about the scope of the doctrine.[2] Not only was the original *Kesavananda* judgment long and full of inner tensions but, many of the justices on the bench that heard it appeared to change their characterizations of what they had meant in the original judgment. The Supreme Court itself seemed to interpret what *Kesavananda* meant in light of later cases, thus adding layers to its own interpretation on an already complex judgment. Most legal commentators, among those individuals as distinguished as Upendra Baxi and H.M. Seervai, appeared to have changed their minds on the matter more than once; and constitutional lawyers as distinguished as P.P. Rao, Fali Nariman, Ashok Desai, and Raju Ramchandran openly wonder whether the confusions created by the doctrine have made it outlive its usefulness.[3]

In this essay I do not propose to resolve all the confusions surrounding the 'basic structure' doctrine. Rather, I would like to offer some theoretical suggestions, or a framework within which this doctrine and its consequences might be understood. I will argue that there are valid grounds on which the Supreme Court could rightly scrutinize even amendments to the constitution, but that the court has often obscured these grounds. I argue that the implications of such a review need not necessarily be anti-democratic, but the court's broad invocation of the basic structure doctrine has often made it appear that this is the case. In the course of elaborating on these arguments I hope to offer some suggestions of how we might think of Indian constitutionalism. I proceed in the following steps. In section one I offer some broad reflections on judicial review as such. I argue that in India judicial review is more a form of modus vivendi than a means of entrenching constitutional values. In section two I argue that judicial review ought not be seen as necessarily anti-democratic. Those who see it as such rest their view upon an impoverished conception of democracy. I propose, very briefly, a democratic conception of constitutionalism. This argument grounds my defence of judicial review of constitutional amendments. I however argue that the court itself has obscured its own intimations of a principled defence by an indiscriminate use of the 'basic structure' doctrine. In section three I apply the theoretical perspective outlined in section two to a number of cases. Finally, I offer some brief conclusions about the future of constitutionalism in India. I must emphasize that this is very much a political theorist's analysis of the large issues at stake and not a lawyer's brief on technical aspects of the cases, though I hope what I have to say will not offend their sensibilities.

Section One

What does it mean for a society to possess a constitution? In normal parlance, and lawyers' discourse, a constitution simply refers to a written document that we know to be 'the Constitution of India'. What else could a constitution be but a document that governs the allocation of institutional power within society, delineates rights and privileges of citizens, and so forth. It is important to remember that the constitution cannot be law in any ordinary sense of the term, for what law is within a legal system can be identified only with reference to its constitution. A constitution is, in this sense, a set of rules of a higher order with reference to which law is identified. What makes the constitution a higher order entity is, amongst other things, the fact that it cannot be changed through the normal law-making procedures of a popularly elected assembly. The constitution, is, in this sense, more deeply entrenched than ordinary law over which legislatures can exercise jurisdiction. This deeper entrenchment protects constitutional rules from simple majoritarian procedures that govern ordinary legislation. This entrenchment is necessary for two reasons. One, the simple fact that prior to identifying what law is, one has to identify *who* has the authority to enact it. That authority cannot itself be the product of ordinary legislation. If we say that parliament has the authority to enact laws we need a higher order law that bestows on parliament this authority in the first place. Parliament does not acquire its authority to enact law in the same way in which laws enacted by it acquire their authority. The second reason for higher order entrenchment is, at least in liberal constitutions, the idea that there are certain substantive constraints on the making of law that no ordinary legislation can override. The relationship between democracy and constitutionalism is often presented as a tension: constitutionalism is presented as a check on the possible threats posed by democracy; democrats in turn find constitutions a constraint on popular will.

The extent to which constitutional constraints over ordinary law-making are entrenched is a matter of degree. As a first approximation, one might say that the more difficult a procedure of amendment, the more entrenched a constitution, in the sense that the more difficult it is to change those higher order rules with reference through which ordinary law is identified. The exemplar of such deep entrenchment is of course the US constitution. Parliamentary systems, at least traditionally, blur the line between constitutionalism and ordinary law-making by having relatively easy procedures for the amendment of the constitution. Indeed, the traditional hypothesis has been that parliamentary systems will, on balance, have weaker traditions of judicial review for one simple reason: as it will be easier to amend the constitution in response to judicial decisions, judicial review will not have much bite, as parliament will find it easy to override judicial review through constitutional amendments. Article 368 enjoins a relatively easy process for amending the constitution. With some qualifications, this hypothesis was borne out during the first seventeen years of Independence. Parliament enacted laws, the judiciary struck them down as being unconstitutional, parliament amended the constitution in consequence and the judiciary went along with the amendments, ceding to parliament the right to amend the constitution. Formally, the judiciary maintained the right to interpret the constitution, but parliament in response could simply change the constitution; it had a more or less unlimited amending power. This view was embodied in two much cited cases: *Sankari Prasad* vs *Union of India*[4] and *Sajjan Singh* vs *State of Rajasthan.*[5] These cases upheld the validity of constitutional amendments that allowed the government to go ahead with land reform legislation in the face of the judiciary striking down ordinary legislation to that effect.

With *Golaknath*, this view of parliamentary prerogative began to change.[6] The court overruled the unanimous decision in *Sankari Prasad* and the majority decision in *Sajjan Singh*. The court now held, among other things, that Article 368 did not permit amendment to fundamental rights guaranteed under the constitution.[7] As many observers pointed out, in part the court may have been moved to take a more assertive stand because of the political uncertainties of the time. Nobody could have vouchsafed with any degree of certainty that Indira Gandhi and the emerging political culture under her would place the same high value on liberal freedoms that Nehru did.

The principal contention in *Golaknath* was this: no constitution could allow for its own subversion. The constitution would be subverted if one of two things happened: either the scheme of allocation of powers within the constitution was modified, or the substantive constraints placed on ordinary lawmaking were violated. In the *Golaknath* and subsequent decisions limiting parliament's right to amend the constitution, there were both apprehensions: could parliament subvert the very process (free elections) through which it acquired its authority in the first place? And could parliament, if left to exercise its powers, take away citizens' fundamental rights including their freedom? The conundrum was this: the written text of the document clearly gave parliament the authority to amend the constitution through a very simple amending procedure. Yet, what was the point of having an elaborate constitution in the first place, if parliament could easily overcome the substantive constraints imposed upon it by the constitution? Why define our fundamental rights, if parliament could change them at will. The critics and supporters of both *Golaknath* and *Kesavananda* picked upon one side of this conundrum. According to the written text of the constitution, parliament did have the authority to amend: an apparently unlimited authority. However, the constitution also delineated substantive constraints. There was, if you like, an inner conflict of constitutionalism. The constitution sought to both entrench higher order rules and made them vulnerable to a special majority. This tension came out in the open as soon as the legislature began to take the constraints of the constitution less seriously

In this sense, the conflicts that ensued in the wake of *Golaknath* and a more active judiciary were inevitable. What was less certain was what the outcome was going to be. In a strange way, as I will argue below, the conundrum has still not been resolved. If someone were to ask the question, 'Who is the final custodian of the Indian constitution?' the answer is far from clear. In order to see the unsettled nature of any answer to this question we need to first reflect upon some general characteristics of independent judicial review and the circumstances in which it takes hold.

It is very difficult to formulate the necessary and sufficient conditions under which independent judicial review takes hold. It used to be a common argument that successful constitutional judicial review is caused and required by strong federalism. The logic for this argument was this: federalism requires an institution to protect complex boundary arrangements; each unit of a federation will, despite incentives to deviate, support the creation and maintenance of some central institution designed to identify non-compliance by others. The logic of this argument was never very persuasive. Why would it necessarily be the case that a state involved in a dispute with a central government would support the creation of another arm of the central government to resolve the dispute? As it transpires in many cases, the nature of the federal arrangement has turned on how judicial power is exercised; and judicial review has often eroded rather than strengthened federalism. In the case of India, which is, in any event, a more strongly centralized state, one could argue that the nature of judicial scrutiny of the centre's intervention in the states has influenced the character of federalism itself.

The legislatures and executives have pretty much followed the judicial lead in defining the federal character of the Indian constitution. It has often been argued that the weakening of Indian federalism during the 1970s and 1980s was a result of single party dominance of the centre and that coalition governments increase the prospects of federalism. However, a simpler explanation implicating the courts can be offered. Arguably, the advisory opinion of the court in 1977, which permitted the dissolution of nine state governments before their term had expired, led to the weakening of Indian federalism. Whatever the other controversies surrounding the Supreme Court's decision in *Bommai*, there has been, following that decision, greater reluctance on the part of the centre to impose presidential rule on the flimsiest of grounds. Arguably, the court has made it clearer than before that there have to be 'substantial constitutional' reasons for dismissing a state government.[8] Even Laloo Prasad Yadav's misrule in Bihar could not quite pass that test. It appears that the character of judicial review could determine the nature and scope of federalism rather than being determined by it.

An analogous argument can also be made about the 'separation of powers hypothesis.' This argument suggests that constitutions that enshrine strong separation of powers amongst the various branches of government would also, in all likelihood, have strong traditions of judicial independence and power.[9] The general presumption has been that judicial review in parliamentary systems should be very weak. However, this thesis has never been quite able to explain why strong traditions of judicial review and the exercise of judicial power are appearing in parliamentary systems which have not traditionally had a strong separation of powers even when there has been no change in the formal distribution of powers. Second, these arguments do not quite explain the variance over time in the exercise of judicial power. This variance can often be best explained by the actions of the judiciary itself. The mechanisms through which judicial review comes to be instituted as a regular practice are often themselves judicial decisions. In India, as elsewhere, it is not simply the formal allocation of powers but an evolving constitutional jurisprudence, exemplified in *Kesavananda* and its successors, that has enhanced the powers of judicial review.[10] I am not sure we have or can have a general theory of the conditions under which constitutional law will evolve in the direction of asserting greater powers of judicial review. It seems that the degree of independence, especially in democratic societies, that a judiciary has is itself a creation of judicial power. The idea that 'judicial review causes itself' is probably as good as any answer to the puzzle of judicial power.

The questions to ask would therefore not be: Under what conditions do courts exercise extensive judicial review? The answer to that is more or less when they want to. The questions are rather these: First, is there any discernible pattern to the exercise of either constitutional review or judicial activism? What are the kinds of issues that occasion the exercise of the court's power? Second, what enables the exercise of judicial power to legitimize itself *vis-à-vis* the executive/legislature. The answer to the first question, in the Indian case, as elsewhere, is that emerging traditions of rights discourse in the court itself[11] generate strong reasons for judicial review. The emergence of a rights based jurisprudence is a worldwide phenomenon and can take strong root even in the absence of a Bill of Rights. However, the exact content of this rights jurisprudence has varied considerably. In the Indian case the courts, and society at large, have been less devoted to a civil liberties rights based discourse. Rather, the courts have legitimized such interventions as they have made largely on the basis of the idea that government ought to be forced to intervene in certain areas to achieve 'substantial goals', whose content is largely defined through the framework set out in the Directive Principles of State Policy. In doing so, the courts have had to strike a balance amongst the competing rights at stake. It is far from clear that the courts have evolved any clear criteria or tests to guide competing interests (say between 'environment' and 'development'), but the goals of equality have given the courts occasion to flex their judicial might.[12]

Court interventions have been widely seen as legitimate, or at least tolerated, because the representative institutions are widely seen as being immobilized, self-serving, corrupt, and incapable of exercising either their basic policy prerogatives or their powers of enforcement.

Even in comparative terms, the exercise of judicial power is increasingly being seen not as a threat to effective majoritarian rule, but as a response to its ineffectiveness. A serious disaffection with majoritarian institutions of accountability makes the exercise of judicial power almost necessary. We are resorting to judiciaries basically because we cannot help but do so.

However, the fact that independent judicial review, even of constitutional amendments, has taken hold has made constitutionalism less rather than more certain in some respects. A couple of large conclusions can be drawn from even a brief survey of Indian constitutional law. First, the question, 'who is the final arbiter of the constitution?' cannot be easily answered. The court has declared itself to be such, but for a variety of contingent reasons its authority to override amendments to the constitution has not been fully challenged since that decision. In parliamentary systems, there is no theoretical reason to suppose that simply because the courts decide on the constitutionality of a particular matter, that matter ought to be considered settled or removed from the political agenda. The reality of constitutionalism has been that the legislature and the judiciary are likely to remain *competitors* when it comes to interpreting the constitution. It is by no means settled who has the final word. The decisions of each are more like one link in a long chain of events that can be played out any number of times. Parliament can pass legislation, the courts can determine its constitutionality, parliament can try to circumvent the courts by amending the constitution, the courts can pronounce that parliament has limited powers of amendment, parliament can ... and so on and on.[13] We have not seen a full-scale assault on judicial interpretation of what the 'basic structure' doctrine requires during the 1990s because of the fragmented political system where no party is in a position to dictate terms to parliament. In the event of any political party gaining enough power to command the power to amend the constitution, it is not clear what the outcome of a judicial–legislative tussle is going to be. If indeed, at some point, any recommendations that the newly constituted constitutional commission might come up with for changes in the constitution are brought before parliament, the ability of the courts to enforce the 'basic structure' doctrine will be seriously tested. It however bears repeating that judicial supremacy in India is not simply a result of a one-time act of constitutional design, but is secured through an ongoing struggle.

Second, the courts face a dilemma: Even if the court establishes itself as the authoritative interpreter of the constitution, the institutional interest of the court is to resolve conflicts over constitutionality while maintaining the legitimacy of constitutional review in the future. Indian judges have, for the most part, been extremely aware of this dilemma. Judges appear to routinely try to anticipate the effects of particular decisions on the popular authority of the court. This makes the major decisions of the court, notwithstanding their own self-presentation, less straightforwardly an application of some high constitutional principle or value. Rather, most judgments are a delicate and *political* balancing of competing values and political aspirations; they seek to provide a workable modus vivendi rather than articulate high values. This is not the place to argue this point at any length, but I would submit the hypothesis that most court decisions can be read as modus vivendis of this. Even *Golaknath,* arguably the strongest judgment in favour of the sanctity of fundamental rights handed down by an Indian court, made a retrospective exception for three constitutional amendments relating to property rights that it might otherwise have invalidated. Similarly, *Kesavananda*, while making a strong statement to the effect that the 'basic structure' of the constitution cannot be amended by parliament, left the door open by being deliberately vague on the content of the 'basic structure'. The *Raj Narain* decision also gave many sides partial victories. It did not overturn Indira Gandhi's election; nor did it allow a constitutional amendment exempting the prime minister and speaker's election from normal challenges. The *Mandal* decisions simultaneously enlarged the scope of affirmative action, but also put limits on it. Arguably the recent *Hindutva* decisions, which have been justly criticized for their odd ideological interpretation of Hinduism, can be seen in this light. At one level these judgments reassert the importance of the Representation of People's Act; at another the courts are reluctant to dismiss a popularly elected government simply because of its ideological views. These examples merely illustrate the sense in which the court's decisions ought to be seen as a modus vivendi that do not put its own authority in jeopardy.

If one looks upon the Supreme Court as, despite its assertions of formal powers, facilitating a kind of modus vivendi, then one can more easily explain why the courts get involved in some matters and not others. For instance, as far as civil liberties are concerned, the courts have been on the whole extremely reluctant to question the presumptive powers of the state in issues like preventive detention and human rights violations. This is because of a perceived sense that Indian public opinion at large shares some of the same security syndromes that drive the state to exercise these powers too frequently in the first place. The courts have, with a couple of exceptions, treaded very gingerly on certain classes of religious disputes. First, Indian courts go to unusual lengths to demonstrate that despite calling for the reform of religious practices they are not *anti-religious*. They have interpreted Indian secularism itself as a kind of modus vivendi rather than as a set of clear principles. Second, the courts have on many occasions shied away from taking a clear stand on religious disputes that they see as very clearly controversial. Arguably the fate of the *Babari Masjid* case is a good example. The case itself has languished in Indian courts for fifty years. When the executive sought an advisory opinion from the Supreme Court, it took two years to deliver one to the effect that it was up to the high courts to decide. The courts have been much keener to supervise executive agencies in corruption investigations than they have been to call executive agencies to account in cases of 'communal' violence.

In the Indian case, the courts' concern for their own authority has meant a reading of the political tea leaves, as it were; the judicialization of politics and the politicalization of the judiciary have turned out to be two sides of the same coin. It is no accident that Indian constitutional law has been relatively unstable, or that the same courts can appear strong and assertive in some areas and not in others. It may be the case that Indian courts have acquired much legitimacy and power not because of the clarity and consistency of an underlying constitutional vision but because of the opposite. One could interpret all of the court's decisions as a modus vivendi between competing group values and aspirations which are sufficiently indeterminate and open ended to keep the players motivated enough to play it. In a way the courts' legitimacy rests precisely on the fact that in its attempt at providing a modus vivendi, it has given a sufficient number of parties enough partial victories to give them an incentive to keep on playing the game.

If this general characterization of the manner in which judicial review is exercised has any plausibility, one should not too readily assume that there is a simple association between the rise of judicial constitutional review and the emergence of constitutionalism. Constitutionalism is a commitment that the interactions of actors be governed by an authoritative set of rules. There is however no reason for supposing that the authority of any set of rules, whether they delineate formal structures of authority or articulate substantive values, can be fixed and insulated from politics simply as a matter of constitutional design. When we claim that some rules carry such authority we are making a statement less about constitutional design than the fact that there is a consensus in society around those rules. I take it to be the case that for strong constitutionalism to emerge there has to be a prior overlapping consensus on the values such constitutionalism would embody. Constitutionalism is the result of social consensus, not institutional design, and is only as robust as the former.

In the Indian case the emergence of constitutionalism is impeded by structural reasons as well. First, enforcement is the Achilles heel of all Indian institutions, the judiciary included. The judiciary has justified its own power by claiming that the government does not enforce its own laws, yet, there is little evidence that judicial intervention leads to better enforcement.[14] Even in cases where the courts were proactive in trying to invite litigation, they were ineffective. As Charles Epps puts it, 'The Indian Supreme Court clearly *tried* to spark a right revolution—*but nothing happened.*'[15] One of the ways in which the courts institutionalize constitutionalism is through a feedback mechanism that affects the legislature and influences public opinion. The legislature resorts to guesswork about the constitutionality of particular legislation before enacting it. I take it to be the case that for a constitutional politics to emerge there has to be some relationship, as mediated by the rule-making of constitutional judges, between the constitutional rules and the decision-making of public officials. Claims about the judicialization of politics would suggest that under certain conditions judges will construct a set of dialogues and collective conversations about the capacities and limits of state power that the legislature and civil society will help perpetuate. It is very difficult to make the case that the judiciary has successfully accomplished that goal. It is not clear that the legislature or the executive has, in any sense, internalized judicial law-making. Evidence for this is scarce, but I hope this large discussion of judicial review will allow me to found this thought: the application of the 'basic structure' doctrine is unlikely to reveal any underlying consistency of principle. It will also be subject to the vicissitudes of a modus vivendi that the judiciary is, in general.

Section Two

Judicial review in India immediately encounters a problem that is in part a result of the length and manifold aspirations of its constitution. How do we identify which portions of the constitution ought to be deeply entrenched and made immune from the whims of a special majority? This is not a question that can be settled with reference to the text itself. Unlike Article 139 of the Italian constitution or Article 112 of the Norwegian constitution,[16] the Indian constitution does not explicitly prevent any part of the constitution from being amended. The paradoxical idea of an unconstitutional constitutional amendment, in straightforward terms, makes less textual sense in the Indian case. Therefore, settling on a basic, unamendable part of the constitution with reference to the text itself would have an odd implication that all aspects of the text ought to be entrenched to the same degree, that is be protected as constituting higher order rules, in which case potentially all amendments could be declared void. On the other hand, thinking of nothing as entrenched would have the opposite consequence: keep the constitution an artifact of passing fancy. In this sense, propounding something like the basic structure based on some doctrine or principle not explicitly contained in the text of the constitution was inevitable. *Golaknath* was one attempt to sort out which constitutional provisions ought to be seen as deserving of higher order entrenchment than others. In effect, *Golaknath* was giving an answer to this question by a simple criterion. The fundamental rights enumerated in Part Three of the constitution deserved more fundamental protections than others. The ruling in *Kesavananda* was an attempt, from another point of view, to answer the same question. It overruled the *Golaknath* view that fundamental rights could not be taken away by the amending procedure, only to replace it by the claim that the court had the power to scrutinize any amendment if it violated the basic structure. The scope for judicial review was extended even further because the court did not adequately define 'basic structure' except through examples; it failed to articulate its reasons for why certain parts of the written constitution were privileged over others. To take a fairly well known example. Suppose one says, as Nani Palkhivala had argued in his briefs during *Kesavananda*, that the principles embodied in the preamble to the constitution be deemed specially protected. In that case, why was 'socialism' allowed to be added to the preamble through a constitutional amendment? Then, having been added, why has the court not thought it fit to make it part of the basic structure in the same way that it has done with 'secularism'? There is nothing in the text of the constitution that can settle questions such as these. What principle can be invoked to determine the content of the 'basic structure'?

I think critics of the 'basic structure' doctrine who criticize it on the grounds that it is anti-democratic have not taken sufficiently seriously the considerations that led to the formulation of the doctrine in the first place: which parts of the constitution, which values and allocation of offices deserved to be deeply entrenched? They see judicial promulgation of this matter as anti-democratic for the simple reason that it replaces the authority of elected assemblies with that of a court, and it makes constitutional change in light of changing circumstances more difficult.[17] They are generally hostile to the idea of deeper entrenchment of higher order rules in the first place; they claim to have a greater preference for democracy at the expense of constitutionalism. This is a very general argument to the effect that constitutionalism is anti-democratic. There is no space here to deal with this argument in detail, but one general line of reply might go something like this: the idea that judicial review in general, and review of constitutional amendments in particular is anti-democratic, because it is a usurpation of the authority of a majoritarian institution, namely parliament, rests upon a particular and misleading view of both democracy and constitutionalism. This argument rests upon construing democracy simply as a form of government. Democracy, on this view, is a set of institutions where the authority to make ordinary laws rests with elected representatives. Both elections and enactment of laws is determined by a bare majority rule. Of course, given the complexity of most democracies, embodied in institutions like second chambers and so forth, enactment of laws is not simply a consequence of a bare majority rule. Nevertheless, the core idea is that democracy is a form of decision procedure embodying some version of majority rule. Constitutional amendments usually require super majorities.

This view of what is democratic, call it the pure procedural view, fails I think to capture the sense in which a constitution is democratic. A constitution is democratic not simply in the ways in which ordinary laws are. Ordinary laws are democratic because they are the enactments of a majoritarian decision procedure. A constitution, by contrast, is democratic because a sovereign people establish it. The people, considered as free, equal, and independent citizens, exercise their constituent power to create a constitution. In employing that power, sovereign citizens institute a particular form of representative government and entrust it with powers to conduct our business and ordinary powers to legislate. These powers are, to use, Lockean language, held in trust and are to be exercised for achieving common ends. On this view, what makes a constitution democratic is not simply the fact that the constitution enjoins a representative government. Rather, the constitution itself is an expression of a deeper democracy, because it is a creation of the people, conceived as free, independent, and sovereign citizens.

If this view has any plausibility, we can think of what constitutionalism means in a new way. A constitution does not simply identify procedures for applying and making laws. This seems to roughly be the view of those who believe that since judicial review of the decisions of a representative assembly are anti-democratic, using the 'basic structure' doctrine to take over parliament's rights to amend the constitution is also anti-democratic. However, a democratic constitution does more. It places constraints upon the ordinary lawmaking activities of the government in order to prevent the usurpation of the *sovereignty of the people* by governments and private institutions. In principle, even decisions produced by a majoritarian decision procedure of a legislative assembly, or an ill judged constitutional amendment, can put the sovereignty of the people at risk if it jeopardizes the set of rights that enable citizens to maintain their sovereign freedom and independence. If this is correct it supplies at least one rationale for judicial review. Judicial review is not anti-democratic in this sense: it is simply one of the mechanisms provided in the constitution to protect democratic sovereignty from usurpation by transient majorities. However, if my view is correct, it also points to a principle that a judiciary ought to be obliged to employ when striking down enactments that are a result of parliament's amending power. The constraint democratic constitutionalism places on judicial reasoning is this: the arguments that the judiciary invokes in its deliberations must be compatible with, or seek to preserve those principles that express and maintain our standing as free and equal citizens. Democratic sovereignty, if it is to have any content at all, is based in the equal freedom, independence, and political jurisdiction of democratic citizens. The best expression of democratic freedom is the fact that we possess equal rights and liberties; these are rights that would be agreed to by free and independent persons and are a part of democratic sovereignty.

How would this test help resolve some of the conundrums that grew around the basic structure doctrine and the case law that followed from it? I can give here no more than a thumbnail sketch of such an account. The purpose of doing so is this. One must clearly articulate what adjudicative principle could justify a doctrine such as 'the basic structure' doctrine. The second is to argue that because the court itself did not clearly articulate such an adjudicative principle and relied on an indiscriminate list of protected items, as both defenders and critics of the court acknowledge, its formulation of the basic structure doctrine is inconsistent and unpredictable in its application.

Some democratic theorists have a prior worry. Suppose for a moment we agree that there should be an entrenched constitution and that the basic structure is a good way of describing the items that should be entrenched, why leave it up to the courts to determine its content? A parliament has done things like amending the preamble of the constitution, why should not a representative assembly rather than the judiciary be the authoritative interpreter of what provisions best express our status as free and democratic citizens.[18] How is it that the Supreme Court has acquired the authority to give content to the basic structure in the first place? This is a powerful theoretical argument which I will not answer directly. However, in the Indian case, the story of why the court became the apparently authoritative interpreter is contextual.

It is worth reminding ourselves that the court did not take on the mantle of ultimate custodian of the constitution entirely of its own choosing. So long as the legislatures were taking constitutionalism seriously, not jeopardizing fundamental rights, violating basic requirements of equality and due process, the courts could continue to defer to parliaments. However, once these were put at risk, could you trust the very institutions that were putting core constitutional values at risk to be a judge in their own cause? Would you expect a parliament that had enacted laws exempting the prime minister and the speaker of the house from normal election laws to honour the constitutional requirement that there be equality before the law? From the point of view of democratic theory it is certainly the case that only a popular sovereign assembly could ideally have undertaken a delineation of the basic structure. It is however a bit facetious to think that parliament as such constituted such an assembly. *Golaknath* had at least left open the possibility that parliament could use its residuary powers to convene such an assembly; but the political prospects of a new constituent assembly being convened are extremely dim.

It bears repeating that my defence of judicial review of amendments to the constitution interprets democracy not simply as a procedure designed to aggregate the balance of preferences through some decision procedure such as majority rule. It is rather a set of institutions that secures the freedom, independence, and equality of all its citizens. That is precisely why democracy requires not just equal political rights such as the right to vote, run for office, majority rule, etc. Other basic liberties are just as essential: freedom of thought and expression, freedom of conscience, freedom of association, the right to pursue one's own conception of the good in a manner compatible with similar rights for others, the right to physical integrity, etc. The judges in *Golaknath* were right in thinking that a basic set of liberal rights is as much part of democratic sovereignty as equal political rights. It is one of the oddities of Indian constitutional discourse that while, on the one hand, there has been a great proliferation in the language of rights, the idea that rights need to be very deeply entrenched and immune from legislative whims has commanded less than complete enthusiasm. This is so for a variety of reasons, but the principal one seems to be this. Many of our distinguished legal commentators continue to see fundamental rights as largely instrumental and subordinate to social and economic equality, or following Marx, a kind of bourgeois illusion that simply detracts from the goals of greater equality. Alternatively, as I suggested above, they see the entrenchment of fundamental rights as a kind of anti-democratic measure against constitutional change. The argument above suggests these fundamental rights are just an expression of democratic sovereignty; an acknowledgement of our equal moral worth, and recognition of us as free and equal citizens. I hope I have made the case that an entrenched constitution is not necessarily anti-democratic if one takes the democratic aspiration in the fullest sense of the term. On this basis there are grounds for limitation of the amending power of parliament.

What of the worry, articulated by Justice Bachawat, in his dissent in *Golaknath* and later echoed by Justices Shelat and Grover, that to constrain constitutional amendment was not only to deprive society of the means to transform its constitution in accordance with changing circumstances but also bind future generations to the present one.[19] On this view, the trouble with entrenching constitutions is that they make us, and future generations, beholden to the constituent power exercised by our ancestors. This objection however misses the way in which entrenching parts of a constitution may preserve *our* sovereign powers. The point of saying that parliament does not have an unqualified right to amend the constitution is not to say that only the founders could exercise their constituent power to create or transform our constitution whereas our parliament does not have such a power.[20] *That* would be to bind the present generation to the previous. It is rather to say that the constitution is a means of expressing *our* democratic sovereignty as free and equal citizens, and any amendment that subverts that sovereignty is unjustified.

Section Three

The suspicion of entrenching rights through limiting the amending power of parliament has however been largely complicated by the right to property. Imagine for a moment a slightly different decision in *Golaknath*. Such a decision could have kept the substance of the *Golaknath* judgment, namely that parliament does not have the right to amend the constitution in a way that abridges fundamental rights. It could however have gone on to say, as *Kesavananda* did, that property is not a fundamental right, or at least in the same sense in which, say, freedom of expression is. I suspect that decision would have had more takers. As it happens, the fear of limiting parliament's right to amend the constitution really derives not from the cogency of arguments based on parliamentary sovereignty but from a fear that entrenchment of fundamental rights would also give immunity to those who claim an unqualified right to property under Article 31 of the constitution. The fourth and seventeenth amendments to the constitution were necessitated by the narrow interpretation of the right to property given by the court that stood in the way of land reforms. Successive amendments not only made changes in the provisions relating to the right to property but also expanded the Ninth Schedule, and many of the cases that come under the 'basic structure' doctrine involve property rights. This is not the occasion to go into the complicated history of property-related constitutional amendments in Indian law. I rather want to make a few remarks on how the perspective outlined above might help us think about these issues.

It is I think plausible to insist, as the Supreme Court has done, that the right to private property cannot be thought of as an unqualified right. It is almost certainly the case that absolute property rights that allow for unlimited accumulation and unregulated exchange worsen over time the economic condition of the disadvantaged and deprive them of the fair value of their liberties. It may be the case that unlimited property rights create, or at least help preserve, social conditions that render many people's claims to be free and equal citizens useless; and under an inegalitarian structure this is even more so. Absolute property rights simply could not be democratically justified to everyone and are not an expression of our standing as free and equal citizens in the same way as say the right to freedom of expression is. To this extent, society as a whole, through its representatives, ought to have the authority to regulate the distribution of property to an appropriate degree. To this extent the courts were right to let stand many of the amendments that facilitated such a redistribution.

Having said this, there is no clear ex ante calculus of what form of redistribution is legitimate; nor is there a clear criterion for distinguishing wanton forfeiture by the state of legitimate rights to property in the name of redistribution from a genuinely productive redistribution scheme. This requires adjudication on a case by case basis. However, the Supreme Court has gone further than simply leaving the room open for curtailment of the abridgement of unqualified rights to property for redistributive purposes. In decisions subsequent to *Kesavananda*, the Supreme Court pulled off the extraordinary feat of ascertaining that directive principles and fundamental rights belong together to the basic structure of the constitution. The court claimed that there was no potential dissonance between fundamental rights and directive principles; they are, in Justice Chandrachud's words, 'like a twin formula for achieving a social revolution which is the ideal the visionary founders of the constitution set before themselves.'[21] The implications of this claim are less than clear. Jurists like Seervai worried that putting directive principles on par with fundamental rights violated the original constitutional compact because clearly it had been the intention of the Constituent Assembly not to put these two aspects of the constitution legally on par with one another, even though as political aspirations they might have the same status. I think Seervai's worries on this matter were a little overblown because, read another way, *Minerva* and *Waman Rao* arguably entrenched the fundamental rights in Part III even more. The judgment could be read as saying that *even if* the directive principles are said to belong to the basic structure, the objectives laid in the directive principles could not justify overriding basic rights. 'To destroy the guarantees given by Part III in order purportedly to achieve the goals of Part IV is plainly to subvert the constitution by destroying its basic structure.'[22]

However, by declaring the directive principles part of the basic structure the court only heightened the confusion about what was to count as the 'basic structure'. Other than a hortatory appeal to the need for a social revolution, the court did not advance reasons for why the directive principles are an expression of the equal standing of free and independent citizens in the same way that fundamental rights are. It also assumed rather than substantiated the claim that there was no potential conflict between fundamental rights and directive principles. Despite the undoubted importance of the directive principles, there are good reasons to think that they cannot be entrenched in quite the same way as fundamental rights, in part because greater indeterminacy attends to what would count as fulfilling those objectives than attends to the enforcement of the latter. One might say, for instance, that a social revolution requires that everyone be guaranteed full employment; but how exactly this is to be achieved is much more indeterminate and not entirely within the control of governments in quite the same way as say enforcing people's right to freedom of expression is. In other words the directive principles give and ought to give enormous leeway to legislatures to determine how they are to be fulfilled: what structure of property rights best achieves the broad aims of the directive principles can be a matter of debate.

If it is allowed that what counts as the 'enforcement' of directive principles is vastly more indeterminate than fundamental rights, making these part of the basic structure is vacuous, in that a potentially vast range of legislative enactments and amendments could be construed as satisfying its requirements. In this form the doctrine has no bite other than giving the court vast judicial leverage. On the other hand, if the court decides that particular amendments violate the basic structure because they contravene directive principles, the court will have to set itself up in a position of determining what the best means are of achieving the goals set up in the directive principles. It is not clear that the court has the competence to do quite that.

The point of the foregoing decision is to found the following thought. The declaration that directive principles are part of the basic structure is both jurisprudentially tendentious and potentially vacuous. It seems more on par with a symbolic statement that does not worry about the conditions of its own realization. It is a bit like adding 'socialism' to the preamble: it could mean nothing or everything.

Is there any harm in declaring the directive principles part of the 'basic structure?' I think there is an indirect harm in the sense that the Indian state and Indian courts have too often relied on the illusion that getting just policy outcomes is largely a matter of getting intentions right, and that the state can achieve these goals simply by administrative fiat. To take an example, rent control laws, tenants' rights against landlords, ostensibly legitimized in the name of the state's intention to ameliorate the condition of the propertyless, arguably inhibited the creation of better urban infrastructure and long-term construction of low-cost housing. This is certainly a debatable matter, but such inordinate emphasis on the promulgation of intent, and less intention to the causal schemes and incentive mechanisms by which such intentions could be realized, has been a weakness of both the Indian state and the Indian judiciary. Despite our abysmal experience with dysfunctional property laws, poor economic growth, slow generation of employment, we still seem to think that correcting these matters is simply a matter of the state's intent and will, and that we can have directive principles enforced in the same way in which we think of fundamental rights. The perspective of democratic equality I outlined above, as one from which to adjudicate matters, does I think undermine the question of the optimal structure of property rights. However, the court would have been better off if they had dealt with matters relating to the place of property rights and its relationship with equality on their own terms, rather than using as unwieldy a doctrine as 'basic structure'.

Section Four

The perspective of democratic constitutionalism I outline above makes it easier to assess some of the other applications of the 'basic structure' doctrine. Even though the court's wading into the deep waters of limiting parliamentary amendments was perhaps an inevitable result of legislative dysfunction, some features of their application of the basic structure doctrine were avoidable. The Supreme Court appears to have been haphazard in defining the doctrine and inconsistent in its applications. It seems to have used the basic structure doctrine as much to expand the scope of judicial power as it has to delineate the core values of the constitution. On the one hand, the basic structure doctrine, the idea that some core values like liberty require higher order protection, did very little to protect these liberties in the face of concrete threats; on the other, they were used to open up new vistas of judicial activism. Add to this the fact that the illustrative list of what counts as the basic structure is indiscriminately varied and inconsistently applied, and one begins to doubt whether the 'basic structure' doctrine, as articulated by the court, has any consistent basis at all.

Several items were mentioned in the original *Kesavananda* judgment as constituting the basic structure: supremacy of the constitution, republican and democratic form of government, secular character of the constitution, separation of powers, free and fair elections, federalism, sovereignty of the country, fundamental rights enumerated in Part III, the unity and integrity of the nation, to which were later added the rule of law, equality, judicial review, and so on. The very nature of these lists suggests that the court has not quite thought through the constitutional *principle* behind the basic structure doctrine. Rather, they picked out items from the text of the constitution without specifying why. It is almost as if the Supreme Court takes the view that we recognize the basic structure when we see it. Many of the items are clearly a necessary expression of our democratic sovereignty as free and equal peoples, but some seem less eligible for entrenchment. It is not clear, for instance, whether federalism, or any particular form of federalism is a necessary expression of democratic freedom. Many items are indeterminate still: does the unity and integrity of the nation imply that a free people cannot of their own accord surrender any territorial claims they might have? Is any particular set of boundaries really necessary to our claims as a free and democratic people? Then what does the injunction to maintain sovereignty mean? Is it compatible with submission to the jurisdiction of supranational institutions through multilateral treaties? Even those items that might be thought of as plausible candidates for entrenchment as part of the basic structure, like secularism, have been inconsistently applied. In *S.R. Bonmai* vs *Union of India*, a landmark case that upheld the dismissal of three BJP state governments after the demolition of the Babari Masjid on the grounds that the principles adhered to by these governments were incompatible with secularism, the court used the basic structure doctrine to defend a core constitutional value: secularism. In the *Hindutva* cases, on the other hand, the Supreme Court refused to acknowledge that the 'basic structure' doctrine might be relevant to determining whether Manohar Joshi, a proponent of Hindutva, had violated the Representation of People's Act by suggesting that Maharashtra might become a Hindu state. Both these cases were complex for a variety of reasons that will have to await another discussion, but two points stand out: the first is that the fact that a value like secularism has been identified as part of the basic structure is no longer a predictor of how it will be used in constitutional discourse. Secondly, both cases underlined that the tension between procedural, majoritarian democracy, and substantive liberal values is real. That however does not mean that liberal values, like fundamental liberties and a secular constitution, are anti-democratic and all one can do is work out a modus vivendi between them. What it means is that the tension can be mitigated only by recourse to higher order constitutional values that assert that these liberal values are just the best expression of our standing as free and equal citizens.

What the court ought to have done was to explain more clearly the rationale for the basic structure doctrine and entrenchment of the values they comprise. The rationale ought to have drawn upon something like the general consideration in favour of entrenchment that I mentioned above, namely the preservation of democracy in a deeper sense: to maintain our integrity as free and equal citizens. This means that any interpretation of the constitution must be justified with reference to the fact that the constitution derives its authority not from the fact that it is a written text bequeathed to us by our ancestors, but by its status as a public charter that is an instrument of democratic sovereignty. Any interpretation of the constitution must be such that it is acceptable to free and equal persons reasoning publicly. The authority of the basic structure can derive only from the fact that any values or laws included in it are essential to preserve our standing as free and equal citizens. Although the court, in cases like *Raj Narain* and *Bonmai* gave intimations of just this understanding, it obscured its own case by including peripheral items under the basic structure rubric. The court often seemed not to be engaging in public reason, that is, deliberating from the point of view of what might preserve democratic sovereignty; rather it seemed to rely on an odd combination of textual deference with the invention of its own principles. Of course, the perspective of democratic sovereignty can be indeterminate in its conclusions. On matters such as property rights, there is no simple answer to what could be justified to free and equal citizens. In such cases, subject to standard constitutional constraints, the court probably ought to act as if the presumption was in the favour of the legislature. The court should not put itself in the position of being the final arbiter of the optimal structure of property right. One could also imagine a wide variety of electoral rules, and possibly forms of government, compatible with free and fair elections.

Here again, there might be some permissible range of disagreement that ought to be left to legislators to work out. On the other hand, if the magnitude of the change in electoral laws implies a fundamental reallocation of powers within society, it is less than clear that special majorities, to use Hidayatullah's phrase, should be given discretion over the matter. I however hope that the standard provided by liberal constitutionalism, though indeterminate, is not entirely vacuous.

In Lieu of a Conclusion

This essay has argued that there are good *democratic* grounds for entrenching certain constitutional principles and making them immune from the whims of even special majorities. However, the Supreme Court has been less than clear on what these grounds are, and its application of the basic structure doctrine has been characterized by the same weaknesses as its use of judicial review in general. Although the court carries enormous authority, constitutionalism—the sense that a polity takes certain values to be deeply authoritative—remains a fragile aspiration. For one thing, the courts have used their powers to facilitate a modus vivendi rather than articulate clear constitutional principles. The terms of this modus vivendi are greatly determined by the courts estimate of prevailing political fissures. Constitutional rules endure in India less because they are internalized as values that set authoritative constraints on behaviour, more because they provide enough occasions for discretionary manipulation to allow the show to go on. At its best, the Supreme Court's exercise of judicial review over the whims of a supermajority has protected the basic institutional framework laid down in the constitution. However, whether it has made the idea that we are all free and equal as citizens more entrenched in the constitutional and political culture of India is debatable. A constitution, said John Adams, 'is a standard, a pillar and a bond when it is understood, approved and beloved. But without this intelligence and attachment, it might as well be a kite or a balloon flying in the air.'[23] Whether we have a constitution in this sense will be tested by how well we weather the process currently under way to undo, through a commission, the work and wisdom of ages. Our current constitution has, as I have argued, its own inner conflicts. The court's mandate ought to be to use its underlying principles to help us navigate these tensions, not to replace the whim of transient legislators by equally indiscriminate whims of its own.

Notes and References

1. 1973 (4) SCC 225.
2. As Justice Matthew put it: 'The concept of a basic structure as brooding omnipresence in the sky apart from specific provisions of the constitution is too vague and indefinite to provide a yardstick for the validity of ordinary law.' See *Indira Gandhi* vs *Raj Narain*, AIR 1975 SC 2299, 2389.
3. For Seervai, see the fourth edition of his magisterial *Constitutional Law of India*, Universal Law Publishing Company, Delhi, 1999; for Upendra Baxi, compare 'The Constitutional Quicksands of *Kesavananda Bharati* and the Twenty Fifth Amendment,' *Supreme Court Cases*, Journal Section, vol. 1, pp. 45–67, with *Courage, Craft and Contention* (Tripathi, Delhi, 1987), Ch 3. Also see Ashok Desai, 'The Basic Structure and Constitutional Amendment' in Venkat Iyer (ed.), *Liberty and the Rule of Law* (Butterworth, Delhi, 2000); P.P. Rao, 'The Basic Structure Doctrine', *The Practical Lawyer*, 1999.
4. 1952 SCR 89.
5. 1965 1 SCR 933.
6. *I. C. Golaknath* vs *State of Punjab* 1967 2 SCR 762.
7. There had been intimations of this doctrine in Justice Hidayatullah's dissent in *Sajjan Singh*. He wrote, 'the constitution gives so many assurances in Part III that it would be difficult to think that they were the plaything of a special majority. To hold that would mean prima facie that the most solemn parts of our constitution stands on the same footing as any other part ... As at present advised, I can only say that the power to make amendment ought not ordinarily to be a means of escape from absolute constitutional restrictions.' *Sajjan Singh*, 966.
8. *S R Bonmai* vs *Union of India* (1994) 3 SCC 1.
9. For instance, John Ferejohn in his 'Law, Legislation and Positive Political Theory', in J.S. Banks and Eric Hanushek (eds), *Modern Political Economy: Old Topics, New Directions* (Cambridge University Press, Cambridge, 1995, p. 208), argues that:

   Nations with traditions and practices of unrestricted parliamentary sovereignty would tend to have judges that are more or less neutral appliers of law to cases. Conversely, those nations that restrict parliamentary sovereignty might be expected to develop traditions of judicial independence and power. Judges in parliamentary systems would not emphasize or notice the discretionary or interpretative elements of their decisions. They would see themselves as parliamentary heads ... One would expect this to be true regardless of the history of the legal system.

It is not clear that this hypothesis is empirically sustainable.

10. See supra, no. 2.
11. This can also be an artifact of the institutional anomalies of Indian law in some instances. For example, most of the environmental litigation is carried out in terms of 'rights' because the system of tort law is relatively weak.
12. Even the *Kesavananda* decision, while designed to protect the right of the courts to nullify constitutional amendments, was intended to provide greater justiciability to the Directive Principles of State Policy than to protect fundamental rights, as was the intention in *Golaknath*. Almost all the Supreme Court's celebrated 'activist' decisions—a constitutional right to a minimum wage, a right to counsel, a right to livelihood, broad remedies against environmental destruction—stemmed from a concern for equality rather than civil liberties. Indeed, civil liberties concerns have been palpably weak in Indian courts.
13. Perhaps something like this is now under way, though not with respect to constitutional amendments. Parliament passed the *Muslim Women's Bill* to override the Supreme Court's interpretation of the CPC in *Shah Bano*. In a spate of recent judgments, the courts seem to be restoring the situation that existed prior to the *Muslim Women's Bill.*
14. So far as I am aware there is no study of enforcement of judicial decisions.
15. *The Rights Revolution*, p. 71.
16. The Italian constitution reads, 'The republican form of the State cannot be the subject of constitutional amendment.' The Norwegian prohibits amendments that 'contradict the basic principles of the constitution'.
17. This argument is put forward by Raju Ramachandran, in an otherwise illuminating essay 'The Supreme Court and the Basic Structure Doctrine', in B.N. Kripal *et al.*, *Supreme But Not Infallible,* Oxford University Press, New Delhi, 2000, pp. 129 ff.
18. See Jeremy Waldron, *Law and Disagreement* (Oxford University Press, Oxford, 2000) and republican critiques of judicial review more generally.
19. 'It is not possible to place society in a strait jacket. The society grows, its requirements change. The Constitution and laws may have to be changed to suit those needs. No single generation can bind the course of generations to come.' *Madhav Rao Scindia* vs *Union of India* 1971 1 SCC 85, p. 473. This echoes Jefferson's famous lament about constitutions that 'no society can make a perpetual constitution'.
20. This seems to be the view of Seervai's magisterial *Constitutional Law of*

India (4th edn, Universal Law Publishing Company, Delhi, 1999). My own view is that the whole invocation of parliament lacking constituent power is a red herring.

21. See AIR 1980 SC 1789, 1806.
22. *Minerva Mills Ltd* vs *Union of India* AIR 1980 SC 1789, 1806.
23. John Adams, cited in Hannah Arendt's *On Revolution* (Viking, New York, 1965), p. 125.

9

INDIVIDUAL AND GROUP RIGHTS
A View From India[1]

NEERA CHANDHOKE

Introduction: The Political and the Theoretical Moment

In the 1980s political theorists raised important questions relating to liberalism and liberal constitutionalism. One of the basic issues that was catapulted on to the agenda of political theory was that of the significance of the cultural community in political life. Liberals have been notoriously shy to acknowledge the value of cultural communities, because historically this strain of thought has positioned itself against any kind of feudal supra-individualist grouping that may truncate individual freedom, and limit the horizons of self-determining rationality. However, from the late 1980s, communitarians were to pose a direct and unambiguous challenge to the idea that the unit of liberal constitutionalism was the dis-embedded, abstract, individual as the bearer of the rights of citizenship. Michael Sandel, one of the leading representatives of this school of thought, was to argue that individuals are embedded in definite systems of meanings, which are given by their cultural community. Community is 'not a relationship they choose (as in a voluntary association) but an attachment they discover, not merely an attribute but a constituent of their identity.'[2]

The insistence that we should recognize the constitutiveness of the modern individual carried important implications for liberal constitutionalism. Should such an argument be accepted, constitutions would have to allot citizenship rights not only to individuals but also to their constitutive cultural communities, codify systems of justice that are embedded within the meaning systems of communities, and abstain from imposing abstract and ahistorical principles of law on societies, as in the Rawlsian vision.

The liberal–communitarian debate is of some interest because it stretched across an entire range of issues that theorists had thought had been settled relating to questions of citizenship or justice. However, a detailed exploration of the debate is beyond the purview of this essay. What is of interest is the way in which the recognition that individuals are constituted by their communities, and conversely the recognition that communities are of value, spilt over into other debates that are significant for India. One such debate that followed the recognition of the value of culture is that of multiculturalism. Theorists were to argue that any given society is composed of many cultures, and that each of these is important to its members. Therefore, these cultures should be granted 'recognition' in the Hegelian sense, of being valued for and in themselves.

To this, the legal philosopher Ronald Dworkin added an important rider: cultural narratives are a precondition for making intelligent judgements about how to lead our lives, as they provide the spectacles through which we identify experiences as valuable. However, the survival of a culture, suggested Dworkin, is by no means guaranteed. Therefore, we must protect cultures from structural debasement or decay. 'We', argues Dworkin, 'inherited a cultural structure and we have some duty, out of simple justice, to leave that structure at least as rich as we found it.'[3]

This was to give rise to the second debate: that of providing supportive social and political environments to cultures that may be vulnerable simply because they are in a minority. Will Kymlicka was to famously argue that some minorities face a disadvantage in relation to cultural membership. On issues that matter to them, minorities are likely to be outvoted and outmanoeuvred,[4] and therefore some cultures should be protected through special legal or constitutional measures above and beyond common rights of citizenship. In other words, if minority cultures are vulnerable because they are weak in relation to majority ones, they should be shielded through a system of group-differentiated citizenship.

As the debate progressed, it became increasingly clear that we can no longer subsume minority under universal rights. Ian Brownlie suggests that fairly reasonable group claims have involved matters that are not covered by universal rights.[5] For instance, the liberal formulation on the right of the individual to her/his culture cannot cope with claims to positive action to maintain the cultural and linguistic identities of communities. Brownlie concludes that in certain important respects the classical approach to the protection of individuals is too limited, and needs the application of additional concepts and principles.[6] Recognition of this lacuna in universal human rights has brought minority rights back on to the political and intellectual agenda, particularly with the adoption of the declaration on the 'Rights of Persons Belonging to National, or Ethnic, Religious and Linguistic Minorities' by the UN General Assembly on 18 December 1992.

However, for India the debate was not new and appeared to cover already familiar terrain. After all, the constitution had recognized the rights of all groups to their own culture and religion. Article 29 (1) of the chapter on fundamental rights lays down that 'Any section of the citizens residing in the territory of India or any part thereof having a distinct language, script or culture of its own shall have the right to conserve the same.' This constitutional provision recognizes that different groups have different cultures; that these linguistic and religious cultures are valuable to their members; and that members of distinct cultures need to be given explicit rights to protect their culture. Note that the right to culture is an individual right, i.e. individuals are granted the right to their culture. No provision is made for those cases where the culture itself may be under threat of dissolution, or where it may be subjected to calls for assimilation. Neither is this right applicable only to minorities. This article, along with Article 30 which guarantees that all religious and linguistic minorities are given the right to establish and administer educational institutions of their choice, constitutes the provision of cultural and educational rights.[7] These two articles have to be read along with Articles Twenty-five to Twenty-eight that grant the freedom of religion in order to comprehend the range of protections afforded to religious groups.

It is tempting to read the Indian constitution in the light of contemporary theories outlined by Joseph Raz and Will Kymlicka. We could, for instance, argue that the founders of the constitution had forestalled the Western theoretical world when it came to differentiated citizenship, and that therefore the makers of the constitution were remarkably prescient.

However, this would be, as I argue later, mistaken for the reasons for the grant by the constitution of the right to cultures to reproduce the conditions of their own existence as historically determined. We cannot graft the reasoning we find today in works of political theory on to historically determined discussions in the Constituent Assembly. Having said that, let me also suggest that contemporary conditions in India are such that we may need to *buttress* and support the reasoning of members of the Constituent Assembly by reference to contemporary theories of multiculturalism and minority rights. This is because it is the multicultural nature of Indian society that is under attack by proponents of Hindutva. The first part of this essay focuses on this aspect. In the second, I want to show that group or collective rights are necessarily identified with minority rights for specific reasons. In the third part I take up the somewhat vexatious issue of how we negotiate the relationship between group and individual rights. I suggest that group rights flow from individual rights and, therefore, have to respect individual rights.

1. Situating Group Rights Historically

The reason why cultural rights were recognized in the Motilal Nehru constitutional draft of 1928 had to do with the *differentia specifica* of the historical situation in the 1920s. This was of course the period when the social base of the Congress widened substantially with Gandhi's entry into the arena of Indian politics. As Gandhi used with some profit the experience he had gained in South Africa in bringing together diverse sections of the people through political mobilzation, Indian society witnessed rapid politicization, as formerly excluded or marginalized communities were welded into a wide-ranging alliance. Indeed, it was during this period that the Congress was to acquire its famed umbrella-like coalitional character. The process of building a mass struggle out of communities who were either actively hostile or wholly indifferent to one another was not, however, without problems.[8]

Those were not happy days for inter-religious alliances. The 1920s had witnessed frequent and large-scale eruptions of communal violence in the early and mid years of the decade. In most parts of Punjab and UP, open rioting scarred the landscape: 88 riots took place in the period 1923–7, which left 400 people dead and 5000 injured. Mahatma Gandhi reportedly threw up his hands and declared that the Hindu–Muslim problem was an insoluble puzzle that he would keep out of. The problem was exacerbated by the rise of Hindu majoritarianism with the formation of the Hindu Mahasabha in 1915. This naturally unleashed tension, fears, and insecurities among the Muslim community, which increasingly turned to the solution of separate electorates institutionalized by the colonial state.

However, the authors of the 1928 document on the constitution were reluctant to acquiesce in the institutionalization of separate electorates. Nonetheless, although Motilal Nehru and Tej Bahadur Sapru rejected separate electorates, they recognized the importance of liberty of religion and cultural autonomy in order to prevent harassment and exploitation of one group by another.[9] In sum, in the 1928 Motilal Nehru constitution the rights of minority communities to their religion and culture were recognized partly to allay the fears of the religious minorities, partly to neutralize the demand for separate electorates by the Muslims, and partly to devise a principle that could regulate inter-group relationships within the Congress coalition. Whereas the broader principle, i.e. *sarva dharma sambhava*, served to regulate relations in general, group rights were granted to create the conditions for a mass struggle as well as to offset the fears of the religious minorities that they would be swamped in a majoritarian India. Therefore, in 1928, the Motilal Nehru constitution granted to *all* religious communities the right to their language, script, culture, and religious practices.

With these considerations in mind, Jawaharlal Nehru was to write a note on minorities in *Young India* on 15 May 1930:

> The history of India and of many of the countries of Europe has demonstrated that there can be no stable equilibrium in any country so long as an attempt is made to crush a minority or force it to conform to the ways of the majority. There is no surer method of rousing the resentment of the minority and keeping it apart from the rest of the nation than to make it feel that it has not got the freedom to stick to its own ways. ... It matters little whether logic is on its side

or whether its own particular brand of culture is worthwhile or not. The mere fact of losing it makes it dear. Therefore we in India must make it clear to all that our policy is based on granting this freedom to the minorities and that under no circumstance will any coercion or repression of them be tolerated ... we can also lay down as our deliberate policy that there shall be no unfair treatment of any minority. Indeed, we should go further and state that it will be the business of the state to give favoured treatment to minority and backward communities.[10]

The Karachi Charter on Fundamental Rights of 1931 reiterated the right to religion and the freedom to profess and practice any religion. It also stipulated that the state should be neutral towards all religions (Clauses 2 and 9 of Article 1). A fresh addition to the list of minority rights in the charter was the right of minorities to cultural autonomy and equal access to educational facilities (Clause 3).

During the second session of the Round Table Conference, a memorandum on the 'Congress Scheme for a Communal Settlement', that was supposedly authored by Mahatma Gandhi, was presented before the Minorities Committee on 28 October 1931.[11] The scheme provided for the protection of culture, language, script, education, the profession and practice of religion, and religious endowment. It also provided for the protection of personal laws, as well as for a proportionate share in the legislature for all communities through joint electorates, protection of minority interests in the central and provincial cabinets, and a fair share for the minorities in the public services. The latter consideration, it was agreed, should be balanced by considerations of merit and efficiency.

The report of the Sapru Committee, which was set up by the non-party conference in November 1944, recommended full religious tolerance, non-interference in religious beliefs, practices, and institutions, and protection of the language and cultures of all communities. In its recommendation number 18, the committee proposed the establishment at the centre and in each of the provinces a minorities commission comprising a representative of each of the communities, which would keep a watch over the interests of the minority communities in the area.[12]

The members of the Constituent Assembly were to uphold the historical commitment made to the minorities since the 1920s. Pandit

G.B. Pant, moving the resolution to set up an Advisory Committee on Fundamental Rights and the Rights of Minorities, explicitly stated that, '[a] satisfactory solution of questions pertaining to minorities will ensure the health, vitality and strength of the free State of India ... now it is necessary that a new chapter should start and we should all realize our responsibility. Unless the minorities are fully satisfied, we cannot make progress; we cannot even maintain peace in an undisturbed manner.'[13]

In 1947, however, the political context was quite different. The country had been partitioned in the name of religion, howsoever fragile the Pakistan movement may appear in retrospect. Therefore, while the members of the Constituent Assembly agreed that the rights of the minorities to their cultures should be protected, they also believed that minorities had no claim to political rights either in the form of reservations in legislatures or separate electorates. Separate electorates had, after all, reaped a bitter harvest.

In this, the assembly performed something of a U-turn, for the Subcommittee on Minorities headed by H.C. Mookherjee, in its report of 27 July 1947, had recommended that seats should be reserved for religious minorities under joint electorates. Secondly, the interests of such minorities should be protected in the cabinets through a convention under a schedule to the constitution. Thirdly, reservations for minorities should be provided for in the public services, but these claims should be balanced against the demand of merit and efficiency. Fourthly, independent officers should be appointed to report to the legislatures on the working of the safeguards.[14]

The Advisory Committee on Fundamental Rights headed by Sardar Patel accepted most of these reservations in its 'Report on Minority Rights' adopted on 8 August 1947. On 27 and 28 August 1947, the Constituent Assembly adopted the entire report of the Advisory Committee. In February 1948, these provisions were incorporated into the draft constitution in Part XIV entitled 'Special Provisions Relating to Minorities'.[15] However, some members of the Advisory Committee, Tajamul Hussain and H.C. Mookherjee, in a meeting of the committee on 30 December 1948, reopened the matter of political rights. The members felt that in the light of changed political conditions (Partition), as the committee had originally made its recommendations in 1947, it was not considered desirable that minorities should have reserved seats in the legislatures. This, it was said, could lead to further separatism; it also conflicted with the ideal of a secular democratic state. On 25 May 1949, Sardar Patel tabled the report of the Advisory Committee in the Constituent Assembly. The report read:

We have felt bound to reject some of the proposals placed before us partly because as in the case of reservation of seats in cabinets, we felt that a rigid constitutional provision would have made parliamentary democracy unworkable and partly because, as in the case of the electoral arrangements, we considered it necessary to harmonize the special claims of minorities with the development of a healthy national life. We wish to make it clear, however, that our general approach to the whole problem of minorities is that the state should be so run that they should stop feeling oppressed by the mere fact that they are minorities and that, on the contrary, they should feel that they have as honourable a part to play in the national life as any other section of the community. In particular we think it is a fundamental duty of the state to take special steps to bring up those minorities which are backward to the level of the general communities.[16]

The position was very clear: the minorities were not invested with political rights.[17]

Pandit Nehru subsequently articulated the compulsions behind the original moves to grant political rights to the minorities. History, he said, had proved that separate electorates had inflicted great damage to the country. Nevertheless, reservations were reluctantly recommended, because it was for the minorities to take the lead and say that they did not want them. '[I]n our heart of hearts', said Pandit Nehru,

we were not sure about ourselves ... but always there was this doubt in our minds, namely, whether we had not shown weakness in dealing with a thing that was wrong. So when this matter came up in another context, and it was proposed that we do away with all reservations except in the case of the Scheduled Castes, for my part I accepted that with alacrity and with a feeling of great relief, because I had been fighting in my own mind and heart against this business of keeping up some measure of separatism in our political domain.[18]

Political reservations, argued Jawaharlal Nehru, would isolate the minority in a democracy, and lead to the loss of goodwill and inner sympathy of the majority. 'So, ultimately the only way to proceed about it—whether from the point of view of the minority or from the point of view of the majority—is to remove every barrier which separates them in the political domain so that they may develop and we may all work together.'[19] Any demand for reservations betrayed a lack of trust in the majority, Nehru concluded.

The shift in Nehru's position can be traced in the main to the drastically altered political situation in the country. When the assembly initially met, there was hope that the Muslim League could be persuaded to join in the deliberations. It was also hoped that Partition could be avoided by the grant of definite assurances. By 1948, when the issue was reopened in the Advisory Committee and subsequently in the Constituent Assembly, Partition had created its own political reverberations. Now the need was to consolidate what had been left of the nation; the need was to prevent any move that might lead to further separatism. Political reservations were therefore dropped as potentially divisive. At the same time, the issue of the educational and cultural rights of different groups was taken seriously.[20]

However, when the Drafting Committee considered the report of the Advisory Committee in its meeting on 1 November 1947, certain modifications were made. Subclause (1) of the recommendations of the Advisory Committee originally read that 'Minorities in every unit shall be protected in respect of their language, script and culture, and no laws or regulations may be enacted that may operate oppressively or prejudicially in this respect.' This, in the process of becoming Article 23 of the draft constitution, was altered to read thus: 'Any section of the citizens residing in the territory of India or any part thereof having distinct language, script and culture of its own shall have the right to conserve the same.' The right was therefore widened to cover *all* sections of Indian citizens: any section of the citizenry had the right to conserve its culture, language, and script, while minorities based on religion or language had the right to establish educational institutions of their choice. This was done in order to allow people who moved from one state to another to preserve their language and culture. This became Article 29 of the constitution.

In the debate in the Constituent Assembly on 7 and 8 December 1947, Clause 2 of the recommendation of the Advisory Committee, which originally read that 'No minority whether based on religion, community or language shall be discriminated against in regard to admission into State educational institutions maintained by the state' was altered. Pandit Thakur Das Bhargava moved an amendment that was adopted by the house. The amended article read: 'No citizen shall be denied admission into any educational institution maintained by the State or receiving aid out of State funds on grounds only of religion, race, caste, language or any of them.' The original clause was meant to prevent discrimination against minorities in admission into state or state-aided institutions. This was converted into a general right of citizens to equality in admissions to institutions established by minorities themselves under the present Article 30 (1).

The Constituent Assembly in its debate on Article 23 rejected the demand that primary education should be in the mother tongue.[21] Begum Aizaz Rasul, Hasrat Mohani , Z.H. Lari, and M.N Kunzru supported the recommendation. Z.H. Lari insisted that educationists had widely accepted that education should be in the mother tongue, and that at many places such an opportunity did not exist for the minorities. His amendment, supported by Karimuddin and Begum Aizaz Rasul, read that any minority having a distinct language and script of its own should be entitled to have primary education imparted to its children in the medium of that language. H.N. Kunzru argued that it was one of the most important rights of the minorities to have primary education imparted in their mother tongue in areas where their numbers were sufficiently large. G.B. Pant, however, rejected the suggestion on grounds of practicality. He in fact dubbed the suggestion as reminiscent of the two-nation theory. Dr B.R. Ambedkar accepted the importance of primary education in the mother tongue, but was reluctant to make it a fundamental right enforceable in a court of law. In sum, while the constitution grants the right to preserve cultures to all groups, minorities have the exclusive right to manage their educational institutions.

Minority Rights and the Contemporary Moment

Admittedly, there is great temptation to interpret the adoption of the principle of group rights in terms of philosophical arguments that hold currency today, namely that individuals need access to their cultures for a variety of reasons. However, this would not only collapse two historically specific moments into one but also two distinct arguments belonging to different genres into one. Because theory is historically specific, theoretical arguments normally, even if not inevitably, address the historical context of their time.

Howsoever portentous the Indian constitution and the thinking on the form of the constitution since the 1920s may have been, the precise reasons that are being offered today in favour of minority rights were *not* a part of historical reasons offered fifty years ago. In effect, the reasons for the recognition that groups should have a right to their culture and religion had a great deal to do with the political situation of the 1920s. The grant of these rights has however become supremely controversial today, and it is time to buttress thinking on group rights by advancing other reasons and justifications that find ready resonance in much of the theoretical literature on the subject. The task, I may add, becomes urgent, for political developments in the country, particularly since the 1980s, have not proved overly felicitous for group rights in general and minority rights in particular. Therefore, even as I suggest that group rights were adopted historically for pragmatic reasons, the contemporary political moment, I believe, demands another form of argument for the grant and the protection of group/minority rights.

This is because, roughly the same time as theories of multiculturalism and minority rights were doing the rounds in the intellectual capitals of the Western world, India witnessed the onslaught of cultural nationalism which, as cultural nationalisms go, was not only exclusive but excessively dismissive of the rights of religious minorities to live on terms of equality in the polity. This lies of course in the nature of cultural nationalism, which seeking to build a unified and undifferentiated culture as the bedrock of the political community, marginalizes those communities whose belief systems may not fit in with those of the majority. Cultural nationalism simply challenges the democratic project of allowing space and recognition to all identities. It calls for the erasure of all specific identities and demands the constitution of a culturally homogeneous nation. This is cause for concern, for cultural or organic nationalism, as history shows us, is constructed on a ritualized and systematic suspicion of strangers (read minority groups), upon the privileging of one ethnic, linguistic, or religious community, and on calls to exterminate 'impurities' in the organic nation.

In India the project of Hindutva does all this: it appeals to the mythic unity of the Hindu people, invokes an ahistorical version of a glorious Hindu past, disparages minority identities, and demands conformity and homogeneity in order to accomplish two tasks. Both tasks, I might add, have serious implications for the future of a plural India in general and for the rights of minorities in particular.

The first task that the project seeks to accomplish is to define the nation in Hindu terms. 'India is essentially a Hindu country. My party emphasizes that India is one nation and not a multinational state,' L.K. Advani of the BJP stated emphatically.[22] Many defenders of Hindutva hold that the party has softened its stand on cultural nationalism after it came into power at the centre in March 1998. Yet Advani, in a speech to the national executive of the BJP in May 1998, stated vehemently that '[o]ur campaign for the Ram mandir in Ayodhya was a testimony to our commitment to the concept of cultural nationalism, without which not only the meaning of secularism but the very identity of India remains undefined.' The report carried this comment on his speech: '[i]n a surprise move, Mr Advani also sought to discount its [the BJP's] new-fangled moderate image by attributing part of its recent growth to the earlier Ayodhya agitation. He referred to the major role played by the issues of Ayodhya, Kashmir and swadeshi in extending the party's social base and consolidating its popular support.'[23] The somewhat troubling implications of this statement are more than apparent.

Secondly, in order to build a homogeneous nation that disallows or subsumes other ways of life, defenders of the Hindutva campaign systematically and insistently denigrate minority communities. In a tenacious, ordered, and subversive mode, the votaries of Hindutva cast suspicion on the moods and motivation of the community Hindutva is largely defining itself against: Muslims. Witness a sampling of some writings in the columns of the *Organizer*. One columnist writes: '[t]he crux of the insoluble Hindu–Muslim problem in India has been the Muslim clamour for being treated as a privileged minority and a master race deserving special rights and more than equal status by virtue of their being the pre- British rulers of India.'[24] Another columnist argues that '[a]dded to all these, is the false notion among the Indian Muslims that they are the descendants of the former rulers of India and, therefore, a superior ethnic lot.'[25] As recently as February 1997, the same columnist asks rhetorically the following question: why do elements of Muslim separatism in India continue to persist after Partition? How can we ensure that the Muslims in India will not seek another Partition on the same grounds? In the post-Partition period, he complains, the policies of the Congress followed the same logic as that of the British Raj and gave constitutional validity to Muslim identity under the deceptive name of minority rights. Having said that, the columnist proceeds to construct perverse stereotypes of the minority community. What we call the Hindu–Muslim question, he argues, is really a conflict between liberalism and obscurantism, between coexistence and confrontation, and between openness and seclusion. Ironically, he appropriates Gandhi for the purpose: '[t]hroughout their freedom struggle, Hindus, including Mahatma Gandhi, talked of getting freedom from one thousand years of slavery, meaning freedom not only from the British Raj but also from the traces of the earlier oppressive Islamic rule since the days of Mahmud of Ghazni. It is thus essential that the Muslims share the Hindu sense of physical, political and mental sufferings and atone for the injustices inflicted on Hindu order under the Islamic rule.'[26]

The thrust of all these diatribes is straightforward and unapologetic. Hindutva seeks to construct and legitimize the definition of the nation in largely Hindu terms by insistently devaluing minority identities. The flip side of legitimization is de-legitimization. L.K. Advani, presenting the 'soft' form of this ideology, has recently stated that his party accepts and celebrates the multi-religious, multilingual and multi-ethnic diversity of Indian society. He is however careful to state that it is united at its core by cultural nationalism. Muslims, he goes on to add, should learn to accept and respect symbols of 'national culture' like Ram, Krishna, Buddha, Mahavir, and Nanak, 'since civilization and culture form the basis of India's national identity'.[27] The cultural symbols that are said to 'unite' Indian society in this formulation are either Hindu or associated with reformist cults arising out of Hinduism.

Indeed, this happens to be the mild, softer version of Hindutva: the amended version, as observers will have it! The continuing majoritarian trends are, however, explicit. Witness Prime Minister Vajpayee's statement in parliament that the building of the Ram mandir in Ayodhya is an expression of the 'national sentiment'. The statement begs the questions: Whose nation? Whose sentiment? The answer is perhaps self-evident; what is important to note is that the ideology of Hindutva seeks to steamroller minority identities and erase constitutionally sanctioned rights in order to institute the one nation, one people notion.

All this inexorably led to the fanning of perverse passions in the cause of demolishing the Babri mosque in order to reverse history. These inflamatory statements were, in other words, to foretell the sequence of events that were to follow. For instance, in 1989 several hundred thousand bricks or Ramshilas made of 'local earth' were taken from five and a half lakh villages and towns scattered over the country by VHP and RSS cadres for the purposes of constructing the Ram mandir in Ayodhya.[28] The Shilanyas brought with it intensification of tensions and hostility, fractured communities and dismembered unities. Expectedly the desire to reclaim history expressed itself in provocative and incendiary oratory against the Muslim community.

Kota in Rajasthan witnessed its first communal riot after 33 years of harmony on 14 September 1989, which left 15 dead. Bihar was the worst hit with communal clashes in Hazaribagh, Sasaram, Darbhanga, Jharia, and Gaya, and elsewhere. Reports of civil liberties organizations revealed that Muslims were dragged out of trains and butchered, localities were destroyed, and entire villages such as Chanderi were burnt down. The personnel of the Bihar Military Police participated actively in the killings, by deliberately targeting Muslims. In Bhagalpur, as the procession carrying consecrated bricks approached Muslim-dominated areas, more and more people joined it and, swelling the numbers to almost 10,000, raised slogans demanding that Muslims should go to Pakistan and asserted that Hindustan is for Hindus. This expectedly led to resistance and bloody communal rioting. Hundreds of Muslims lost their lives in this carnage.[29]

The story was to repeat itself in 1990 when L.K. Advani traversed the country from Somnath to Uttar Pradesh in a Toyota vehicle disguised as a *rath*. The kind of hysteria that was whipped up in the process was unprecedented, with youths offering him cups of blood signifying their readiness to commit martyrdom, young children went to meet him armed with bows and arrows, and sadhus and women anointed his forehead with a *tilak*, often of blood. Once again, after the Babri mosque was demolished, the communal riots that erupted all over the country were arguably the worst since Partition.

After the BJP government came to power leading a coalition in 1998 and then in 1999, we have repeatedly seen the insistent physical targeting of the Christian minority in Gujarat, Orissa, and Uttar Pradesh. The Vishwa Hindu Parishad, for instance, has stated repeatedly that Christians must Indianize and sever links with churches abroad. Acharya Giriraj Kishore stated firmly that 'there is no point in having a dialogue unless and until they change their ways and accept that Christianity is not the only way to salvation.'[30] Indeed, this is only the milder form of denigration, for random groups attached to the Sangh Parivar have targeted the Christian minority in various ways from burning churches to murdering missionaries. Christmas in Gujarat is ridden with tension, even as Christians are repeatedly and insistently marked out for violence and worse.

What is more upsetting is the fact that dominant sections of the state and civil society seem to share the assumptions of Hindutva.[31] In *Manohar Joshi* vs *Nitin Bhaurao Patil* and eleven other cases known collectively as the Hindutva cases, the court was faced with the use of communal rhetoric in elections under the Representation of the People Act 1951.[32] The election of Shiv Sena/BJP candidates in the December 1987 elections to the state assembly in Maharashtra had been challenged as constituting corrupt practices under the act cited above. In an appellate judgement, whereas the Supreme Court found Bal Thackeray, among others, guilty of promoting interreligious hatred, it also managed to legitimize 'Hindutva' as a way of life in India. The use of the term, the court ruled, does not amount to corrupt practice during an election. No interpretation, stated the court, can confine the meaning of *Hindutva* to the narrow limits of religion alone, or equate it with fundamentalist Hindu religious bigotry. Hindutva, the court was to further argue denotes the content of Indian culture and heritage.

> [T]he term Hindutva is related more to the way of life of the people in the subcontinent. It is difficult to appreciate how in the face of these decisions the term 'Hindutva' or 'Hinduism' per se, in the abstract, can be assumed to mean and be equated with narrow fundamentalist Hindu religious bigotry, or be construed to fall within the prohibition in [section 123(a) or 93a).[33]

As Hindutva, stated the court, cannot be equated with fundamentalism, an appeal to Hindutva is not an appeal to religion, nor does it connote hostility to all persons who do not practice religion. Such words may be used in a speech to '*promote secularism* or to emphasize the *way of life* of the Indian people and the Indian culture or ethos or to criticize the policy of any political party as discriminatory or intolerant.'[34]

This is a deeply flawed judgement, institutionalizing and legitimizing, as it does, discriminatory practices and communal oratory. It is also however an indication of the dissolution of the national consensus on the rights of minorities to either their religion or to be represented in the public spaces of national culture (which is constituted by Hindutva) on their own terms. When groups are so denied space or visibility in the national arena, they are delegitimized and devalued simply because they have been excluded from the national vision. Cultural nationalism consequently delegitimizes those who do not find place in the mythologies of nationalism. Cultural nationalism, it appears, has been one of history's more serious mistakes, precisely because it gestures towards who is included and who excluded in the construction of the nation.

In sum, though group rights have been granted by the constitution, political practices have challenged the right of minority groups to their culture and religion. Therefore, it is time to reinforce the thinking on group rights by the addition of supplementary reasoning.

II. Group Rights and Minority Rights

Given the drastically communalized political situation in the country, it is obvious that we cannot just repeat or reiterate the arguments that were made when the group rights principle was accepted by the leadership of the freedom movement and by the members of the Constituent Assembly for pragmatic reasons. Alternatively, the defenders of the principle recognize that the political situation is somewhat different in the here and now, and that the extant historical situation demands a related but a different argument. In other words, we may find that though revisiting history is essential for our purpose, it is not sufficient to resolve ineluctable dilemmas, and that new political events and trends have forced us to shift/expand the grounds for defence. Before doing so, however, two small clarifications may be appropriate here. One, human rights usually pertain to the sovereign citizen of modern individualism. Thus, the right to freedom of religion is an individual right, and is a subset of the right to freedom. When we speak of minority rights, however, we speak of *group* rights; that is, the right of the group to maintain and perpetuate its practices and culture.

Secondly, I wish to clarify my use of the term minority here. A minority is a group that is numerically smaller in relation to the rest of the population; it is non-dominant to the extent that its values are either inadequately represented or not represented in the public sphere or in the constitution of societal norms; it possesses characteristics that differ from those of the majority group and, more importantly, wishes to preserve these characteristics. This definition of a minority is relational to the majority in terms of numbers, in terms of domination or lack of domination, in terms of possessing characteristics that are distinctive, and in terms of its desire to preserve these distinctive characteristics even if they conflict with the sensibilities of the majority.[35]

Having said that, let me begin this part of the argument with a focus on the individual right to culture.[36] Now, culture is an amorphous concept, but we can for the purposes of this argument conceptualize it as follows. Culture, let me suggest, provides its members with the cognitive and evaluative resources (I use the term resource not instrumentally but in the sense of historically constituted stocks of assets) to 'think with' or 'think through'. In other words, culture gives us assemblages of meaning that help us not only to negotiate our life and our experiences, but also to evaluate them as worthless or worthwhile, valuable or valueless, moral, immoral, or amoral. Alternatively, culture gives us the resources that enhance and deepen our personal faculties of reflection and judgement, even as we appropriate and pattern the world in the sense of making it comprehensible. The imperative of making the world intelligible, to map it into comprehensible categories is, as social psychologists have recognized, perhaps the first, even the most primary requirement, of human beings. Without access to the resources that help us to interpret and evaluate the world, we are simply left clueless.

Certainly, our use of the concepts provided by our culture may be so unguarded and unreflective, so unthinking and imperceptible, that we may not even realize that we are seeing the world through these lenses. Individuals do not for most of the time think consciously about why they think in a particular way, for cultural understanding is subterranean, pervading deep structures of cognition. What is important is that without access to the resources of our cultures we are rendered defenceless, bewildered, and lost. What is more important is that culture is not a structure; as a set of cognitive and evaluative resources it constitutes an openended system of meanings that can be interpreted by various individuals in different ways. Therefore, even as cultures constitute individuals, individuals renegotiate cultures.

Correspondingly, common access to the same structures of meaning constitutes a cultural community. This, however, does not mean that members of a community make the same sense of the world or that they cannot interrogate the meaning systems handed down by the community. Culture merely gives us the wherewithal to make sense of the world, but what we make of the world is another story. The moot point is that as communities provide a referent for understanding, individuals tend to identify with the cultural community.

Therefore, if we deny individuals access to his or her culture or community we not only deny them access to the cognitive and evaluative resources that aid their perception, we deny them fulfilment. As it is these very resources which allow an individual to identify with the community, denial of them diminishes individuals irreparably. There is more, for if the individual identifies with her community because this community provides her with the resources that aid cognition and evaluation, then her well being and her self respect are intimately and closely tied to the well being and self respect of the community. Therefore, if the community is, in Anthony Appiah's words, 'dissed' or if it is devalued, degraded, or subjected to perverse stereotypes, the self image of the member is simultaneously devalued. 'Slighting my culture,' writes Raz, 'holding it up for ridicule, denying its value, and so on, hurts me and offends my dignity. It is particularly offensive if the slight bears the imprimatur of my state or of the majority or official culture of my country.'[37]

In sum, I suggest that cultures and communities are a good for the individual, and that access to this good is of such overriding importance that we should secure this access through the grant of a right. The question that can logically follow is: if cultures are a good for the individual, why do we need only minority rights? Should not the right of each individual to culture and community be secured, irrespective of whether she/he belongs to the majority or the minority?

Note that if we place this argument, that access to culture is of overriding importance, in the context of formal equality, we will naturally arrive at the conclusion that each person counts equally and, therefore, all should have equal rights. This is both just and fair. However, as countless critics of formal equality have suggested, such actions may serve to reproduce existing inequality in society. To treat an unequal society equally is to perpetuate unequal distribution of assets. Equally, since different social weights are attached to different ways of life in any given society, minorities necessarily suffer from historically constituted discrimination and disadvantages. To treat every group equally will be to reproduce inequality among groups. In any case, the majorities do not suffer from the same disadvantages as minorities. Therefore, we need to treat minorities differently in accordance with the principle of substantive equality.

Gregory Vlastos provides us with a particularly graphic example of this. Suppose a New Yorker x, he argues, gets a letter from Murder Inc. threatening his life. To counter this threat several policemen and plainclothesmen are ordered to guard him over the next few weeks at a cost which is several times higher than the per capita cost of security to other citizens during the same period. Will this involve a departure from the general principle of equal right of all citizens to the security of their persons? Surely not. The allocation of greater resources and manpower to x's security, is not because he has a greater right to security than others. 'The greater allocation of community resources in x's favour, is made precisely because x's security rights are equal to those of other people in New York.'[38] Without the allocation of greater resources, x's security levels would plummet to zero, and therefore he should be given additional support to bring his security level up to normal.

The argument allows us to comprehend that we will have to treat cases of unequal placement unequally, in order to equalize access to the distribution of some good. There is nothing contradictory about an argument that states that, (a) we need to distribute rights unequally to ensure equality, or that (b) we protect whatever rights people already possess through the institutionalization of measures that the majority does not require, for the latter are already secure in their possession of the good.

We adopt both these courses, differential rights and protective measures, to realize the fundamental assumptions of equality. As Vlastos puts it: 'An equalitarian concept of justice may admit just inequalities without inconsistency if, and only if, it provides grounds for equal human rights which are also grounds for unequal rights of other sorts.'[39] If we apply these arguments to the case in hand, that is, the right of the members of minority groups to their cultural community, the identification of group with minority rights can be seen as both justified and fair.

Now at this point someone may legitimately object that our concern is with the right of the individual to culture; the fate of the community is not our concern. Communities decline, our objector can argue, because its members do not think it worthwhile to either invest in or regenerate the community. The onus, he can point out, rests on the members and the members alone. This is however an argument strongly reminiscent of apologetics for the marketplace. The flawed ideology of the market has been subjected to enough opprobrium and censure to bear repetition. What is important for the purpose of this argument is that we will probably be able to trace the reasons for the decline of minority cultures to the social environment. Cultures dwindle because they have been subjected to sheer indifference, intentional neglect, and deliberate dismissal. Languages decay because they have been purposefully marginalized (take the case of Urdu), groups lose historical memory because their histories have been denigrated and dismissed, communities lose their self-respect because they have been stereotyped in perverse ways.

In short, both the causes for the decay of minority groups, as well as the remedies for this, *have to be sought in wider society.* We can hardly place the responsibility for maintaining the community on its members, when other groups who are in a position to affect the fate of the community target it insistently and incessantly. In any case, whatever be the specific cause of decline, in the interests of equality and rights we need to halt or reverse it through the institutionalization of supportive environments for minority cultures. This is in perfect consonance with the demands of substantive equality, which suggests differential treatment for groups that require different treatment. Therefore, whereas majorities already have an advantage, inasmuch as their culture is reflected in the polity, minorities suffer from disadvantages which must be rectified in order to make them equal.

Individual and Group Rights

Secondly, our objector may wonder why individual rights to culture are not sufficient. The fact that we can easily reduce the right of cultural communities to exist, maintain, and reproduce themselves to the right of the individual to culture is debatable. For one, individual rights to the cultural community does not by any means guarantee that the community itself will be allowed to flourish or be respected. There is absolutely nothing, let us acknowledge, in the grant of a right that *guarantees the good the right is a right to*. For instance, we can state that p has the right to x, y, z by virtue of n, but we cannot guarantee that x, y, or z will be available to p. Unless we take steps to ensure x, y, or z are there for p to access, individual rights do not make sense. Communities have to *exist* for individuals within them to have rights.

However, as has increasingly become clear, minority communities that are profoundly vulnerable *cannot secure their own existence and reproduction* if wider social and political processes threaten them either through deliberate destruction or through 'benevolent neglect'. In such cases, the state will have to intervene in order to secure a supportive social and political environment for the minority group. There are very good reasons for doing so, for cultural narratives are widely recognized as a precondition for making intelligent judgements about the world. Bearing this in mind, let me hazard four propositions on minority rights.

1. Constituent communities are of overriding importance to their individual members as they provide them with cognitive and evaluative resources that help these members to render the world intelligible.
2. If the constitutive community is subjected to perverse and demeaning stereotypes, or ethnic targeting, this compromises the self-respect of the individual in the first case, and her right to life in the latter case.
3. It further follows that the right of the individual to life, dignity, and culture rests upon the *antecedent* right of the cultural community to exist, to reproduce its practices, and to be respected.

4. In this case we need to think of group rights as *conditional* rights, which enable and actualize individual rights. In other words, just as individuals need access to food in order to actualize the right to life, they need access to a flourishing culture so that their right to culture is actualized. This does not by any means entail that individuals have to stay locked within their cultures. We give to an individual the right to food, after which she can fast or diet, which is not our concern. Similarly, we should secure the right to culture by providing supportive political and social conditions, after which the direction in which the individual moves on is not our concern.

The point is that the move from individual rights to group rights can only be made when we recognize that the efficacy and validity of individual rights is *dependent* upon, or is contingent upon, the existence of group rights. If cultural communities are a good for the individual, this should be of enough overriding importance for us to secure access to cultural communities. However, the effectiveness of this right, recollect, depends on the existence of an active and flourishing community. Therefore, if a culture is decaying in a plural and a majoritarian society, or if a culture is sought to be assimilated into the majority culture, we have an obligation to institute a supportive social and political environment for that culture to flourish.

Since, as argued above, it is almost impossible for us to actualize individual rights when groups are targeted, group rights can be conceptualized as *conditional* rights for individual rights. They cannot be *reduced* to individual rights. The two rights are substantially different and will require the institutionalization of different measures. This is discussed in the last section. Now, however, let me move to another issue: that of the clash between individual and minority rights.

III. Some Problems with Minority Rights

Group rights is not however such a straightforward solution, for the rights of communities to their religion and culture can easily conflict with the rights of the members of the group to freedom and to equality. As history has shown, the moment a religious community stakes its claim to be considered the bearer of rights, it tends to suppress either dissent or any questioning of its credentials, let alone efforts to privilege civic rights over the obligations of the member to the community.

Consider the following case. In May 1995, the Supreme Court of India had to decide on an issue that had been raised by three special leave petitions. The issue simply was whether marriage between two persons professing the same religion dissolves if one of the partners converts to another religion. In this case, three Hindu married men had converted to Islam and married a second time. Subsequently, one of these men converted back to Hinduism abandoning his second wife, who continued to be a Muslim, and a child without adequate maintenance in accordance with the personal codes of Islam.

In its judgement on the 10 May 1995, the Supreme Court declared that unless an existing marriage was dissolved, bigamy is void and punishable under section 494 of the Indian penal code. The court ruled that the Hindu Marriage Act of 1955 does not recognize that conversion has the effect of dissolving the earlier marriage. It requested the central government to set up a committee to enact a conversion of religion act to check the abuse of religion, as well as to chart out a uniform civil code under the provision of Article 44 of the constitution. The act should provide that a citizen who abandons his religion cannot remarry unless he divorces his first wife. The judgement held that 'the second marriage of a Hindu husband after embracing Islam being violative of justice, equity, and good conscience would be void on the ground of natural justice.' The judgement went on to hold that though freedom of religion is at the core of our culture, 'religious practices, violative of human rights and dignity and sacerdotal suffocation of essentially civil and material freedoms, are not autonomy but oppression.'

Ten years earlier, in a similar judgement that aroused a political storm, Justice Y.V. Chandrachud had expressed concern over governmental inaction in enacting a uniform civil code for women. Interestingly, in both cases, the honourable justices had linked the question of gender justice to lack of national feeling among the minority community. In the earlier case the court had ruled that 'a common civil code will help in the case of national integration by removing disparate loyalties to laws which have conflicting ideologies.'

What is interesting for our purpose is that in 1995 the decision of the court led to violent reactions by the spokesmen of the Islamic community. Dr Sadiq, a Shia leader from Lucknow, stated that the Supreme Court verdict on bigamy was a contravention of the Islamic shariat and that it was not acceptable to the Muslim community. A stronger statement was made by the All India Muslim Personal Law Board, which urged the government to delete Article 44 of the constitution, and to declare that it did not intend to enact a uniform civil code. A large number of ulemas and Islamic jurists all over the country declared the decision of the court as open interference in Muslim personal law and declared that it was unacceptable to the Muslim community. The head of the board, Maulana Abul Hasan Ali Nadvi, stated that Muslims were required by religion to obey laws laid down in the Koran and the Hadith on matters relating to marriage, divorce, inheritance, will, and property.

Something of the same kind had happened in the Shah Bano case. The decision of the court had been met by marches, demonstrations, protest statements by self-styled patriarchal leaders of the community. That the woman had become the site for the construction of community identity and rights as a community was evident in the statement of the Jamiyat- al-ulema-i-Hind, which tellingly commented: 'the demand [for a code] is tantamount to a fundamental departure from the position that, in the presentday situation where the Muslim community is deeply entangled in a struggle for the search and safeguard of its self-identity, it is only personal law that can be a permanent guarantee of its preservation'. The statement is self-explanatory: the boundaries of the community were in both cases erected on the rubble that ensued from the collapse of gender injustice, and individual rights had suffered in the conflict between two rights.

Negotiating Individual and Group Rights

We thus arrive at the core of the problem faced by theories of minority rights. The call to view the individual in abstraction from the minority community carries the problem that justice will accrue neither to the individual nor to the community. However, the call for group rights can carry an equal number of dangers, for there is no guarantee that a group that asks for rights will be willing to grant rights to its own members.

Therefore, whereas we can argue that group rights provide the *pre-*

conditions for individual rights, we discern a problem the moment we recognize that groups can truncate the rights of their members to freedom or equality in the name of group identity. It may even be a part of the process whereby groups seek to represent themselves as coherent for the purposes of acquiring rights. Therefore, by no stretch of logic can we assume that a group which demands special rights in the body politic will as a matter of course extend these rights to its own members. We may, therefore, have to design practices and policies to protect the members of groups, even as we design policies and practices to protect the group in society.

It is true that political compulsions oblige us to accept practices that are deeply unfavourable to, say, gender justice: personal codes for one. There is, however, no reason, I suggest, why we cannot work out a politically and morally consistent position in this matter, or that the contingencies of political life do not prevent us from drafting out such a position on contentious issues. This has a twofold advantage. It will help us to approach the topic from a principled position, rather than from one that can be construed as paternalistic or opportunistic. It will also aid us in supporting members within the community who are struggling for reform in an ethical and principled manner. It is to the development of such a politically consistent, principled position that the argument in the succeeding section is addressed.

In a prefatory manner, we need to recognize that in this specific context we are really speaking of two genres or classes of rights. Neither can these rights be conflated, nor do they issue from the same kind of argument. These two sets of rights differ in their individualistic and communal aspects: they represent two distinct human goods, they derive their value from two separate human needs, and they are backed up by two altogether different philosophical arguments.

Firstly, individual rights—I refer specifically to civil rights to freedom and equality—address the capacity of the person to be a thinking, reflective being; a being who is able to question certain givens. On the other hand, community rights address the need to belong. As *identity* rights they refer to the quest for situatedness. The second right *situates* the individual and gives her a sense of her own moorings; the first one *allows the individual to question this setting.* Group rights are asserted against the wider society if and when the rights of that group are violated.

Individual rights are asserted both against community diktats and state regulations.

Certainly, these two sets of rights can be complementary: my right to my religion depends on the existence and the flourishing of my religious community . However, it is more than possible that these two rights may conflict. Admittedly, the conflict is not peculiar to these two sets of rights alone. Recall that rights have always conflicted with one another, famously the right to property and the right to equality. Nothing prevents various rights from clashing with one another even as nothing allows harmony between different sorts of rights. This is partly because rights are asserted from different moral positions, and partly because different rights are asserted in different historical periods that reflect the concerns of that particular age. After all, the political concerns of definite historical periods can be distinctive for that period, and need have nothing to do with the preoccupations of other historical ages.

Bearing this in mind, let me now recapitulate the argument advanced in this essay in favour of minority rights in order to suggest how the relationship between individual and group rights can be resolved. I have argued that:

1. The right of a community to exist and thrive has as its raison d'etre the belief that community is a substantive good for its members. Note, however, that I have privileged community not in itself *but because it enhances our conception of what it means to be human.* The right of the community to exist, to maintain, and to reproduce itself is a *precondition* for individual rights, for there is nothing in the act of asserting a right that guarantees the good that right is a right to. We have to establish the good through intentional actions, so that the right in question becomes meaningful. I began with the right of the individual to her cultural community as an individual right; I then arrived at the notion that the existence of a flourishing cultural community is a precondition for the individual to exercise that right. Therefore, by all notions of logic, the rights of the community cannot *substitute* for individual rights as they are the *preconditions* for individual rights.

Let me illustrate this point with an analogy. The socialist tradition of human rights insists that social and economic rights are indispensable to the meaningful exercise of political and civil rights. An individual who is forced to beg for charity or one eking out subsistence on the margins of society cannot be free. The point is well taken. Now consider this: we have a benevolent despot who grants a minimum income to all, who sees that no one is indigent or poverty-stricken, but who in the process takes away the right to freedom itself. If he, in other words, grants the right to food and to other material conditions of life, and takes away the right to freedom as authoritarian regimes do, he deprives the individual of core rights.

Now, one of the vital aspects of the core right to freedom is that we can demand that we be provided with the conditions that make freedom meaningful. If however we *acquire access to these conditions at the expense of the right itself*, consider the consequences. It may after all happen that the despot at some point of time deprives us of these material conditions. We cannot ensure that he will not do so: he has given us material goods as a matter of will, and takes them away as such. However, as our right to assert rights has been taken away from us, we will not be able to demand material conditions as a matter of right. We have simply lost the right we possessed to do so. We are left weaponless, because the *preconditions of that right have been substituted for that right itself.* Will that satisfy our proponents of socialism? Surely not.

My case for group rights is based on precisely this kind of reasoning. Group rights, which are meant in this chapter to secure individual rights, cannot substitute for individual rights. We cannot *replace individual rights with the preconditions of these rights*, for, in the end, we may be left with neither.

2. Let me now come to the second point why group rights cannot substitute for individual rights. The source of rights in the natural rights tradition is the moral nature of the human being, because the individual possesses moral worth. Therefore, violations of human rights are intrinsically wrong because they compromise the dignity of the human being, and treat her in ways that are less than human. The minimum condition a democratic, political community has to fulfil is that the human being must be treated with dignity. Below this we cannot permit ourselves to fall.

Arguably, for an individual to be treated with dignity for the reasons specified above, we must also treat her constitutive group with dignity. If however that constitutive group violates this dignity, if it *violates the very dignity it was meant to protect,* we betray the basic presumptions of the grant of group rights. The protection of human dignity requires as a precondition the treatment of the constitutive group with dignity; but a precondition, as argued above, cannot substitute for the right itself. Group rights have been designed for the purpose of covering some of the flanks of rights. They cannot replace human rights, *for the beginning and the end of my concern with group rights is the concept of human dignity.* This cannot be infringed for any reason

3. Thirdly, as I argued earlier, the principles of substantive equality tell us that groups which are disprivileged in the body politic must be granted special rights to their identity. Now, one of the principles of political consistency is that the argument must be generalizable. If this is so, then the same argument that we apply to the question of minority rights in society should be capable of proving relevant for analogous situations, that is, for individuals within the minority group itself via *the principle of political consistency.* To grant vulnerable groups in society special protection and withhold this protection from the vulnerable sections within the group would be both politically inconsistent as well as morally flawed.

Therefore, if minority communities seek revaluation in the dominant discourse through demand for respect and recognition, the minorities within the communities can equally seek revaluation through the demand that their identity should be respected. In short, if this strategy is available to groups in society, the same strategy should be available to minorities and individuals within the community. The same principle can thus give us an argument that applies across the board to both the minority community and the individual within the community. Consequently, if group rights are granted to minority communities on the grounds that their location in the body politic requires special treatment, then the argument that the same reasoning be applied to the sections *within* communities is both logical and moral.

Conclusion

Human rights exist on a dual level, that of the community and that of the individual. The ultimate aim is to provide conditions in which individuals can flourish. It is, of course, desirable that both sets of rights complement each other, but if such harmony is not forthcoming, the rights of the community will need to be 'trumped' by the rights of the individual.

Therefore, we need to think of community rights as *conditional* rights, and *when that right is overridden, it is not overridden by consequences, but by a concern for the core rights.*[40] While we still acknowledge the primacy and the priority of a right, we allow exceptions to be made, not on any other consideration but on the ground of core rights. The only ground for limiting a right is the need to uphold a core right.

Notes and References

1. A detailed argument on this issue has been made in my earlier work, *Beyond Secularism: The Rights of Religious Minorities*, Oxford University Press, New Delhi, 1999.
2. Michael Sandel, *Liberalism and the Limits of Justice*, Cambridge University Press, New York, 1982, p. 150.
3. Ronald Dworkin, *A Matter of Principle*, cited in Will Kymlicka, *Multicultural Citizenship*, Clarendon Press, Oxford, 1985, p. 83.
4. Will Kymlicka, *Liberalism, Community, and Culture,* Oxford University Press, Oxford, 1989.
5. Ian Brownlie, 'The Rights of Peoples in Modern International Law', in James Crawford (ed.), *The Rights of Peoples*, Clarendon Press, Oxford, 1988, pp. 1–16 in 2–3.
6. The second claim identified by Brownlie, i.e. to land, is applicable to the case of tribals in India and indigenous people in settler countries. The third specific claim relates to secessionist movements. What is of interest to me here is the first claim identified by Brownlie, i.e. the demand for positive action for the maintenance of cultural identity. Ian Brownlie, 'The Rights of Peoples', p. 4.
7. Article 30 reads that '(1) All minorities whether based on religion or language, shall have the right to establish and administer educational institutions of their choice. (2) The state shall not, in granting aid to an educational institution discriminate against any educational institution on the ground that it is under the management of minority, whether based on religion or language.'
8. It is perhaps worth noting in this context that Gandhi drew religious groups into the freedom movement as groups and not as atomized individuals. Critics of his strategy have pointed out that he widened rather

than closed religious differences through the pursuit of this strategy, but arguably his recognition of the strength of religious identification in the country propelled him to adopt this strategy. His act, as Ravinder Kumar points out, 'was an act of faith and hope that different religious communities, through common struggle against the British government, would fuse their identities into a new nation held together by certain common objectives and certain shared ideals.' Ravinder Kumar, 'Nationalism and Social Change', in *Essays in the Social History of Modern India.*, Oxford University Press, New Delhi, 1983, p. 29.

9. In 1927, thirty prominent Muslims met in Delhi on a common platform to surrender separate electorates provided that Muslims were given representation in the legislative councils of Punjab and Bengal in proportion to their population, that one-third of the seats were reserved in the Central Legislature for Muslims, that Sind was recognized as a separate province, and that reforms were introduced in the North Western Frontier Province. The Congress was reluctant to accept these terms, and the Muslim League stayed away from the All Party Conference that had met to draw up a constitution because of the rejection of reservation of seats.
10. Jawaharlal Nehru, 'Note on Minorities', *Jawaharlal Nehru: Selected Works*, vol. 4 (ed.) S. Gopal, Jawaharlal Nehru Memorial Fund, 1st Srs, Orient Longman, New Delhi, pp. 259– 60.
11. See Iqbal A. Ansari. (ed.), *Readings on Minorities Documents and Perspectives,* Institute of Objective Studies. Delhi, 1996, vol. 2, pp. 145–50.
12. *Constitutional Provisions of the Sapru Committee,* Padma Prakashan, Bombay, 1945.
13. *Constituent Assembly Debates,* vol. 2, 20–27 January 1947, Lok Sabha Secretariat, New Delhi, p. 331.
14. B. Shiva Rao, *The Framing of India's Constitution. Select Documents,* vol. 2, N.M. Tripathi, Bombay, 1968, pp. 396–402.
15. Article 292 and 294 of the draft constitution provided for a reservation of seats in proportion to the population of religious minorities under joint electorates in both the central and the state legislatures. This provision was to be reviewed after ten years. Article 296 provided that the claims of religious minorities shall be taken into consideration along with the consideration of merit and efficiency in appointment to public services. Article 299 provided for the appointment of special officers at the central and state levels to report on all matters relating to the safeguards provided for minorities.
16. B. Shiva Rao, *The Framing of India's Constitution. Select Documents,* vol 2, pp. 416–17.

17. The Sapru Committee recommended that ten per cent of the seats in the Union legislature would be reserved for special interests. The remainder of the seats would be distributed among the religious communities. These communities would also be represented on the union executive. In the interests of national unity, it was proposed that Muslims be persuaded to opt for joint electorates with reserved seats. The committee recommended that the reservation of seats for religious minorities in the central assembly should be at par with those of the Hindus, despite the great disparity in popular strength.
18. *Constituent Assembly Debates,* vol. 8. pp. 329–30.
19. Ibid., p. 331.
20. On 19 April 1947, the Constituent Assembly sub-committee on Cultural and Educational Rights of Minorities, in its interim report, made certain suggestions. These were based on K.M. Munshi's note circulated among the members of the sub-committee on 16 April 1947, under the direction of the Fundamental Rights Committee. The note sought adequate protection of the right of the minorities to their language, script, primary education in the mother tongue, and non-discrimination in state aid to minority schools. The sub-committee prepared an Interim Report of 19 April 1947 that carried the following recommendations.

    (1) All citizens are entitled to use their mother tongue and script thereof, and to adopt, study or use any other language and script of their choice.

    (2) Minorities in every unit shall be adequately protected in respect of their language and culture, and no government may enact any laws or regulations that may act oppressively or prejudicially in this respect.

    (3) No minority whether of religion, community or language shall be deprived of rights or discriminated against in regard to admission into State educational institutions, nor shall any religious instruction be compulsorily imposed on them.

    All minorities, whether of religion, community or language, shall be free in any unit to establish and administer educational institutions of their choice, and they shall be entitled to state aid in the same manner and measure as given to similar State-aided institutions.
21. When this report came to be considered in the advisory committee, considerable controversy erupted. The clause seeking to protect the mother tongue was seen as superfluous and was deleted, though K.M. Munshi argued at great length that the clause had a precedent in the Polish treaty, which was later incorporated in the Polish constitution. Objections were raised that the right to establish and administer educational institutions

would perpetuate communal institutions, and that the state should not aid these institutions. However, the committee passed the clause by a majority vote. The advisory committee thereby recommended that minorities in every unit will be protected in respect of their language, script, and culture, and that no laws or regulations may be enacted which may operate oppressively or with prejudice in this respect. Secondly, no minority, whether based on religion, community or language, shall be discriminated against in regard to admission to state educational institutions, nor shall religious instruction be imposed upon them. Thirdly, all minorities, whether based on religion, community or language, shall be free to establish and administer educational institutions of their choice, and that the state in providing for aid to schools shall not discriminate against such institutions. The Constituent Assembly on 1 May 1947 adopted these clauses without any modification, with the exception of sub clause 2, which had stated that no religious instruction will be imposed on the minorities. This was deleted.

22. Interview on CNN on 29 May 1991. Cited in Gyanendra Pandey, 'The Civilized and the Barbarian: The "New" Politics of Late Twentieth Century India and the World' in idem (ed.), *Hindus and Others. The Question of Identity in India Today*, Penguin Books, New Delhi, 1993, pp. 1–23, p. 15.
23. Bhaskar Roy 'BJP Must Improve Performance says Advani', *Times of India*, 3 May 1998, p. 1.
24. V.P. Bhatia, 'The Panipat Syndrome', *Organiser*, 10 Dec. 1995, p. 13.
25. Ram Gopal, 'The Mystery of Wailing Muslims. Ailing Hindus', *Organiser*, 16 Feb. 1997, pp. 2, 17, p. 2.
26. Ibid., pp. 2, 17.
27. *Pioneer*, 14 June 1997
28. The village elders and pujaris had consecrated the bricks by wrapping them in saffron cloth, worshipping them for several days, and carrying them in processions throughout the country to the radial spot at Ayodhaya. Conversely, the earth, which was dug up in Ayodhya for the foundation stone laying ceremony, was redistributed to different parts of India. All in all, when the foundation stone ceremony or the Shilanyas began on 9 November 1989, 2,500 VHP and Bajrang Dal volunteers had brought 1,67,063 Ramshilas to Ayodhya. Among them were three silver-coated bricks brought from Gujarat and Ghaziabad. *Hindustan Times*, 8 Nov. 1989.
29. The close co-relation between the routes of Ram shila puja, the communal violence of September-October, and the electoral gains of the BJP in

the 1989 elections is clear. Analysts estimate that out of the constituencies the BJP won in the 1989 elections, 47 were in those areas which had seen wide-scale rioting: Gujarat, Madhya Pradesh, Bihar, Rajasthan, and Uttar Pradesh. In the state assembly elections in March 1990, the BJP won in Madhya Pradesh, Rajasthan, and Himachal Pradesh, and secured a large number of seats in Gujarat and Maharashtra. In 1991, the BJP became the second largest party in parliament with 119 seats, expanding its vote share from 11.4 per cent in 1989 to 19.9 per cent in 1991. The rest is history: the demolition of the mosque and the transformation of the party into a party of government leading a coalition at the centre in the 1998 and 1999 elections.

30. *Hindu,* 11 March 2001, p. 1.
31. The Supreme Court had to decide whether 12 elected representatives in the BJP/Shiv Sena government in Maharashtra, that included the Chief Minister Manohar Joshi and the Shiv Sena chief Bal Thackeray, had engaged in corrupt practices under the Representation of the People Act. Section 123 (3) of the act makes appeals to religion, race, caste, community, or language, or the use of or the appeal to religious and national symbols for the purpose of winning the election or for prejudicely affecting the election of any other person, corrupt practices. Section 123 (a) of the act prohibits the promotion of feelings of enmity or hatred between the people on grounds of religion, race, caste, community, or language for the purposes of winning the election or for prejudicing the prospects of any other candidate winning the election. The court found several of the accused, including Bal Thackeray, guilty of promoting religious enmity and hatred. *Manohar Joshi* vs *Nitin Bhaurao Patil,* 1995, 7 SCALE 30 , *Ramesh Yeshwant Prabhoo* vs *Prabhakar Kasinath Kunte and Ors,* 1995. 7 SCALE 1, and ten others
32. AIR 1996. SC 796, also 1996, (1) SCC 169. Thackeray wrote an inflamatory editorial in the journal *Samna* on 8 December 1992, which is held to have sparked off the riots in Mumbai. In 1993 the Congress government in Maharashtra set up the Srikrishna commission under Justice B.N. Srikrishna to inquire into the riots. Six cases were filed by the police against Thackeray for inflammatory writing. In 1996 the Shiv Sena government withdrew four of the six cases and left two pending. In July 2000 the Congress/NCP government in Maharashtra decided to arrest Thackeray, a move that prompted the latter to make even more inflammatory statements. Three Shiv Sena ministers and the Law Minister in the Central Government resigned on the issue. On 25 July Thackeray was arrested under Section 153 (a) of the penal code, and produced before

the additional chief metropolitan magistrate of the Bhoiwada court. B.P. Kamble dismissed the case on the grounds that it was time barred.

33. Cited in Brenda Cossman and Ratna Kapur, *Secularism's Last Sigh*, Oxford University Press, Delhi, 1999, p. 20.
34. Ibid., p. 21, emphasis mine
35. However, the delineation of these characteristics may not result in what can be euphemistically termed the minority 'problem'. (I am using the term 'problem' synonymously with an issue that has become contentious, and that seems irresolvable because views around it are irreconcilable.) The status of minorities does not become a problem either when their numbers are smaller than that of the majority, or when they are inadequately represented or not represented at all in the public sphere and societal norms, or when they form distinctive groups that possess specific attributes, or when this group shows a sense of solidarity in wanting to preserve its characteristics. The minority 'problem' arises when the wish to preserve these distinctive attributes in the form of symbolic practices, or in the demand for autonomy, is politically constructed as being unacceptable to the majority. It is when the majority perceives and interprets these practices as offensive or, more importantly, when the majority represents these practices as offensive, that the status of minorities is translated into a political problem. Alternatively, it is when the majority seeks to stifle the identities of minorities by demanding that they assimilate, and when the minority resists the erosion of its identity which the call of assimilation entails, that we have a political problem on our hands. The logical culmination of this is the construction of a phenomenon called majoritarianism, and the converse phenomenon called minorityism. If a minority group is not averse to assimilation—after all the Welsh people have assimilated into English society—we do not face a problem. On the other hand, the insistence of Irish Catholics to preserve their specific religion constitutes a political problem. Equally, when majorities are content to let other groups live their lives in relative independence, as under the millet system found in the Ottoman Empire, the problem does not arise in quite this way.
36. I am perfectly cognizant of the fact that religion cannot be conflated with culture, but religion is one of the defining moments of culture, and therefore I employ the two terms interchangeably.
37. Joseph Raz, 'Multiculturalism. A Liberal Perspective', *Dissent*, Winter 1991, p. 72.
38. Gregory Vlastos, 'Justice and Equality', in *Theories of Rights* (ed.) Jeremy Waldron, Oxford University Press, Oxford, pp. 41–76 , p. 19.

39. Gregory Vlastos, 'Justice and Equality', p. 49.
40. To my mind, there are four such core rights: the right to life, liberty, equality, and the right to assert rights. The right to assert rights is particularly important because different rights are asserted at different times in response to different situations. For instance, the entire issue of displacement has thrown up a new right: the right to habitat. Therefore, people must have the right to assert rights even as we discover new conceptions of what it means to be human, for after all rights supervene upon a category we call human.

10

SEX EQUALITY, LIBERTY, AND PRIVACY
A Comparative Approach to the Feminist Critique[1]

MARTHA C. NUSSBAUM

> Introduction of Constitutional Law in the home is most inappropriate. It is like introducing a bull in a china shop. It will prove to be a ruthless destroyer of the marriage institution and all that it stands for. In the privacy of the home and the married life neither Art. 21 nor Art. 14 have any place. In a sensitive sphere which is at once intimate and delicate the introduction of the cold principles of Constitutional Law will have the effect of weakening the marriage bond.
>
> —Delhi High Court, in *Harvinder Kaur* vs *Harmander Singh*, 1984

Privacy and Feminist Politics

The pursuit of sex equality through constitutional law has sometimes taken a detour through the disputed and murky concept of privacy. The United States, lacking an explicit provision for sex equality in its constitution, and having failed in the 1960s to amend it to add one, revived the once-discredited tradition of substantive due process; that is, of reading substantive rights into the notions of 'life and liberty' in the due process clauses of the Fifth and Fourteenth Amendments, closely analogous to Article 21 of the Indian constitution. The tradition had gone into eclipse after a period early in the twentieth century, during which substantive due process was used by the court to strike down a number of socially progressive laws protecting the rights of workers, including minimum wage and maximum hours laws. The court had held that such laws violated rights of employers, and that these rights derived constitutional status from the vague notion of 'life and liberty'. Criticism of these decisions mounted, within and outside the court, until the key case, *Lochner* vs *New York*,[2] was finally overruled in 1934—after the court had, in the interim, invalidated 200 pieces of progressive economic legislation.[3] After this, substantive due process was viewed for a long time as a retrogressive and discredited strategem.[4]

Thirty years after the overruling of *Lochner*, however, in a range of cases dealing with contraception and abortion, the US Supreme Court again returned to the due process clause and the allegedly substantive rights contained in it, recognizing a right to privacy that was admittedly nowhere explicit in the constitution. In a famous and much-discussed opinion, Justice Douglas claimed that 'specific guarantees in the Bill of Rights have penumbras, formed by emanations from those guarantees that help give them life and substance.'[5] Declaring unconstitutional a Connecticut law that made the use of contraception by married couples illegal, Justice Douglas argued that a right to privacy resides in the 'penumbras' of several explicit provisions, including above all the due process clauses, but including, also, the Fourth Amendment's strictures against unreasonable and unwarranted search and seizure, the First Amendment's guarantee of freedom of speech (which was interpreted to have freedom of association in its 'penumbra'), the Third Amendment's prohibition of quartering of soldiers in people's houses in time of peace, and the Ninth Amendment's tantalizing remarks about other rights 'retained by the people'. Other cases soon followed, recognizing this right in areas highly relevant to women's equality: most notoriously, *Roe* vs *Wade*,[6] which recognized a woman's right to abortion.

Is privacy a useful concept and one that gives good guidance in law and public policy? Also, is it a concept that helps law advance the cause of sex equality? I shall answer 'no' to both these questions. A generally negative answer to the first question has been been given before, most influentially by Judith Jarvis Thomson in her pathbreaking and deservedly much-cited paper.[7] I shall be agreeing with Thomson that the interest in protecting privacy is really a cluster of distinct interests, although it is not important to my argument to take sides on the disputed question of whether it is always best to regard the privacy interest as *derivative* from these other interests.[8] We could however accept Thomson's conclusion that privacy is essentially a cluster concept best analysed in terms of a plurality of distinct interests, without thereby concluding that it is a useless or even pernicious concept for legal and political purposes, or a concept ill-suited to advance the interests of sex equality. I shall also argue for the latter position, appealing to considerations most of which are familiar from a tradition of feminist criticism that links American and Indian feminists.

I shall not, however, agree with some very influential voices in that tradition, concluding that the notion that we need to replace privacy is simply that of equality.[9] Instead, I shall argue that we articulate the issues in the most perspicuous way if we recognize, in addition to the interest in equality or non-subordination, a plurality of distinct human liberties as all deserving state protection. Among these are some that have been associated with the concept of privacy: for example, the freedom to be free from unreasonable and unwarranted search and seizure, the freedom of movement and travel, the freedom of association, the freedom to control in certain ways the public use of information about oneself. While these, I shall argue, should not be swept under the umbrella of privacy, they also should not be, and could not be, funnelled into equality. Thus we are left with what we might have thought we had all along: a plurality of distinct vital human interests, all of which should be enumerated, and all in need of constitutional protection.

While many scholars have analysed the role of privacy in constitutional law and related political and legal discourse simply by reference to the US experience, focusing on India helps such an analysis move forward. It is always valuable to look at how issues of vexing complexity arise differently in different cultural contexts, because comparison helps both cultures clear their heads by attaining a fresh perspective on distinctions that each has come to regard as habitual. The Indian constitutional tradition, during its fifty years of life, has both committed itself firmly to sex equality and, more recently, has introduced a right of privacy modelled on the US privacy right as recognized in *Griswold* and *Roe*. Exploring the tensions that have arisen between privacy and equality in the Indian tradition, we will see, I believe, new and strong reasons to distrust the notion of privacy, and some promising paradigms of how that concept may be replaced by a public recognition of both an interest in equality and a plurality of distinct interests in liberty as all deserving state protection.

The Indian constitution, and the tradition of interpretation that articulates it, are in some ways better equipped than the US constitution to recognize both the interest in equality and a plurality of distinct liberty interests, precisely because it leaves less room for vague and confusing appeals to privacy, filling more of the gaps by an explicit discussion of equality and of other specific protected interests. It also happens, however, that in recent years Indian constitutional jurisprudence has borrowed wholesale the problematic privacy jurisprudence of the US Supreme Court, using it to fill gaps in the understanding of protected liberties in areas ranging from unwarranted search and seizure to informational privacy to bodily integrity and personal autonomy. I shall argue that this direction has generated a number of confusions, some familiar, some less so. Looking at the confusions, and especially at their dire consequences for issues of sex equality, helps us see why it is always problematic to rely on this messed-up notion. Such a stratagem can eventually lead only to confusion, and to setbacks for women's interests.

I shall begin, therefore, with some preliminary discussions of cultural context and comparison, and of some significant differences between the US and Indian constitutional traditions. I shall then introduce the most important feminist objections that have been made to privacy as an organizing concept, and sketch my own preferred approach, referring, as I do so, to important Indian cases. My treatment of the cases will focus on the long-contested issue of 'restitution of conjugal rights', but I shall consider also significant cases that deal, respectively, with issues of police surveillance and solitary confinement. (I shall leave aside the informational area in this essay, though I shall refer to it briefly.)

Privacy and Cultural Difference

Before the argument can even begin, we need to establish that we are entitled to speak of the concept of privacy when addressing Indian culture. There is a familiar canard about non-Western societies, that they don't ascribe the same value we do to privacy. This canard gets a particularly tenacious grip on talk about India, as Westerners who come to India briefly often feel that they lack expected sorts of privacy there, and that, sadly, nobody cares. This sentiment was vividly, if chauvinistically, expressed by Paul Ehrlich in *The Population Bomb*, when describing a taxi ride in Delhi:

> The streets seemed alive with people. People eating, people washing, people sleeping. People visiting, arguing, and screaming. ... People, people, people, people. As we moved slowly through the mob, hand horn squawking, the dust, noise, heat, and cooking fires gave the scene a hellish aspect. Would we ever get to our hotel?[10]

This extraordinarily chauvinistic description (which might suggest that Ehrlich has never visited New York) is nonetheless typical of a way in which many Americans react when they visit a strange culture where the general sense of strangeness combines with particular experiences of difference, and indeed India does provide such particular experiences. Americans are likely to be surprised, for example, by a relative absence of regard for or interest in the personal solitude of the proverbial 'room of one's own' in family customs across class and region. Personal solitude is at least one of the things that is not too misleadingly connoted by the term 'privacy'.

These experiences of course show us nothing about whether there is a value of privacy in Indian culture—even if we could assume that there is such a thing as 'Indian culture', or that the places a middle-class American visitor visits give us any representative idea of that hypothetical entity. They show that India draws certain concrete lines in different places from America. If however we consider the general meanings of 'privacy' typically acknowledged as most salient in American legal and philosophical discussions of these matters, Indians also mark each of the notions as salient, and ascribe some positive value to their protection.

1. *Information*. 'One of the human interests most commonly associated with the term 'privacy', and sometimes said to be the primary or only such interest,[11] is the interest in controlling the access to and dissemination of information about oneself. Not surprisingly, in India as in America, and probably every other place in the world, people recognize that certain types of information about oneself are privileged;

that one is entitled to conceal such information, and that it is bad for outsiders to publicize it without consent. Case law in India prominently recognizes the confidentiality of medical records,[12] and there are similar issues about other personal information, about libel and slander, about the entire range of so-called privacy concerns of an informational character.[13] People's preoccupations in these areas are not very different from the preoccupations of Americans, although, of course, concrete lines are drawn differently in different places.

In general, it would be extraordinary if there was any human culture in which people were not concerned with secrecy and the concealment of personal information; certainly literary works from all around the world persistently revolve around such themes. Even in cultures in which there is virtually no personal solitude we nonetheless discern a keen concern to protect personal information from access. One does not have to have a secluded bedroom to have a secret.[14]

2. *Modesty and Surveillance of the Body.* Another interest very commonly associated with the term 'privacy' is the interest in controlling access to one's body: by touch, sight, and other forms of surveillance. Some would argue that this interest is reducible to the interest in control over personal information; but most theorists generally agree that there is a distinct further interest in protecting one's person from unwanted observation or touch.[15]

Here differences of class, sex, and region construct major internal differences within each nation, but again, we can say that in India as in the United States, there is a deep concern for keeping certain parts of the body, and certain bodily acts, hidden from the sight of others, and also a more general concern that, whatever one is doing, one should not be watched without one's consent. Indian lines are drawn differently from American ones in some concrete cases: but here it is India, on the whole, that more jealously guards the relevant areas of privacy. There is no stratum of society in which people do not seek an unobserved place for urination and defecation. Poor people sometimes walk an extremely long way from their dwellings in order to find such privacy.[16]

Lest someone suggest that this concern reflects a borrowing of Western values, let me quickly mention that it is among the most ancient and deeply traditional concerns of both Hindu and Muslim cultures.

The Quran, famously, enjoins modesty for both men and women, and modesty on both sides entails not looking in lascivious ways at the bodies or activities of others.[17] There are times when the symmetry of these provisions is ignored and the protection of modesty is applied to women only, but Muslim writers frequently note that this is a distortion of the tradition.[18] As for ancient Hindu law, along with the elaborate focus on rules for bathing, tooth-brushing, etc., there is equally elaborate focus on rules for privacy in urination and defecation.[19] In general, one must never urinate on the roadway, in rivers or water, on grassy or beautiful spots; one should urinate and defecate away from human habitation and not upwind of such a habitation. These ancient prohibitions apply, of course, only to the 'twice-born' castes, but they generate a social norm to which others, too, are responsive. Certainly the idea that public urination is a violation of religious law plays at least some role in generating enduring social custom.[20]

Of course, although Americans sometimes talk as if we value this sort of privacy highly, we actually do not have nearly as strong a sense of impropriety about public excretion. Men urinate more or less anywhere they need to, although occasionally this is punished by law.[21] Women are permitted the same courtesy in certain contexts, such as that of public running. Even semi-public defecation is a commonplace in any long-distance race, where the Portajohns always have long lines and runners do not want to lose ten minutes from their time.[22] By contrast, in India it is utterly unacceptable for a woman to urinate in public, even when circumstances make this a highly desirable option.

Indian customs also prescribe an intense concern with modesty in personal dress: women still rarely wear shorts, and athletic clothes typically cover the legs and at least the shoulders. In the US, of course, one would not need to have any such thoughts about modesty, as the only clothing that would cause dismay would be an entirely topless outfit for a woman, or total nudity for a man.

Finally, privacy with regard to the dwelling place has also been recognized in Hindu law from ancient times. Cases dealing with new windows or doors that enable someone to overlook another person's dwelling place allude to a customary 'right of privacy' in this regard, and cite ancient sources for it.[23]

As this observation already indicates, law in India reflects this anxious concern for privacy in the sense of modesty, protecting to almost absurd lengths a person's right to control the access of others to any sight of the person. Section 509 of the Indian Penal Code of 1860 makes it a crime to intrude upon the privacy of a woman with the intent of insulting her modesty. (This is only one of the numerous laws dealing with issues of modesty, which have lately been used as a major resource in feminist struggles for protection against sexual harassment).[24] Furthermore, even though such laws are more likely to protect middle-class than working-class women, there is at least some legal recognition that the value of privacy extends to all: in a 1962 case involving a police raid on a brothel, the court found it legally unacceptable that the police officer walked into a prostitute's bedroom 'without even the civility of a knock or warning to her to prepare for the intrusion'.[25] As we shall see, the issue of unreasonable searches assumes a large place in Indian privacy jurisprudence.

Another sign of the value attached to privacy in this sense is found in laws governing housing construction. Elaborate easement laws prohibit construction in which one person's window will command a view through another person's window: a property owner, to ensure that this does not happen, may acquire an easement over the property of a neighbour, preventing him from erecting such a window. This principle is based on Hindu customary law and has existed in codified form since 1773. In some states it is judicially enforced under the Indian Easements Act of 1882.[26] Obviously this approach, the rationale for which focuses on the modesty of women, is ill suited to present-day urban living.

3. *Autonomy or Liberty.* It is however a third aspect of the concept of privacy (or an alleged such aspect) that is most at stake in our cases concerning sex equality: this is the interest in decisional autonomy or liberty in certain areas especially definitive of the self. It is this decisional type of privacy that is invoked in *Griswold* and *Roe*, and it is this aspect, too, that most centrally figures in Indian cases concerning the restitution of conjugal rights. I shall shortly be arguing that this is the aspect of 'privacy' most misleadingly brought under that concept, but I need to discuss it at least briefly, as it has frequently been suggested by some American feminists that the interest in self-governed choice is an outgrowth of 'Western individualism', and is foreign to non-Western cultures.[27]

We might stop with the Preamble to the Indian constitution, which states in the most unequivocal terms that the liberty and dignity of the individual are central aims of the nation. It however seems to me important to state, too, that Indian male traditions attach an extremely high value to decisional autonomy for males, and that more recent feminist traditions insist on asserting this same value in the case of women. Rabindranath Tagore was among the leaders: his character Mrinal, in the 1914 short story 'Letter From a Wife', writes to her husband, 'I found myself beautiful as a free human mind'—and it is this conception of herself that led her to leave a life in which she could have no decisional freedom. She invokes longstanding (if dissident) Hindu traditions of female liberty in her defence: the Rajput queen Meerabai, who left her husband and became an itinerant singer in service of her conception of god. [28] Today, in women's organizations in India, the same idea is ubiquitous. Women strive for greater control over finances, working conditions, the daily conditions of existence.[29] Often the precedent of India's own independence struggle is invoked: just as India could only become independent of her colonial oppressor by pursuing economic and political self-sufficiency, so too women will only be free from their oppression at the hands of men when they achieve a measure of economic and political control and autonomy. This is more or less a cliché of the Indian women's movement; it's what women's banks, women's labour unions, and even literacy programmes for girls, are seen as all about: increasing control over the important decisions that make one's life. (It works: female literacy has been shown to be the single most important factor in enabling women to hold down the number of children they bear.[30])

To some extent I have simplified the complex and tangled concept of privacy by focusing on these three issues only. I hope however that this cursory treatment suffices to establish that we are not engaging in mindless acts of colonialism when we approach India with questions about privacy in view.

The US and Indian Constitutions: Fundamental Rights, Equal Protection, Due Process

I shall now set the stage for discussion of the Indian cases by characterizing some of the central features of the Indian constitution, and comparing it to the relevant features of that of the US. India, like the

US, has a written constitution with an enumerated list of fundamental rights; it also has a Supreme Court that is the final interpreter of the constitution, and which has increasingly seen its function as similar to that of the US Supreme Court. Thus judicial review of statutes has become increasingly common in India, though it was not so initially; US cases are frequently cited as precedents.

Several differences between the two documents are important for the tradition I am about to discuss. First, the Indian document is in many respects much more explicit than its US counterpart in regard to the rights and entitlements of citizens enjoying constitutional protection. The Fundamental Rights are in some central cases described as positive entitlements to which 'All citizens shall have the right', rather than simply in terms of what legislators may *not* do. The US document is typically negative in its expression, and consequently vague about positive entitlements.[31]

Moreover, whether positively or negatively described, the Indian rights are typically set out in considerable detail. First, each particular right is discussed at greater length, with a clear intent to resolve certain disputes that have plagued the US tradition. Thus, for example, Article 15, concerning non-discrimination on grounds of religion, race, caste, sex, or place of birth, contains an explicit provision for affirmative action for both lower castes and women and children.[32] The endless debates and agonies of the US context are thus avoided—unless opponents of affirmative action should prove able to amend the constitution. At the same time, although the non-discrimination provision is still confined to public accommodations, there is an explicit and rather broad definition of the extent and nature of those accommodations, plainly designed to resolve troublesome issues of discrimination that plague specific minorities. Second, there is simply a larger list of explicit entitlements, including equality of opportunity in public employment, freedom of association, the right to form labour unions, the right of travel and freedom of residence anywhere within the nation, the free choice of occupation, a prohibition of traffic in human beings and of forced labour, and so forth.[33] US constitutional law has had to arrive at some of these liberties by a much more indirect route. The right to travel, for example, has been read into the meaning of the word 'liberty', as it occurs in the due process clause of the Fifth Amendment.[34]

Article 13 of the Indian constitution explicitly invalidates all 'laws in force' that are inconsistent with the list of Fundamental Rights, although it remains disputed whether 'laws in force' includes the personal laws.[35]

Although the Indian list of rights is on the whole more explicit than its US analogue, two omissions from the US list are striking, and will concern us in what follows. The Indian constitution has no analogue of the US constitution's Eighth Amendment, forbidding 'cruel and unusual punishments', although there is an extensive guarantee of habeas corpus and a prohibition of certain types of arbitrary preventive detention. Nor is there an analogue of the US constitution's Fourth Amendment, prohibiting unreasonable and unwarranted searches and seizures.[36]

The Indian constitution contains analogues of both the due process clause of our Fifth and Fourteenth Amendments and of the Equal Protection clauses of our Fourteenth Amendment. Article 14 states: 'The State shall not deny to any person equality before the law or the equal protection of the laws within the territory of India.' Article 21 states: 'No person shall be deprived of his life or personal liberty except according to procedure established by law.' As we shall see, these provisions, and especially Article 21, have been the primary avenues through which our privacy jurisprudence has made its way into Indian law, although Article 19's list of concretely enumerated rights has also played an important role.

The Indian framers were, of course, well aware of the US history of substantive due process in the *Lochner* era, and were extremely wary, early on, of any expansive use of Article 21, seeing how the US analogue had been used to strike down progressive economic legislation.[37] Indeed, in revising the draft document, the Drafting Committee deliberately substituted the phrase 'procedure established by law' for the phrase 'due process of law'. In other words, they aimed at making the document more friendly to actual legislation and to invite less due process surveillance. It appears that they meant to discourage judicial scrutiny of any legislation that was enacted by normal legislative procedures. This fact was cited in an early case, *A. K. Gopalan* vs *State of Madras*,[38] as evidence that the framers did not intend that laws should be judicially evaluated with reference to some independent benchmark of justice. That decision took a very cautious view of the judicial role with reference to Article 21, although its six separate opinions left it very unclear precisely how cautious the role was understood to be. Clearly, the case left a lot of room for judicial scrutiny of actual procedures established by law, at least in certain types of cases other than the type (preventive detention) actually being considered. As time passed, and the US use of substantive due process to protect rights to contraception and abortion made due process look less retrograde and more promising, the mood of the Indian judiciary shifted, and thus the uses of Article 21 with which I shall be dealing became a possibility.[39]

Notice that the Indian document contains a number of resources for the empowerment of women that the US document lacks. First of all, it contains an explicit provision of non-discrimination on the basis of sex, and an explicit interpretation that this is not to be taken to be incompatible with affirmative action programmes aimed at the improvement of the lot of women.

Second, the explicit attention to freedom of assembly, freedom of travel, equality of opportunity, and labour rights sets up a favourable situation for women who may need to appeal for protection of just such rights in connection with their pursuit of social equality. These freedoms, of course, are among those that are most commonly infringed on grounds of sex.

Third, the understanding of equality in the Indian document is explicitly, and from the outset, substantive rather than abstract and formal, in that it is made clear that special protective legislation advancing the interests of a disadvantaged group should not be construed as impermissible discrimination. A primary complaint of the US feminist tradition has been that the legal understanding of equality in the tradition is purely formal: thus, so long as laws treat everyone the same, it doesn't matter if this uniformity of treatment reinforces hierarchy.[40] Feminists have urged instead that equal treatment, and equal protection of the laws, be understood substantively, as requiring an end to systematic hierarchy and discrimination. This idea is however already well entrenched in Indian constitutional jurisprudence. The bare formal idea of treating everyone similarly never had much attraction for the Indian framers, who understood that their task centrally involved breaking up existing hierarchies, and that success in that task would require a lot of differential treatment.[41] That is, we are told in no uncertain terms that the goal of equal dignity and non-discrimination may, and indeed should, be pursued by treating women differently. In short, the framers understood the goal of equality in terms of an end to systematic hierarchy and discrimination, based on both caste and sex.

Against Privacy: Four Feminist Arguments

At this point we are ready to introduce the most common criticisms that feminists have made against the use of the concept of privacy in US constitutional law. These criticisms, although initially articulated with reference to US law, have become common currency in the international feminist movement.[42] In each case, I shall introduce the argument and then turn to the Indian situation to see how that legal tradition helps us assess the feminist charge.

1. *Too Diffuse and Unclear.* Privacy, it is claimed, is simply too diffuse and unclear a concept to serve any useful legal role.[43] This objection has been made by many scholars, not all of them feminists, but it is an important part of the feminist charge. The claim is that the concept is not just a cluster concept, or a concept in need of further specification: many core concepts of constitutional law are like this. The claim is that the concept is so extremely unclear and amorphous that judgments of what falls under it are highly likely to be arbitrary and wilful. This is a feminist issue, because arbitrary judgments are especially likely to express the views of current convention or the current arrangement of power. That complaint has frequently been made in reference to the death penalty. It has been argued that any vague phrase, for example the vague concept of 'heinous and horrible' murders, will conduce to arbitrary judgments, and, in the US context, to racially discriminatory application of the death penalty.[44] The issue appears to be no less salient with the concept of privacy.

Indian legal thinkers have made precisely this point, so we should not think that the concept has acquired a superior clarity of definition in the Indian legal or non-legal tradition. The Press Commission of India in 1982 opined that 'Privacy is a very nebulous concept and criteria which may constitute its violation cannot be drawn up.'[45] Rajeev Dhavan, an eminent authority on the seclusion and information aspects of privacy, summarizes the situation in this way:

> Even in its constitutional context, it is not clear as to what 'privacy' means and how far the right to privacy extends. So far, the concept of 'privacy' has

been used as a persuasive linguistic device. 'Privacy' is a nice-sounding emotive phrase which persuades people that the Court is doing nice things.[46]

This contention has merit. One probably could map out a reasonably coherent cluster-concept of privacy that would cover the informational and seclusion-and-modesty related interests that were identified above.[47] If we leave out the area of personal liberty and autonomy, which is the most serious source of confusion, we would be left with a concept that is no vaguer than many legal concepts, and one that might usefully be demarcated further through an evolving legal tradition. However, the special problem that arises when we consider so proceeding is that privacy, even so delimited, covers a large number of distinct areas of law: the law of the press, the law of torts, laws relating to housing, and, in the area of modesty, the criminal law. It seems far better to demarcate precisely what citizens have a right to, and a right to be free from, in each of these areas, rather than simply to assert that they have 'a right to privacy'. Or rather, the statement that they have 'a right to privacy' does absolutely nothing in indicating how to shape these diverse areas of law, until we enumerate the distinct privacy interests at a much more concrete level.

2. *Privacy as Protection of Male Bad Behaviour.* The central argument in Catharine MacKinnon's internationally influential critique of the privacy concept is that appeals to privacy have routinely functioned to insulate bad behaviour, and behaviour that is, in J.S. Mill's sense, 'other-regarding', affecting the interests of others, from state scrutiny. 'In this light', MacKinnon writes, 'a right to privacy looks like an injury got up as a gift.'[48] Thus, appeals to the alleged privacy of the home have routinely accompanied defences of the marital rape exemption, and of non-interference with domestic violence and with child abuse. It is not that in principle people don't sometimes grant that a showing of coercion voids the presumption of non-interference. However, as MacKinnon says, 'the problem is getting anything private to be perceived as coercive'. In the marital home, there is a presumption of consent. What this means is that there is a presumption that anything a man does in the marital home is all right. As MacKinnon states: it is not women's privacy that is being protected here, it is the male's privacy. Recognizing a sphere of seclusion into which the state shall not enter means, simply, that males may exercise unconstrained power. In effect, the male's action within

his own home is viewed traditionally as, in Mill's terms,[49] a self-regarding action; an action that implicates no interests other than his own—because traditionally women and children are not considered, for either legal or ethical purposes, as separate individuals with separate interests.

More generally, MacKinnon, Carol Pateman, and other feminist critics look at the whole history of the public/private distinction, and see in it a stratagem through which men have claimed for themselves an unlimited exercise of power, among whose primary uses has been the subordination of women. The Greek distinction between the *polis* and the *oikos*, one of the most foundational sources for our modern public/private distinction, functioned in exactly this way. As Aristotle articulates it, it is the distinction between a sphere in which a man is an equal among equals, constrained by demanding norms of reciprocity and justice, and a sphere in which he rules as a king.[50] The rule of a man over a wife is subtly distinguished by Aristotle from his rule over slaves: the kingly husband is supposed to take his wife's views into account in some way. Even so, both forms of royal rule are even more strongly distinguished from the rule practiced among citizens, which is not kingly rule at all, but rather a 'ruling and being ruled by turns'. Similarly, John Locke's state of nature, yet another formative source of modern Western traditions of privacy, is a realm in which one is not bound and may do as one likes: it is 'a state of perfect freedom to order their actions, and dispose of their possessions and persons as they see fit, within the bounds of the Law of Nature'.[51] Of course this means that those with power get to exercise it unconstrained. The private domain is thus defined as a domain in which the powerful have a sway unlimited by considerations of equality and reciprocity.

What this history tells us is that even when appeals to privacy appear to protect the interests of women (or children), we should be sceptical, asking whose interests are really advanced. Laws that protect the modesty of women from violation by the eyes or even the touch of a stranger appear in one way protective of women; and they have been used by feminists who hope to squeeze progressive results out of antiquated codes. However, the concept of womanly modesty is inextricable from the history of patriarchy, and it subjects women to asymmetrical limitations on their freedom. The prohibition on outraging womanly modesty is just the flip side of the prohibition of immodest behaviour on the part of a woman who might wish to wear clothing of her choice, or to walk with freedom in the world. Even in the very immodest US, which some time ago abandoned norms of modesty in dress, the legacy of these asymmetrical controls survives in things like the (relative) difficulty of public urination for women (even though women, unlike men, can arrange to urinate without revealing their genitals).

Another related way in which the appeal to privacy does harm is that it shores up traditional hierarchies surrounding marital heterosexuality. What gets protected is the privacy of the marital couple in the conjugal home.[52] Same-sex couples and even unmarried heterosexual ones are less likely to achieve the same protection.[53] Thus *Griswold* vs *Connecticut* defended the right to contraception as a right of married couples, and it was only later, in *Eisenstadt* vs *Baird*,[54] and on grounds of equal protection, not privacy, that the same protection was extended to unmarried individuals. Privacy is also class-linked. If certain forms of behaviour are protected on the grounds that they take place in the 'private zone' of the home, then people who don't have such a convenient zone of privacy will be disadvantaged. Thus call girls, who operate out of their home or in expensive hotels, may achieve protections that are denied to streetwalkers.

For all these reasons, feminists have thought it unwise of American jurists to seek protection for certain key rights to liberty of women by sliding them into the all too capacious envelope of privacy. The right to contraception and to abortion, as I shall later discuss, are not very naturally linked with the notion of privacy as either confidentiality/secrecy or modesty/seclusion. People can take birth control pills when all the world is watching, and many people make no secret of this. Abortion by its very nature is always done with others present, and is no more secluded than any other medical procedure; if it is at the present time more confidential than some procedures, this is largely because of the climate of hostility surrounding it. What is at stake in contraception and abortion is decisional autonomy or liberty. The issue is whether a certain life-defining choice will or will not be open to a woman (or, in the case of contraception, also to a man). When we say, 'These decisions are respected because they are private', we allude to the old idea of the protected sphere, and we raise all the problems associated with that distinction. As we shall see, this can eventually prove quite harmful to women's interests.

Because I have referred to the Western tradition of the private/public divide as the source of my problem, I have again raised the question: do Indian traditions contain the basis for a comparable worry. Most emphatically, they do. Traditional Hindu law gives the household considerable autonomy. At the same time, one of the central prerogatives, and indeed duties, of the householder is strict control over the women of the house: chapter 9 of the *Laws of Manu* states that women are by nature untruthful, lustful, and in need of constant supervision, and so the husband must arrange that this be done. In this way, the idea of the household as a protected sphere of male authority is established.

In keeping with this general picture, marriage is thought to imply consent to sexual intercourse, so there is no traditional concept of rape in marriage. Certainly, traditional sources are quite critical of cruelty and violence in the home (unless there has been adultery), but even violence of a quite remarkable type has at times been countenanced under the doctrine of implied consent. The issue is compounded by the traditionally low age of marriage. Can a girl of ten or eleven by any stretch of the imagination be presumed to consent to sexual intercourse? Even so, as we shall see, that proposition has been energetically defended.

An especially pernicious development of the idea of male rule over the household took over during the time of British domination, with British connivance, resulting in a keen interest in justifying even extremely cruel conduct as simply within the husband's husbandly prerogative. In an extremely impressive article, historian Tanika Sarkar has investigated the rhetoric surrounding the tragic death of Phulmonee, a girl of 10 or 11, who was raped by her husband, Hari Mati, a man of 35, and died of the resulting injuries.[55] Sarkar convincingly shows that in reaction to British domination of external political life, nationalists turned inward, boosting the idea of male autonomy in the home as the one cherished zone of self-rule, 'the last pure space left to a conquered people'; this autonomy was understood to be built around the submission, and indeed the much-praised and allegedly voluntary suffering, of women. Nationalists of this stripe resisted internal demands for reform of child marriage, painting them as subversions of their cherished (but really constructed) traditions.[56] The British were complicit in this development: they understood that leaving the subject a sphere of self-rule was to their advantage, and thus they actively assisted in the codification of personal law and the privatization of marriage and family.

Appeals to the privacy of the home were then invoked to resist efforts to raise the age of consent to marriage, and to oppose any attempt to prosecute men like Hari Mati—who was not guilty of rape under law, given that his wife was above the statutory limit of 10.[57] In short, anyone who takes up the weapon of privacy in the cause of women's equality must be aware that it is a double-edged weapon, long used to defend the killers of women.

Let us now turn to recent cases on the question of 'restitution of conjugal rights', where we shall see, I believe, that the appeal to privacy muddies the waters, setting women up for a most unfortunate reversal. The remedy of forcible restitution to the conjugal home is not originally Hindu in origin; it derives from British ecclesiastical law.[58] As articulated in the Hindu Law of Marriage, it can be claimed by either husband or wife, and it frequently operates as a prelude to divorce in the modern era, in that a person who obtains an order of restitution that is not obeyed can use this fact as a ground for divorce.

The idea of forcible restitution has an infamous history, going back to the time of Phulmonee's death.[59] A young woman named Rakhmabai, from a rich family, was given a good education by her reformist stepfather, a prominent Bombay doctor. At age 11 she was married to one Dadaji Bhikaji Thakur, but she continued to live with her parents because her stepfather opposed early consummation of marriage. As the years passed, Dadaji proved idle and ignorant; he also contracted tuberculosis. He kept trying to persuade Rakhmabai to come live with him, but he was unsuccessful. Eventually, he filed a lawsuit (in 1884, when she was twenty) for restitution of conjugal rights. (He apparently chose this procedure rather than more traditional ones available within the caste, in order to get his hands on her money, which the caste procedures would not have enabled him to do.) Rakhmabai went public, writing an anonymous letter to the *Times of India* describing her complaint:

> We [Hindu women] are treated worse than beasts. We are regarded as playthings—objects of enjoyment to be unceremoniously thrown away when the temporary use is over ... Reduced to this state of degradation by the dictum of the Shastras, looked down upon for ages by men, we have naturally come to look down upon ourselves. Our condition, therefore, cannot ... be improved, unless the practice of early marriage is abolished and higher female education is largely disseminated.[60]

The case became a rallying-point for reformers, on the one hand, and traditional guardians of male authority on the other. Rakhmabai disobeyed the order of restitution, and was about to be sentenced to six months in jail, when a committee of reformers intervened on her behalf. Because the court was unwilling to enforce the decree, Dadaji eventually accepted a property settlement. The marriage was never legally dissolved, and Rakhmabai never remarried, although Dadaji did shortly thereafter. Rakhmabai got a medical degree in England and worked as a doctor in Bombay until her retirement in 1917, after which she remained active in social reform causes until her death in 1955 at the age of 91. She always dressed as a Hindu married woman until Dadaji's death in 1904, after which she dressed as a widow.

This famous case sets the stage for our recent cases, establishing that extremely important liberty interests for women are on the line in the debate over the ancient remedy of forcible restitution.

The recent uproar over restitution begins with another famous case. A well-known movie actress from Madras, Sareetha, was sued for restitution of conjugal rights by her husband, Venkata Subbaiah.[61] She had married him while still an unknown high school girl, and the two had separated before her career began, largely as a result of quarrels over her desire to be an actress. Seeing that she was rich and famous, her husband apparently wanted either to get her back or to obtain a substantial financial settlement. In a much-heralded and dramatic opinion, Justice[62] Choudary of the Andhra Pradesh High Court declared the relevant section of the Hindu Marriage Act unconstitutional, on grounds that it violated Article 21's guarantee of 'life and liberty'. Drawing on the US tradition of privacy-right jurisprudence and explicitly citing *Griswold* and *Roe* as precedents, he declared that Article 21 implies a right to privacy, which must be understood to be implicit in the meaning of 'life and liberty', given that it had already been established (see below) that 'life' means not *mere* (animal) life, but a properly dignified human life. The remedy of restitution is 'a savage and barbarous remedy, violating the right to privacy and human dignity guaranteed by Art. 21 of the Constitution'. Justice Choudary also held, in a separate argument, that the remedy was unconstitutional too on equal protection grounds, violating Article 14.

The privacy arm of the argument was not entirely unprecedented: as we shall see below, such a right had been recognized in the area of search and seizure. However, the application to women's liberty interests, following the US line, was entirely new—and, I shall argue, somewhat unfortunate. It is not that the opinion does not make a compelling feminist argument. Indeed, its eloquence is most impressive:

> [T]he purpose of a decree for restitution of conjugal rights ... is to coerce through judicial process the unwilling party to have sex against that person's consent and free will ... It cannot be denied that among the few points that distinguish human existence from that of animals, [the] sexual autonomy an individual enjoys to choose his or her partner to a sexual act is of primary importance. Sexual expression is so integral to one's personality that it is impossible to conceive of sexuality on any basis except on the basis of consensual participation ... [I]t cannot but be admitted that a decree for restitution of conjugal rights constitutes the grossest form of violation of an individual's right to privacy. Applying Professor Tribe's definition of right to privacy, it must be said that the decree for restitution of conjugal rights denies the woman her free choice whether, when and how her body is to become the vehicle for the procreation of another human being. Applying Parker's definition, it must be said, that a decree for restitution of conjugal rights deprives a woman of control over her choice as to when and by whom the various parts of her body should be allowed to be sensed. Applying the tests of Gaiety and Bostwick, it must be said, that the woman loses her control over her most intimate decisions. Clearly, therefore, the right to privacy guaranteed by Ar. 21 of our Constitution is flagrantly violated by a decree of restitution of conjugal rights.

As one can see, Justice Choudary had clearly devoted much thought to the concept of privacy. Indeed, he is quite frank about its slippery multiplicity: '[I]t must be admitted that the concept of right to privacy does not lend itself to easy logical definition ... partly because ... the concept was thrown up in great haste from a miscellany of legal rock and stone and partly because of the inherent difficulties in defining such an elusive concept.' On the other hand, he is satisfied that 'any plausible definition of right to privacy is bound to take [the] human body as its first and most basic reference for control over personal identity. Such a definition is bound to include [the] body's inviolability and integrity and intimacy of personal identity, including marital privacy.' It was therefore enough for him if he could show that on all the major understandings of the right to privacy that focus on the body and its integrity, that right, was violated by the law in question.

The question is, however, why one should have brought the issue of bodily integrity and liberty under privacy in the first place. Surely it does not naturally belong there. Justice Choudary's reference to 'marital privacy' betrays the difficulty: the traditional concept of 'marital privacy' militates precisely against women's liberty and bodily integrity. It is that very concept that makes it so difficult, even today, to get marital rape criminalized and domestic violence prosecuted. Surely, if what was wanted was a right of control over one's body, that right would much more naturally have been read out of Article 19's guarantee of freedom of movement, travel, and residence (as the surveillance cases suggest), or out of various aspects of the Criminal Code forbidding assault and rape. If it was felt that a separate right had to be recognized to give this area sufficient protection, why not say directly that Article 21's guarantee of life and liberty involves protection of the very basic right of sexual autonomy, the right to refuse sex one does not want, without which, as the judge eloquently states, human life is more bestial than human. Why bring privacy into it?

Well, someone will say, why not? It is a vague but by and large positive notion, and it generally suggests that one is doing something good. I have however said enough to indicate why it is a dangerous way of doing good. Mention the traditional idea of marital privacy, and people will immediately start thinking of the traditional patriarchal household. In that household, women have no sexual autonomy so the argument has a certain tendency to undercut itself.

Indeed, it was with reference to the traditional ideal of the household that the justice was eventually overruled. At approximately the same time, a restitution case was heard in the Delhi High Court. The court argued directly against the Choudary opinion, which had created a stir, holding that the remedy of restitution was not unconstitutional under either Article 14 or Article 21.[63] (The arguments in the opinion were so pointed that the justice even ridiculed as errors obvious printing errors in the Andhra Pradesh opinion.) The essence of the Delhi argument, as can be seen from my epigraph, is that the intimate nature of marriage makes the application of constitutional principles inappropriate. The opinion also insisted that the restitution decree did not really enforce sexual intercourse and thus could not be counted as a judicial invasion of 'marital privacy'. Of course, the opinion itself appealed to the traditional notion of marital privacy in its judgment that the constitution should stay out of marriage.

In 1984, in a different case, the Supreme Court sided with the Delhi court and against Justice Choudary.[64] Conjugal rights, held the justices, are 'inherent in the very institution of marriage itself'. Quoting from the Law Commission's 1955 report on the Hindu Marriage Act, they write that 'the essence of marriage is a sharing of common life, a sharing of all the happiness that life has to offer and all the misery that has to be faced in life ... Living together is a symbol of such sharing in all its aspects.' The decree of restitution thus 'serves a social purpose as an aid to the prevention of break-up of marriage.'

As for the claim that the law violates women's bodily integrity, the justices opined that the law contained 'sufficient safeguards ... to prevent it from being a tyranny'. In particular, a woman who does not want to obey can always pay a fine, 'provided he or she has properties to be attached'. To the appellant's contention that 'in the social reality of the Indian society, a divorced wife would be materially at a great disadvantage', the justices say yes, this is correct. Therefore in the particular case they order the husband to pay maintenance to the wife and to pay the legal costs of the appeal.

Now we can see that what happened, on the face of things, was that the whole strategy of appeal to Article 21 was denied. I would however argue that it was easy to deny it because of the way in which the alleged right was framed, as a right of privacy, for it was then so easy to say, look at our concept of marital privacy. Surely that concept is threatened not by a kindly law that helps people live together and work out their differences, but by the cold hand of constitutional law, that enters in to break up the sanctity of the marital home. Perhaps the Supreme Court would have refused to recognize any liberty-right for women here, no matter how framed. However, surely the appeal to a concept deeply identified with the allegedly seamless unity of the patriarchal family, and with the presumption of consent to sex in marriage, did no good in staving off this result.

I have so far not mentioned another especially interesting aspect of Justice Choudary's opinion: his appeal to equal protection. He acknowledges that formally the law is neutral: either husband or wife can petition for a decree of restitution. But then, in keeping with the less formalistic and more substantive understanding of equality in Indian constitutional traditions, he says that the reality is otherwise. The enforcement of such a decree, especially given that it may result in the conception of a child, will alter the wife's life in a way that it could not possibly alter the husband's. It 'cripples the wife's future plans of life'.

> As a result this remedy works in practice only as an engine of oppression to be operated by the husband for the benefit of the husband against the wife. By treating the wife and the husband who are inherently unequal as equals, Section 9 of the Act offends the rule of equal protection of laws. For that reason [it] should therefore be struck down as violative of Article 14 of the Constitution.

One could not have a more succinct statement of MacKinnon's feminist position on equality, although, as I have noted, this understanding is traditional in Indian law and radical only in the US context.[65] Choudary recognizes that formal equality does not guarantee substantive equality: we must look at social context and history. But then he goes further: when we so look, we find that formal equality is actually incompatible with substantive equality. This is the line of reasoning used in some US cases involving race (separate but equal schools, formally neutral bans on interracial marriage);[66] but US courts have never stated the principle so clearly in the context of sex equality.[67] This extremely progressive aspect of the case was, unfortunately, briefly stated and far less emphasized than the privacy argument. It was denied by the Delhi court and overruled by the Supreme Court, but with no comment. The critique, like Justice Choudary's argument, focused on the privacy issue. I believe that here, as in the US cases involving race, the equality line is ultimately the more productive and progressive one.

These cases dramatically illustrate the dangers that face women jumping on the privacy bandwagon. Privacy is inherently a retrograde value, linked with the idea of a protected patriarchal sphere of authority. What, then, should be the feminist approach?

I believe that we cannot make much progress for women without utterly rejecting the idea of a protected private sphere within which the law does not meddle. The privacy tradition typically conflates two ideas of the protected sphere: a spatial idea (the home as a privileged *place*), and an institutional idea (marriage as a privileged *relation*). It seems to me very clear that the protection of an institution under cover of the notion of privacy is simply mistaken: the fact that people are linked as husband and wife does not entail that the law has no business in that relationship. As for the appeal to a special place, or sanctuary, this seems more plausible, and in some areas (for example, that of unwanted surveillance) it may appear appealing. Typically, however, such an idea of home as a protected place has served to insulate family *relationships* from legal scrutiny; as I shall argue in the following section, it also serves to give special privileges to those whose harmless activities take place in that place, even though they might be just as harmless when conducted elsewhere. Even the liberties that we most closely associate with the idea of home as a protected place (for example, the right to be free from unreasonable and unwarranted search and seizure) would be better understood to protect persons and their property whether or not they are at home and whether or not they have a home. Thus the idea of home as a protected place remains at least questionable.

It seems to me that we should begin by adopting Mill's distinction between self-regarding and other-regarding acts. If an act is other-regarding (with impact for the interests of non-consenting others), it gets no special protection by being placed in a home rather than elsewhere. If harm is caused to a person, that harm is the business of law, no matter where the harm occurs. (I shall shortly turn to the question of protecting self-regarding acts, or acts involving the interests only of the agent.) Furthermore, as this must be explicitly stated, women and children are persons, not aspects of a male super-person. In short, bad behaviour receives no greater sanction by being indulged in within the bosom of the family.

On the other hand, MacKinnon's suggestion that we can do all we need to do by appealing to equal protection and an end to hierarchy and domination seems to me insufficient. Such an appeal succeeded in overturning US anti-miscegenation laws because they really did shore up an existing 'White Supremacy'. It shows some signs of making progress in the contested terrain of abortion, where it was at least recognized in *Planned Parenthood* vs *Casey*[68] that the denial of abortion rights to women does have a serious equality aspect: women, and not men, are being forced against their will to support fetal life.[69] In the Indian cases it seems sufficient to show the unconstitutionality of the remedy of restitution.

But of course there may come a time when the races in the US are equal; and even when the sexes are equal we would still want to overturn, or so I think, laws that forbid a person to marry the person of her choice, and laws that give one person the right to bring back an unwilling partner to the conjugal home. Some feminists may say that there would be no such laws in a regime of sex equality, but I think that we cannot be so certain, and we don't want to stake our liberty on that supposition.[70] Surely if we think of the parallel area of race, we can imagine the interest in enforced separation becoming detached from an interest in shoring up domination. If blacks were equal, they might well still wish to preserve the purity of the black race, as so many influential African-Americans do. Suppose such African-Americans succeeded in passing an anti-miscegenation law designed to ensure racial purity and continuity. That law, I would argue, would be invidious and unacceptable—in a different way from the old anti-miscegenation laws, but unacceptable all the same.[71] Similarly, in a regime of sex equality, a law denying women access to abortion would still be objectionable on grounds of liberty, even if the equality issue no longer existed. That is just to say that there are certain cherished areas of human freedom that need protection. Among these are the freedom to leave a marriage when one wishes, and the free choice of a marital partner. Those liberty interests need express protection, and they do not get that protection from equality alone.

One can see that the US justices were in a bind: the US constitution is so relatively thin on enumerated liberties that they had to grasp for something, and privacy looked like one way of plugging an egregious gap.[72] Even so, it was, a defective way. Whether or not the political difficulty we have had with this issue would have been in any sense mitigated by starting from a different analysis, a different analysis seems required, for the reasons given: it is always dangerous to opportunistically use a set of concepts implicated in such a shady history. As the Indian example shows, such a tactic can all too easily backfire. The Indian constitution offers more appealing options, among them the freedoms of movement, assembly, and travel. Also, as I have suggested, if those were found lacking one could have argued directly from the concept of 'life and liberty' itself, as Justice Choudary in effect did.

3. *Privacy as a dubious way of protecting self-regarding acts*. As for acts that do no harm to others, and that are in Mill's sense self-regarding, it seems unclear, again, that the concept of privacy does useful work in helping us see when and how these acts should be protected.[73] Does something harmless become less worthy of protection because it occurs

in what is defined as 'public space'? Now of course when an act moves out of the home into the 'public space' new questions need to be raised, such as the effects of the act on non-consenting onlookers. Frequently however there are no such issues, and yet acts are given less protection anyhow, simply because they do not take place in someone's home. Initially, contraception was protected only in the marital home, and the actions of activist Bill Baird, in giving out contraceptives publicly to unmarried undergraduates, were not protected until the equal protection-based decision intervened. This was wrong: contraception is a pure self-regarding act, and the state has no business meddling with it, no matter where the relevant transactions take place. Again, the recent tendency, in European law, to protect homosexual sodomy on grounds of the privacy of the home suggests a pernicious distinction: if men have sex in their own dwelling place, it is legally protected. On the other hand, if they frequent a bathhouse, even if all the people there are consenting and un-offended, the act no longer enjoys the same protection. One might add that here again we see how privacy works to shore up traditional hierarchies: for 'the home' and 'the family' are paradigmatic heterosexual institutions, and gay male culture, especially, has been sceptical about them, preferring to cultivate other forms of association, called 'sex publics' by theorist Michael Warner.[74]

Again, a high-class call girl who works in good hotels or in her own dwelling will be protected (in some conceptions of privacy as it relates to prostitution), whereas a call girl who solicits on the street will not be protected, even though the sex act itself will not be witnessed by any impressionable children or any other non-consenting party. Again, public, nude dancing before a consenting and eager audience is likely to be unprotected, whereas the same dance performed in the home will be protected.[75] The use of pornography was protected in *Stanley* vs *Georgia*,[76] on grounds of the privacy of the home; this precedent would not give protection to the use of pornography, equally not involving children or non-consenting parties, in an adult store.

These examples require us to note that the public/private distinction, as it is routinely applied in such cases, is not the same as a distinction between places where there are non-consenting parties around and places where there are no such parties. If it were, then it would at least be very close to Mill's distinction between self-regarding and non-self-regarding acts. As we have however seen, there are plenty of times where there are non-consenting parties in the 'private' space of the home. Outside it there are many spaces and places where there are only consenting parties: sex clubs, bathhouses, dance clubs, sex stores (assuming that they bar entry to minors below some reasonable age of consent). It is only in a portion of the space denominated 'public' that Milleans need to be worried about effects on the non-consenting, and it is very clear that defenders of 'public morality' are not focused on the issue of consent. Justice Scalia put it vividly when he said, in his dissent in *Romer* vs *Evans*, that the purpose of Indiana's law against public nudity 'would be violated, I think, if 60,000 fully consenting adults crowded into the Hoosier Dome to display their genitals to one another, even if there were not an offended innocent in the crowd.'[77] Justice Scalia is right about the Indiana nudity law, but then that shows us that the public/private distinction does not track the Millean distinction.[78]

In short, a self-regarding act does not deserve less protection, if it really remains self-regarding, by being in some space denominated 'public'. I note that this is a particularly grave issue when we consider the rights of homeless persons who, in the US, have sometimes been denied their right to freedom from unwarranted search and seizure by reason of their homeless status. Also, if it were to be inequitous and unwise, in this regard, for the legal system of the US to rely on the spatial notion of the private sphere, regarding the home as a privileged sanctuary rather than seeking to distinguish protected areas of liberty from other areas of human conduct, we can see that it would be all the more unwise in a nation such as India, where quite a large proportion of people[79] live on the streets in relatively unprotected dwellings.

My Indian cases once again show the wisdom of bewaring of such a use of the 'private' to defend harmless acts only when they take place in a protected sphere. The first cases to recognize a right to privacy in connection with Article 21 were those involving police surveillance. In the first of these, *Kharak Singh* vs *State of Uttar Pradesh*,[80] the dissenters recognized such a right, and in the second, *Govind* vs *State of Madhya Pradesh*,[81] the majority recognized the right, citing American privacy cases from a variety of distinct areas, including search and seizure, but also including the Fourteenth Amendment privacy right cases *Griswold* and *Roe*. As I have mentioned, the right to privacy is invoked in these cases because the Indian constitution has no analogue of our Fourth Amendment prohibiting unreasonable and unwarranted searches and seizures.

At issue was a state police regulation, framed in accordance with directives provided by a national Police Act, according to which people who had a criminal record or were in other ways suspected of 'a determination to lead a life of crime' could be subject to unannounced domiciliary visits, often in the middle of the night, and could also be followed and spied on when outside the home. Justices Mathew, Iyer, and Goswami, citing the 1877 US case *Munn* vs *Illinois*, opine that 'liberty' in Article 21 should be given an expansive interpretation:

> Is then the words 'personal liberty' to be construed as excluding from its purview an invasion on the part of the police of the sanctity of a man's home and an intrusion into his personal security and his right to sleep which is the normal comfort and a dire necessity for human existence even as an animal?

The justices then, as we might expect, bring in the notion of privacy, holding that a right to privacy in one's home is implicated in the meaning of liberty. Citing the dissent in *Kharak Singh*, they hold that 'in the last resort a person's house, where he lives with his family, is his "castle", that nothing is more deleterious to a man's physical happiness and health than a calculated interference with his privacy ...' Once again, the sacred privacy of the householder in his dwelling place.

Significantly, the justices do understand that the actions of the police threaten important human liberties even when they are not directed at the 'sanctity of the home', and they do mean to call into constitutional question not only the domiciliary visits, but the whole pattern of police spying.[82] However, at this point they turn to the enumerated liberties of Article 19, holding that freedom of movement must also be given an expansive construction. Again, citing the dissenters in *Kharak Singh*, they opine that it is not 'mere freedom to move without physical obstruction and ... movement under the scrutinizing gaze of the policeman cannot be free movement.' Freedom of movement

> must be movement in a free country, i. e. a country where he can do whatever he likes, speak to whomsoever he wants, meet people of his own choice without

any apprehension, subject of course to the law of social control, and that a person under the shadow of surveillance is certainly deprived of this freedom.

The question then is, why all the fuss about privacy, if the key issue in the case is understood to be one of personal liberty and autonomy? ('Individual autonomy', say the justices, is 'perhaps the central concern of any system of limited government'.) Domiciliary visits seem to be bad in just the way surveillance outside the home is bad: they deprive a person of liberty to move around, talk to people, and the like. Again, the justices know that privacy is a slippery notion: 'The most serious advocate of privacy must confess that there are serious problems of defining the essence and scope of the right.' Nonetheless, they indulge in a vague and diffuse rhetoric about the sanctity of the home, and even refer to aspects of marital sanctity that have no evident connection to the case: 'Any right to privacy must encompass and protect the personal intimacies of the home, the family, marriage, motherhood, procreation, and child rearing.' What does this have to do with shadowing a person not charged with or even suspected of any concrete crime? What is wrong with this surveillance, in short, does not become right when they do it in public. The justices know as much, and thus it is utterly unclear why they need the appeal to privacy at all. Freedom of movement would appear to suffice. If however they believe that the offence acquires additional dimensions of harm when the home is visited, then it would seem better to spell out the relevant liberty in something like the way of the US Fourth Amendment, which could be read into Article 21 as easily as could the red herring privacy.[83]

I believe that *Govind* is an important opinion and one that, in its basic holding, strikes a delicate balance between the state's interest in surveillance and the individual's right to liberty. Thus I do not mean to object to the general line of the court's impressive argument.[84] I intend only to question the detour through the concept of privacy, which I believe to have been unnecessary for the basic line of the court's argument.

4. *Privacy as an irrelevant rubric for important interests*. Privacy has functioned, in both US and Indian law, as a rubric under which to introduce into the constitution interests that are not otherwise explicitly recognized in it. It is a gap-filler, and as such, easier than the process of constitutional amendment. Even so, it is conceded by most who survey

the history of the cases that a fair number of the interests that come in that way are oddly grouped under that rubric. As I have already said, privacy is an odd way of protecting the right to obtain contraception, given that contraceptive products are publicly sold, as much as are toothbrushes, and their use is, if anything, less private than the use of toothbrushes: women take their pills anywhere they happen to be, whereas they won't brush their teeth just anywhere. Only a confusion of contraception with sex acts could make us think of contraception as a private act, in the sense of secluded and shielded from view. Abortion, similarly, is not a private act. It usually takes place in a clinic or doctor's office, with a number of parties present. It has nothing to do with privacy as seclusion and modesty (or at least no more so than other medical procedures), and nothing to do with confidentiality of information (or at least not more so than other medical procedures). We shall see that the Indian cases that use substantive due process to introduce previously unenumerated rights are similarly dealt with all over the map, although Indian jurisprudence is somewhat more self-aware in recognizing the limits of the privacy concept, and therefore it is not introduced where its introduction would be most blatantly peculiar, as we shall see when we turn to prisoners' rights. If however we are going to recognize unenumerated rights under substantive due process without appeal to the concept of privacy in even a small number of cases, then why should we rely on it at all in cases which we must strain to squeeze under the concept?

There can be no clearer demonstration of this issue than one of India's most eloquent and vivid Article 21 cases, *Sunil Batra* vs *Delhi Administration*, discussing the extent of personal liberty possessed by prisoners on death row.[85] (India and the US are alike in retaining capital punishment.) Mandatory solitary confinement for death-row prisoners is held unconstitutional on grounds of Article 21 and Article 14. Article 14 is used to attack the punishment as 'arbitrary': 'The treatment of a human being which offends human dignity, imposes avoidable torture and reduces the man to the level of a beast would certainly be arbitrary and can be questioned under Art. 14.' Article 21 is violated because among the rights to liberty guaranteed by that article is now held to be a 'right to society'. In the words of the opinion (ornate and rhetorical even by Indian standards!):

> A few books, yes; newspapers? No. Talk to others? No; save echoes of one's own soliloquies; no sight of others except the stone ... This segregation ... is violation of the primordial gregariousness which, from the beginning of the species, has been man's social milieu and so constitutes a psychic trauma, when prolonged ..., even in our ancient land of silent mystics and lonely cavemen. For the great few, solitude sometimes is best society but for the commonality the wages of awesome seclusion, if spread over long spells, is insanity. ... Just think, not of the contemplative saint but of the run-of-the-mill mortal. Cage his lonely person and monitor his mind and mood with a sensitive understanding. Then you know that moments bear slow malice; hours hang heavy with ennui; days drop dead, and lonely weeks wear a vicious stillness; for sure, weary months of singleness, with monotonous nights, made more hurtful by the swarms of mosquitoes singing and stinging, and in many cells, by the bloodthirsty armies of bugs, invisibly emerging from nocturnal nowhere, to hide and bite, make for lunacy.

The actual legal argument is a tangled one, as it attempts to bring the right to society under procedural rather than substantive due process. I shall not analyse that aspect of the opinion. What interests me is that the justices plainly see the need here to recognize a dimension of human liberty previously unenumerated. It is a dimension that could not, even if stretched, be brought in under a right to privacy. Therefore they don't try. They simply go directly to the concept of liberty, arguing that 'liberty'in Article 21 itself implies the right in question.

This seems to me basically the right strategy. Why use 'privacy' as a gap-filler at all, given its other difficulties, when we see that one may perfectly straightforwardly, through an incremental process of judicial interpretation, get the rights from the place they really reside: the notion of liberty?

Constitutions and Capabilities

The moral of this investigation, it seems to me, is that constitutions protect a rich plurality of distinct human interests. One might do well, I suggest, to think of the goal as that of protecting a wide range of distinct human capabilities, meaning the ability of people to do and to be certain of things of central human importance.[86] Each of the central human capabilities is distinct in quality from all the others. Thus, it is always dangerous to reduce one constitutional value to another one, or to understand one constitutional value in terms of another. One risks losing the distinctive nature of the vital human interest involved. Privacy has served too long as a catch-all value, into which values of very different types (equality, freedom of movement, freedom of association) have been siphoned, without adequate thought about their distinctive nature. If this process has seemed inevitable in the US context, where the constitution does relatively little to enumerate a wide range of liberties and equality interests that deserve protection, it is surely far from inevitable, and indeed most unwise, in the Indian context, where the constitution supplies ample resources for the protection of distinct liberty and equality interests as the very human capabilities they are.

Each constitutional tradition must draw upon its own resources of text and history. I therefore make no concrete suggestions for either legal tradition; I confine myself to a general philosophical recommendation. What I would favour, to sort our way out of this mess, is a three-pronged approach:

1. A reliance on equality and equal protection where the relevant issue involves systematic hierarchy and subordination. Often, in cases involving sex, this will be the most relevant line, and may prove sufficient to protect the interests that need protecting.
2. A general presumption of a Millean kind against the prohibition of self-regarding acts, whether in public or in private: the state will have to make a strong showing if it is to defend the prohibition of such acts. (In some cases, as with seat belt and helmet laws, the state may best achieve its purpose by showing that the putatively self-regarding act actually has big other-regarding effects, through medical costs undergone by all citizens.)
3. The enumeration of specific human liberty interests that are of especially central importance for protection from interference: as India has done with the right to travel, the free choice of occupation, the right of prisoners to human society, etc., and as the US has done with the right to freedom from unwarranted search and seizure and cruel and unusual punishments. Control over information about oneself—the aspect of a constitutional right to privacy most reasonably denominated 'privacy'—can be recognized through a plurality of distinct strategems in the various areas of law (torts,

press, constitutional law) in which informational issues arise.[87] These may be called 'privacy rights' if one wishes, though, as I have said, the plurality of different areas of law in which they arise makes it implausible to speak of a unitary 'right to privacy'. Meanwhile, various liberty interests now covered under privacy, such as the right to marital choice, to contraception, and to abortion, need to be extricated from the privacy morass and introduced through a more straightforward route—although it is beyond my practical political expertise to state how, in the case of each constitutional tradition, this can best be done. The human capablities at stake in this debate are too important to leave them in trust to privacy, that most untrustworthy and compromised of concepts. Certainly in matters of sex equality, to turn to privacy is indeed to dress up an injury and call it a gift.

Notes and References

1. An earlier version of this essay, was presented at a symposium on the right to privacy at the American Philosophical Association Eastern Division, 30 December 1999. It was then presented in Delhi at a conference honouring the 50th anniversary of the Indian constitution. For a very brief discussion of related ideas, see my 'Is Privacy Bad for Women?', *The Boston Review* 25 (April/May 2000), 42–7.

   I am grateful to Sonia Katyal, Joshua Fairfield, and Chad Flanders for research assistance; to Marc Galanter and Wendy Doniger for answering my questions about Indian traditions; to Indira Jaisingh for conversations in 1997 that greatly helped me think about some of these issues; to Joshua Cohen and Judith Jarvis Thomson for helpful conversation at the Philosophical Association meeting; to Chad Flanders, Andrew Koppelman, David Strauss, Cass Sunstein, Richard Posner, R. Sudarshan, and Iris Young for helpful comments on a previous draft; to Catharine MacKinnon for ongoing conversations about these issues that have shaped my thinking about them in fundamental ways.
2. *Lochner* vs *New York*, 198 US 45 (1905); the dissents by Justice Harlan and, especially, Justice Holmes are, justly, more famous than the majority opinion. The court held unconstitutional a New York statute providing that no employee shall 'work in a biscuit, bread or cake bakery or confectionary establishment more than sixty hours in any one week, or more than ten hours in any one day.' This was held to violate the right to

contract that was held to be part of 'liberty' as protected by the Fourteenth Amendment.

3. The turning point came in *Nebbia* vs *New York*, 291 US 502 (1934), when the court upheld mandatory minimum prices for milk, holding that the economic difficulties of milk producers 'could not be expected to right themselves through the ordinary play of the forces of supply and demand. ... [N]either property rights nor contract rights are absolute; for government cannot exist if the citizen may at will use his property to the detriment of his fellows, or exercise his freedom of contract to work them harm.' This common-sense observation might seem in the Indian context too obvious to need stating; in the US context, it was (and in some ways still is) a radical thought.
4. On the widespread condemnation of *Lochner*, and reasons for it, see G. Stone, L. Seidman, C. Sunstein, and M. Tushnet, *Constitutional Law*, 3rd edn, Little, Brown, Boston, 1996, pp. 814–38.
5. *Griswold* vs *Connecticut*, 381 US 479 (1965).
6. 410 US 133 (1975).
7. Judith Jarvis Thomson, 'The Right to Privacy', *Philosophy and Public Affairs* 4 (1975), 295–314. Thomson's article is well known in India, and is cited in a number of Indian Supreme Court opinions.

   Not coincidentally, Thomson's own influential analysis of the abortion right does not make use of the notion of privacy, preferring an analysis in terms of equality, stressing that women are unequally made to bear the burden of supporting fetal life: see 'A Defense of Abortion', *Philosophy and Public Affairs* 1 (1972), 47 ff. Her analysis of abortion has become more influential in recent years in the legal world: see, for example, Donald Regan, 'Rewriting *Roe* vs *Wade*', 77 *Michigan Law Review* 1569 (1979); Andrew Koppelman, 'Forced Labor: A Thirteenth Amendment Defense of Abortion', 84 *Northwestern U. Law Rev.* 480 (1990). Cass R. Sunstein, 'Pornography, Abortion, Surrogacy', ch. 9 of *The Partial Constitution* Harvard University Press, Cambrdige, MA, 1993; and see Ruth Bader Ginsburg (now a Justice of the US Supreme Court), 'Some Thoughts on Autonomy and Equality in Relation to *Roe* vs *Wade*', *North Carolina Law Review* 63 (1985), 282 ff.; Catharine MacKinnon, *Feminism Unmodified*, Harvard University Press, Cambridge, MA, 1987, pp. 93–102; MacKinnon, 'Reflections on Sex Equality Under Law,' *Yale Law Journal* 100 (1991), 1281–324. Should this argument about the unequal burden of pregnancy seem bizarre, for after all, only women get pregnant, we might helpfully consider a hypothetical law that required all and only African-Americans to donate kidneys for the life-support of children who need kidneys.

This would be unconstitutional under US law on grounds of equal protection, even if it were the case that only African-Americans were available as kidney donors, because it imposes a burden on a group on the basis of a 'suspect classification'. One good thing about this argument, in the area of abortion, is that it enables us to bypass the interminable metaphysical debate about whether the fetus is a person, as a law imposing an unequal burden on the basis of a suspect classification would be unconstitutional even if the people benefited were full-fledged human beings. See Sunstein's extensive discussion of these matters.

8. For a response to Thomson on this issue, see Thomas Scanlon, 'Thomson on Privacy', *Philosophy and Public Affairs* 4 (1975), 315–22.
9. See Catharine MacKinnon, 'Privacy vs Equality: Beyond *Roe* vs *Wade*', in MacKinnon, *Feminism Unmodified*, pp. 93–102; MacKinnon, *Toward a Feminist Theory of the State*, Harvard University Press, Cambridge, MA, 1999, pp. 190–4; see also MacKinnon, 'Reflections on Sex Equality Under Law', *Yale Law Journal* 100 (1991), pp. 1281–1324. Another analysis that replaces privacy with equality is that of Cass Sunstein, in 'Pornography, Abortion, Surrogacy', ch. 9 of *The Partial Constitution*, Harvard University Press, Cambridge, MA, 1993. MacKinnon's new casebook on sex equality (forthcoming), far more international than most such technical treatises for lawyers, cites Indian decisions (including the case from Andhra Pradesh that I shall discuss) as supportive of her general approach.
10. Paul R. Ehrlich, *The Population Bomb*, Ballantine, New York, 1968, p. 15.
11. See various writings on privacy by Richard A. Posner.
12. See *Mr. X* vs *Hospital Z*, AIR 1999.
13. See Rajeev Dhavan, *Only the Good News: On the Law of the Press in India*, Manohar, Delhi, 1987, ch.8 ('Protecting Privacy').
14. See Jean Briggs, *Never in Anger*, Harvard University Press, Cambridge, MA, 1970, a study of the Utku, an Eskimo people who, on account of climate and poverty, lived at extremely close quarters, all family members in a single room. Briggs shows that habits of reticence and guardedness were very carefully cultivated in this community.
15. See, for example, Judith De Cew, *In Pursuit of Privacy: Law, Ethics, and the Rise of Technology*, Cornell University Press, Ithaca and Cornell, 1997.
16. See the description of several such daily routines in Leela Gulati, *Profiles in Female Poverty: A Study of Poor Working Women in Kerala*, Hindustan Publishing Company, Delhi, 1981.
17. See Quran 24.30 and 24.31; for a good discussion of these verses, see Huma Ahmed-Ghosh, 'Preserving Identity: A Case Study of Palitpur', in

Zoya Hasan (ed.), *Forging Identities*, Westview Press, Boulder, CO, 1994, 169–87.

18. See other citations and discussion in my *Women and Human Development*, Cambridge University Press, Cambridge, 2000.
19. See the summary of these rules given in P.V. Kane, *History of Dharmasastra (Ancient and Mediaeval Religious and Civil Law)*, vol. II, Part I, Bhandarkar Oriental Research Institute, Poona, 1941, pp. 648–51.
20. The focus of the ancient legal texts is on the behaviour of men, but not because women are freer to behave immodestly. As we shall see, it is because women are understood to be acting, always, under male supervision and control. A classic locus for this idea is *Laws of Manu*, ch. 9.
21. See Dan Kahan on shaming penalties, discussing the penalty for public urination in Hackensack, N.J., where offenders had to scrub the streets with a toothbrush.
22. The practice is even recommended in print. Typical is this pre-race advice from Bob Glover and Shephard, *The Runner's Handbook* (Penguin, New York, 1996): 'Make a final bowel movement and empty your bladder. Don't be modest. Your comfort is at stake and the bushes may be your only choice.'
23. See P.V. Kane, *Hindu Customs and Modern Law*, Pune, 1944, pp. 99–100.
24. On some of the complexities of this feminist strategy, see my 'The Modesty of Mrs. Bajaj: India's Problematic Route to Sexual Harassment Law', forthcoming, in a volume on sexual harassment edited by Catharine MacKinnon and Reva Siegel. For an excellent general discussion of difficulties caused by the concept of modesty in pursuing women's interests, see Flavia Agnes, 'Protecting Women Against Violence? Review of a Decade of Legislation, 1980–89', *Economic and Political Weekly* 27 (25 April 1992). See also Surendra Chaher, 'Outraging the Modesty of a Woman: Inter-Spousal Perspective', *Journal of the Indian Law Institute* 32 (1990), 527–35.
25. *In re Ratnamala*, AIR 1962 (Mad. 31, 35). See discussion in E. Jeremy Hutton, Krishnan S. Nehra, and Durvasula S. Sastri, 'The Right of Privacy in the United States, Great Britain, and India', in Richard P. Claude (ed.), *Comparative Human Rights*, Johns Hopkins University Press, Baltimore, 1976, pp. 127–60.
26. See discussion in Hutton, Nehra, and Sastri, ibid., at pp. 152–3.
27. For examples of such rhetoric, and for the problematic character of these and related appeals to difference, see the excellent discussion in Uma Narayan, *Dislocating Cultures*, Routledge, New York, 1997.
28. See discussion in my *Women and Human Development*, ch. 1; and, also

my 'Beautiful as a Free Human Mind: Women, Human Development, and the Spirit of Santiniketan,' recently published in Santiniketan Cultural Journal edited by Amita Sen.

29. For many examples, see my *Women and Human Development*, especially Introduction and ch. 1. See also Kalima Rose, *Where Women are Leaders: The SEWA Movement in India*, Vistaar, Delhi, 1992.
30. See Amartya Sen, 'Fertility and Coercion', *University of Chicago Law Review*, 1998.
31. Thus the US First Amendment: 'Congress shall make no law respecting an establishment of religion, or prohibiting the free exercise thereof; or abridging the freedom of speech, or of the press; or the right of the people peaceably to assemble, and to petition the Government for a redress of grievances.' The Fourth Amendment: 'The right of the people to be secure in their persons, houses, papers, and effects, against unreasonable searches and seizures, shall not be violated, and no Warrants shall issue, but upon probable cause, supported by Oath or affirmation, and particularly describing the place to be searched, and the persons or things to be seized.' The Eighth: 'Excessive bail shall not be required, nor excessive fines imposed, nor cruel and unusual punishments inflicted.'
32. The full text of Article 15: (1) 'The State shall not discriminate against any citizen on grounds only of religion, race, caste, sex, place of birth or any of them. (2) No citizen shall, on ground only of religion, race, caste, sex, place of birth or any of them, be subject to any disability, liability, restriciton or condition with regard to (a) access to shops, public restaurants, hotels and places of public entertainment; or (b) the use of wells, tanks, bathing ghats, roads and places of public resort maintained whole or partly out of public funds or dedicated to the use of general public. (3) Nothing in this article shall prevent the State from making any special provision for women and children. (4) Nothing in this article or in clause (2) or article 29 shall prevent the state from making any special provision for the advancement of any socially and educationally backward classes of citizens or for the Scheduled Castes and the Scheduled Tribes.'
33. Article 19 states: 'All citizens shall have the right (a) to freedom of speech and expression; (b) to assemble peaceably and without arms; (c) to form associations or unions; (d) to move freely throughout the territory of India; (e) to reside and settle in any part of the territory of India; and (f) to practice any profession, or to carry on any occupation, trade or business.' Once again, the further text of the article makes it clear that these guarantees do not prevent the state from making laws advancing the interests of disadvantaged groups.

34. See *Rockwell Kent* vs *John Foster Dulles*, 357 US 116: 2 L. (ed.) 2d 1204 (1958). The case concerned alleged Communists who were denied passports on that account. The court wrote: 'The right to travel is a part of the "liberty" of which the citizen cannot be deprived without due process of law under the Fifth Amendment ... [A historical inquiry] shows how deeply engrained in our history this freedom of movement is. Freedom of movement across frontiers in either direction, and inside frontiers as well, was a part of our heritage. Travel abroad, like travel within the country, may be necessary for a livelihood. It may be as close to the heart of the individual. as the choice of what he eats, or wears, or reads. Freedom of movement is basic in our scheme of values.' Thus India guaranteed its citizens freedom of travel before the US did so.
35. See, *State of Bombay* vs *Narasu Appa Mali* (1952) in which two eminent judges held that the term 'laws in force' did not include personal laws. Some of the cases to be discussed below revisit this question.
36. Another difference: The analogue of US Fifth Amendment prohibitions of double jeopardy and compulsory self-incrimination (in Article 20) contains no due process clause in the internal language of that article itself.
37. The founders conferred with several US Supreme Court justices, especially Justice Frankfurter; the difficulties of the *Lochner* era forming a substantial part of those discussions.
38. AIR 1950 SC 27.
39. For one account of the relevant history, see David G. Barnum, 'Article 21 and Policy Making Role of Courts in India: An American Perspective', *Journal of the Indian Law Institute* 30 (1988), 19–44.
40. For the most influential critique of this understanding of equality, see Catharine MacKinnon, *Feminism Unmodified, and Toward a Feminist Theory of the State*; see also discussion in my 'The Feminist Critique of Liberalism', ch. 2 of *Sex and Social Justice*, Oxford University Press, New York, Oxford, and Delhi, 1999.
41. See Marc Galanter, *Competing Equalities*, Oxford University Press, Delhi, 1984.
42. The work of Catharine MacKinnon, in which these criticisms are most influentially articulated, is well known in India; in my experience with feminism in India, I would say that MacKinnon's work is the best known non-US feminist writing.
43. This is the central theme of Thomson's critique of privacy: see above. As I have mentioned, Thomson's article is cited in India cases; and her general point is also made by Indian legal writers: see Rajeev Dhavan, n. 45.

44. See discussion in my '"Secret Sewers of Vice": Disgust, Bodies, and the Law', in Susan Bandes (ed.), *The Passions of Justice*, New York University Press, New York, 2000.
45. *Report of the Second Press Commission (1982)*, 77 pr. 43, cited in Rajeev Dhavan, *Only the Good News*, p. 341.
46. Dhavan, op. cit.
47. De Cew's book (see n. 15 above) does something like this relatively well, with these aspects, but it seems to me that when it tries to extend the concept to cover decisional autonomy things go less well. For another useful discussion, with some responses to privacy-sceptics, see Ruth Gavison, 'Feminism and the Public–Private Distinction', *Stanford Law Review* 45 (1992), 1–46.
48. Catharine MacKinnon, 'Privacy v. Equality', *Feminism Unmodified*, Harvard University Press, Cambridge, MA, 1987, p. 100.
49. Though of course Mill was one of the staunchest opponents of this way of thinking about women and the household: see his *The Subjection of Women* (1869).
50. See Aristotle, *Politics*, I.1.
51. John Locke, *The Second Treatise on Government*, Macmillan, Library of Liberal Arts, Macmillan, New York, 1988, p. 4. See the good discussion in Judith DeCew, *In Pursuit of Privacy*, ch. 1, and also Carol Pateman, *The Disorder of Women: Democracy, Feminism, and Political Theory*, Stanford University Press, Stanford, 1989.
52. On the inherently conservative nature of the privacy right, see the analysis by Thomas Grey in 'Eros, Civilization, and the Burger Court', *Law and Contemporary Problems* 43 (1980), 83–100.
53. On this see Lauren Berlant and Michael Warner, 'Sex in Public', *Critical Inquiry* 24 (1998), 547–66. See also Michael Warner, *The Trouble with Normal: Sex, Politics, and the Ethics of Queer Life*, The Free Press, New York, 1999, reviewed (favourably) by me in *The New Republic*, 3 Jan. 2000.
54. 405 US 438 (1972); in a 6–1 decision, the Supreme Court declared unconstitutional a Massachusetts statute prohibiting the dispensing to unmarried persons of any contraceptive device. The holding was that the law violated the Equal Protection clause of the constitution by denying to unmarried persons the protection afforded to married persons. Significantly for my argument, the relevant acts were done in public: Bill Baird, a contraception advocate, had dispensed contraceptives to crowds of undergraduates at Boston Universtiy.
55. Tanika Sarkar, 'Rhetoric Against Age of Consent: Resisting Colonial Reason and Death of a Child-Wife', *Economic and Political Weekly*, 4 Sept. 1993, 1869–78. Reprinted (revised) in her book *Hindu Wife, Hindu*

Nation: Community, Religion and Cultural Nationalism, Permanent Black, Delhi, 2001.

56. Sarkar shows in detail that consent-based alternatives, even in ancient India, were summarily dismissed as aberrations. She notes that authority for child marriage comes only from Raghunandan, a late and local authority, and yet it is converted into a sine qua non of the Hindu family and Hindu religion.
57. The British judge who heard the case in which Mati was prosecuted for homicide, simply fell back on the law: 'Neither judges nor Juries have any right to do for themselves what the law has not done.' He then went on to say that probably the husband didn't realize that sleeping with a ten-year-old by force would cause damage. All the British authorities involved went out of their way to make no criticism of the allegedly traditional Hindu custom; indeed, they opined that marital age was a question 'with which no Government could meddle and no Government ought to meddle.'
58. See the opinion by Justice Choudary, cited below.
59. This famous case has been discussed in many places, including Sarkar's article. I base my discussion here on Meera Kosambi, 'Gender Reform and Competing State Controls over Women: The Rakhmabai Case (1884–1888)', in Patricia Uberoi, (ed.), *Social Reform, Sexuality and the State*, Sage Publications, Delhi, 1996), 265–90.
60. Cited in Kosambi, p. 271.
61. *T. Sareetha* vs *T. Venkata Subbaiah*, AIR 1983 Andhra Pradesh 356. See my discussion of the case in *Sex and Social Justice*, Oxford University Press, New York, 1999, Introduction and ch. 3. For extensive discussion of changes in family law, see Indira Jaisingh, *Justice for Women*, Goa 1997; Upendra Baxi, *Towards a Sociology of Indian Law*,Satvahan, Delhi 1986, ch. 3; Archana Parashar, *Women and Family Law Reform in India*, Sage Publications, Delhi, 1992; Ratna Kapur and Brenda Cossman, *Subversive Sites: Feminist Engagements with Law in India*, Sage Publications, Delhi, 1996; Patricia Uberoi, 'Introduction: Problematising Social Reform, Engaging Sexuality, Interrogating the State', in Uberoi (ed.), *Social Reform, Sexuality, and the State*, Sage Publications, Delhi, 1996, and also her article 'When is a Marriage Not a Marriage? Sex, Sacrament and Contract in Hindu Marriage', in the same volume, pp. 319–46.
62. In India, not only members of the Supreme Court, but also those of appellate courts are referred to by the title 'Justice'.
63. *Harvinder Kaur* vs *Harmander Singh Choudhry*, AIR 1984 Delhi 667.
64. *Saroj Rani* vs *Sudarshan Kumar*, AIR 71 (1984) 1562 SC.
65. Indeed, MacKinnon cites this case in her casebook to make her argument.

66. See *Brown* vs *Board of Education of Topeka* 347 US 483 (1954), declaring that separate but equal schools violate equal protection; *Loving* vs *Virginia*, 388 US 1 (1967), declaring unconstitutional, on equal-protection grounds, a Virginia law forbidding interracial marriage; the law, held the court, was but a device to uphold 'White Supremacy'.
67. Though they have in some areas recognized the basic idea: for example, Judge Posner's opinion in *Carr* v *General Motors* recognizes that the asymmetry of power in the workplace means that formally similar jokes and comments had substantively very different meanings.
68. *Planned Parenthood of Southeastern Pennsylvania* v *Casey*, 505 US 833 (1992).
69. See references above to equality-based analyses of abortion, beginning with J. Thomson, who is cited in the Supreme Court's opinion.
70. Similarly, we probably do not want the equality argument to be the only one protecting a woman's right to choice in abortion, for if the sexes were to be equal, then, on the MacKinnon/Sunstein analysis, a law outlawing the procedure would pass constitutional muster. We need to recognize an interest in decisional autonomy here, in addition to the equality interest. For the rest of this chapter, however, I shall discuss abortion no further; and I do not propose to examine its complex history in the Indian context.
71. See Derrick Bell, *Race, Racism, and American Law* (3d ed. 1992) at 89–90, who regards this as a more complex case than I do.
72. See, on this, Judge Richard Posner, *Sex and Reason*, Harvard University Press, Cambridge, MA, 1992, p. 328, on the recognition of the privacy right in *Griswold*: 'A constitution that did not invalidate so offensive, oppressive, probably undemocratic, and sectarian a law would stand revealed as containing major gaps.'
73. For similar considerations, see Richard Posner, *The Economics of Justice*, Harvard University Press, Cambridge, Mass., 1981, ch. 11.
74. See Warner, *The Trouble with Normal*, cited above.
75. See *Barnes* vs *Glen Theatre, Inc*, 501 US, 560 (1991). The case concerned an Indiana club, the Kitty Kat Lounge, which featured nude dancing. Only consenting adults were present. Another issue that became evident in the case was that of class distinctions: the lower court (which had ruled the law unconstitutional) made the point that nude dancing on the stage of the Chicago Lyric Opera was permitted. The Supreme Court, overruling the opinion, did not address the issue of class.
76. 394 US 557 (1969).
77. *Romer* vs *Evans*, 517 US at 574–5. For my Indian audience: the Hoosier Dome is a large stadium in Indiana used for sporting events. One has to buy a ticket to enter, and so the issue of offence to non-consenting

bystanders in the public square should not be raised by the imagined display, any more than by the display of football violence that actually takes place there.

78. See Grey, 'Eros, Civilization, and the Burger Court', cited above.
79. In Bombay, the figure for such 'pavement dwellers' has been estimated to be over 30 per cent of the population—personal communication, Sheela Patel, SPARC (an organization representing the interests of pavement dwellers in Bombay).
80. AIR 1963 SC 1295.
81. AIR 1975 SC 1378.
82. The actual holding is complex: they say that it is possible that the whole pattern is unconstitutional, but for now they will simply hold that the state needs to show a compelling interest in public safety if it is to apply these procedures to a particular individual.
83. A closely related issue is that of 'modesty' as a rubric under which to criminalize sexual harassment: see my 'The Modesty of Mrs. Bajaj'. Mrs. Rupan Deol Bajaj was harassed at a private party that was repeatedly characterized as including 'the élite of society'. She herself stated to the press, 'I am not a woman from the roadside', as if such a woman, working with her body in full view of all, might possibly have no modesty to outrage.
84. Here I am in full agreement with Upendra Baxi in his Introduction to Baxi (ed.), K. K. Mathew, *Democracy, Equality and Freedom*, Eastern Book Co., 1978, Lucknow, pp. lxxiii-lxxv.
85. AIR 1978 (SC 1675).
86. I elaborate and defend this approach in *Women and Human Development: The Capabilities Approach*, Kali for Women and Cambridge University Press, Delhi and New York, 2000.
87. See, for an Indian case, *Mr X.* vs *Hospital Z*, AIR 1999 (SC 495), which recognized a right to privacy in the area of confidentiality of medical records, although it also held that this right could be suspended in cases where harm to others is at issue. (The plaintiff was HIV positive and was about to marry; what concerned the court was the health interest of his prospective wife.) This Millean decision seems entirely appropriate. (This is not however generally agreed, and the case is being challenged by some feminist groups who see women as increasingly victimized by men who do not divulge their AIDS status: personal communication, Flavia Agnes, April 2000.) As for the right in question, it could be framed under substantive due process without recognizing a fully general 'right to privacy' governing all the areas we have been discussing, as a right to the confidentiality of certain sorts of intimate records.

11

The Pursuit of Social Justice*

A. VAIDYANATHAN

Background

A free, democratic state and an egalitarian society were ideals that held strong appeal to the leaders of the Indian nationalist movement. Explicitly articulated on numerous occasions by the Indian National Congress, they were eventually incorporated in the constitution of the Indian republic and throughout the past fifty years they have held a central place in the rhetoric of politics and influenced public policy to a significant degree.

To be sure, the concepts of equality and social justice, which form the foundation of the constitution, are at odds with the premise of inequality of status by birth embedded in the traditional values and practices of Indian society. Moreover, those who accepted the liberal concepts of freedom and democracy did not share the same ideas on social justice or instruments for achieving them. These ideological differences, together with diverse caste, class and regional interests, found their echoes in the debates in the Constituent Assembly. The shape and content of the constitution, as it eventually emerged, was clearly a compromise between diverse and often conflicting viewpoints.

That they managed to accommodate these differences without compromising the centrality accorded to 'freedom, equality, and social justice' is a tribute to the sagacity and skills of the constitution makers.

The Preamble asserted the basic resolve of 'We the People of India' to secure social, economic and political justice and equality of status and opportunity to all its citizens. The compromises came in the way the operative clauses were structured and detailed. Elections to the legislatures and parliament based on universal adult franchise laid the basis for broad-based democratic institutions. The provisions regarding fundamental rights sought to guarantee all citizens certain essential 'negative freedoms', in particular freedom of speech, association, and religious affiliation and eqality of access and treatment in specified spheres (including legal processes, education, and public employment). Making these rights justiciable gave them a great deal of force, which has been further strengthened by the courts taking the view that they are a part of the basic structure of the constitution.

Provisions bearing on social justice were principally those relating to affirmative action and the Directive Principles of State Policy. The need for positive discrimination in favour of socially and educationally backward classes had acquired political salience in some parts of the country well before Independence. The first steps towards caste-based reservations in education and public employment were taken in the old Madras presidency as early as the 1920s.

The constitution carried this further by incorporating explicit provisions for mandating reservations of Scheduled Castes and Tribes in elected legislative bodies and provisions enabling reservation in public employment and education for these groups. There was also a general provision enabling reservations in public employment for other backward classes which, in the opinion of the state, were not adequately represented in the services. Job reservations, it was stipulated, should be consistent with efficiency in administration and viewed as essentially transitional measures. That their scope and duration have since expanded and got entrenched is another matter and one which reflects the way the balance of political power has evolved.

The Constituent Assembly was sharply divided on the issue of positive welfare rights to give concrete content to the concept of social justice. In the event, they decided against giving them mandatory or even enabling force. Instead they were incorporated in the sections on Directive Principles of State Policy which were made explicitly non-justiciable. Any serious effort at radical redistribution of wealth from the rich to the poor was also effectively restrained by making the right to property a fundamental right. (This is the only positive economic right to be included in this section.) Its conservative interpretation by the courts further restricted the scope for redistributive measures.[1]

Nevertheless, Directive Principles were expected to, and did, provide a frame of reference for judging the goodness of public policy around which public opinion could be mobilised democratically. Dr Ambedkar's observations on this have proved prescient:

> whoever captures power will not be free to do what he likes with it. In the exercise of it, he will have to respect these instruments of instructions which are called Directive Principles. He cannot ignore them. He may not have to answer for their breach in a court of law. But he will certainly have to answer for them before the electorate at election time.[2]

Evolution

The constitution gives an idea of the society which is sought to be built and also defines the space and the framework of action to realise the vision. The actual course of this quest has been shaped by several factors. There are inherent difficulties in defining the content of social justice. These difficulties are evident in the long and ongoing debate on this issue among social philosophers. At one extreme are those who see egalitarianism as a state where there is no inequality in access to resources and opportunities. A thoroughgoing redistribution of ownership of means of production is seen by some as a necessary and sufficient condition for its attainment. At the other extreme are those who believe that such a state is impossible to attain. Rapid growth and diversification of production is, in their view, the most effective way of eliminating poverty and deprivation. They stress the importance of inequality as a source of incentives for innovation and growth.

In between are a wide range of views on achieving justice without equal distribution of wealth and incomes through some form of a welfare state. Progressive taxation of income and wealth, public provisioning of education and health, public ownership of strategic sectors, active state intervention to ensure basic needs, full employment and social security have figured prominently, though in varying combinations, in the traditional concept of a welfare state. The ongoing debate on the concept of social justice has since veered towards assurance of basic needs (defined more broadly and inclusively than per capita income) and enlarging the range and freedom of choice to everyone, and to the disadvantaged in particular, to realize their potentials.[3]

These changes at the level of ideas, combined with responses to evolving experience and, to an important degree, the shifts on balance of power in the Indian polity have shaped Indian political and policy debates on this issue. The Congress Party, which has held power over much of this period, initially proclaimed its commitment to building a 'socialist society' by redistribuiton of wealth through land reforms, expanding public ownership, and government regulation of the private sector. The major part of new investments and most new investments in key sectors (the so-called 'commanding heights') were accordingly reserved for the public sector. Private sector activities were sought to be strictly controlled and financial institutions were nationalised.

Attempts at land reform were thwarted by landed interests because of their control over local bureaucracy responsible for maintenance of land records, their clout in the arena of state politics, and the legal constraints imposed by the constitutionally guaranteed right to property. The complex intermeshing of caste and class, a distinctive feature of India, made political mobilization for radical land reform extremely difficult.[4] Expansion of the public sector and controls on the private sector did not make much of an impact on the distribution of income or the concentration of wealth and power in the private sector.[5] With overall growth being modest in the face of unprecedented acceleration in population growth, the pace of poverty reduction was very slow. During the sixties there was widespread apprehension, with some evidence to support the thesis, that inequality and unemployment may be worsening.

This led to a significant shift of emphasis from redistribution of wealth and incomes to assurance of basic minimum living standards. Old controversies over land reform, checking concentration of private wealth, and growth versus distribution have not ended. They remain alive but one cannot miss the changing emphasis in the discourse on the subject. Indira Gandhi fought and won a dramatic electoral victory in 1970 on the Garibi Hatao slogan. The slogan acquired credibility as substantial resources were actually committed to poverty alleviation programmes. The aim was to directly help the poor to acquire or expand their productive asset base and provide them with assured employment. Within a very short span of time virtually every party, covering the entire ideological spectrum, adopted it as part of their manifestos.

Over the years poverty alleviation schemes have grown in number and, more importantly, the resources committed to them have also grown rapidly.

Assessment

Critics from both the right and the left are unhappy with the results achieved so far. There is indeed much to be dissatisfied about: the pace of growth and diversification in economic activity has been modest and below expectations; inequalities in wealth and income have not been reduced; an unconscionably large proportion are poor even by the rather austere norms of minimum living standards accepted by the government; universal literacy is yet to be realized ; a large proportion of children drop out without completing elementary education; incidence of malnutrition and disease is high; and basic health care facilities are inadequate and inefficient. Indeed in all these respects disparities between regions, between males and females, and between socio–economic groups remain acute. The fact that India's performance in these areas compares unfavourably with many developing countries is often cited as indicative of failure.

Most of the above propositions are factually well founded and can therefore scarcely be questioned. However, an inadequate or disappointing pace of improvement is obviously not the same thing as lack of improvement. In terms of the GDP growth (aggregate and in per capita terms) India's performance during the second half of the twentieth century has been much higher in comparison to that in the first half of the century and comparable to the long-term growth rates recorded by countries of the 'developed' world. However, performance nowadays tends to be judged not by long-term historical experience but by the experience of post-war Japan, the so called newly industrializing economies and, more recently, China. These have posted sustained GDP growth rates of 7–8 per cent or more per annum in recent decades in comparison to India's average of 4 per cent a year. However, growth experience needs to be viewed from both perspectives, not only one of them.

This consideration is also relevant in assessing progress in the field of education and health. It is undeniable that the accomplishments are far short of the goals to which the Indian state was committed and by comparison with the achievements of many other third world countries. This should not however detract from the fact that literacy rates of the population, school enrolment rates of children, and mean years of schooling have risen steadily and substantially, and that there has been a progressive narrowing of regional, gender and class/caste disparities.[6] Much the same is true of health and sanitation. The reduction of infant and adult mortality rates, wider access to protected water supply, and the creation of a public health network are indicative of improvement despite their many serious deficiencies of coverage, quality and accessibility to the neediest segments.

As for poverty, while there is room for difference of opinion on the extent of reduction, the weight of evidence points to a reduction during the past 3–4 decades. Given the 'poverty line', the proportion of poor people in the population is basically a function of the mean per capita consumption and the inequality in its distribution. Available evidence shows no significant changes in inequality of consumption expenditure. As per capita real consumption has been rising, one would expect the incidence of poverty to decline. However differences of opinion persist over the extent of this decline and, of late, even on whether it has actually declined.[7]

Evidence on other aspects of inequality is more mixed. Limited success has been achieved in securing ownership rights to tenants, ensuring security of tenure, and regulation of rents. The amount of surplus land acquired under ceiling laws is meagre, and the extent actually redistributed even more so. Indeed, even in the more successful cases of reform, as in Kerala, West Bengal, and Karnataka, while the number of beneficiaries is large, the extent of land distributed to the landless and erstwhile tenants has been relatively small. The incidence of tenant cultivation has actually increased in some regions. The index of concentration of landownership shows no decline. The emergence of reverse tenancy has, on the other hand, resulted in an increased concentration of operational holdings in some parts of the country.[8]

The proportion of the nation's capital stock owned by the public sector has increased. But most of the public investment has been financed out of borrowings and the net returns to their investment has been low.[9] Consequently, the expansion of the public sector achieved little by way of reducing inequalities of income in the private sector. Nor did controls and regulations reduce the extent of concentration of ownership and control in the private sector. Given the difficulties of obtaining reasonably accurate information on household incomes and wealth (especially from the better-off households), data on distribution of wealth in the private sector (and changes within it) have to be treated with a great deal of caution. Indirect evidence suggests worsening of inequalities in some respects: Thus inter-regional disparities in per-capita agricultural production have increased;[10] the expansion and improvement of irrigation, a key determinant of increases in land productivity, has benefited larger farmers more than the small ones;[11] disparities in productivity of irrigated and rainfed land has increased.[12] The proportion of population dependent on wage labour and of employment in the unorganised sector, both of which are characterised by relatively low incomes and high insecurity, has increased. However, real wage rates of casual labour seem to have generally increased in both rural and urban areas at any rate since the early 1970's.[13]

At the same time, viewed in a broader perspective, one can see several signs of weakening in entrenched social inequalities and growing political assertiveness of the underclass. One important manifestation of this is the change in the social composition of the landowning classes. Evidence is accumulating that upper-caste dominance in rural land ownership has significantly declined and that the 'backward' castes, (including the Scheduled Castes) have substantially increased their share in land ownership. This is documented in a number of recent village studies in different parts of the country.[14]

Several factors seem to have contributed to this trend: The increasing tendency of the well-to-do upper castes to move out of agriculture by investing their surpluses in non-farm activities and in higher education; the weakening of their power and hence capacity to enforce traditional arrangements *vis-à-vis* tenants and labourers; and the acquisition of resources by working in urban areas, sometimes in other states and, on occasion, even abroad. While government may have failed to implement land reforms, the existence of the legislation seems to have helped the bargaining strength of the landless, the land poor and tenants *vis-à-vis* upper-caste landowners.

The proportion of rural population depending on wage labour has risen significantly and an increasing number of labourers depend on casual rather than regular employment on a seasonal or annual basis.[15] These trends are widely viewed as undesirable on the ground that it reflects dispossession of small and marginal farmers of their land; that wage labour is exposed to exploitation and that casualization increases the scope for it. However, much (perhaps most) of the 'proletarianisation' of rural labour is on account of the growth of rural population relative to land. Regular employment is no doubt declining, much of it on account of a virtual elimination of traditional, exploitative forms of attached labour. While casual labourers face greater uncertainty about finding work, they are also free from dependence on a particular employer. The shift from payments in kind determined by custom to cash wages reflecting the balance between supply and demand reduces the scope for exploitation, even as it gives them greater freedom over the disposition of their income. Available evidence shows no significant change in duration of employment of an average labourer; and real wage rates have everywhere risen, though modestly.

The traditional social and political power structures in village India have also greatly loosened as a result of the progressive commercialization of the rural economy, increasing interactions with bureaucrats, politicians and regional/ national political parties. The spread of education, positive discrimination in higher education and public employment has contributed to greater awareness and, perhaps more importantly, helped create a nascent middle class and political leadership in these groups. The numerous reported instances of Scheduled Castes, most of whom are labourers, refusing to perform their traditional roles are indicative of their assertiveness. Successful pressures for extension of the scope and duration of reservations is another. The manner in which allocations for poverty alleviation programmes, ostensibly meant for their benefit, are managed has also begun to attract their critical attention. The cumulative effect of these forces on the balance of social and economic relations (especially in rural areas) has been to give the underclass an increasing voice to articulate their claims in the political arena, and actively seek a greater share in political power.

These are significant steps towards a more democratic and equitable society, but only the first ones. The impact on living conditions of the underprivileged and on equality of opportunity has so far been quite modest. Nor has there been a radical change in the caste–class composition of the power élite. Hard evidence may be lacking, but few will dispute the widely shared impression that key positions in business, public bureaucracy, the media, and other major arenas, where power is exercised, continue to be dominated by the affluent and educated. The emergence and dramatic growth of new business houses and the upward mobility of sections of the underclass facilitated by affirmative action are welcome signs, but the power élite is still dominated by the upper rungs of the social hierarchy. They are the principal beneficiaries of the power patronage, corruption and employment generated by the vast increase in resources expended by public agencies. At a more fundamental level, the society is a long way from eradicating prejudices, exclusions, discrimination, and attendant inequities based on caste, community, and religion.

The fluidity in Indian politics combined with growing awareness and participation of the backward castes, Scheduled Castes and Tribes has even enabled the latter to challenge, weaken and, in several regions, dislodge the upper castes' hold on political power. The assertiveness of the underprivileged, unsettling as it may be, is far from being undesirable: it is to be welcomed in order to make democracy more meaningful. The upper classes however feel threatened by this trend. Their hold on power has weakened. Their opportunities have been restricted by the high proportion of public sector jobs and admissions to higher education covered by caste-based reservation and the progressive extension of its scope and duration. Not surprisingly, a significant section of them attribute the heightening of communal and caste tensions, fragmentation of political parties, weak governance, spread of corruption, slow growth of the economy and the resulting instability to the 'pampering' of Scheduled Castes and Tribes, and backward castes and communities, for political gain.

Regional, caste, communal, and ideological conflicts are endemic to the Indian polity. So long as Congress controlled power over most part of the country, these contradictions and conflicts were contained and managed within the party. With the decline in the Congress's hold, they are coming more and more into the open. The collapse of communist regimes in the USSR and East Europe, and the profound changes in the character and policies of the Chinese regime have resulted in a severe erosion of socialism as an ideology around which the have-nots could rally. The emergence of regional and caste-based parties seems to be more in the nature of a process of regrouping and realignment of forces induced by the above developments rather than an autonomous resurgence of the underclass.

Corruption is indeed widespread. But bribes given and taken by the under-class account for an insignificant part of the phenomenon. Tax evaders, businessmen, contractors, bureaucrats and politicians, who account, both as perpetrators and as beneficiaries, for the bulk of corruption, all belong to the richest 10 or 20 per cent of the population.

Nor are poverty alleviation programmes (inclusive of elementary education, health, water supply and food subsidies) the cause of erosion of resources available for investment. Indeed, the allocation for some key components, especially elementary education and basic health care, are inadequate even to maintain the quality of services provided by existing facilities, not to speak of achieving universal coverage and improving their quality.

The pro-poor interventions suffer from numerous and well-known deficiencies: they are fragmented, poorly designed, and prone to huge leakages; benefits do not reach intended beneficiaries in full measure.[16] To a large degree this is because these very programmes have been seized and exploited by the political class and the bureaucracy to extend their patronage networks and share the spoils of office, often for personal gain. Nevertheless, they can scarcely be dismissed as being of no consequence. They have generated substantial additional employment, provided effective relief in times of severe drought and even helped maintain, if not improve, real wage rates.[17] They have also enabled, even if only to a modest degree, more and more of the underprivileged to avail of opportunities for advancement.

In any case, poor-oriented programmes are not the principal reason for the large and growing fiscal deficit. Far more important is the slow growth of government revenues relative to expenditure, the soaring costs on account of salaries and benefits for government employees, interest payments, and implicit subsidies. The government budget which showed a modest revenue surplus till the late 1970s went into deficit during the early 1980s. The deficit has increased rapidly and in 1998–9 stood at 5.7 per cent of GDP. The growing dependence on borrowed funds has led to a galloping increase in interest payments which currently account for 30 per cent of revenues.[18] Unrecovered costs on account of all publicly provided goods and services have risen over two and a half times from 1987–8 to 1994–5; they were less than the total public sector plan outlays in the former year, but in 1994–5, exceeded the latter by 30 per cent.[19]

Any programme for fiscal stabilization must therefore concentrate on tighter tax administration, administrative reorganisation to contain the size of the government establishment, adopt a salaries/benefit policy more in line with the capacity of the economy, and reduce subsidies. Budget speeches make ritual references to these issues, but very little is done to seriously address them. The reasons are clear: strong action on these matters would adversely affect the interests of the relatively well-to-do, comprising not only the business and professional classes but also large farmers, government employees, and those in the organized, unionized sectors.

Those who pay, or are liable to pay, direct taxes belong to these groups. The belief, underlying recent tax reform, that lower rates will be more than compensated by a dramatic increase in compliance, have been belied.[20] Laxity and corruption in tax administration remain serious problems.

Public sector employees have managed, through trade union pressure, reinforced by their strategic positions in the country's government, to secure increases in their emoluments and benefits at a much faster rate than other sectors. Restructuring of administration necessary for greater efficiency cannot even get started in the face of their strong resistance.

When it comes to cutting subsidies, the only relatively serious effort during the last decade has focussed on food and fertilizers. This effort has been frustrated by the argument that they are anti-poor. While there is some merit in the argument (at least as far as food subsidies are concerned), it has also provided a convenient alibi to distract attention from the much larger subsidies in electricity, water, public transport, higher education and urban amenities. The bulk of the benefits from these accrue directly or indirectly to the relatively well off segments of the rural and urban populations.[21] Raising user charges and restructuring organizations (into autonomous but trimmer, more transparent, accountable and financially self-reliant entities), necessary to tackle the problem will also affect them far more adversely than the poor. Upper-class resistance to these reforms is therefore very strong. Though far less numerous than the poor, they have been able to prevent or neutralize any attempt to address these issues.

Impact of Globalization

One would have expected that the necessity to reduce the fiscal deficit and find much needed resources for infrastructure investments would have forced a change of attitudes. There are some signs that this is beginning to happen but they are as yet very anemic. No credible action capable of making a significant difference is visible. Instead the élite have chosen to take refuge in the belief that the new economic policy of liberalization, globalization, and privatization will solve the problems by accelerated economic growth.

Not that the new economic policy commands universal and unqualified support from all segments of the élite. The working classes, especially those with secure jobs protected by law and trade unions in the public and private sectors, oppose the reforms. They have good reason to fear that their jobs and bargaining power are at serious risk. On the other hand, the indigenous business class, while welcoming internal liberalization, has become apprehensive of competition from imports and foreign companies. Their enthusiasm about globalization has distinctly cooled. Farmers would support reduction of trade restrictions if it means higher prices for them. But since the likely gains are uncertain and uneven across regions the enthusiasm is rather muted. On the other hand, they strongly oppose any attempt at reduction of subsidies on inputs. Apprehensions of increasing influence of multinationals and foreign governments on domestic policy and the spectre of a new imperialism have led to a broader opposition to globalization at the ideological level.

Enthusiasm for globalization is greatest among the educated middle class. A large section of them have already tasted the substantial benefits from migration to developed countries.[22] This aspect of globalization has been in process for several decades and has quicknened over time. In so far as greater integration, of the world economy leads to lowering of barriers to migration; this class stands to benefit. It also expects to benefit from the entry of multinational corporations and the attendant increase in domestic job opportunities and emoluments for skilled and professional personnel.

Influential segments of the élite thus support, though in varying degrees and for diverse motives, liberalization and globalisation. They evidently see the potential gains for themselves but also seek to rationalize it as beneficial for the economy as a whole. In doing so they ignore, or at any rate make light of, well-grounded concerns about its detrimental, and some positively harmful, consequences.

The spread of modern mass media (especially television) has become an increasingly powerful influence in shaping the desires and aspirations of third world populations regarding the kind of goods they would like to possess and the lifestyle they would like to adopt. This has been reinforced by the aggressive advertising of products of multinational corporations. Attracted by the potentially huge market India offers, more and more of them are setting up or expanding their manufacturing base in the country. Expectations of the kinds of jobs and lifestyle people would like are changing much faster than their means to realise them. The gap is not only larger at the base of the socio-economic pyramid in comparison to those near its apex, but it is probably also widening faster. Superimposed on the large initial disparities, and the generally low living standards, this portends a further aggravation of social tensions.

There is also the larger question about the desirability of indiscriminate adoption by the third world of the consumption patterns of the 'developed world'. The viability of these lifestyles is under serious question even in the 'developed countries'. It is widely recognized that profligacy in their consumption is the root cause of depletion of natural resources and degradation of the environment worldwide. A drastic change in consumption patterns is seen to be essential to arrest and reverse these trends in the interests of long term sustainability. However, these considerations do not have any significant impact on the perceptions and attitudes of those who make and sell products or those who buy them in the third world.

Governments of the third world (including India) have become helpless spectators and, increasingly, active perpetrators of the mindless race to modernity. The attendant consequences for the environment and sustainable use of natural resources in countries like India are compounded by the huge demand for third world natural resources (especially energy and forests) to sustain the living standards of the rich countries and by the tendency of their firms to shift polluting activities to the third world, where environmental standards and their enforcement are far less rigorous.

Globalization and the spread of MNCs have also larger political consequences. The third world and the developed world start from highly unequal positions in terms of resource endowments relative to population and of technological capability. Thanks to the new Intellectual Properties Regime, technological upgradation through imitation and adaptation has become much more difficult and expensive. A proactive strategy to acquire mastery over modern technology and the capacity to innovate new techniques, which some countries of East Asia have so successfully pursued—is in principle open to India. However, both the Indian government and Indian industry have chosen the softer, and shortsighted, option of using collaborations and joint ventures as the vehicle of technological progress. Implicit in this is the prospect of continued, possibly increasing, dependence on foreign knowhow.

Whether MNCs can be effectively made accountable to comply with domestic laws on par with domestic business is another issue. The MNCs have immense resources and political clout in their home countries. Their power to interfere and influence policies of host governments to serve their interests is evident from the experience of several other countries. Apprehensions in India on this account are therefore legitimate. The implications of free movement of finance capital between countries and its volatility for the ability of domestic policy to ensure a stable economic environment have also been highlighted by recent experiences. One does not have to accept the thesis of an emerging New Imperialism to recognize these as genuine concerns.

Globalization, as it is currently unravelling, also gives rise to concerns about the perpetuation and further strengthening of the unequal relations between nations. Attempts to work out international agreements to address these problems, and build rule-based arrangements for trade, capital, and technology flows, and environmental regulation, have run into serious difficulties. The experience of negotiations on trade, intellectual property rights, and environment provides ample evidence of the unwillingness of the rich to concede that resource depletion and environmental deterioration is due to their high consumption levels, and to accept fair share of the responsibility for concerted global action. On the other hand, they have unabashedly used their power to protect and promote their interests in ways palpably inimical to the interests of the third world. While the growing interest in rule-based international arrangements is a welcome development, the fact remains that the terms of these agreements are highly unequal, and institutions for their enforcement are dominated by the rich.

Prospects

In sum, the erosion of their political power, a perception that the present arrangements have unduly restricted their economic opportunities, and the belief that globalization opens up vast new vistas for them, has led to a palpable weakening of the élites' interest (even belief) in transforming the system from within. More important, it has eroded its appreciation, not to speak of acceptance, of moral and political compulsions of public action to correct deeply entrenched inequalities and ensure that all citizens are enabled to live a decent, dignified life. On the contrary, it has resulted in a transformation in their attitudes to positive discrimination, poverty alleviation, and social security for the underprivileged from one of apathy to one of hostility. The already serious divide between the élite and the underprivileged has widened.

Without an ideology that can unite the have-nots for positive action, caste and religion have become more and more the basis for political mobilization. The emphasis of these formations is on seeking privileges by way of subventions and preferential treatment for various state favours which end up benefiting a minority among the underprivileged. They have not shown as strong an interest in advocating programmes which will lead to a sustained, broad-based improvement in the living condition and opportunities for their constituents. Attempts at fostering an alternative ideology based on nationalism and majority religion have failed to correct these tendencies; on the contrary, they are adding fuel to religious conflicts, violent politics, and other tendencies decidedly inimical to the ethos of democracy.

These tendencies naturally cause widespread concern about the future of Indian democracy and its ability to achieve social justice. Nevertheless, one must also take note of several positive features: the conduct of elections involving several hundred million voters regularly, in an orderly manner, and without undue violence; the high level of voter turnout; the openness and intensity of political debate; the existence of a free and vibrant press; and the functioning of the judiciary have all been widely acclaimed. Also noteworthy is the demonstrated capacity of the system to deal with numerous complex problems, often serious and sometimes potentially explosive, with resilience and flexibility but without sacrificing the basic framework defined by the constitution. Some at least of the constitutional amendments were an attempt to adapt in the light of evolving experience. Others which went against the basic spirit of the constitution were checked by the courts (the concept of basic structure being an example) and (as in the case of the emergency) by the electorate.

Thanks to the media and the NGOs, deficiencies, failures, and abuses by government and important problems (civil rights, untouchability, corruption, social discrimination, droughts and famines, environment) are in the public gaze and critical scrutiny has forced governments to pay attention and take corrective action. The public distribution system, flood and drought relief, the national social security schemes for the poor, and anti-poverty programmes are all examples of constructive responses to public pressure. Mounting criticism of waste and ineffectiveness of anti-poverty programmes was one of the factors that led to a revival of interest in panchayati raj and the passage of the 73rd and 74th Amendments to the constitution.

The creation of representative local bodies chosen through mandatory elections and vested with responsibilities for local development is a far-reaching step. That state and central politicians, who stand to lose power by implementing these provisions, legislated these amendments is significant. Their resistance to actually parting with their power is understandable. But they eventually have to concede space and resources to local bodies.

The 73rd and 74th Amendments have created an irrevocable space for local politicians to press for greater resources and power to local bodies. These pressures are gaining strength and will, sooner or later, have to be accommodated. Together with the provision for mandatory elections and reservations for Scheduled Castes/Tribes and women, democracy in India promises to become wider and deeper.

The rapid growth of non-governmental organizations is another major positive development. By strengthening institutions in civil society, they are strengthening democracy. NGO activists have made a significant contribution by bringing issues relating to equity and environment to public attention and seeking remedies through mass mobilization and judicial interventions. Equally important, and significant, is their active involvement in developmental activities at the grass-roots level. Besides helping local communities (especially the less privileged) to take better advantage of resources available under state funded programmes, many are experimenting with innovative techniques and participatory approaches to local development. They also show much greater concern for equitable sharing of benefits and environmental issues. A noteworthy feature of the NGO movement, and one which to some extent compensates for the apathy of the élite to issues of sustainable and equitable development, is that it is attracting a substantial and apparently growing number of educated youth at the cost of lucrative professional careers.

Conclusion

Viewed strictly from the perspective of the present, one is apt to be overwhelmed by the intense state of ferment in society, the contradictory and confusing happenings and the frustrations of living amidst violence, widespread corruption, and apparently growing disorder. The system is ridden with narrow loyalities; there are worrisome anti-democratic tendencies and even the modest goals of social justice as envisaged by the constitution-makers remain to be fulfilled. If however one were to view the evolution of the Indian polity in a historical perspective one cannot but be impressed by the fact that so vast and diverse a country has managed its affairs in a democratic framework, that democratic institutions and processes have taken deep roots, that it has given more and more voice to and space for the underprivileged. There can be little doubt that the constitution has been worked in a manner that has strengthened democracy and made sustained, if modest, progress towards a more just social order. The apparent changes and drift can be seen as reflections of deep changes in society and the attendant realignment of forces. Both positive and negative tendencies are in evidence. No one can predict how and what balance between the two will be struck and whether the results will be to propel India to become an even more vibrant democracy moving further towards a juster social order. However, the experience of the last fifty formative and difficult years gives reason for cautious confidence that it will.

Notes and References

* Revised version of paper presented at a conference organized by UPIASI, New Delhi, 23–5 January 2000. The revisions have benefited from comments and suggestions from C.T. Kurien, Manabi Majumdar, V.K. Natraj, M.S.S. Pandian, S. Neelakantan, Satish Saberwal, R. Sudarshan and participants at the seminar. I would like to thank, without implicating, all of them. I would also like to thank Ms. Syamala for typing the paper through several revisions.

1. The land reforms programme, the major redistributive measure attempted by the state, suffered an early and severe setback as a result of the Supreme Court's judgements in the *Kameshwar Singh* and *Bela Banerjee* cases (both in 1954). The court held the impugned legislation in both cases to be violative of fundamental right to property on grounds that compensation was arbitrary and unjust. Several other land-reform legislations were also struck down on similar grounds. And in 1967, the court went further to challenge the power of parliament to amend the provisions relating to fundamental rights. Subsequently, in the *Kesavananda Bharati* case (1978), it softened its stand on the issue. However, when reviewing a series of constitutional amendments seeking to put the land-reform laws beyond judicial challenge, the court held (in the *Minerva Mills* case) that amendments should not compromise the basic structure of the constitution. The tension between right to property and promotion of equality remains unresolved. (For a detailed account of the judgements see, Kamal Jeet Singh, *Distributive Justice in India: A Socio-Legal Study*,

Reliance Pub. House, New Delhi, 1985). This is not to suggest that the courts were the only impediments of land reform. Politics, as Sudarshan has pointed out, was, and remains, an important factor, but the courts' judgements clearly assisted the opposition to radical reform. See R. Sudarshan, 'The Political Consequences of Constitutional Discourse', in T.V. Sathyamurthy, ed., *State and Nation in the Context of Social Change*, OUP, Delhi, 1994.

2. Quotation as cited in Paul A. Appasamy, *et al.*, *Social Exclusion from Welfare Rights in India*, International Institute of Labour Studies, ILO, Geneva, 1995.
3. For a recent discussion of these issues see the writings of A.K. Sen.
4. For a critical assessment of the reforms in Kerala, see K.N. Raj and Michael Tharakan, 'Agrarian Reform in Kerala and Its Impact on the Rural Economy', CDS Working Paper, Trivandrum; on Karnataka, see Abdul Aziz and Sudhir Krishna, eds, *Land Reforms in India*, vol. 4, Sage, New Delhi, 1992. The role of intermeshing between caste and class in shaping the politics of Indian land reform is highlighted in my 'Employment Situation, Emerging Perspectives', *EPW*, December 1996; and 'Agricultural Development: Imperatives of Institutional Reforms', *EPW*, December 1996, by comparing it with the Chinese experience.
5. See GOI *Reports of the Committee on Distribution of Income and Wealth*, 2 vols, 1964 and 1969; R.K. Hazari, *The Structure of the Private Corporation Sector*, Asia Pub. House, Bombay, 1966.
6. See Vaidyanathan and Nair (eds), *Elementary Education in India*, Sage, New Delhi, 2001.
7. This issue has resurfaced in current discussions on the impact of liberalization and structural adjustment and the incidence of poverty during the 1990s. See Gaurav Dutt, 'Has Poverty Declined Since Economic Reforms:Statistical Data Analysis', *EPW*, December 1999. A Vaidyanathan, 'Poverty and Development Policy', Kale Memorial Lecture, Gokhale Institute of Economics and Politics', Pune, 2000.
8. The National Sample Survey, which provides by far the most systematically compiled data on the subject, shows that there was no significant or sustained change in the degree of inequality in land ownership (measured by the Gini Coefficient) in most states; inequality in operational holdings, on the other hand, shows a sustained (and in some a sizeable) increase in a majority of states. H.R. Sharma, 'Distribution of Land Holdings in Rural India, 1953–4 to 1991–2', *EPW*, March 1994; also Ravi Srivastava, 'Changes in Contractual Relations in Land and Labour

in India', *Indian Journal of Agricultural Economics*, July–Sept. 2000, for a more up-to-date picture of these changes.

9. The share of the public sector in the country's total capital stock (net reproducible wealth) rose from 18 per cent in 1950–1 to 45 per cent in the early 1970s. The expectation that this would result in an increasing proportion of profit and property incomes accruing in the public sector, and thereby reducing inequalities in private incomes, has been belied. The rate of return (both on capital employed and on net worth) earned by government enterprises has been much lower than that of the private corporate sector. In 1950–1, the major part of public investment was financed by its own savings, but over the years this has declined sharply and now stands at 10 per cent. (A summary of the relevant data is given in A. Vaidyanathan, *The Indian Economy: Crisis and Response*, Orient Longman, Chennai, 1995.)
10. The relevant data are summarized in A. Vaidyanathan, 'Poverty and Economy: The Regional Dimension', in John Harriss, *et al.*, *Poverty in India: Research and Policy*, Oxford University Press, Delhi, 1992.
11. Thus the proportion of cultivated land reported to be irrigated has risen in all landholdings of all size classes; but while this proportion rose from 26.6 per cent in 1953–4 to 41.6 per cent in 1991–2 in holdings below 1 ha, it rose from 6.1 per cent to 25.1 per cent among holdings of more than 10 ha. The relevant NSS data are summarized in A. Vaidyanathan, *Water Resource Management: Institution and Irrigation Development in India*, OUP, Delhi, 1999.
12. A. Vaidyanathan, 'Impact of Irrigation on Productivity of Land', *Journal of the Indian School of Political Economy*, Pune, 1997.
13. During the 1950s and 1960s real wage rates in rural areas were generally stagnant and in several states even declining (see A.V. Jose, 'Real Wages, Employment and Income of Agricultural Labourers', *EPW*, March 1978). However, since the early 1970s they show a rising trend in a majority of states. The relevant data are presented in A.V. Jose, 'Agricultural Wages in India', *EPW*, June 1988 and Vaidyanathan, 1996.
14. For Tamil Nadu, see S. Guhan, 'Palakurichi: A Resurvey', Working Paper, Madras Institute of Development Studies (MIDS), Chennai, 1983; S. Guhan and Joan Mencher, 'Irivelipettu Revisited', Working Paper, MIDS, Chennai, 1984; S. Guhan and K. Bharathan, 'Dusi: A Resurvey', Working Paper, MIDS, Chennai, 1984; K. Sivasubramanian, 'Irrigation Institute in Two Large Multi-Village Tanks of Tamil Nadu', Ph.D. Dissertation, University of Madras, 1995; Haraka Yanigisawa, *A Century*

of Change: Caste and Irrigated Lands in Tamilnadu 1860s–1970s, Manohar, Delhi, 1996. For Karnataka, see Aziz and Krishna 1992. This trend is also reported by a few recent unpublished village surveys in Telengana and coastal AP.

15. National Sample Survey estimates show that wage and salary employees as a proportion of all workers rose from 25 per cent in 1972–3 to 42 per cent in 1993–4. Over the same period, those working in casual wage labour rose from 78 per cent of all wage/salary employes in 1972–3 to 84 per cent in 1993–4. Wage and salary employment is more conspicuous in urban areas, but much the larger part of it consists of regular employment. Casual wage labour constitutes a much smaller, though rising, proportion of wage/salary class. See *Sarvekshana*, July–Sept. 1996.
16. These criticisms also apply to the reservations policy. The reservation quotas are not fully met; and those who benefit from them are largely concentrated in the minority of these groups who have already moved up the scale of education and incomes. It is also arguable that the impact of reservation in admissions to higher education has been substantially eroded by extending reservations in the teaching profession and the consequent fall in the quality of teachers.
17. S. Mahendra Dev, *India's (Maharashtra) Employment Guarantee Scheme: Lessons from Experience*, Indira Gandhi Institute for Development Research, Mumbai, 1995; Raghav Gaiha, 'Do Rural Public Works Influence Agricultural Wages?', *Oxford Development Studies*, 25, 3, 1997.
18. Reserve Bank of India, *Report on Currency and Finance 1998–9*, Mumbai.
19. S. Mundle and M. Govinda Rao, 'The Volume and Composition of Subsidies in India 1987–9', *EPW*, May 1991.
20. The ratio of direct tax collections to GDP rose from 1.9 per cent in 1990–1 to 2.8 per cent in 1995–6. It has however remained more or less stagnant since. That of excise duty has actually fallen steadily from 4.3 per cent in 1990–1 to and 3 per cent in 1998–9. GOI, Ministry of Finance, *Economic Survey 2000–2001*.
21. For example, implicit subsidies on education (other than elementary education) amounted in 1994–5 to an estimated Rs.15,000 crores, most of it for high school and university education. Those having access to these levels of education are mostly concentrated in the top 20 per cent of the population. Subsidies on irrigation, fertilizers, and electricity, which amounted up to Rs. 32,000 crores in 1994–5, are partly a reflection of inefficiencies in their production and distribution and partly due to underpricing. Part of the high costs is due to an inflated labour force

whose emoluments put it among the top 20 per cent of the population. At the same time, benefits of irrigation and fertilizers are largely concentrated among the better-off farmers. Those with farms of over 2 ha. constitute less than a fifth of the holdings but account for over 60 per cent of the irrigated area and pumpsets.

22. At the end of the 1980s the number of Indians who have voluntarily emigrated to Europe, North America and Australia is estimated at over two million. Another two million were in the Gulf countries. Emigration to the USA, Canada and the Gulf has been increasing during the 1980s. See Vinod Kadria, *The Migration of Knowledge Workers: Second Generation Effects*, Sage, New Delhi, 1998. The educational composition of migrants is not known. A high proportion of recent migrants to the USA and Canada are highly educated professionals. The proportion is relatively small in the Gulf. The number of highly educated Indians abroad can be conservatively placed at one million. This compares with 21 million people (as enumerated in the 1999 census of population) who have graduated; and around four million who have postgraduate degrees. This means that one out of every twenty young people graduating from Indian universities has emigrated. The proportion among postgraduates would be much higher.

12

The Long Half-life of Reservations

MARC GALANTER

The furore over the implementation of the Mandal Report[1] marked a transition. Mandal and its reception recapitulated the unresolved tensions in the constitutional scheme of compensatory preference to modify India's social structure. These tensions in turn resonate with the conflicting and paradoxical notions of the equality that India has embraced so decisively in defining itself as a nation.

The constitution established a regime of formal equality spanning a society of legendary hierarchy. It contemplated a government that would take various measures to mitigate prevailing inequalities in wealth, education, and power. In pursuing this mandate, government was specifically forbidden to employ the ascriptive categories of caste, religion, and race. This ban on 'communal' measures was subject to a massive and singular exception: the state was empowered to utilize these forbidden categories to remedy the accumulated disabilities suffered by those at the bottom of the caste hierarchy (the Scheduled Castes) and at the margins of Indian society (the Scheduled Tribes). The explicit provision for these groups is the core of the policy of compensatory discrimination that is one of the distinctive themes of the Indian constitution.

The Mandal report can serve as a convenient marker along the winding path followed by India's 'affirmative action' policies. The ambiguities that have bedevilled these policies are reflected in the uncertainty about their name. Originally, the overall policy was nameless;[2] the various measures that embodied it were referred to as 'reservations' or 'special treatment' or 'preferential treatment' or 'concessions'. Most of those writing about it have been content to label it 'reservations' without connecting that device to any wider principle or goal.[3] In the 1950s Professor Alexandrowicz proposed 'protective discrimination', and this has been taken up by some writers on the subject and is raised in the courts.[4] My later proposal of 'compensatory discrimination' gained some currency, particularly among comparativists, but also remained a niche term.[5] There are others, such as 'positive discrimination', 'benign discrimination', and 'reverse discrimination'; many writers and judges use more than one of these terms, treating them as synonyms.[6] All seem fated to be overwhelmed by the borrowed American term 'affirmative action', which began to be used in the early 1980s.[7]

On first encounter, we might dismiss this new terminology as yet another instance of uncritical adoption of American terms and of a wider and unreciprocated receptivity to American law.[8] However, perhaps there is more here. Conveying at least an oblique reference to the American experience, it signals a tendency to regard Indian developments not as intractably unique, but as a complexly particularized instance of fundamental issues about disadvantaged segments of the population in 'meritocratic' democracies. The sense of mutual relevance is expressed in a burgeoning transnational discourse. Just a year ago I participated in a meeting in St Louis in which academics and practitioners from India, South Africa, and the United States exchanged views on their affirmative action programmes; the Indian experience was considered a source of lessons that might be relevant in other settings.[9]

The Mandal Solution

Apart from the untouchables and tribal peoples, the constitutional policy of preference also authorized measures for 'other socially and educationally backward classes'. From its inception the commitment to these 'Other Backward Classes' has been haunted by a series of persistent and unanswered questions: how wide a layer of Indian society is included? How are they to be selected? What is the role of caste in that selection? What benefits should they receive? Finally, what relation does this bear to the core commitment to the untouchables and tribals? Although more people, more money, more jobs and more programmes are involved in preferential measures for Scheduled Castes and Tribes, the scattered measures for OBCs have involved more controversy in the courts and, for the last decade, on the streets and in the legislatures. The Mandal Report boldly essayed to slash through the conceptual and policy tangles that beset the designation of OBCs, and in large measure its resolution has been institutionalized by the government and the courts.

From the outset it was unclear whether the Other Backward Classes category was meant to include a wide middle band of castes and communities situated 'above' the Scheduled Castes and Scheduled Tribes, and excluding only prominently well-advantaged groups at the top. Alternatively was it intended to catch those whose advantages were far below the average, comparable in circumstance to the Scheduled Castes and Scheduled Tribes? Put in another way, was the backwardness of the Other Backward Classes to be relative to the average or to the top? Mandal opts for the expansive view, and this has now been ratified by the government and by the Supreme Court.

Similarly, long-standing questions about whether caste groups are the backward classes on whom preferences can be conferred and the precision with which their backwardness needs to be measured achieved some resolution after Mandal—at least for now. Mandal identifies the Other Backward Classes on the basis of caste. Like its predecessors, the report displays some difficulty separating out two ways of talking about caste in connection with backwardness. Castes may be the social *units* whose backwardness is to be measured; alternatively, caste may be a rank or status that serves as a measuring rod for determination of the backwardness of social units. The significance of distinguishing them is evident if we consider what it means to eliminate the 'caste test': the alternative to castes as units is to measure the backwardness of families or occupations or individuals; a substitute to caste as a measuring rod is to base eligibility on such criteria as poverty/illiteracy.

Mandal employs caste in both senses. It uses castes as the units whose backwardness is going to be measured (along with jati-like formations among non-Hindus), and it proposes to use caste standing as the measuring rod. It identifies the Other Backward Classes as those 'considered as socially backward by others'[10] and it seems willing to accept varna as a useful summation of standing,[11] noting that three-quarters of the respondents to its questionnaire identified 'the three upper Varnas ... [with the] dominant castes'.[12] Its emphasis on caste rank is somewhat obscured by wrapping it in a complex test involving eleven criteria, but these are weighted to emphasize traditional measures of low status (perceived rank, manual labour, and female participation in the labour force).[13]

There are further problems in ascertaining the conditions that actually prevail among the groups in question. The appearance of precision in applying the commission's criteria is dissipated by a serious methodological flaw. These caste groups have not been counted in the census since 1931; the extrapolation of community population figures for half a century, on the assumption that all communities experienced equal growth rates,[14] renders suspect many of the commission's findings about relative conditions.

The shaky foundation for determining the backwardness of caste groups raises the question of whether it might be possible to select beneficiaries by an 'economic test' of wealth or income. Indeed, the Mandal Commission purports to have included the 'value of family assets' among the things it measured.[15] Even if the political will were present, there is reason to doubt the capacity of government to effectively implement an 'economic test' of backwardness. Those attracted by such a test should reflect on the inability of the government to cope with the task of identifying the Bhopal victims. For all its complexities, looking for traces of a single event in the population of a delimited area is less demanding than ascertaining the wealth or income of all the candidates for backward class status. For the time being, such a policy is administratively out of reach.

To the inexactness with which the beneficiaries are identified, the Mandal scheme adds some features that belie its apparent modesty and precision. The quantum of reserved places required by a reservation can be calculated in either of two ways. A reservation—for example, the 27 per cent of places in central government services that is recommended by Mandal—can be treated as a *guaranteed minimum*, so that the reservation ensures that if a smaller number of beneficiaries are selected in open competition, the results are adjusted to add additional members of the beneficiary group up to the level of the reservation.

Alternatively, a reservation can be designed to allocate seats *over and above* those gained by the beneficiaries in open competition. Mandal clearly opts for the *over and above* method.[16] This portends a very sizable increase in the intake of Other Backward Classes. Curiously, so far as I know, the permissibility of these *over and above* reservations has not been the subject of constitutional challenge in recent years, although a generation ago several courts found them objectionable.[17]

Who would occupy all these places? Schemes of reservation tend to reproduce within the beneficiary class the same kind of clustering that the reservation is meant to remedy. That is, those among the beneficiaries who already enjoy the greatest advantages obtain a disproportionately large share of the benefits. That result might be mitigated by use of income ceilings or by compartmentalizing the reservation. Mandal never mentions the use of income and explicitly rejects the use of compartments.[18] The report is quite sanguine in its recognition that the

> major benefits of reservations and other welfare measures for OBCs will be cornered by the more advanced sections of the backward communities. The chief merit of reservation is not that it will introduce egalitarianism amongst Other Backward Classes when the rest of the Indian society is seized by all sorts of inequalities. But reservation will certainly erode the hold of higher castes on the services and enable OBCs in general to have a sense of participation in running the affairs of their country.[19]

Unquestionably, the top layers and the most prosperous among the Other Backward Classes would secure a disproportionate share of the benefits and those at the bottom of these groups would get little. Resources would be redistributed from the least advantaged members of the most advantaged groups to the most advantaged members of less advantaged groups who are themselves above the mean on most indicators. The numbers of the lowly would provide the basis for the promotion of the fortunes of their well-off cousins. The Mandal Report's concern with the distributive consequences of selection *vis-à-vis* the upper castes is combined with a cool indifference to the distributive consequences within the OBC group. This contrast troubled the Supreme Court, which insisted that government curb the regressive features of the reservation scheme by requiring measures to remove the 'creamy layer' of 'socially advanced persons/sections' from the designated backward classes.[20]

The Paradox of Equality and the Limits of Compensatory Preference

The policy of compensatory discrimination is premised on the understanding that in a regime of formal equality and open competition, members of a previously victimized group, burdened by accumulated disabilities, will fall further behind (or gain too slowly). The solution is to draw a line between the realm of formal equality and a separate zone of compensatory preference. In this protected zone, the former victims can nourish their accomplishments and enlarge their capabilities until the day that the protective barrier can be lowered and the special protections dismantled.

This protective policy harbours an ironic tension, for the conditions of victimization that invite compensatory treatment are not distributed neatly in all or none fashion, but are matters of degree. Alongside paradigm groups of victims like the untouchables and the descendants of enslaved American Blacks are others with a lesser but sometimes substantial claim that they too suffer from a cumulative impairment of their ability to compete. The presence of a model of compensatory treatment generates plausible claims to extend its coverage to additional groups of beneficiaries. The range of variation among beneficiaries invites gradation or modulation to make benefits proportionate to need. However, in whatever way these policies are extended, they create new discontinuities, for there is still a point at which we say protective treatment ends here and formal equality begins. There is always a group just across the border with a claim that the abrupt step is unfair. There are always urgings to avoid such unfairness by a continuing modulated system of protections articulated to the entire range of need or desert. However as we shave away the arbitrariness of special protection for some, to accord each a due measure of special protection, we dissolve that arbitrary line that separates formal equality and protective treatment, and in doing so abandon the constitutional policy of compensatory discrimination for something very different: a world of allotments according to desert.

Is this where Mandal is heading? The report identifies its aspiration as 'equality of results'.[21] Does this mean a world of proportional representation by descent groups in all spheres of activity? Mandal seems to have a more complex vision, condensed into a revealing fable that contrasts urbane Mohan, the child of an urban middle class educated family who lives in an environment full of enrichment and sound guidance, with rustic Lallu, a child of uneducated low-caste parents who lives in a village remote from schools and lacking encouragement and cultural stimulation.[22] Positing that each 'had the same level of intelligence at the time of their birth, it is obvious that owing to vast differences in social, cultural and economic factors' Mohan will 'beat [Lallu] by lengths in any competitive field. Even if Lallu's intelligence quotient was much higher as compared to Mohan, chances are that the former will lag far behind the latter in any competition where selection is made on the basis of "merit".'[23] 'If merit also includes grit, determination, ability to fight odds, etc., should not the marks obtained by Mohan and Lallu be suitably moderated in view of the privileges enjoyed by the former and the handicaps suffered by the latter?'[24]

Does equality of result mean a race in which the competitors are handicapped so precisely that each reaches the finish line at precisely the same instant, so that the event has been transformed from a race into a companionable non-competitive run? Or alternatively, does it mean that outcomes are proportionate to qualities deserving of reward? Although the story of Lallu suggests that outcome should reflect native endowment, presumably we are not to equate this endowment per se with moral desert. In this story, native ability is combined with the personal qualities of grit and determination (assuming these are entirely independent of favourable family endowment); the latter ensure that his talents will be used effectively to the benefit of society. Is reward deserved for using one's talents? Or for displaying admirable qualities like grit? Or in order to benefit society? Alternatively, are we to assume that all of these will be closely correlated? In any event, 'merit' in the sense of current performance is to be 'moderated' in order to isolate a truer 'merit' that is obscured by the privileges and handicaps that envelop the individual.

In keeping with its mandate, Mandal aspires to far less than comprehensive 'equality of results'. Its proposals are fashioned to offset differences in privileges and handicaps between members of different castes. Within the protected group as a whole it has no objection to conventional un-moderated measures of merit. However, among the crores of Backward Classes there are present those same disparities in favourable location, family support, and other circumstances that separated Lallu and Mohan. Do not these, too, call for measures to filter out the effects of undeserved privilege and handicap, and to make reward proportionate to effort, courage, and other qualities that represent desert?

Mandal is surely correct in its intuition that compensatory discrimination cannot do everything. Reservation is a crude device that is inherently incapable of eliminating all the effects of unearned privilege and undeserved handicap. But then, if the policy of protective treatment for disadvantaged groups cannot be universalized to address all the arbitrarinesses and unfairnesses of life, Mandal seeks to generalize it to all the less advantaged descent groups in Indian society.

However, generalizing protective treatment to all groups dissolves the original and distinctive national commitment to the core beneficiary groups, the Scheduled Castes and Scheduled Tribes. The reservation device becomes not an exceptional tool of inclusion but a scheme of communal allotments. Programmes that utilize group identity to redistribute scarce rewards carry high costs and should be used sparingly and for limited objectives. Focusing on achieving ever finer distributive adjustments abandons the great and achievable purpose of limited use of compensatory discrimination: releasing the suppressed energy, imagination, and creativity of the excluded. Compensatory preference may be a viable policy for breaking barriers and forced draft inclusion of excluded groups; it cannot secure a chimerical 'equality of result' throughout India's social order.

Looking Backward from the Post-Mandal World

To the makers of India's constitution half a century ago, the task for compensatory discrimination in the new Indian state was to tear down the barriers of exclusion and promote the incorporation and participation of the historically excluded and isolated groups. These policies were seen as a complement to the commitment to an active welfare state that would quickly ameliorate the condition of India's masses, providing an additional boost to ensure that the poorest would not be left behind. The now evident inability or disinclination of government to achieve that welfare state, even to fulfill its baseline commitments relating to elementary education and drinking water, was hidden from the constitution-makers. The violent exclusionary aspects of inequality were vivid and palpable, and dismantling them was foremost in minds of the founders. The effective performance of equalizing measures was scarcely a visible problem. Besides, the notion that the constitutional scheme was a mandate for government pursuit of substantive equality, embraced by the Supreme Court a generation later[25] and invoked by Mandal, was remote from their understanding.

The policy of compensatory preference sought to remedy a state of affairs in which location in the caste structure was a key determinant of individual performance. The expectation was that preferential treatment, in conjunction with other policies of enlarging opportunity, would diminish the overriding effect of group membership. This would, it was expected, be facilitated by the decline of caste, which would lose its salience and be replaced by social formations more appropriate to modern conditions. The endurance of caste and its emergence as the major recruiting ground of electoral politics would surely have surprised those who designed the policy of compensatory preference. Although they anticipated a decline in the salience of caste, they did imagine that benefits conferred on members of backward groups would have a multiplier effect, percolating to other members of those groups and promoting a general improvement. A great deal of such spillover of benefits may be observed. However, at the same time, the founders underestimated the rise of individualism and the extent to which benefits, especially higher echelon benefits like medical education, would be appropriated by individuals with little spillover to the backward community.

Again, the constitutional design was based on the expectation that government employment would continue to be the principal focus of ambition and power; indeed, it might have been anticipated that its role would increase in the new activist state. Thus no provision was made for preferential hiring in private employment. While the beneficiaries of affirmative action are deflected into government service, the dynamic and growing part of the economy is in the private sector. The private sector envisioned by the constitutional generation was one of domestic firms, now out from under colonial penetration, contributing to import substitution and self-sufficiency. They could not anticipate globalization: the movement of capital into India, the dynamism and autonomy of the private sector, and transnational mobility of skilled labour, including many of the beneficiaries of compensatory discrimination who take their augmented human capital overseas.

Compensatory discrimination was envisioned as self-liquidating. Although the ten-year period specified by legislative reservations was grossly insufficient, there was an expectation that preferential treatment on a large scale would be temporary. Even if reservations were here for as long as might be planned, somewhere out there in the middle term, they would end. Although there were occasional spasms of interest in constriction, programmes haven't diminished and the number of eligible beneficiaries has multiplied. It seems to have been widely accepted as a permanent feature of the Indian polity. (The notion that permanent protection is needed curiously mirrors the original hierarchic ideology that caste forever measures inherent human ability.)

The broader the class of beneficiaries and the more expansive the benefits, the greater the threat that the essentially transitional and exceptional arrangements contemplated by the constitution will ossify into permanent arrangements. After half a century of experience with reservations, there is still no serious evaluation of their performance or achievement. Such evaluation would entail both broad aggregate data and richly contextualized accounts.[26] Such empirical information will not answer the question of what to do about compensatory discrimination policy, but it can help to redirect the debate from chimeras to the actual accomplishments and deficiencies of these policies.

A serious programme of compensatory preference must include measures for self-assessment and a design for it to dismantle itself. The constitutional provisions for legislative reservations have been renewed for the fifth ten-year instalment. Even though authorization for compensatory discrimination is technically independent of this renewal of the constitution's mandated legislative reservations, renewal does provide an occasion for national debate about the design of the policy. Rather than yet another mechanical extension, could one imagine a future renewal based on a critical assessment of the working of the policy, its accomplishments and shortcomings? One might imagine a well articulated scheme that included, for example, a short-term enhancement of reservations to be followed by a graduated phasing out over, say, fifty years, tapering down as specific performance goals are achieved. Measures for inclusion in élites should be complemented with more broadly based measures to enlarge opportunities. For all its failures in implementation, India's policy of compensatory discrimination has been remarkable in its scope and generosity. It is time to upgrade its effectiveness while acknowledging the limits of what can be accomplished with it.

Notes and References

1. *Report of the Backward Classes Commission*. 7 vols. in 2 (1980).
2. As in, for example, what I believe was the first book-length treatment of the subject: Ratna G. Revankar, *The Indian Constitution: A Case Study of Backward Classes,* Fairleigh Dickenson University Press, Rutherford, NJ 1971.
3. E.g. G.P. Verma, *Caste Reservation in India: Law and the Constitution,* Chugh Publications, Allahabad, 1980; B.A.V. Sharma and K. Madhusudhan Reddy, (eds), *Reservation Policy in India,* Lights & Life Publishers, New Delhi, 1982; A.K. Vakil, *Reservation Policy and Scheduled Castes in India,* Ashish Publishing House, 1985, New Delhi; D.N. Sandanshiv, *Reservations for Social Justice: A Socio-Constitutional Approach,* Current Law Publishers, Bombay 1986; Vinay Chandra Mishra (ed.), *Reservation Crisis in India: Legal and Sociological Study on Mandal Commission Report,* Bar Council of India Trust, New Delhi 1991.
4. C.H. Alexandrowicz, *Constitutional Developments in India,* Oxford University Press, 1957, Bombay, p. 57; Anirudh Prasad, *Reservation Policy and Practice in India: A Means to An End,* Deep & Deep, New Delhi, 1991.
5. Galanter, *Competing Equalities*, Oxford University Press, New Delhi, 1984. In his *Equality, Reservation and Discrimination in India* (Deep & Deep, New Delhi, 1982), Parmanand Singh used 'compensatory discrimination and 'protective discrimination' interchangeably. A recent comparative symposium in an Australian journal was subtitled 'A cross-national assessment of programs of compensatory discrimination'. *Law in Context,* Special Issue, vol. 15, no. 2 (1999).
6. For example, C.L. Anand, *Equality, Justice and Reverse Discrimination* (Mittal Publications, Delhi, 1987), refers in his Introduction to policies of 'special treatment' or preferential treatment' going by the name of 'protective discrimination' or 'reverse discrimination' and refers to 'the

different affirmative action programmes', an early invocation of that American term.

7. By 1985, Justice Desai used it as a synonym for compensatory discrimination. *K.C.V. Kumar* vs *Karnataka*, 1985 (1) SCALE 832, 843.
8. Upendra Baxi, 'Understanding the Traffic of "Ideas" in Law between America and India', in Robert M. Crunden (ed)., *Traffic of Ideas Between India and America*, Chanakya Publications, Delhi, 1985; Rajeev Dhavan, 'Borrowed Ideas: On the Impact of American Scholarship on Indian Law', 33, *American Journal of Comparative Law* (1985) 505.
9. A report of the conference sessions is found at 'Rethinking Equality in the Global Society', 75 *Washington University Law Quarterly* 1561–1676, 1997; the papers delivered there will appear in a volume edited by Clark D. Cunningham, *et al.*, A related example of the transnational discourse is, Clark D. Cunningham and N.R. Madhava Menon, 'Race, Class, Caste ...? Rethinking Affirmative Action', 97 *Michigan Law Review* (1999), 1206.
10. Mandal, I, p. 52.
11. Mandal, II, pp. 14, 17.
12. Mandal, I, p. 44.
13. Ibid., p. 52.
14. Ibid., p. 55.
15. Ibid., p. 52.
16. Ibid., p. 58.
17. *Competing Equalities*, pp. 455–7.
18. Mandal, I, p. 57. In *Indra Sawhney* vs *Union of India*, 1992 S C C (L & S) Supp 1, the Supreme Court indicated compartments might be used for the most backward, but the court does not require the use of this device.
19. Mandal, I, p. 57.
20. *Indra Sawhney* vs *Union of India*, 1992 SCC (L & S) Supp 1, at 475–6. Combining income ceilings with communal criteria of backward class membership has been countenanced by the courts since the 1970s. See *Competing Equalities*, pp. 263–6. What is new is that now they are viewed as constitutionally mandated.
21. Mandal, I, p. 22.
22. Ibid., p. 23.
23. Ibid.
24. Ibid.,
25. In *State of Kerala* vs *N.M. Thomas*, A.I.R. 1976 SC 490 the Supreme Court read the constitution's equality provisions as a general obligation on the state to produce substantive equality, blurring the special status

conferred by the constitution on the problem of caste inequality. See *Competing Equalities*, Ch. 11, Sec. D.

26. The complexities of the actual working and effects of these schemes is revealed in such telling accounts as Jonathan P. Parry, 'Two Cheers for Reservations: The Satnamis and the Steel Plant', in Ramchandra Guha and J. P. Parry (eds), *Institutions and Inequalities: Essays in Honour of André Beteille*, Oxford University Press, New Delhi, 1999; Oliver Mendelsohn and Marika Vicziany, *The Untouchables: Subordination, Poverty and the State in Modern India*, Cambridge University Press, Cambridge, 1998.

13

The Expected and the Unintended in Working a Democratic Constitution

GRANVILLE AUSTIN

Introduction

The content of the Indian constitution, its distinctive character, and the society for which it was designed—and in which it has been worked—make this democratic foundation document especially worthy of study. The experiences of its working are instructive for new nations and for those with greater longevity as democracies.

Chief Justice Marshall said in 1821, 'A Constitution is framed for ages to come, and is designed to approach immortality as near as human institutions can approach it. Its course cannot always be tranquil.' This has been no more and no less true of the Indian constitutional experience than that of other peoples.

The members of the Constituent Assembly, who met in New Delhi from 1946 to 1950, laid the foundation for an independent, republican India They knew what the country needed and what they intended it should have: national unity and integrity, democracy, and a social revolution to better the lot of the mass of citizens. These they knew in practice as well as in theory, for they *were* the Government of India while they were drafting the new constitution.

The Constituent Assembly wore two hats: one as the nation's provisional parliament, the other while drafting the constitution. Vital in themselves, these goals were understood to be essential to each other. Social revolution was not to be pursued at the expense of democracy, and the country could not be truly democratic unless a social revolution had established a more equitable society. Without national unity little progress could be made toward either social–economic reform or democratic government. Equally, without democracy and reform, India was unlikely to remain united. The goals were inseparable.

The founding fathers and mothers had spun what I think of as a seamless web. The strands of unity, democracy, and social revolution had to be strengthened together. Over-attention to, or slackness in, any strand would detrimentally affect the web. National leaders often called the goals the three pillars of socialism, secularism (meaning loyalty to nation over faction), and democracy. They were to be the national creed.

Before proceeding, I should like to unburden myself of several propositions that I think are both obvious and indisputable and that underlie this analysis of Indian constitutional patterns since 1950.

First, constitutions do not *work*. They are inert. They are *worked* by the citizenry and their leadership. As Dr B.R. Ambedkar told the Constituent Assembly: 'it's our responsibility now; we can't blame our troubles on anyone else.' Secondly, the fact that any people are able to govern themselves democratically is an act of faith even more than one of reason, particularly because constitutions and their institutions may shape men's actions, but they cannot improve human character. Democracy is a messy business: subject to greatness, meanness, and error. Constitutional government is work in progress; a matter of never-ending adjustments. Each generation must cope with it anew.

Keeping the Web's Strands in Harmony: Fundamental Questions

The first generation that had to work the new constitution was the one that had created it. As Marshall had predicted, tranquillity was not their lot. The issues they faced as they settled into harness and the way in which they coped with them would establish patterns of political behaviour that would both preserve the seamless web and come near to destroying it. I shall examine examples of these in this essay.

Within months of the constitution's inauguration, Prime Minister Nehru and his government were confronted with three fundamental questions: Should constitutional principles be diluted to cope with the perceived realities of governing? How much might one of the web's strands be sacrificed in favour of another without destroying the whole? Finally, what was to be done about conflicts within one of the strands? Governments since then have had to finds answers to the same questions in the context of the seamlessness of the web. The conundrum first arose when it appeared impossible to pursue the democracy and social revolution strands harmoniously because articles in the constitution stood in one another's way, especially articles within the Fundamental Rights.

For example, those articles providing for special assistance to advance the educational and economic condition of the 'weaker sections', or the 'backward classes', of the society, those for assuring to all citizens equality under the law, and those broadly prohibiting discrimination on such grounds as caste, race, and sex were found by a high court to be in conflict. In Madras state there existed the 'Communal General Order' according to which admission to government-supported medical and engineering institutions was by a quota system reserving places for lower-caste persons and limiting the number of persons from the upper castes. Although the 'CGO' pre-existed the constitution, it was consonant with provisions in the constitution designed to improve the lot of the weaker sections.

A Brahmin lady in Madras challenged the CGO as unconstitutional because it denied her equality under the law. The Madras High Court upheld the lady's petition, and the Madras government appealed the decision to the Supreme Court. The court upheld the High Court, thwarting the constitution's provisions and the Nehru government's policy of social revolution. To overcome the difficulty, Nehru led parliament, in the First Amendment, to amend the constitution to the effect that its provisions against discrimination on the grounds of caste, sex, etc. and those assuring equality under the law should not bar legislation providing for special consideration for the backward classes.

Concurrently, in 1950, the government came to believe that the freedom of expression guaranteed in the constitution was in conflict with the need to protect national unity and integrity (within which it implicitly included domestic stability). The judiciary had upheld certain types of speech the government believed to be provocative and needed to be curbed. For instance, S.P. Mookerjee was calling for the annulment of Partition. Nehru's government thought that this at the least endangered relations with Pakistan and might bring about a war between the two countries. The Supreme Court upheld the right of Romesh Thapar to circulate the communist publication *Crossroads* in the state of Madras which the government of Madras had refused. (There was then a communist revolt taking place in a section of the state, and the Communist Party of India was calling for the government's violent overthrow.) Home Minister Sardar Patel thought that the Supreme Court's action in upholding Thapar's rights 'knocks the bottom out of our penal laws for the control and regulation of the press'.[1] The freedom of expression guaranteed in the Fundamental Rights, an essential part of the democracy strand of the web, had come into conflict with the unity and integrity strand. Therefore, also in the First Amendment, the government added to Article 19 that freedom of expression should not prevent it from imposing 'reasonable restrictions' on speech in the interests of the security of the state, friendly relations with other states, public order and decency or morality.

Adding the qualifying term 'reasonable' brought a paradox within the original conflict, for early drafts of this amendment included the restrictions, but not the qualifying word 'reasonable'. Nehru seems to have concurred with this as chairman of the parliamentary select committee examining the draft, but he reversed his position at the last moment, apparently in response to sentiment in the committee advocating the inclusion of 'reasonable'. The paradox was that this attempt to curb speech actually strengthened its freedom. Now, the courts could rule on what were 'reasonable restrictions' on the freedom of expression.

Overshadowing at the time even these critical issues was the matter of property, which brought the democracy and social revolution strands of the web into great conflict. As we know, Article 31 in the constitution's Fundamental Rights stated that no person might be deprived of his property save by the authority of law, and that government might acquire property for a public purpose. The article also stated that the law acquiring the property should specify the amount of compensation for it or the principles upon which compensation was to be based. Yet, among the 'freedoms' in Fundamental Rights Article 19 was the 'right' to hold property and to carry on any occupation, trade, or business, each of which might involve the possession of property.

High Court and Supreme Court invalidation under Article 31 to several state zamindari abolition laws,[2] of laws acquiring land for refugee resettlement, and of laws for the takeover of commercial and industrial undertakings for their socialization or better management, put the government's social revolution programme in jeopardy. Equally so, court decisions under Article 19 forbidding the government of Uttar Pradesh from nationalizing privately operated bus lines threatened government intentions to build a socialist economy. To the dismay of Nehru and many of his colleagues, the democracy and social revolution strands of the web, each enshrined in the Fundamental Rights as well as elsewhere in the constitution, again conflicted.

To resolve the conflict, parliament added other provisions to the First Amendment. It made several drafting changes in the property article (Article 31), and to the 'freedoms' article (Article 19) it added that the government could engage in a business even to the exclusion of private citizens: in this case, operate public transport to the detriment of private enterprise. Far more radical, the amendment created a hierarchy of laws, with the highest category beyond the constitution's reach. State land reform law placed in a new schedule to the constitution (the Ninth Schedule) were not to be subject to judicial review. The expectation of leaders at the time was that the new schedule would be used to protect only land laws.

Conditions in the country, the situations leading to the First Amendment's enactment, and the devices in the amendment itself, presaged patterns that would have their effect on the country's constitutional system for years to come. The amendment set the pattern of amending the constitution to give the seamless web's social revolution strand precedence over the democracy strand; a precedent that would be taken to an extreme length in the early seventies in the Twenty-fourth and Twenty-fifth Amendments. The First Amendment initiated the practice of curbing the courts', and specifically the Supreme Court's, jurisdiction regarding certain matters. Although innocently intended when created in 1951 (several officials of the time have told me that no one imagined the later misuse of the Ninth Schedule), this innocence was severely jolted thirteen years later when the government gravely misused the schedule. Then, a short time before Nehru's death (1964), the central government moved an amending bill that would have placed 124 state land laws into the schedule only to have a parliamentary joint committee toss out 88 of them as unfitting. More startling was member of parliament G.S. Pathak's assertion that the laws should go into the schedule because some of them 'are of doubtful validity ... [or] may be open to attack. We want to immunize all these acts.'[3]

The patterns reappeared in 1970. Now the prime minister was Jawaharlal Nehru's daughter, Indira Gandhi. Adverse Supreme Court decisions in two property cases upset her greatly. In one the court struck down the government's 1969 nationalization of fourteen commercial banks—an action long a staple of Congress Party socialist political speech, but undertaken at that moment to vanquish a political opponent. In the other the court ruled unconstitutional the president's order abolishing the privy purses and privileges accorded to the so-called princes when they brought their feudal states into the Indian Union between 1947 and 1950. In 1971 Indira Gandhi, having restored Congress's majority by her great victory in the parliamentary elections, was eager to consolidate her power. She chose amendment of the constitution as her device, and the Twenty-fourth and Twenty-fifth Amendments were the result. She was supported by the socialists and ex-communists of the Congress Forum for Socialist Action. The first of these amendments stated that parliament could amend the constitution by way of addition, variation, or repeal, and that, were such an amending bill passed, the president had to give it his assent. The second amendment provided that the two most socialist articles in the non-justiciable Directive Principles of State Policy took precedence over certain of the Fundamental Rights: the 'freedoms' of Article 19, equality under the law in Article 14, and the provisions of the property Article 31. Some of the amendments' protagonists believed that these would bring about real social reform, and they did facilitate the nationalization of mines and factories. For other proponents, Indira Gandhi among them, they were populist manoeuvres. India, S.N. Mishra said, had socialism without democracy.

The pattern of isolating the courts and establishing parliamentary supremacy over interpretation of the constitution would be vastly strengthened five years later. Frustrated by the Supreme Court's unwillingness to overturn the 'basic structure doctrine', which stated that parliament might amend the constitution if its basic structure were left intact, propounded by the court in the 1973 Fundamental Rights case, the government moved a drastic amending bill. The Forty-second Amendment, justified as necessary 'to spell out expressly the high ideals of socialism, secularism, and ... [to] give the Directive Principles precedence over those fundamental rights that had frustrated the Principles' implementation',[4] re-emphasized the language of the Twenty-fourth Amendment and added that no constitutional amendment could be questioned in any court on any ground Radically, the amendment gave all the (non-justiciable) Directive Principles precedence over the key fundamental rights just mentioned. The amendment also sharply reduced the Supreme Court's jurisdiction by transferring matters like land reforms and election disputes to yet-to-be established tribunals. At this time (1975–7), under Indira Gandhi's Emergency, the constitution's Fundamental Rights were suspended and thousands of the government's political opponents were placed under preventive detention.

The democracy strand of the web had been all but severed in the name of socialism from the seamless web's social revolution strand. The pattern initiated by Nehru for constructive purposes had been taken to its logical extreme: socialism had gone from creed to slogan. Worse, the goal of social revolution had been invoked to consolidate authoritarian rule: Indira Gandhi's rule over the country.

The Forty-second Amendment and the other Emergency amendments, building on the First, Twenty-fourth and Twenty-fifth, meant that the legislative and executive branches of government had triumphed over the judiciary for custody of the constitution. Moreover, the judiciary was no longer to be a co-equal branch of government. The high courts, as well as the Supreme Court, were to be brought to heel. Sixteen high court judges were punitively transferred from their home courts because they had ruled against the government in habeas corpus cases brought by persons detained under the Emergency.

Nehru had genuinely and publicly supported judicial independence. Although he made amply clear his view that the courts should not impede executive branch programmes of social–economic 'engineering', he insisted that the Supreme Court's decisions be obeyed. Yet, because parliament had authority under the constitution to amend it, 'it becomes our duty to see whether the Constitution so interpreted was rightly framed and whether it is desirable to change it ... to give effect to what really ... was intended or *should have been intended*' (emphasis added).[5] While asserting parliamentary supremacy, Nehru, the impatient democrat and social revolutionary, could not have imagined the depradations of the Forty-second Amendment.

Conversely, Nehru's daughter, beginning early in the 1970s, decided to both subvert the Supreme Court's independence and curb its jurisdiction. She and her ministers attacked the judiciary openly, and in 1973 she superseded three Supreme Court judges to install her own choice as Chief Justice of India—ignoring the convention that the seniormost justice of the court should become the Chief Justice. Changing the composition of the court to make it more 'forward looking' had been advocated for a year or more by a brilliant ex-communist member of Indira Gandhi's circle, Mohan Kumaramangalam, and like-minded others. This was to complement the parliamentary supremacy achieved by the passage of the Twenty-fourth and Twenty-fifth Amendments. Indira Gandhi, however, had more personal intentions. She wished to remove from the court a justice who might rule against her when her election case came to the court on appeal from the Allahabad High Court.

This case, initiated in a 1971 election petition by a disgruntled and defeated opponent, was inching its way through the judicial system. If she were found guilty of the corrupt election practices with which she had been charged, she would have been barred from elective office for six years.

The practice that had begun in Nehru's time, of faulting the courts rather than the Congress Party for failures to implement socialist reform, gathered momentum under Indira Gandhi. Apparently oblivious to the contradiction, Congress Party rhetoric continued to attack the courts for failures to achieve socialist progress while, within its own councils, repeatedly bemoaning its failures to pursue the social revolution. Both the democracy and social revolution strands were distorted by the party's attacks on the judiciary and its own unfulfilled promises of social–economic reform.

Preventive Detention and the Seamless Web

Several of the incompatibilities and conflicts among the strands of the web that confronted government under the new constitution could also be got round, although not resolved, by a device other than amendment: preventive detention.

The framers had believed they would need to perpetuate this device inherited from the British because they would have to deal with the exigencies of governing that they already faced as the government and as leaders of the provisional parliament. In one of the document's paradoxes, they provided for it in the constitution's Fundamental Rights. Arrest and imprisonment under preventive detention laws is singular because it is an action taken by a civil official of the executive branch of government, not one taken by police within the judicial–criminal justice system. An individual could be detained by executive order for three months or longer depending upon the report of an Advisory Board, which was when his detention met the judicial system. Parliament was empowered to authorize detentions for indefinite periods without Advisory Board reviews (Article 22 (7)).

Although an offence against the democratic strand of the web, one can understand its use in the context of the time. For example, S.P. Mookerjee's calling for the annulment of Partition appeared to endanger national security. Members of the Communist Party of India were detained in Calcutta and elsewhere because the party was preaching armed overthrow of the government and leading an actual revolt at the heart of the country. Feudalist landholders were opposing social revolution reforms, often repressing tenants' and agricultural labourers' attempts to benefit from them. Some landholders, particularly in Rajasthan, were arrested rather than tried because, as Nehru asked in parliament: What poor tenant would dare testify against a *jagirdar*? Strikes in industrial and agricultural enterprises and famine conditions in parts of the country sometimes led to hoarding and other economic offences, so individuals were detained to prevent interruption in the supply of essential supplies and services.

The central and state governments used detention in the name of protecting national security, pursuing the social revolution, protecting public order and democratic institutions, and against common criminals. This article in the chapter on Fundamental Rights, was used to infringe citizens' other fundamental rights, liberty (Article 21), and the freedoms of speech and movement (Article (19). When employed against ordinary criminals, many reasonable individuals, lawyers, and judges consider detention a 'necessary evil', convictions being difficult to obtain when witnesses are intimidated.

The president promulgated the first prevention detention ordinance a month after the constitution's inauguration. Appropriate legislation followed and the central government thereafter renewed this act every few years. Most state governments enacted their own legislation in the name of public safety and order, and preventive detention was on the statute book from 1950 to 1977, barring the years 1969–70 when the central government lacked the votes in parliament to continue an expiring act in force.

Preventive detention was also authorized by proclamations of national emergency, such as those in 1962, 1971, and Indira Gandhi's internal Emergency in 1975. During these periods, appeal against detention was crippled by the suspension of the right to move the courts for the protection of the Fundamental Rights, all of which had been suspended. The 1962 and 1971 emergencies were scarcely challenged when proclaimed, but were severely criticized when the government maintained them for years after their original justification had disappeared—apparently because it believed that the extensive powers provided were convenient. Other pieces of legislation, like the Conservation of Foreign Exchange and Prevention of Smuggling Activities Act, provided for detention. The Forty-second Amendment provided that parliament might make, and no article in the Fundamental Rights should prevent it enacting, laws for the prevention of anti-national activities and the formation of anti-national associations. Enforced through preventive detention, this new Article 31–D, in the hands of Indira Gandhi and her son Sanjay, would have been the final log on the pyre of Indian democracy. Indeed, during Indira Gandhi's years as prime minister, use of detention against political opponents and personal enemies soared.

Detention has been used against activists working for reform in rural areas. As the activities and influence of reformist private voluntary organizations increase, as the 'million mutinies' of citizen activism increasingly make themselves felt, it seems a fair prediction that dominant groups and individuals in rural areas will importune local officials to detain 'troublemakers'. If this should become a recurrent phenomenon, government will have sided with society's oppressors.

The Web and Centralized Governance

The centralized federalism of the 1935 Government of India Act, largely incorporated by the framers into the constitution, was intentionally increased by governments over the years to strengthen the seamless web, and by political parties and individual political leaders for their own purposes. Unintentionally, the pattern of increased centralization weakened each of the web's strands and eventually harmed the fortunes of parties and political leaders.

Above all, independent India under its new constitution needed unity, for its peoples and its administrative divisions had never been one. For instance, until the framing period the country had had two broad divisions: 'British India', administered directly by the imperial government in New Delhi, and the 'Indian States', administered by hereditary princes under the watchful eye of the British. More important, the society was made up of compartments of caste, class, religion, language, and cultural and geographical loyalties. The leadership feared these would doom efforts at national unity and integrity and condemned them 'communal'. For Nehru and many of his colleagues and successors, casteism, especially, and regionalism and linguism, were 'communal' and therefore obstacles to their national goal of 'secularism'. All were enemies of national unity *and* democracy and socialism.

Their answer to 'communalism' was 'secularism', by which leaders meant much more than Muslim–Hindu harmony. They meant the blurring or the removal of the many distinctions, the compartments, that characterized society and their replacement by an overreaching sense of Indianness. This 'secularism' was essential for the achievement and preservation of national *integrity*, as they termed it. However, this degree of 'secularism' could not be achieved, given the country's make-up. The leadership was really talking about national *integration*, a condition unnecessary for national integrity: fifty years have shown that the compartments cohabit successfully with only very partial integration. To bring about unity the framers drafted a centralized constitution, whose provisions were reinforced by the presence of a mass party led by charismatic leaders who believed they had the capability and the duty to administer the country their way, but democratically.

This mix-up in terminology led to continued expression of anxieties for national unity and integrity that was understandable. When it has occurred, conflict among castes, classes, and religious communities has upset public stability, but rarely has it threatened national integrity. This applies also to conflict, typically over economic issues, between states, between them and the central government, and between state capitals and the states' internal groups. The exceptions have been Tamil, Sikh, and Naga separatist sentiment in the 1950s and segments of Sikh and Kashmiri sentiment in more recent times. Even these have not fulfilled fears of and predictions regarding the 'balkanization' of the country. Yet, anxieties about the danger to unity have persisted. They have taken a prominent place in Independence and Republic Day speeches into the 1980s—sometimes by politicians wishing to distract attention from other problems. Today, national unity and integrity are generally accepted as having been achieved, although contrary sentiments exist in the vale of Kashmir. The search for uniformity continues among the believers in 'Hindutva', who preach cultural and political uniformity for the nation, which would only destroy it.

Communalism was seen as the enemy of the social revolution. Sectarianism and socialism cannot walk hand in hand, said U.N. Dhebar when Congress president in the 1950s. The leadership, with few exceptions, shared a belief, almost a faith, in a humanitarian socialism. This had to be pursued democratically, with the basic principle being an economy managed by the central government with a national planning commission as its instrument. Established in February 1950, the Planning Commission grew powerful for two decades as the central institution of the managed economy. According to responsible critics, it came to apply a single model to the economic development of all the states, and the chief ministers charged that the National Development Council, established to coordinate the commission's efforts with their governments, became a rubber stamp for central government policy. With economic development increasingly in state hands, the commission has lost much of its influence.

Over-centralization of development through socialism and central planning has had little emphasized effects, denying the country much talented input. The emphasis on the public sector and de-emphasis of the private kept private initiative and entrepreneurship at all levels of society from contributing to economic development. Denying state governments full participation in economic planning and development also excluded sources of insight, ideas, and expertise—besides being undemocratic.

Centralization took many other forms. Parallel to the Planning

Commission was the Finance Commission, provided for in the constitution, whereas the former was not. It reigned powerfully as the mediator on revenue matters between the centre and the states, and was generally praised for its efforts. Other, informal sub-constitutional institutions were typically dominated by the centre. For example, the prime minister, as chairman, dominated the annual conferences of chief ministers. The zonal councils were chaired and dominated by the central home minister, which caused K.M. Munshi, then a governor and earlier a member of the Constituent Assembly, to predict their ineffectiveness as instruments for the coordination of policy and administration.[6]

The fullest expression of centralization came in the constitution's 'Emergency Provisions'. Under these, the entire nation or an individual state could be governed from Delhi, transforming the federal system into a unitary one. The justification for the former was a threat to national security from external aggression or 'internal disturbance'—a term altered in 1978 to 'armed aggression' by a constitutional amendment. The justification for the latter was a situation in which the government of a single state could not be carried on in accordance with the provisions of the constitution, a power commonly termed 'President's Rule'.

The national emergencies of 1962 and 1971 constituted the height of centralization until Indira Gandhi's Emergency of 1975. Although day to day centre–state administrative relations under the constitution were little affected by these two emergencies, New Delhi ruled the country unitarily, the state governments were obliged to do New Delhi's bidding (although several more or less successfully resisted), and civil liberties were in its hands. As mentioned above, these emergencies were continued in force years after the 'emergency' had passed. The public criticized these extensions less as administratively excessive than as evidence of the central government's and the Congress Party's creeping authoritarianism.

President's Rule proved to be the most controversial article in the Emergency provisions because it was frequently abused by the central government to work its will on state governments, often for partisan political purposes. Used thus, and also in situations where there had been no breakdown in constitutional governance, President's Rule was anti-democratic. Nehru used it first in 1951 in Punjab, against President Rajendra Prasad's remonstrances, to impose the Congress Working Committee's will on the chief minister there. In 1959 the centre dismissed the elected government of Kerala. Congress governments in New Delhi often used President's Rule to rid itself of opponents in the states. Of the 57 instances of President's Rule from 1951 to 1987 (leaving aside the mass dismissals of state governments by the Janata Party in 1977 and Indira Gandhi in 1980), the Sarkaria Commission on centre–state relations reported its view that 23 had been inevitable, 15 had been without allowing other claiments to power to test their strength, and 13 had been when the ministry had commanded a majority in the state legislature. Therefore, some 50 per cent had resulted from central manipulation. Indeed, it appears that in many instances the governor's letter to the president calling for President's Rule had been ghost-written in the home ministry in Delhi.

Of course, centralization meant power. Nehru's prestige gave him enormous power, and he enjoyed it while occasionally being ambivalent about using it. Although a tough political fighter, he typically directed his authority toward constructive, national ends, not toward personal aggrandizement. Overburdened by the responsibilities of office, he several times threatened to resign as prime minister.

Things changed under his daughter. For Indira Gandhi, centralization first began as a means, later to become an end in itself. In 1966 she had the task of any prime minister: to lead her party to victory in the forthcoming elections. When Congress won with a reduced majority, due to its own poor record, she knew she had to win on her own. After she split her own party and succeeded brilliantly in the 'delinked' parliamentary elections of 1971, power achieved through centralization became an end. She and her gullible courtiers used socialist rhetoric to lead her idealistic and complaisant parliament to amend the constitution so that its future shape would lie in her hands. As I have noted earlier, she attacked the Supreme Court's independence by appointing her own choice as chief justice. During the 1970s, she augmented her own power by letting the 'federal' organization within the Congress party atrophy and making state party and government officials dependent upon her favour. Whereas to her father dissent was part of the democratic process, although it could anger him, for the daughter dissent was seen as disloyalty and even 'anti-national' activity.

However, her concentration of power was not yet done. To preserve herself in office, she had 'her' Emergency proclaimed, her opponents imprisoned by the thousand, her compliant parliament protect her hold on office by enacting a constitutional amendment that legalized actions that a high court had found illegal in her election case (the Thirty-ninth Amendment)—an act that Law Minister Ram Jethmalani in February 2000 called the most anti-democratic since Independence.

Finally, during her Emergency three of her loyalists, S.S. Ray, Rajni Patel, and H.R. Gokhale, her law minister, secretly drafted the Forty-second Amendment. This, discussed above, plus the Twenty-fourth and Twenty-fifth Amendments, so marginalized the judiciary that the three branches of government were effectively reduced to two. Indira Gandhi then equally effectively reduced those two branches to one, using parliament when she needed it, and ruled the country by herself, aided by son Sanjay and his coterie—the latter exercising what was commonly referred to as an 'extra-constitutional authority'.

This period, these actions, at once marked the height of centralization and the low point for democracy in the country, brought about by the personalization of government and greed for power. Fortunately for citizens, the Janata Government (1977–9) restored the constitution and democracy under it and repaired much of the damage wrought during the Emergency.

Although the achievement of social revolution, 'socialism', had been invoked for the Forty-second Amendment's destruction of democracy (as the Emergency had been justified as necessary to preserve national integrity against the threat of public disorder) and for the Twenty-fourth and Twenty-fifth Amendments' serious challenges to democracy, social revolution itself benefited little if at all. If Prime Minister Gandhi ever had been more than sentimentally keen on using social revolution, she was unwilling to take the political risks entailed. The justification sometimes offered, that centralization grown to over-centralization brought the nation greater unity, was erroneous. It actually set back the cause of national unity by alienating state government leaders and many citizens.

Yet, along with the negative effects of centralization and, worse, over-centralization, we should acknowledge its significant benefits and, apart from the extreme examples we have been discussing, they did remarkably little harm. On the plus side, centralization built heavy industry and infrastructure and fostered the country's economic integration. It forced cooperation on the unwilling, and strengthened the psychological foundations of Indianness. The extreme taught valuable lessons. Foremost among these, as the constitution's draftsman, Dr B.R. Ambedkar, had said, is that in politics, Bhakti, or the path of devotion, 'is a sure road to degradation and to eventual dictatorship'. One doubts that Indira Gandhi's Emergency will be repeated. The second great lesson is that governance overly centralized beyond a certain point benefits neither administration, nor democracy, nor the social revolution, nor national unity and integrity. It is inimical to all. This lesson learned has produced serious consideration of, and significant moves toward, decentralization.

The Seamless Web's Anonymous Strand: Culture

Another pattern, less tangible while being highly visible, has influentially affected all three strands of the seamless web. I term this fourth strand 'culture'. Leaving aside the justly admired art, dance, music, literature, and religious scriptures that mark the country's culture, I speak of the characteristics of daily living. The interaction of government and elements of these aspects of the national culture have profoundly affected the constitution's working, the quality of governance, and, therefore, the credibility of government.

Predominant among these is that India's is a survival society. By this, I mean that lacking institutional safety nets, citizens are struggling to survive: the poverty-stricken struggle for two chappatis where they have one. They, as Duncan Derrett has put it, are attempting to break out of 'the stoical patience of a people expecting nothing beyond subsistence and regarding prosperity as a temporary and delusory windfall.'[7] The better-off fight to stay where they are, fearful of slipping down the economic ladder. The rich strive to make their pile before they lose the contacts that led to their wealth. To these ends, 'everything is personalized and politicized': jobs, appointments, promotions, school entrance, grades in university examinations, academic grants to individuals and institutions, arrests and convictions (or lack of them), and more.

For elected and appointed officials and civil servants, the struggle to survive produces the personalization of government. Well known, the phenomenon consists of putting 'me first and not the country, which takes teamwork', according to Bangalore High Court Justice H.G. Balakrishna.[8] P.N. Haksar thought 'our civil services ... are committed, first of all to themselves and their nuclear family ... [and beyond this to] making secure the future of our sons and daughters ... and, if possible ... the members of our subcaste, caste, community and region.'[9] This deeply embedded cultural characteristic, resting on the scriptural injunction to aid one's own, makes reform in a scarcity economy incredibly difficult. Societies do not change their ethos swiftly or easily.

This phenomenon needs no further description here, but its effect on the social revolution and democracy strands of the web can scarcely be overemphasized. 'The struggle for career advancement is greatly influenced by the surrounding moral atmosphere of the struggle for existence of different classes and groups in society. This has provided ample opportunities for corruption, and indeed for collective self-aggrandisment at the expense of the poor', according to R.C. Dutt.[10]

Among elected and appointed officials, these characteristics, plus the downward indifference characteristic of a hierarchical society, cause politicians to tend to treat the vote 'as no more than an endorsement by the people in favour of the continuation of their rule', wrote Dhirubhai Sheth. They 'manipulate casteist and communal sentiments ... rather than ... improving performance on the economic front ... There is no pro-poor programme; there are only pro-poor slogans.'[11] Another way of putting this is that policies and programmes are announced but not implemented, and that there is a slow but inexorable erosion of government credibility.

Sheth's mention of slogans brings us to another cultural characteristic with a related impact on the credibility of government. This might be called the empty promise syndrome, but it is better described as the gap between word and deed. 'Rhetoric from the housetops, but no implementation', was the description to me of a justice of the Supreme Court. The noted political economist, H.K. Paranjpe, thought this characteristic not a 'gap', but 'the word being equivalent to the deed'.[12] Alternatively, as educationist and poet Prem Kirpal expressed it, 'there is a dichotomy between belief and practice'.[13] A declaration of intent imposes no necessity to ascertain that the action has actually been carried out.

The make-believe air that this gives to public policy is nowhere more apparent than in Congress Party declarations about land reform. In party publications these show a clear pattern. At a Working Committee or other high-level meeting, the failure to implement previously announced programmes is admitted, followed by self-castigation. The reasons for failure are then analysed: such as the party having lost touch with the masses and its officers having been distracted by the 'greed for office'. Finally, after ardent pledges to do better implementing socialism, a new programme is announced, exceeding in ambition the goals whose non-fulfilment had just been deplored.

Looking back, I find that the credibility that Nehru and his government inherited from the Independence movement sustained them for some years. The greed for office among Congress members that he and others idealistically deplored harmed credibility little. It was small in scale and hardly surprising in a party newly come to office. Indira Gandhi's government's credibility was high during the early 1970s, but declined thereafter, although her personal popularity remained high with the mass of citizens. Along with absence of progress toward social revolution, a major cause of this decline was the perceived effect of 'money power' on elections. A second, growing and ever more prominent, was the extension of money corruption from peon to prime minister. This personalization of government for power or pelf is today a common topic of conversation, marking the death of the age of idealism. Leaving aside the ethical aspect of the phenomenon, personalization reinforces downward indifference, as Sheth has pointed out, and often destroys efforts in aid of the common weal. The public's mistrust of politicians is visible evidence of this, along with the popularity of non-elected bodies like the Election Commission and the Supreme Court. Although the courts' reputation is comparatively higher, and the Supreme Court is still held in high repute, the judicial system as a whole, and a criminal justice system stained by the corrupt and brutal police, no longer has the public's confidence.

Yet, the increasing scramble for advantage by elected officials within the civil services and among citizens broadly reveals something more positive. This pattern reveals society to be moving from rigidity toward openness. Caste-based and other group-based lobbying and voting, however self-serving, demonstrates growing participation in governance and the weakening of society's hierarchy. Caste continues to be a major repressive force in society, but it is also a focus for political mobilization as the lower orders strive for their share of the nation's goods. This is messy, but it is democracy and the social revolution in action. Because the country's interest groups, in general, are horizontal, their political aggressiveness does not endanger national integrity.

Equally significant is the widespread birth of citizens' self-help efforts. Ranging from institutions with extensive programmes like Consumer Research and Education in Ahmedabad to organizations pursuing women's and Dalit's rights to non-governmental organizations of varying quality and effectiveness to endeavours by voluntary organizations of a few educated men and women who have settled in villages to learn as well as to assist, these efforts, and villagers' reaction to them, promise to change society. They are evidence of social awakening among those providing and receiving help, and of determination to reform society when government will not. Democracy's breezes are slowly stirring the country.

Finding Fault

Human beings typically are not at their best when assigning themselves responsibility for weaknesses or difficulties in their own governance or when disciplining themselves to reform. It seems to me that Indians and Americans are little different in this respect. Although inconsistencies in the constitution forced the First Amendment's enactment, the resort to amendment also established the patterns of faulting the courts for the government's and the Congress Party's own failures in programme implementation, and of amending the constitution to get around Supreme Court decisions. Successive governments appear not to have appreciated the hazards entailed in re-examining the constitution's first principles, for the several constitutional reviews that have been conducted so far have done harm as well as good, and the Janata Party's restoration of the constitution after Indira Gandhi's Emergency has been an exceptional achievement.

Confronting the discrepancies within the Fundamental Rights affecting the seamless web's three strands, Nehru, especially, blamed the courts and then looked to repair the constitution over President Rajendra Prasad's words of caution. Impatient, Nehru gave orders in October 1950 to prepare a draft amendment. Four months later he formed a cabinet committee on the constitution to wrestle with the issues of compensation for property taken, the issues of free speech, and special consideration for the backward classes. The First Amendment, as we have seen, produced dangerous, unintended consequences while assisting social revolution.

In 1954, the government and the party had such grave doubts about the suitability of the constitution for effecting the social revolution that the Congress Working Committee established a sub-committee to seek the necessary changes, and instructed Home Minister K.N. Katju to set up a commission to consider legal and judicial reform. The formation of the Law Commission was the primary result of this initiative. The anti-judiciary sentiment revealed in the sub-committee's report to the working committee was so harsh that Nehru, as chairman, had to scotch it, substituting his own specific recommendations for amendment of the constitution, especially the property article. (Judicial decisions had proved wrong Nehru's and K.M. Munshi's assurances to the Constituent Assembly that use of the term 'compensation' in Article 31 would not invite judicial scrutiny of state zamindari abolition legislation.)

C. Subramaniam's 1964 committee to follow up the Congress Party's Democracy and Socialism resolution amounted to an interim review. It straightforwardly criticized the party's failures to implement social revolution legislation. The third review lasted the six years from the *Golaknath* decision in 1967, which declared the Fundamental Rights to be beyond parliament's power to amend, to the Supreme Court's 1973 ruling that parliament had the power to amend the entire constitution *provided* it did not damage its 'basic structure'. This landmark decision was the court's response to parliament's enactment of the Twenty-fourth Amendment, which intended to end judicial review of constitutional amendments, and the Twenty-fifth Amendment's giving two of the Directive Principles supremacy over certain of the Fundamental Rights.

The fourth review, by a committee of Congress Party stalwarts and Indira Gandhi loyalists, began formally in February 1976 and ended with the Forty-second Amendment's passage in November that year. This, as we have seen, ended democracy in the name of the social revolution and of protecting national unity—although it was actually designed to perpetuate Indira Gandhi in power. The Janata Party's great review during 1977 to 1979 restored democracy and the constitution to the country.

When politicians did not blame the constitution itself for their own shortcomings, they often chose between two scapegoats: the judiciary in general and the Supreme Court in particular, or the bureacucracy for its lack of commitment to social revolution.

Then came a review that I think of as the constitutional revolt of 1983. Constructively intended, constructively conducted, and undertaken within the constitutional system, this was more important than is generally realized. State governments that were in opposition party hands, and several Congress-ruled state governments, silently, in a series of meetings and manifestos, called for changes in centre–state relations. These ranged from textual changes in the constitution to changes of practice that would lessen central government 'interference' in state affairs and make the states partners with the centre in national governance.

Attempting to defuse the revolt, Indira Gandhi appointed the Sarkaria Commission to study and to make recommendations for reform in centre–state relations. The device succeeded for the short term, but the impetus for decentralization had been given a good start. The Sarkaria Commission published a well-researched, thoughtful report that should be a guide for future reforms.

Conclusion

The founding fathers and mothers, in drafting a constitution providing for representative government with adult suffrage to empower and to unite citizens and by framing the Fundamental Rights and the Directive Principles and the articles protecting and assisting citizens, entrenched democracy in India. These provisions made the constitution a social-democratic manifesto. The constitution's very existence has been a powerful force for change.

This leap of faith that an apparently rigid, hierarchical society was flexible, capable of changing and reforming itself, has been justified by time. The evidence, some of it lacking in charm, is all around us in the changing composition of legislatures, in the political mobilization of Dalits and others, and in electoral turnouts that dismiss and create governments.

The leaders' leap of faith was that constitutional democracy and a constitutionally-pursued social revolution would unite 350 million individuals—as the population then was—into one citizenry, even as their fears of the dangers from society's compartments has been justified. Slow progress toward full democracy and social revolution does not disprove this. The leaders' goal, call it their dream, of 'secularism', meaning social diversities living compatibly, expressed the essence of Indian 'civilization'. The trend toward the dream is strong, although it has enemies among those with fantasies of uniformity.

The constitution's establishment of an independent judiciary headed by the Supreme Court has proved critical for the survival of democracy and to some progress in the social revolution. Itself, the court has gone from handing down many conservative/technical rulings to judicial activism, using as its instrument public interest litigation. The definitions of 'law' and 'justice', once heatedly debated because thought so wide apart, seem to have come close enough to allow this. The court's propounding of the basic structure doctrine was an act of great judicial statesmanship. Happily, the Supreme Court no longer is (if it ever was), nor is seen to be, the great enemy of social revolution. At the same time, the judiciary has been lax in serving the broad public. The country's criminal justice system is tattered, the judiciary and the governments in the states have not reformed the subordinate judiciary, and the bar has shown itself more preoccupied with the welfare of its members than that of its less affluent clients.

Yet, if the courts supplant the legislatures and executives as the principal engines of social reform, whether from their own pride (currently a small trend) or from the other branches' irresponsibility, it will dangerously imbalance the relationship among the strands of the seamless web and the three branches of government. We await evidence that the country's executives and legislatures will live up to their responsibilities.

Although it has brought about major changes in society and politics, the social revolution has passed by 'the poverty-stricken masses'. The shame here first belongs to those not poverty-stricken who so care for their own survival that they are indifferent to the condition of their fellow citizens. They include citizens, legislators who have not enacted reform laws, and ministers, central and state, who have not led their subordinates in implementing laws in existence. Government by majority, 'democratic' though it may be, will produce or perpetuate society's inequities, and iniquities, until a sense of civic responsibility causes citizens and officials to ameliorate them. Government in India will regain credibility only when there are no longer forgotten Indians.

The cultural characteristics described earlier continue to be the principal adversaries of the seamless web's democracy and social revolution strands. India will not have fulfilled the promise of the constitution until citizens and the leadership overcome these adversaries.

National unity and integrity seem to be well beyond danger, although indifference to sensible forms of decentralization could severely strain them. The report of the Sarkaria Commission and, included there, the memoranda submitted to it by state governments, is an excellent source of ideas. There are far, far more forces holding India together than pulling it apart. Strongest among these is a sense of Indianness and common purpose and a multiplicity of economic ties.

Defining political watersheds is as chancy as defining geographical ones is easy. I shall however risk calling Indira Gandhi's Emergency, and the constitutional amendments enacted during it, as the nation's constitutional watershed. The Emergency was less an aberration in the country's politics than an accumulation of patterns: from 'cooperative federalism' to over-centralization of government; from social revolution as creed to slogan, and the 1970s' radical, doctrinaire style of Indira Gandhi's followers; from Nehru's democratic, if charismatic, leadership to succumbing to his daughter's pursuit of power for power's sake; from public service as a civic, national duty to a means for enriching oneself; from respect for the role of the political opposition in a democracy to treating it as an anti-national enemy (and imprisoning its members); from leading parliament to intimidating it into obedience; and from criticizing the judiciary to attempting to subvert it.

The scare given citizens by this accumulation of patterns, by the Emergency's oppressions, has convinced them that it must never recur. Events demonstrated to citizens, and they may have absorbed the lessons that a citizenry lazy about its democratic privileges almost deserves to lose them; that in essence eternal vigilance is the price of liberty, and that they are not blameless. These trends reflect society. As an American cartoon character said, 'We has met the enemy and they is us'. One is disposed to believe that the net effect of the Emergency and of the years that concluded with Rajiv Gandhi's assassination is that citizens have accepted their constitution, as they had not fully done before.

The Emergency changed the character of political party arrangements. It broke the Congress's grip, and Indira Gandhi could not restore it after her return to office in 1980. Nor could the 'sympathy wave' of 1984, resulting from Prime Minister Indira Gandhi's assassination that elected Rajiv Gandhi, do so for long. With room, other parties have grown, political participation has increased, and state governments have assumed a larger role in national governance—denied by Indira Gandhi's emasculation of them after 1971. Although the resulting coalition governments in Delhi have caused unease and frantic talk of 'hung parliaments', in all likelihood the new political flexibility is for the better. Among other things, thought is now being given to decentralization. In the country's situation, the participation of the so-called regional parties at the centre, i.e. coalition governments, is a symptom of increased national unity, not of integrity threatened.

I conclude with a grand and cheering paradox. Although the sins of omission and commission of past governments have shaken democracy, and although the credibility of governments and politicians has dropped to a level that appears to endanger constitutional government in India, the democratic ethos, the principle of representative government, seems deeply rooted among citizens. It has taken time for the constitution to become secure. In the future, government or the citizens may slight or ignore it, yet it is accepted as the nation's foundation document, some say the new *dharmasastra*. It has given citizens standards by which to measure performance, to vote for or against their representatives. Citizens treasure it for the same reason that fifteen decades ago they welcomed the British judicial system: because it has given them a voice previously denied them by society's traditional hierarchy.

A final remark: All these years the citizen's lot has been improving, even if slowly, and government in the country has been functioning, and this is something we non-functionary historians and analysts should not forget.

Notes and References

1. Sardar Patel, letter to Prime Minister Nehru dated 3 July 1950; Durga Das, *Sardar Patel's Correspondence 1945–1950*, Navajivan Publishing House, Ahmedabad, 1973, vol. 10, p. 358.
2. Zamindars were tax farmers who collected revenues from peasant tenants, paid an established amount to the ruler of the time, and kept the remainder for themselves—putting them in a position to rack-rent tenants.
3. *Lok Sabha Debates,* Third Srs., vol. 32, no. 3, col. 366.
4. Quoted from the amendment's Statement of Objects and Reasons.
5. *Parliamentary Debates*, vol. 12, pt. 2, col. 8832–16, May 1951.
6. *Constituent Assembly Debates*, vol. 11, no. 11, p. 979.
7. J. Duncan M. Derrett, 'Social and Political Thoughts', in A.L. Basham (ed.), *A Cultural History of India,* Oxford University Press, New Delhi, 1989, p. 131.
8. In an interview with me.
9. P.N. Haksar, *Premonitions*, Interpress, Bombay, 1979, p. 201.
10. R.C. Dutt, 'Indian Bureaucracy in Transition', in Bidyut Sarkar (ed.), *P.N. Haksar, Our Times and the Man*, Allied Publishers Pvt Ltd., New Delhi, 1989, p. 40.
11. D.L. Sheth, 'Social Basis of the Political Crisis', in *Seminar*, Jan. 1982.
12. Paranjpe in an interview with me.
13. Kirpal in an interview with me.

14

THE ORIGINS OF THE ELECTORAL SYSTEM
Rules, Representation, and Power-sharing in India's Democracy*

E. SRIDHARAN

Democratic Constitutions as Power-sharing Devices

Democratic constitutions pertain primarily to means rather than to ends. They lay down the ground rules of government and politics, usually undergirded by certain foundational principles, including fundamental rights, the rule of law, an implicit or explicit concept of justice, and the like. However, constitutions can also be interpreted as historic social compacts reflecting the state of a nation or nation-in-the-making at a specific historical moment, their subsequent career reflecting the evolution of the nation and the state. Constitutions can also, usually secondarily and indirectly, prescribe ends or outcomes, such as national unity, stability, integration, development, distributive justice, etc. From both these perspectives, constitutions are effective in nation-building if they conduce to power-sharing in such a way that all sections of the nation or nation-in-the-making feel that the constitution embodies justice, protects their core interests, gives them a fair share of representation in the structures of power and a stake in the order created. This essay makes a preliminary attempt at viewing the Indian constitution as a device for power-sharing, and hence for building a united India in which all citizens can feel they have a share in power and a stake. The focus will be on *one particular aspect* of the rules of the game of politics that is a key to representation and hence to power-sharing, *namely, the electoral system*, and the evolution of debates about it. The electoral system will be viewed in the context of other features, such as federalism and fundamental rights, including their subset, minority rights and reservations for historically disadvantaged groups, which crucially impinge on representation and, hence, power-sharing.

The essay deviates from the theme of constitutional ideas and political practices as it is more about a debate that did not take place; a blind spot rather than an explicit debate about the merits of alternative electoral systems for representation and power-sharing in a society plural along multiple axes: religious, linguistic, regional, caste, tribal, etc. However, the blind spots in the history of constitutional and political debate are often instructive. An underlying premise is that power-sharing of a kind that is felt to be fair by all groups in society, including minorities and historically disadvantaged groups, is *a necessary condition for voluntary loyalty and national integration in the long run in a diverse society with a history of conflicts*. This does not mean that I judge an electoral system by the yardstick of how perfectly it represents all the groups in the population. Exact proportionality in representation may be an impossibility. Yet a purposive nation-building effort, or even just a society and a leadership aware of the interests of all its members, has to continually review its system of representation to ensure that the entire citizenry feel that their interests are recognized in the system and opportunities created for them to find fulfilment.

The essay develops as follows over the next four sections. In the second section, after outlining the existing electoral system, I outline the evolution of the Indian party system, particularly the period since 1989 when it took off on a trajectory that it was never intended to do by the electoral system chosen after Independence. That is, it became a multiparty system characterized by large and unwieldy coalition governments, in a society increasingly politicized along communal, caste, and regional lines. I then outline, in the third section, the various proposals for electoral-systemic reform that have been mooted in public debate since the late 1990s in response to the emergence of such a party system and such governments, and such perceived politicization of social cleavages. In the fourth section, I return to the origins to investigate how the electoral system was originally chosen, that is, whether its merits were debated in relation to possible alternative systems, what effects it was intended to produce or avoid, whether its current effects half a century later were ever anticipated, whether any alternatives were seriously considered and why they were rejected and the existing system adopted. Finally, in the fifth and concluding section, I pull together the threads. The essay focuses on the importance of the electoral system for representation and power-sharing, both in the context of the various reform proposals at the beginning of the twenty-first century, and when it returns to examine its origins and evolution, and the debate or lack of it, around it.

The Emergence of a Multiparty System, Coalition Governments, and Politicization of Social Cleavages

The Indian electoral system is a single-member district, simple-plurality system in which voters (over the age of 18 since 1989) cast a single ballot to choose a single representative to the lower house of parliament (Lok Sabha) or the state legislative assembly, the candidate with the largest number of votes, even if only a plurality, getting elected to represent that constituency. There are 543 constituencies that send a single member each to the Lok Sabha (two members are nominated). This first past the post (FPTP) system, in common parlance, was adopted shortly after Independence, following debates in the Constituent Assembly (1946–9) and parliament (1950–1) just prior to the adoption of the Representation of the People Act, 1950 and 1951, and the first general elections of 1952. At that time, there were a significant number of two-member constituencies, and some three-member constituencies, in which one or two seats were reserved for Scheduled Castes (SCs) or Scheduled Tribes (STs), but in which the electoral formula remained the FPTP one, candidates getting elected on the basis of the number of votes cast. However, in these constituencies, voters had two or three ballots and had to cast them for different candidates. Multi-member constituencies were abolished in 1961, following which the electoral system has been the single-member FPTP system.

This electoral system produced a party system in the elections from 1952 to 1984, in which the single largest party won only a plurality of the votes but got a majority of the seats, and formed a single-party majority government. In all elections from 1952 to 1984, the single largest party which formed a majority government was the Congress, except in 1977 when it was the Janata Party—formed by almost the entire non-Communist opposition. The single largest party never got a simple majority, the maximum percentage of votes received being 48 per cent by the Congress in 1984, but always got a majority, several times a two-thirds or (in 1984) even a four-fifths majority.

However, the party system changed from 1989. The past five general elections in India, in 1989, 1991, 1996, 1998, and 1999, have resulted in hung parliaments and, as a consequence, minority and/or coalition governments. Even the Congress government of 1991–6 was a minority government for the first two-and-a-half years of its term. The other post-1989 governments did not last the full term; indeed less than a year each. The first of these was the Janata Dal-led National Front minority coalition of prime minister V.P. Singh, dependent on the support of both the right-wing Bharatiya Janata Party (BJP) and the Left Front, followed by the Janata Dal splinter group led by Prime Minister Chandra Shekhar with a tenth of the Lok Sabha (Lower House) supported by the much larger Congress Party, and the two United Front minority coalition governments of prime ministers Deve Gowda and I.K. Gujral, dependent on the support of both the Congress and most of the Left Front. The National Front and the two United Front governments were large coalitions (five to ten governing parties) which were dependent for their parliamentary majority on supporting parties. The BJP-led coalitions governing since March 1998, and again since October 1999, the latter formally called the National Democratic Alliance, were even larger coalitions. These coalitions have been some of the largest in the world in terms of the number of governing parties.

The decline of the Congress vote to below the (varying) critical threshold at which a vote plurality translated to a seat majority led to hung parliaments and coalition politics. The long-term reasons for this were: the desertion of the Congress by sections of its erstwhile base, including rich peasants, SCs and Muslims, in large parts of the country; the inability of the Congress to incorporate newly-mobilized groups such as farmers and intermediate castes; also at least partly because of the decline in the internally democratic and grand-coalitional character of the party following the Congress split of 1969 and centralization under Indira Gandhi.

Another significant trend over the past decade in Indian politics is the rise of identity politics, including Hindu majoritarianism manifested in the rise of the BJP and the like-minded Shiv Sena in Maharashtra. Identity politics is also represented by the Kashmiri Muslim secessionist insurgency since 1989, and regional parties with an ethno–cultural platform in several states, including the Dravidian parties in Tamil Nadu, the Akali Dal in Punjab, the Telugu Desam in Andhra Pradesh, and the Ahom Gana Parishad in Assam, besides continuing secessionist insurgencies in Assam, Nagaland, and Manipur, and movements within some states to secede and form new states in parts of existing large states. The latter movements have led to the formation of three new states in November 2000—Uttarakhand, Jharkhand, and Chhattisgarh—carved out of Uttar Pradesh (UP), Bihar, and Madhya Pradesh (MP), respectively. The rise of caste-based parties like the Bahujan Samaj Party (BSP), and to a lesser extent the Samajwadi Party in UP and the Rashtriya Janata Dal (RJD) in Bihar, also reflect the rise of identity politics.

The principal points I wish to make are that *both the traditional justifications for the FPTP system*, in general and in India, including in the Constituent Assembly debates which I will discuss shortly, which are namely *that it produces stable single-party majority governments, and that its aggregative imperative leads to national integration as against splitting the party system along 'ethnic' (broadly defined, including religio–communal, caste, regional–ethnic, cultural, etc.) lines, have been belied in practice for a decade now*.

Two questions arise: first, are coalitions unstable and short-lived due to the logic of the first past the post (FPTP) electoral system? I have argued in detail elsewhere that this is indeed the case, while emphasizing that coalitions have the advantage of being more broadly representative.[1] The principal reason is that the seat–vote disproportionality of the FPTP system induces instability between the parties of the ruling coalition and the opposition, on the one hand, and tensions between the coalition partners, on the other. This is because even a small swing in votes can effect a much larger swing in seats. Therefore, power can shift between opposing coalitions quite dramatically, and coalition-making parties have an incentive to try to split the opposing coalition by every means, the payoff being potentially high. Likewise, a small swing in popularity leading to even a small swing in votes between coalition partners can lead to a large swing in seats, potentially decimating some parties while boosting others, dramatically altering their bargaining power. This is in contrast to what happens under the proportional representation (PR) system, where vote swings, which are rarely dramatic, lead to only roughly proportional swings in seats. This leads to the question: would a shift to some form of proportional representation lead to more stable coalition governments? In short, could PR usher in a shift from majoritarian democracy to what Arend Lijphart has called a consensus democracy?[2] Or would it lead to even greater fragmentation of the party system? If the former, then there is a possible rationale for a shift to proportional representation of some kind, like the shift towards the German-style mixed FPTP-list PR system that Japan and New Zealand have effected in the first half of the 1990s in their own variants.

Second, is the rise of such 'ethnic'—communal, caste-based, regional nationalist/separatist—political parties and movements, and the social and psychological cost in terms of the fears of majority domination, political marginalization, and cultural submergence, and the furies they unleash, ultimately rooted, at least in part, in the majoritarian character of the FPTP electoral system? I argue elsewhere that is substantially the case.[3] The argument, in a nutshell, is that groups so distributed as to be in a minority in most parliamentary or state assembly constituencies would find it difficult to win party nominations and get elected so long as ascriptive criteria influence, and are seen by party managers to influence, voting behaviour, which is substantially the case. Minority groups would then tend to be systematically under-represented, and deprived of a proportionate share in power, perhaps even to the extent that preservation of their minimum material interests and cultural identity would be felt to be threatened, while 'ethnic' majorities or pluralities would tend to be magnified in elected legislatures and executives. If this is the case, is there again a possible rationale for considering a whole or partial switch to proportional representation? It could reduce the magnification of pluralities to steamroller majorities.

All the possible minorities are vulnerable to steamroller majoritarianism at the national and/or state levels if polarization along the relevant majority–minority faultlines takes place, with all the consequences that such developments can unleash: suspicion, fear, perceived powerlessness, fury, violence, backlash, instability, chaos, and even national disintegration. This points to the need to qualify the political system's majoritarian tendencies in the interest of long-term social and political stability.

One way of doing so, without changing the electoral system, is to define the fundamental rights more precisely, especially as regards the extension of individual rights to derivative group rights, with special attention to religion, places of worship, cultural heritage sites and structures, place names, language, script, educational rights, particularly medium of instruction and optional language facilities, second official language status in the states, and the like. Such an extension of individual fundamental rights to derivative group rights and freedoms can be intellectually justified.[4] This would qualify majoritarianism by limiting the range and extent of basic policies and institutions which can be altered by legislative majorities or by executive fiat.

A second way, and one which is not a policy option but a development that has to come about in the natural course of political evolution if it is to happen at all, is the reconstruction of an umbrella party, like the Congress was in its heyday, with coalition politics being played out within the party, and electoral politics not being played out along lines of social cleavage.

A third way, not in contradiction to at least the first, is to change the electoral system to some variant of PR, or to introduce multi-member constituencies even if still following the FPTP formula (as in Japan's multi-member plurality system over 1950–93). This would both ensure better representation of minorities, especially the minorities most vulnerable to under-representation, and that coalition and/or minority governments are more faithfully representative of the popular vote as well as more stable, and hence coherent in terms of policy and governance. There would be a need here to simultaneously ensure that PR's tendency towards extreme fragmentation of the party system by undermining the FPTP system's incentive to aggregate votes, and hence to build social coalitions, is checked.

Recent Proposals for Electoral-Systemic Reform

There have been a slew of proposals for electoral reform over the past few years. I mention here only those few which go beyond reforming the existing single-member district, FPTP system, technically, the single-member district, single, non-transferable vote, simple plurality system, to consideration of features of alternative electoral systems, particularly.[5] Most of these proposals have been motivated by concern about the prospects of effective governance as well as of power-sharing which derived from the experience of the post-1989 hung parliaments and coalition and/or minority governments, political instability, and especially since 1996, perceived disproportionate or pivotal power of small and/or regional parties in coalition governments. Some of these proposals had also been motivated by the possible fresh delimitation of constituencies after the end of the constitutional freeze on delimitation after the 2001 census. Fresh delimitation could lead to changes in the share of seats in the Lok Sabha of several states, and at least lead to redrawing the boundaries of existing constituencies.[6] Although the Ninety-first Constitution Amendment, passed by parliament in August 2001, extends the freeze of the inter-state allocation of seats in the Lok Sabha for another twenty-five years, until 2026, it is an open question how politically sustainable this amendment is, quite apart from the question of its desirability, which is debatable. It is quite possible that it may be challenged after the 2011 census if not even earlier.

The two major proposals that have been discussed in the Law Commission of India's Working Paper, 'Reform of Electoral Laws' (January 1999) are: first, the introduction of a mixed FPTP-cum-PR system akin to the German model, consisting of the introduction of a list system in addition to the FPTP system based on single-member territorial constituencies, and, second, a two-ballot majority run-off system.[7] The mixed system would consist of an increase of 25 per cent, or 138 seats, in the permitted maximum of 550 seats in the Lok Sabha, taking the new total number of seats to 688. These additional seats would be filled on the basis of list PR, in which parties would publish a list of nominees before the election. There would be no need for a second ballot since the allotment of seats would be on the basis of vote share. However, both the additional PR seats allotted and the vote share that would be taken into account to fill these would be at the state level, with additional PR seats allotted proportional to states' population shares, with small adjacent states being clubbed together, and likewise vote shares in such states. Only recognized parties, national and state, would be eligible for the additional PR seats.

The second system discussed but not recommended by the Commission, is a majority run-off system where only candidates polling over 50 per cent of the votes cast get elected from single-member territorial constituencies under the existing FPTP system. If no candidates get a simple majority, a run-off election is held in which only the first two candidates of the first round contest, the winner of these being elected. An important provision is that negative votes are allowed, which will be counted as valid votes cast. This run-off system finds support in both of the consultation papers of the National Commission to Review the Working of the Constitution, released in early 2001, except that they do not endorse the negative vote, and by some eminent persons including former president of India, R. Venkataraman and former chief election commissioner, M.S. Gill.[8]

The justification given for considering these changes and for recommending the first of them is that very often the winning candidate receives only 30–35 per cent of the votes cast, resulting in a wastage of the remaining 65–70 per cent of the votes, the will of the majority going unrepresented as the seat–vote disproportionality is very great. Therefore, the introduction of mixed FPTP-list PR will make the system less disproportional. However, the part of the proposal that restricts the allocation of additional list PR seats only to recognized parties narrows the menu of choice, and in effect makes the system more proportional only among the existing established parties at the national and state levels, weighting it against the emergence of new and small parties. Furthermore, the Commission rejects a total switch over to list PR.

There are two principal justifications given for the run-off system. First, 'to cut down, or at any rate, to curtail the significance and role played by the caste factor in the electoral process. There is hardly any constituency in the country where any one particular caste can command more than 50 per cent of the votes. This means that a candidate has to carry with him several castes and communities, to succeed'.[9] Second, 'the negative vote is intended to put moral pressure on political parties not to put forward candidates with undesirable record ...'.[10] The NCRWC's consultation paper, 'review of Election Law, Processes and Reform Options' argues that the 'multiplicity of political parties, combined with our Westminster-based first-past-the-post system results in a majority of legislators and parliamentarians getting elected on a minority vote.'[11] This is said to undermine the representative character of elected legislators, although this issue was never raised in public debate or in party positions during the years of a Congress plurality in vote share resulting in substantial majorities in parliament, even though the system then was also characterized by precisely the fact of substantial numbers of legislators and parliamentarians getting elected on a minority vote. The NCRWC consultation paper recommends the run-off system for two reasons. First, it would result in legislators who have a simple majority of the vote, thus resolving the problem of representative character. Second, 'it also makes it in the self-interest of various political parties to widen their appeal to the electorate.'[12]

The Election Commission of India also seriously considering for the first time a possible change of the present electoral system to majoritarian (run-off) system/ list system/mixed system or any other system, albeit cautiously adding that the 'need is to start a national debate so as to have a broad national consensus on this very fundamental subject'.[13]

If we examine these justifications, we find that the argument for partial PR and the implied or explicit critique of the FPTP system is nothing new, the same arguments having been advanced and debated decades ago the world over, and in the Constituent Assembly debates too. *Then why has it become salient today?* The reason is clearly that for a decade since 1989, the FPTP system has resulted in hung parliaments and minority and/or coalition governments with their attendant instabilities rather than parliamentary majorities and stable one-party governments. Indeed, the thrust is not on proportionality so much as stabilizing the existing major parties by reducing the disproportionalities among them. Similarly, the run-off system strengthens the two largest parties at the constituency level, being actually *less* proportional than the choices expressed by the electorate in the first round of voting in which voters choose from an unconstrained menu of options, in contrast to the run-off round when the supporters of third and more parties have to vote for one or the other of the two run-off candidates. This actually reduces the menu of choice by forcing an artificial lumping of political options into two major alliances. The majority that it produces for the elected legislators is a *manufactured* one, in which vote–seat disproportionality is greater than under FPTP elections. This system has not been used for parliamentary elections anywhere in the world and is used only for presidential elections in France, Portugal, and Algeria.[14] As for the ostensible reason advanced of its conducing to reducing caste conflict, it could well result in bipolar caste conflicts, say between Forwards and Backwards, with Scheduled Castes (SCs) and minorities playing a balancing role. In addition, it would do nothing to reduce the other viciously divisive politics that has seen growth over the past decade, namely, minority-baiting communalism; indeed, it may create conditions favourable to communal polarization that may result in a totally majoritarian politics in which minorities that are not locally concentrated may be virtually excluded from representation.

Political parties have not taken explicit positions on electoral-systemic reform, although it should be noted that the Bharatiya Jana Sangh in the 1950s and 1960s supported PR. It was under-represented in terms of seats in relation to its vote share. However, the BJP is now a beneficiary of the FPTP system, winning a third of the seats in 1999 with under a quarter of the votes, while the Congress with a greater (28 per cent) but more thinly spread vote share won only 21 per cent of the seats. The BJP no longer makes any mention of PR. Another noteworthy point is that all the reform options recently mooted, whether the run-off system or the mixed FPTP–PR system with relatively high cut-off points for representation in the second tier, favour the large parties and discriminate against the small ones, notwithstanding the justification for such proposals being the supposedly unrepresentative character of legislators elected on only a plurality vote or the disproportionality effect of the FPTP system.

Going Back from the Present to Examine the Origins

In light of the fragmentation of the national party system, particularly its increasing coincidence with social cleavages, the possible redistribution of the states' shares of seats in the Lok Sabha at some point in the future after 2001, the demands for greater representation by reservation of seats for women, following that for SCs and STs, and within that a quota for Other Backward Classes (OBCs), all reflecting the present electoral system's disproportionalities, and the proposals for electoral-systemic reforms, it would be interesting to look back to the Constituent Assembly and early parliamentary debates on the electoral system to examine whether the FPTP system's implications for representation and power-sharing were thoroughly debated, and whether its possible consequences were anticipated.

The Constituent Assembly was extremely aware of India's heterogeneity and sensitized to the issues of representation of various groups in legislatures, cabinets, and public employment. These issues arose in debates over the fundamental rights, minority rights, and the articles of the draft constitution, including those of provincial governments. However, these debates centred on the then four-decade-old issue of joint versus separate electorates and representation, including reservations for minorities and SCs and STs. Explicit debate on the merits of alternative electoral systems did not take place except in the context of amendments moved almost entirely by members of the Assembly belonging to the Muslim minority. Hence, *the debate on alternative electoral systems and their dynamics and implications for representation and, hence, power-sharing over time, was a debate that did not really take place.* Even to the extent that it did, it did not reveal a deep understanding of the dynamics of either the FPTP system or of various PR formulae. Rather, there was a pronounced tendency to assume as somehow natural the familiar Anglo-Saxon FPTP system.

This tendency was there in the draft constitution prepared by the constitutional adviser, B.N. Rau, based on the reports of various committees of the Constituent Assembly which submitted these reports between April and August 1947, with these being placed before the Drafting Committee on 27 October 1947. The draft constitution tended to assume the single-member constituency and FPTP system, but also had multi-member constituencies to be filled by a multiple-ballot, distributive-vote, quota system, at least for reserved constituencies (at that time reservation for religious minorities was also accepted).[15] That is, referring to the Fourth Schedule, point 34, 'Where at an election in a territorial constituency, a poll is taken for the purpose of filling more than one seat, a voter shall have as many votes as there are seats to be filled on the poll, but shall not be entitled to give more than one vote to any candidate.'[16] Thus, the distributive vote meant that in a multiple-ballot system, voters could not 'cumulate' their ballots on a single candidate, called the cumulative vote. The cumulative vote system would tend to help minority groups to get at least some candidates elected by voters casting two or more, or all their votes, for their favoured candidate. Rau was strongly influenced in favour of the FPTP system notwithstanding his study of various PR systems during his travels to several Western countries in October 1947, though he concedes that there was 'general agreement even among the critics of proportional representation that the application of the system is a necessity in the case of countries with self-conscious racial or communal minorities.'[17]

Prior to preparing the draft constitution based on the reports of the various committees of the assembly, he circulated a questionnaire at the first meeting of the Union Constitution Committee on 5 May 1947, and another questionnaire to the Provincial Constitution Committee, also at its first meeting on the same date. Question 23 asked: what should be the (a) composition; (b) franchise; (c) electorate; (d) constituencies; (e) method of election. The only response to the first questionnaire that touched upon (d) and (e) was that of Shyama Prasad Mookerjee, who favoured equal electoral districts and single-member constituencies, but multi-member constituencies where seats were intended to be reserved (at that time for religious minorities too).[18]

Likewise, responses to the same question from members of the Provincial Constitution Committee, were as follows. Of the five who responded, Rajkumari Amrit Kaur suggested PR with multi-member constituencies, P. Subbarayan and B.G. Kher suggested FPTP in single-member constituencies with PR in reserved multi-member constituencies, and Brijlal Biyani FPTP single-member constituencies.[19] What this implies is that though there was an assumption of continuity of the FPTP system, the issue was not decided and that some members did suggest PR and multi-member constituences if only for reserved constituencies. However, the underlying assumption of the carry-forward of the FPTP system was very strong.

This assumption appears to have been implicitly accepted by most members of the Constituent Assembly, as indicated by the absence of a systematic and focused debate on the effects of various electoral systems on the pattern of representation. The only references to it were in debates that focused largely on minorities and the issue of the electoral system, questioning the merits of FPTP, and were raised largely by members belonging to minority communities. Below are some illustrative snatches from the scattered debate on the electoral system to be adopted.

In the debate on the draft constitution, Z. H. Lari (UP, Muslim) advocated PR by single transferable vote (STV) or cumulative voting.[20] He cited Ireland, which then had been ruled for fifteen years by one party although PR supposedly favoured a multiplicity of parties, and France had a plethora of parties despite FPTP. He also argued for an elected, not appointed, cabinet on the Swiss model, making it easier for minorities to get represented in the cabinet, and recommended minority reservation in legislatures and public services though not in the cabinet.

Hussain Imam (Bihar, Muslim), in the same debate, recommended PR with large (10–12 member) multi-member constituencies, one or two per administrative district, on the grounds that effective opposition would be possible only under PR, citing the under-representation in seats in comparison to votes, and hence the ineffectiveness of the Socialists, in UP.[21] This was a justification of PR on explicitly party-political grounds rather than concerning representation of minorities. The only other such justification was one in an earlier debate (Debate on Report on Minority Rights) in which D.H. Chandrasekharaiya (Mysore State) moved an amendment for the PR system in all elections, preferably by single transferable vote (STV), or if not, by single non-transferable vote (SNTV) on the grounds that the FPTP system over-represents the majority or plurality party, and also to ensure better minority representation.[22]

An indirect critique of FPTP was made in the debate on the legislative assembly in the larger debate on the Principles of a Model Provincial Constitution. Saiyid Mohammed Saadulla (Assam, Muslim) moved an amendment to raise the scale of representation from one representative per lakh of population to one per two lakhs.[23] Omeo Kumar Das (Assam, General) said in the debate on the amendment moved by Saadulla that the scale of representation should be lowered from 1 per 100,000 to 1 per 75,000 in Assam because 'there are many backward communities and these communities have no chance of getting elected in bigger constituencies'.[24] Rev. J. J. M. Nichols–Roy (Assam, General) supported this for better representation of hill tribes which inhabit large, low-density territories, citing the North Cachar Hills as an example.[25] This was supported by Gopinath Bordoloi (Assam, General) for the Assam tribes, and Lakshminarayan Sahu (Orissa, General), citing tribes in Orissa, and Jaipal Singh (Bihar, General), citing tribes in the Jharkhand region.[26] They were all keenly aware that smaller constituencies in the FPTP system would better enable communities with a small population to be more proportionately represented, especially if territorially concentrated.

The closest the assembly came to an explicit debate on FPTP versus PR was on 4 January 1949 (before the proposal for reservation of seats for religious minorities was dropped in May 1949) when Kazi Syed Karimuddin (CP and Berar, Muslim) moved an amendment (no. 1415) to clause 5 of Draft Art. 67 on the composition of parliament, in which he recommended PR by cumulative voting and attacked FPTP and single-member districts for promoting the tyranny of the majority and for the wasted votes of the collective majority of voters unrepresented in governments formed by a plurality victory.[27] He raised the issue of PR versus reservations for minorities, and attacked religion-based reservations of seats, then still under consideration, indeed, broadly accepted under Draft Art. 292, because such members elected under joint electorates would not be true representatives of their communities. *He favoured abolition of reservation if PR was introduced but not if it was not.* He made an explicit linkage between PR and abolition of reservation, the crucial issue being the representation of minorities and their assured share in power. He was supported by K.T. Shah (Bihar, General) who moved an amendment proposing PR by STV for political, not communal, reasons, and recommended states as constituencies, that is, very large, multi-member constituencies lending themselves to highly proportional outcomes.[28]

Mahboob Ali Baig Sahib Bahadur (Madras, Muslim) supported PR by STV, again for political reasons, because it favoured a strong opposition, citing Pandit H. N. Kunzru on supporting PR and STV for the Upper House.[29] Sardar Hukam Singh (East Punjab, Sikh) also favoured PR rather than reservation for minorities as it did not violate individualist principles. He argued: 'My position is that if separate electorates are detestable and if reservation of seats is objectionable, then some method has to be devised by which the rights of minorities can be safeguarded and this is the only method suggested in the amendments that can be considered.'[30]

Interestingly, Ambedkar opposed PR on the grounds that it presupposes literacy, and also *because it does not ensure a share of representation and power as do reservations*. In his words:

I submit that PR is really taking away by the back door what has already been granted to the minorities by this agreement [he had in the earlier part of his speech favoured a majority–minority deal on joint electorates in exchange for reservations], because PR will not give to the minorities what they wanted, viz., *a definite quota* [emphasis added]. It might give them a voice in the election of their representatives. ....[31]

What comes across in the very sketchy and fragmented debate on the choice of an electoral system is that while the issues of representation and power-sharing were keenly felt by all, the central trade-off contemplated (and accepted until the turnaround in May 1949) was the abolition of separate electorates and the introduction of joint electorates under an FPTP system of voting, more assumed than seriously debated, in exchange for reservation of seats in the legislature for minorities (and for STs). In other words, the majoritarian character of the FPTP system was sought to be tempered by the introduction of an essentially *consociational* feature such as reservations. This was a mixture of opposites since what later came to be called consociationalism recognizes explicit group rights in a way essentially at odds with the individualist premises of the FPTP system. The option of a non-consociational system of representation based on liberal individualist premises such as the PR system, which tends to better represent minorities and small parties without having to resort to reservations, was never seriously debated or even understood.[32] Nor was the multi-member single-ballot plurality system of the Japanese type (1950–93), or other PR alternatives such as the SNTV system, both of which are more proportional than FPTP but are operable in an illiterate electorate.

The early parliamentary debates on the Representation of the People Bills of 1950 and 1951 did not reveal any informed and detailed discussion on the consequences of possible alternative electoral systems for the pattern of representation and, by implication, power-sharing. Indeed, the members were not even clear whether the constituencies were going to be single or multi-member and whether the electoral formula was to be FPTP or some other. This is revealed by interventions such as those of Hussain Imam (Bihar, Muslim):

In this Bill no provision has been made as to how the constituencies are to be delimited. Do we want to have single-seated constituencies or multi-seated constituencies? Nor has it been mentioned here whether we are going to have proportional representation or the distributive voting or cumulative voting ... Do we wish to have the anomaly of the British electoral system by means of which minorities in a three-cornered contest can get a larger number of seats in the House than the voting recorded at elections? ... I wish that there should be a Select Committee to ascertain the wishes of the House as to how we wish to be represented.[33]

Ajit Prasad Jain (UP, General), in the same debate, also criticized the vagueness of the bill on constituency size (number of members) and electoral formula, and whether, if there was to be a multi-member constituency, there was to be cumulative or distributive voting.[34] He endorsed single-member constituencies except for the reserved seats. The same criticism of vagueness about constituency size and electoral formula in the bill was echoed by M. A. Ayyangar (Madras, General), leading Ambedkar to promise that there would be a bill that would deal with these two issues.[35]

As a result of these interventions, The Representation of the People Act of 1950, as originally enacted, spelt out a system of both single-member general constituencies and multi-member constituencies, the latter by implication being for those constituencies in which some seats were to be reserved for SCs and STs. It did not however make explicit the plurality formula (FPTP), this being assumed.

The fact of the electoral formula being FPTP and general seats being single-member and reserved seats multi-member, comes out only in the RPA 1951, section 63 on Method of Voting: 'In plural member constituencies other than Council constituencies every elector shall have as many votes as there are members to be elected, but no elector shall give more than one vote to any one candidate.'[36] This also brings out the distributive voting rule for such constituencies. That the FPTP or plurality-rule formula is implied comes out in Ambedkar's remark, referring to the Constituent Assembly's resolution endorsing distributive voting (with reference to Art. 332 (5) on tribal constituencies), thus implying multi-member constituencies in which an SC or ST seat is reserved rather than reserved constituencies in which only an SC or ST candidate can contest.[37] If the latter, Ambedkar said, then there is no need to refer to distributive voting (which implied at least two ballots); it would have been one man, one vote (the implied default FPTP system). The FPTP formula is also implied in Section 65 of the Act on Equality of Votes: 'If after counting of the votes is completed, an equality of votes is found to exist between any candidates, and the addition of one vote will entitle any of those candidates to be declared elected, the Returning Officer shall forthwith decide between those candidates by lot ...'[38]

Lastly, the FPTP formula or plurality rule *for both single-member general and multi-member reserved constituencies* is clearly spelt out in the Representation of the People (Conduct of Elections and Election Petitions) Rules 1951, Rule 48 on Declaration of candidates elected, for both : '... the Returning Officer shall ... forthwith declare the candidate or candidates to whom the largest number of valid votes has been given, to be elected.'[39]

What is however interesting is that by this time, just before the first general elections of 1952, there was hardly any debate on either constituency size or the related issue of electoral formula, as regards their effect on representation of small parties or minorities. The SC and ST representation issue was resolved by reservation under joint electorates and plurality-rule multi-member constituencies. The debate did not veer in the direction of either changing the formula towards some form of PR, which would have benefited small parties and minorities, especially territorially dispersed minorities, nor moving towards larger, multi-member constituencies under the existing plurality formula (as in Japan's multi-member plurality-rule electoral system, 1955–93), which would have ensured better representation for both small parties and minorities, including perhaps assuring SC and ST representation without recourse to reservation.

The next and most illuminating debate on the electoral system as regards representation took place during the Two-Member Constituencies (Abolition) Bill in 1961. The move to abolish two-member (and the few three-member) reserved constituencies for SCs and STs originated in the demand for such abolition by some SC members, on the administrative grounds of size, multi-member constituencies being very large in area and population, and difficult to cover in an election campaign without incurring inordinate costs, and more importantly, on the grounds that SC and ST members in such constituencies felt that they would gain in importance in single-member reserved constituencies. Thus, as A. K. Sen described it:

> The Scheduled Caste and Scheduled Tribe members have been pleading for a long time that the system which would give reservation in their favour and give the best possible effect is one which would enable them to stand from single-member constituencies and which would thus prevent the possibility of Scheduled Caste and Scheduled Tribe members being tacked on with members standing for general constituencies.[40]

There was opposition to the abolition from general constituency members who feared the possible reservation of their constituencies for SCs and STs. As Mahavir Tyagi (UP) put it:

> This Bill goes against the interests of the Scheduled Castes ... my submission is that the representative character will deteriorate to a great extent if single-member constituencies are created. ... As soon as you reserve a constituency for Scheduled Castes, 80 per cent of the population of that constituency will feel frustrated because their sons cannot offer themselves as candidates from their home constituency.[41]

There were also objections raised on administrative grounds, of the complications necessarily arising from the bifurcation of the assembly constituencies in each double-member parliamentary constituency, and further, the double-member assembly constituencies within such parliamentary constituencies. Opposition members also feared that opposition strength constituencies would be declared single-member constituencies reserved for SCs or STs.[42]

Mahavir Tyagi (somewhat prophetically, and presaging the criticisms of the Bahujan Samaj Party over three decades later) also raised the fear of SC members being unrepresentative of their community because they would be dependent on a majority of non-SC voters to be elected.[43] The bill, however, went through. After this debate the electoral system for the Lok Sabha has not undergone any basic change as regards constituency or electoral formula, and hence the electoral system's effects on the representation of small parties and minorities, and further, its effects on power-sharing.

Conclusion

Looking back in the light of the changes since 1989, it is interesting to note how deeply entrenched the assumption of the appropriateness of the FPTP system was in the Constituent Assembly debates, the early parliamentary debates, and the Lok Sabha debates up to 1961 on the electoral system. In particular, in the debate on the Two-Member Constituencies (Abolition) Bill, 1961, *the debate never went in the direction of achieving greater proportionality of outcomes, or reducing the effective threshold of representation, even by adopting larger, multi-member constituencies (with or without multiple ballots) while retaining the plurality-rule formula*, leave alone moving towards any form of PR.

Essentially, three broad types of electoral system were available for choice, given a largely illiterate and politically poorly informed electorate (thus ruling out systems that assume considerable political information such as the STV among PR systems or the alternative vote among plurality systems). These are plurality systems, PR systems, and semi-proportional systems. The latter include the single non-transferable vote and the cumulative vote. In India, just after Independence, the British FPTP system was the default system and, as we have shown, adopted largely by default without a discriminating and informed debate on alternatives. Plurality systems, like the single-member constituency FPTP system, favoured the largest parties and tended to under-represent political and other minorities. PR systems, while being proportional in outcomes, especially in large, multi-member constituencies, and enabling better representation of small parties and minorities, would run the risk not only of fragmented legislatures but also the fragmentation of the party system over time along religious, caste, linguistic, regional, and tribal lines.

However, it was also within the realm of possibility to adopt semi-proportional systems which were operable by an illiterate electorate. Two variants possible were the single SNTV and the cumulative vote system. In the SNTV system, voters in multi-member constituencies using the plurality rule, have only one vote. Candidates are selected by the plurality rule. In a four-member constituency, for example, the top four candidates by votes received get elected. This system is more proportional in outcomes than simple plurality. Another variant that enables small parties and minorities to get their candidates more easily elected is the cumulative vote system, a special case of the limited vote system. In this, voters in multi-member constituencies using the plurality rule for election, have more than one vote but fewer than the number of candidates (hence limited vote). If they are allowed to 'cumulate' their votes on only one candidate, this becomes the cumulative vote system, while if they have to cast not more than one vote per candidate, it is called the distributive vote system. The two-member and three-member constituencies that existed until 1961 were, in embryonic form, distributive vote systems. Both the SNTV system and the two limited vote systems, cumulative and distributive, are special cases of the multi-member plurality rule system. These systems, particularly SNTV and the cumulative vote system, give political and other minorities a better opportunity of electing their preferred candidate, and while inducing greater competition for votes among two or more candidates belonging to the same party in a multi-member constituency, and hence weakening parties to some extent, not exerting as much centrifugal pressure on parties as PR systems. The more proportional outcomes under PR and semi-PR systems is because such systems, even semi-proportional systems based on the plurality rule, lower the effective thresholds of representation.

Contemporary research on comparative electoral systems has shown that there are *effective thresholds of representation* determined by the combination of electoral formula and district magnitude, especially the latter, which are a barrier to small party representation. The issue of effective thresholds and proportionality is complicated by the fact that the effective threshold is a range rather than a fixed percentage, and can be conceived of as having an upper and a lower bound. The upper bound is the threshold of exclusion, or the maximum percentage of the vote under the most unfavourable conditions, that may be insufficient for a party to win a seat. Anything over this guarantees a seat. The lower bound or threshold of representation (or inclusion) is the minimum percentage of the vote, under the most favourable conditions, that can win a party a seat. The exact effective threshold in any particular system would lie somewhere between these upper and lower bounds and would be determined by district magnitude, the electoral formula, and the number of competing parties.

Lijphart arrives at an average upper threshold of 100%/M+1 vote percentage, where M is the district magnitude.[44] That is, for a party to win a seat, it would in a 10–seat district have to win at least 9 per cent of the vote, in a 5–seat district, at least 17 per cent. These are much lower percentages than anything conceivable under FPTP. For example, in a small (for PR systems) district of 5 seats, one-sixth of the votes would be sufficient to win a seat but not one-tenth, whereas in a 10-member district, one-eleventh would be sufficient. Compare these cases with an average effective threshold of 35 per cent of the vote under FPTP in an Indian single-member constituency for general elections over 1952–84, and likewise for post-war elections in the UK, Canada, Australia, New Zealand, and the US (Congressional).[45] Lijphart has, with Taagepera, modified his formula for an effective threshold to 75%/(M+1) which yields even lower effective thresholds for every district magnitude. By this formula, the effective threshold under FPTP is 37.5 per cent, while for a 5–seat district it falls from one-sixth to 12.5 per cent or one-eighth.[46]

It never appeared to strike anyone in the Constituent Assembly and early parliamentary debates on the electoral system that multi-member plurality systems falling in-between FPTP and PR, would radically reduce the effective threshold of representation, thus enabling SCs, STs, smaller caste groups, and religious minorities to be more proportionately represented *without* the device of reservation, not to speak of more proportionate representation for smaller parties. A multi-member plurality system would also be as easy to implement in a largely illiterate population. In retrospect, reservation of constituencies for SCs and STs, especially the single-member constituencies since 1961, and especially the ending of rotation of reserved constituencies since 1976, has led to precisely what Mahavir Tyagi warned against (although he was not motivated by concern for SC representation), that SC members would be dependent on non-SC voters, and hence would be unrepresentative of their community's interests and, in turn, defeat the purpose of reservation. This criticism finds an echo in the dissatisfaction with SC MPs of existing parties manifested in the rise of the Bahujan Samaj Party in the 1990s notwithstanding four decades of reservation. Furthermore, reservation as a device to ensure representation can lead to snowballing demands for reservation for more and more groups and sub-groups as, for example, in the demand for women's reservation, the further demand for reservation for OBC women within any women's quota, and the demands by some Muslim groups for reservation for Muslims.[47]

To sum up, this essay has attempted to retrace the debate on the origins and adoption of India's electoral system. The single-member constituency, FPTP system was adopted in the Constituent Assembly and early parliamentary debates, not so much from a focused debate on the merits of alternative electoral systems as regards their effects on the representation of parties and social groups, but from a default assumption that the FPTP system was somehow natural, carried forward largely unconsciously from British and British colonial practice since 1935. There was an awareness that this system would tend to under-represent territorially dispersed groups like the SCs and Muslims, but that was sought to be remedied by the device of reservation, guaranteeing representation, rather than by electoral-systemic engineering. If the recent proposals on electoral-systemic reforms mentioned earlier in this essay are any indication, the state of knowledge and debate on the effects of alternative electoral systems remains extremely rudimentary.

Notes and References

* The author would like to thank S. K. Mendiratta of the Election Commission of India for his help with historical records and data, and Yogendra Yadav and Zoya Hasan for comments on an earlier draft. The usual disclaimer applies.

1. E. Sridharan, 'Principles, Power and Coalition Politics in India: Lessons from Theory, Comparison and Recent History', in D.D. Khanna and Gert W. Kueck (eds), *Principles, Power and Politics*, Macmillan, New Delhi, 1999, pp. 270–90.
2. Arend Lijphart, *Democracies: Patterns of Majoritarian and Consensus Government in Twenty-one Countries*, Yale University Press, New Haven, 1984
3. See E. Sridharan, 'Does India Need to Switch to Proportional Representation? The Pros and Cons', in Paul Flather (ed.), *Recasting Indian Politics: Essays on a Working Democracy*, Palgrave, London, 2002 (forthcoming).
4. See Nalini Rajan, 'Multiculturalism, Group Rights and Identity Politics', *Economic and Political Weekly*, vol. XXXIII, no. 27, 4 July 1998, pp. 1699–1701.
5. The debate on this in India has only just begun with the working paper, 'Reform of Electoral Laws', of the Law Commission of India, discussed at a public symposium in New Delhi on 23–4 January 1999. The working

paper (pp. 9–17) recommends increasing the number of seats in the Lok Sabha by 25 per cent (of the maximum of 550) to 138, these seats to be allotted to candidates of political parties on the basis of their pre-declared list (the list system) according to the parties' vote share in states, some smaller states being lumped together in territorial constituencies. For example, Andhra Pradesh with 42 Lok Sabha seats would have 11 extra seats to be filled on a party vote share basis going down the party list. A more recent set of proposals are those contained in the two consultation papers issued as interim output of the National Commission to Review the Working of the Constitution: 'Review of the Working of Political Parties Specially in Relation to Elections and Reform Options', and 'Review of Election Law, Processes and Reform Options'.

6. The government decided on 31 August 2000 to continue the freeze on the number of seats in the Lok Sabha and state legislative assemblies until 2026 but to set up a Delimitation Commission to re-fix the number of seats reserved for Scheduled Castes and Tribes and to readjust and rationalize parliamentary and state legislative assembly constituencies. See Alistair McMillan, 'Delimitation, Democracy and End of Constitutional Freeze', *Economic and Political Weekly*, vol. XXXV, no. 15, 8 April 2000, for projections of seats lost or gained by states in the event of inter-state reallocation of seats on the bases of the 1991 and projected 2001 censuses. The latter projection shows that Tamil Nadu (6) and Kerala (3) will lose 9 seats, the southern states 11 seats, while the Hindi-speaking states will gain 15 seats, UP alone gaining 7.
7. Law Commission of India, working paper, 'Reform of Electoral Laws', Jan. 1999.
8. National Commission to Review the Working of the Constitution, 'Review of the Working of Political Parties Specially in Relation to Elections and Reform Options', and 'Review of Election Law, Processes and Reform Options'. See also, Election Commission of India, 'Electoral Reforms (Views and Proposal)', 1998.
9. Ibid., p. 34.
10. Ibid., p. 34.
11. National Commission to Review the Working of the Constitution (NCRWC), consultation paper, 'Review of Election Law, Processes and Reform Options', Jan. 2001, p. 33.
12. Ibid., p. 37.
13. Election Commission of India, 'Electoral Reforms (Views and Proposal)', 1998.
14. Arend Lijphart, *Electoral Systems and Party Systems: A Sudy of Twenty-*

seven Democracies 1945–1990, Oxford University Press, Oxford 1994, pp. 18–19.

15. B. Shiva Rao, *The Framing of India's Constitution: Select Documents*, vol. III, Indian Institute of Public Administration, New Delhi; N.M. Tripathi, Bombay, 1967, pp. 119–20.
16. Ibid., p. 120.
17. B.N. Rau, *India's Constitution in the Making*, 2nd edn, Allied Publishers, Bombay 1960, p. 327. See his ch. 17, 'Systems of Representation', pp. 315–27, for a flavour of his strong inclination towards FPTP and antipathy to PR.
18. B. Shiva Rao, *The Framing of India's Constitution: Select Documents*, vol. II, Indian Institute of Public Administration, New Delhi: N.M. Tripathi, Bombay, 1967, pp. 531–2.
19. Ibid., p. 628.
20. *Constituent Assembly Debates* (*CAD*), vol. VII, pp. 299–300, 8 Nov. 1948.
21. CAD, vol. VII, pp. 303–4, 8 Nov. 1948.
22. CAD, vol. V, pp. 273–4, 28 Aug. 1947.
23. CAD, vol. IV, pp. 660–1, 18 July 1947.
24. Ibid., pp. 662–3, 18 July 1947.
25. Ibid., pp. 663–4, 18 July 1947.
26. Ibid., pp. 666–7, 664–5, and 672–3, respectively.
27. CAD, vol. VII, pp. 1233–5, 4 Jan. 1949.
28. Ibid., pp. 1236–8, 4 Jan. 1949.
29. Ibid., pp. 1244–5, 4 Jan. 1949.
30. Ibid., p. 1250, 4 Jan. 1949.
31. Ibid., p. 1263, 4 Jan. 1949.
32. Even a scholar like Ambedkar did not seem to understand the workings of PR as revealed by his remark that PR was not compatible with parliamentary democracy (CAD, vol. VII, pp. 1261–3, 4 Jan. 1949.
33. *Parliamentary Debates (Part II—Proceedings Other than Questions and Answers) Official Report*, vol. IV, 1950 (1–20 April 1950), p. 3046.
34. Ibid.
35. Ibid., p. 3068–9.
36. Representation of the People Act 1951, Section 63.
37. *Parliamentary Debates (Part II—Proceedings Other than Questions and Answers) Official Report*, vol. XI, 1951 (21 April 1951 to 14 May 1951), pp. 8349–51.
38. Ibid., Sect. 65.
39. Representation of the People (Conduct of Elections and Election Petitions) Rules 1951, Rule 48, p. 203.

40. *Parliamentary Debates, Second Series*, vol. L, 1961 (13th Session), pp. 344–5.
41. Ibid., pp. 356–8.
42. Ibid., p. 421, intervention by B. C. Kamble.
43. Ibid., pp. 863–4, intervention by Mahavir Tyagi.
44. See Lijphart (1994), p. 26
45. See Lijphart (1994), p. 17, Table 2.1
46. See Lijphart (1994), pp. 182–3, note 29.
47. See the paragraphs, 'On Reservation in Public Employment, Legislature, etc.', in the Comprehensive Resolution on National and International Questions adopted by the Markazi Majlis-e-Mushawarat of the All India Muslim Majlis-e-Mushawarat, on 27 Jan. 2001, in *Muslim India*, March 2001, pp. 128–9.

15

DECENTRALIZATION AND LOCAL GOVERNMENT

The 'Second Wind' of Democracy in India[1]

PETER RONALD DESOUZA

The arguments on 'decentralization and local government', in the context of a modern nation state, have been doing the rounds in India for well over a hundred years. Although the intellectual frame of the debate has changed, as the imperatives of governance have changed with India moving from colonial to independent rule, the formal questions remain the same with regards to the need, normative and material benefits, nature of the exercise, and experience of decentralization. In this essay I shall address these questions in relation to the latest phase of decentralization in India, the 73rd Constitutional Amendment and after. At the outset I must mention that I shall be looking only at rural decentralization, not urban decentralization associated with the 74th Constitutional Amendment, as the internal dynamics of the two domains are qualitatively different. The focus here will hence only be on panchayati raj institutions.

Historical Overview

First a brief historical overview. For purposes of framing the current debate, the concern with decentralization can be seen to have passed through the following major phases. The first involved the various policy initiatives of the colonial period. The second refers to the constitutional assembly debates. The third concerns the various post-independence committees, and the fourth represents the period of the 73rd Constitutional Amendment and after (henceforth CSAA).

Although the early concern with decentralization can be traced to the period after the uprising of 1857, when the colonial administration sought to 'transfer responsibility for roads and public works to local bodies',[2] because of severe financial pressure the major policy statement concerning decentralization is associated with Lord Ripon. In his Resolution on Local Self-Government of 18 May 1882 he advocated decentralization because it would promote the goals of 'administrative efficiency', 'political education', and 'human development'. Paragraphs 5 and 6 of the Resolution actually state these goals quite unambiguously. 'It is not primarily with a view to improvement in administration that this measure is put forward and supported. It is chiefly designed as an instrument of political and popular education' ... and 'as education advances there is rapidly growing up all over the country an intelligent class of public spirited men who it is not only bad policy but sheer waste of power to fail to utilize.'[3] These ideas of Ripon were out of step with the colonial administration and can be attributed to his public life in England when he associated with groups such as the Christian Socialists and reformers such as Sidney Herbert. For Ripon, development of a vibrant local self-government system was an important goal but 'in the British India of 1882, the Viceroy was almost alone in his liberalism'.[4] This spirit of decentralization, however, did not carry very far. What evolved, in spite of various subsequent committees such as the Royal Commission on Decentralization (1907), the *Report of Montagu and Chelmsford on Constitutional Reforms* (1918), the Government of India Resolution (1918)[5] etc. was a hierarchical administrative structure based on supervision and control. The administrator became the focal point of rural governance.

While the debates during the colonial period concerned the most appropriate strategy for effective governance, whether centralization or decentralization, the debate in the Constituent Assembly on panchayati raj was more fundamentally grounded. There were two viewpoints in contestation here, that of Gandhi presented by his followers, and that of Ambedkar. At the heart of this contest were two different views on, (i) the nature of politics, (ii) the basic unit of politics and the edifice that was to be built with it, (iii) the constitutional status of panchayati raj, and (iv) the intrinsic character of the village. These four issues remain relevant in the current phase of decentralization. The contrasting ideas of the 'good society', and their derivatives, is at the heart of the contestation on decentralization today.[6]

Village *swaraj* was the centrepiece of Gandhi's vision of an independent India. This followed from his fundamental opposition to parliamentary democracy which he saw as perpetuating domination and from his belief in an economy of limited wants and based upon local production, resources, consumption and technologies. Very eloquently he outlined this vision of the village republic, his 'good society', in the issue of *Harijan* of 26 July 1942:

> My idea of village swaraj is that it is a complete republic, independent of its neighbours for its vital wants, and yet interdependent for many others in which dependence is a necessity. Thus the village's first concern will be to grow its own food crops and cotton for its cloth. It should have a reserve for its cattle, recreation and playground for adults and children ... The village will maintain a village theatre, school and public hall. It will have its own waterworks ensuring a clean water supply. This can be done through controlled wells or tanks. Education will be compulsory up to the final basic course. As far as possible every activity will be conducted on a cooperative basis. There will be no caste, such as we have today with their graded untouchability. Non-violence with its technique of *satyagraha* and non-cooperation will be the sanction of the village community. ... The government of the village will be conducted by the Panchayat of five persons annually elected by the adult villagers, male and female, possessing minimum prescribed qualifications. These will have all the authority and jurisdiction required. Since there will be no system of punishments in the accepted sense, this Panchayat will be the legislature, judiciary, and executive combined to be operative for its year in office. Any village can become such a republic without much interference.[7]

Such village republics would be interlinked in a set of

> ever widening, never ascending circles. Life will not be a pyramid with the apex sustained by the bottom. But it will be an oceanic circle whose centre will be the individual always ready to perish for the village, the latter ready to perish for the circle of villages, till at last the whole becomes one life composed of individuals, never aggressive in their arrogance but ever humble, sharing the majesty of their oceanic circle of which they are integral units ...[8]

In this extensive statement one can see Gandhi's belief in the primary harmony of social existence, the essentially cooperative nature of social exchange, and the importance of face to face relationships. Central to his vision was the privileging of the local over the distant. Participation in politics therefore became an integral part of public life. Gandhi's stature and the appeal of his vision caused some of the members of the Constituent Assembly to argue for it to be the political model for Independent India.[9] Dr. B.R. Ambedkar opposed this suggestion, viewing village India differently and believing that the path of the future lay in a constitutional parliamentary democracy. In strong language he denounced the proposal to make the village the basic unit of the political system:

> It is said that the new Constitution should have been drafted on the ancient Hindu model of a state and that instead of incorporating Western theories the new Constitution should have been raised and built upon village panchayats and District panchayats ... They just want India to contain so many village governments. The love of the intellectual Indian for the village community is of course infinite if not pathetic ... I hold that the village republics have been the ruination of India. I am therefore surprised that those who condemn provincialism and communalism should come forward as champions of the village. What is the village but a sink of localism, a den of ignorance, narrow-mindedness and communalism? I am glad that the Draft Constitution has discarded the village and adopted the individual as its unit.[10]

Ambedkar's remarks, rooted in an experience of oppressive caste and feudal structures in rural India, provoked a storm of protest because they were so hostile to the Gandhian vision and more subtly disrespectful of the Mahatma himself. The village, for Ambedkar, represented regressive India, a source of oppression. The modern state hence had to build safeguards against such social oppression and the only way it could be effected was through the adoption of a parliamentary model of politics and a rejection of the idea of 'oceanic circles'. Ambedkar's remarks caused a furore, with Professor N.G. Ranga, Alladi Krishnaswami Aiyer, K. Santhanam, Shibbanlal Saxena, and others expressing their disagreement and lamenting that the village, which was an essential feature of Indian social and political life, found no recognition in the constitution.

A compromise was forged and Panchayati Raj Institutions (PRIs) found place in the non-justiciable part of the constitution, the Directive Principles of State policy, as Article 40. It stated 'The State shall take steps to organize village panchayats and endow them with such powers and authority as may be necessary to enable them to function as units of self-government.' I have discussed these two viewpoints at some length because they draw attention to the crucial issue that confronts all attempts at decentralization, *the structures of power in rural India.* Faced with these structures we, today, must examine the potential of PRIs to undermine them through an expansion, extension, and deepening of democracy in India. In the four decades since the adoption of the constitution, PRIs have travelled from the non-justiciable part of the constitution to one where, through a separate amendment, a whole part is devoted to it, i.e., part IX, schedule XI. Let me now briefly traverse this journey.

The earliest committee to study decentralization issues was the Balwantrai Mehta Committee which was appointed in 1957 to study community development projects and the national extension service, and to assess the extent 'to which the movement had succeeded in utilizing local initiatives and in creating institutions to ensure continuity in the process of improving economic and social conditions in rural areas.' The report was quite visionary and one can see in it the élan of the early years of independence. There was a sense of the problem and a sense of responsiveness to it. It offered solutions along two broad axes: (i) administrative decentralization, for effective implementation of the development programme, and (ii) control by elected bodies of this decentralized administrative system. The Balwantrai Mehta committee held that community development would only be deep and enduring when the community was involved in the planning, decision, and implementation process. However, the PRI structure which was introduced in most parts of the country as a result of this report did not develop the requisite democratic momentum and failed to cater to the needs of rural development. There are various reasons for this, such as, (i) political and bureaucratic resistance at the state level to a sharing of power and resources with local-level institutions, (ii) the takeover of these institutions by the rural élite who cornered a major share of the benefits of the various welfare schemes, (iii) the lack of capability at the local level, and (iv) the absence of political will of grass-roots leaders.[11]

Recognizing that PRIs had failed to live up to their early promise, the Ashoka Mehta Committee (1978) was appointed to inquire into the working of PRIs and to suggest measures to strengthen them. It considered the PRI experience post-1959 as having passed through three phases: (i) ascendancy (1959–64), (ii) stagnation (1965–69), and (iii) decline (1969–77). The Ashoka Mehta Committee felt that a combination of factors had conspired to undermine PRIs, such as an unsympathetic bureaucracy, absence of political will, lack of involvement in planning and implementation on a substantial scale, fuzziness with respect to the role of PRIs, i.e., are they merely an administrative agency or are they also an extension of rural local government? And of course, the domination of PRIs by the economic and social rural élite. The committee recommended that the district should be the basic unit since it was a viable administrative unit for which planning, coordination, and resource allocation were feasible and for which technical expertise was available. The states of Karnataka, Andhra Pradesh and West Bengal passed new legislation based on the Ashoka Mehta Committee Report. However, flux in politics at the state level did not allow these institutions to develop their own political dynamics. This post-1978 period was an unstable one in state politics.

Next appointed was the G.V.K. Rao Committee (1985) constituted to take another look at the various aspects of PRIs. The committee was of the opinion that a total view of rural development must be developed in which PRIs must play a central role in handling people's problems. More thinking on PRIs was initiated by the Committee for the Concept Paper on Panchayati Raj Institutions (CCPPRI), also known as the L.M. Singhvi Committee (1986). The *gram sabha* was considered as the base of a decentralized democracy, and 'PRIs have to be viewed as institutions of self-government which would actually facilitate the participation of the people in the process of planning and development flowing from and as a part of the concept of self-government ... It recommended ... that local self-government should be Constitutionally recognized, protected and preserved by the inclusion of a new chapter in the Constitution.'[12] It also viewed with dismay the irregularity of elections and engaged with the issue of the role of political parties in panchayat elections, stating that non-involvement should be consensual rather than through legislative fiat.

This suggestion of giving PRIs constitutional status was opposed by the Sarkaria Commission, but the idea nonetheless gained momentum in the late 1980s, especially because of the endorsement by Prime Minister Rajiv Gandhi who introduced the 64th Constitutional Amendment Bill in 1989. The bill was defeated in the Rajya Sabha in 1989 and a subsequent bill, the 74th Constitutional Amendment Bill, was introduced by the National Front government which could not become an act because of the dissolution of the 9th Lok Sabha.

The foregoing is a short sketch of a centuries' long engagement with the issue of decentralized democracy. It gives one a sense of the parameters of the debate, the goals, the means adopted to achieve these goals, and the obstacles encountered. The CSAA, therefore, had a fund of ideas to draw from: ideas that were critical of decentralization[13] as well as supportive of it.[14] The thinking that produced the CSAA was not a response to pressure from the grass-roots, but was a response to an increasing recognition that the institutional initiatives of the preceding decades had not delivered, that the extent of rural poverty was still much too large, and that the existing structure of government needed to be reformed. It is interesting to note that this thinking emanated from the central and state governments.

The 73rd Amendment Act (CSAA)

The new phase of decentralized democracy in India hence begins with a paradox. A very centralized instrument, a constitutional amendment, is used to empower a very decentralized activity, panchayati raj. This paradox is based on a belief in a promise that the CSAA will deliver, that when a sensitive and properly designed structure of local government is put in place it will overcome the hurdles currently confronted by rural development initiatives, and will bring about genuine self-government. Let me now examine this promise by identifying the problems faced by the pre-CSAA PRI system. The 73rd Constitutional Amendment should be seen as a response to these problems. The principal problems are:

Irregular elections and supersession: The pre-CSAA PRIs went into decline because many of the procedural conditions for vibrant institutions of local government were either ignored or subverted. In consequence, in most states elections to these bodies were not held regularly. Once constituted, PRIs continued for long periods. The threat of replacement, so vital for accountable government, was hence never real. In addition, there were prolonged periods when PRIs were superseded.

Insufficient devolution of powers: The problem that has dogged PRIs has not only been that there was no clear delegation of powers but also those that were delegated were insufficient to the tasks at hand. Hence PRIs were unable to exhibit any degree of autonomy either in implementing anti-poverty programmes, in preparation of local plans, in undertaking integrated local development, in hiring or disciplining staff assigned from other departments. Insufficient administrative and financial powers reduced the PRI to becoming merely an administrative extension of the centralized structure, implementing decisions and plans taken elsewhere rather than by the PRIs themselves.

Bureaucratic resistance: The inadequate transfer of powers to the local level was coupled with a bureaucracy that did not want to lose its status and power, as would have been the case in a decentralized democracy. To report and be accountable to panchayat-level representatives, in a rural society such as in India where a 'Sarkari' position symbolizes status, was considered as a lowering of this status. Besides ceding the power to plan, allocate, and implement to PRIs, the state bureaucracy also resisted being directed by elected representatives at the PRI level, seeking as they did to issue rather than remain those receiving directives.

Domination by rural élites: The devolution of powers, however limited, without the commensurate political reform, i.e., greater representation to deprived sections of the people such as Dalits, Adivasis, and women, through a quota system, and commensurate economic reform, i.e., land reforms, meant that rural élites, especially the dominant castes and the feudal landowners, came to corner the benefits of the centrally sponsored schemes because of their control, through various means, of local administration. This spawned a whole network of beneficiaries such as contractors, landlords, local politicians and bureaucrats, bank officials, and party leaders who siphoned off funds meant for rural development. Inadequate representation of the more deprived sections of the people meant that the targeted beneficiaries were unable to break into this oligarchic rural environment.[15] The first *India: Rural Development Report 1999*, when reflecting on the overall failure of rural development, given that there are still 200 million rural people in poverty in the 1990s, observed that 'an elaborate system of patronage, thriving on the disempowerment of the poor and hapless, distributes largesse to a chosen few at the cost of multitudes and characterizes rural India.'[16]

Unsatisfactory working of gram sabha: The *gram sabha*, which was supposed to be the base of local government, the jewel in the PRI crown, actually failed to function as envisaged. S.P. Jain lists some of the experiences of the *gram sabha* before the CSAA.[17]

(a) Meetings called mostly on the directives of the *zila parishad* or panchayati *samiti* level, i.e., pressures from higher levels of administration,

(b) meetings called mostly without prior notice,

(c) people from other villages found it difficult to attend these meetings,

(d) prescribed number of meetings not called,

(e) proxy meetings at times were convened and proceedings were written even without the knowledge of those who attended,

(f) attendance was found larger if the visit to the meeting of some leader or senior officer was announced,

(g) in situations where collection of subscriptions and contributions was to be made, people generally avoided such meetings,

(h) appropriate rules governing the procedure of *gram sabha* meetings were not framed,

(i) items such as preparation of village production plans, formulation of village plan, fixation of targets and information about new activities were generally the prerogative of officials,

(j) since most of the people attending the *gram sabha* were not aware of their role in the formulation of village plans, etc., they attended as silent listeners,

(k) proceedings of the *gram sabha* were mostly not properly recorded and never reported to the panchayat or panchayat *samiti*. There was no follow-up action.

(l) unwillingness of the *Sarpanch* and other *Panchas* to convene meetings, and

(m) the personal and caste-based nature of village politics.

These factors, together with the absence of political will—as state-level leaders were worried about the challenge from PRI level leaders—meant that during the decades following the Balwantrai Mehta Committee report (1957) PRIs did not emerge as a genuine level of local self-government in India. They were, at best, merely instruments of decentralized administration.

Features of the CSAA

In response to these constraints experienced by PRI over the three decades since 1957, the Narasimha Rao government piloted and passed, on the basis of a general consensus, the Constitution 73rd Amendment Act on 22 December 1992. After ratification by over half of the state assemblies and after obtaining the assent of the President the Act came into force on 24 April 1993.[18] There are some radical features in the act. They seek to address some of the problems encountered by PRIs in previous years, such as, (i) granting PRIs constitutional status, (ii) empowering socially and economically disadvantaged groups, i.e., Dalits, Adivasis, and women, (iii) ensuring free, fair, and regular elections, (iv) keeping terms fixed, (v) identifying a list of items which would fall under the jurisdiction of PRIs, and (vi) addressing the issue of PRI finance. The principal features are as follows:

1. The centrality of the *gram sabha*, as a deliberative and decision-making body, for decentralized governance.

2. A uniform three-tier PRI structure across the country, with the village, block, and district as the appropriate levels. States with populations of less than twenty million have an option not to introduce the intermediate level.

3. Direct election to all seats for all members at all levels. In addition, the chairpersons of the village panchayats may be appointed members of the panchayats at the intermediate level and chairpersons of panchayats at the intermediate level may be members at the district level: MPs, MLAs, and MLCs may also be members of panchayats at the intermediate and district levels.

4. In all the panchayats, seats are to be reserved for SCs and STs in proportion to their population, and one-third of the total seats to be reserved for women. One-third of the seats reserved for SCs and STs will also be reserved for women.

5. Offices of the chairpersons of the panchayats at all levels will be reserved for SCs and STs in proportion to their population in the state. One-third of the office of chairpersons of panchayats at all levels also to be reserved for women.

6. The legislature of the state at liberty to provide reservation of seats and offices of chairpersons in panchayats in favour of backward classes of citizens.

7. Average panchayat to have a uniform five-year term and elections to constitute new bodies to be completed before the expiry of the term. In the event of dissolution, elections to be compulsorily held within six months. The reconstituted panchayat to serve for the remaining period of the five-year term.

8. It will not be possible to dissolve the existing panchayats by amendment of any act before the expiry of its duration.

9. A person who is disqualified under any law for elections to the legislature of the state or under any law of the state will not be entitled to become a member of a panchayat.

10. An independent State Election Commission (SEC) to be established for superintendence, direction, and control of the electoral process, and preparation of electoral rolls.

11. Devolution of powers and responsibilities by the state in the preparation and implementation of development plans.

12. Setting up of a State Finance Commission once in five years to revise the financial position of these PRIs and to make suitable recommendations to the state on the distribution of funds among panchayats.

Concerns post-CSAA

With the passage of the CSAA the states then passed their own conformity legislation. For a comprehensive understanding of the body of rules that governs the PRI structure in the states one needs to bear in mind the process through which the existing body of rules emerges. There are three stages involved. (i) At the start is the constitutional amendment (CSAA) that sets the framework and identifies the parameters within which the body of rules is to be developed. (ii) This is followed by the conformity legislation of states that translates the CSAA into the furniture of local government, i.e., establishing offices, prescribing powers and functions, recommending procedures, developing linkages between this level of government and others, etc. The conformity legislation (principal legislation) recognises that there will be new contingencies which will have to be addressed in the future and hence it contains clauses that allow state governments to prescribe new rules without going through the legislative process. (iii) This contingency provision gives rise to a substantial body of rules (delegated legislation) which emerge through government orders (GOs) and which in actuality are the source of a great deal of authority within the panchayat system. This opening for the state governments to intervene (read control) comes about through the language of some of the key clauses in the conformity acts. These clauses use language such as the 'state may by notification' or 'subject to such rules as may be made under the proviso to article ... the government may alter ...' which allow the state to withdraw, curtail, extend, override the authority of the PRI system. An observer of local government has found that states such as Andhra Pradesh and Karnataka have used the route of delegated legislation in preference to principal legislation.[19]

PROVISIONS FOR CONTROL OF PRI BY STATE GOVERNMENTS (RELEVANT SECTIONS)

No	*State Powers*
1	State govts' powers to formulate rules and to make changes in the content of schedule
2	Delimitation responsibility of govt not SEC
3	State governments' power to appoint officials
4	State govts manage PRI affairs when delay in elections
5	State govts' powers to dismiss *sarpanch*, etc.
6	State govts to cancel resolution or decision of *panchayats*
7	State govts' power to dissolve panchayats
8	State govts' power to inspect records/works
9	Finance Commission report recommendatory not mandatory

In spite of this control by the state governments, these three sets of rules must be seen as creating a legal structure that represents a political opportunity in which representative parliamentary democracy is combined with direct democracy. This combination of representative and direct democracy institutions is seen as synergistic, and it is expected that this initiative will result in an extension and deepening of the democratic process in India.[20] The CSAA should be seen as an attempt to occupy the empty spaces of politics in this vast polity. As its passage, especially now after eight years of its working, some critical concerns have been raised which need to be noted and assessed. I shall now briefly comment on them in terms of the domains within which they are discussed. The evaluation is in terms of five domains: (i) legal, (ii) administrative, (iii) fiscal, (iv) planning, (v) political.

In the Legal *Domain*

(i) Recognizing that there is often a shadow between precept and practice, the first significant observation concerns the legal language of 'shall' and 'may' in the CSAA. These operative words result in some provisions being mandatory on the states, when they frame their conformity acts, and some being non-obligatory. Some of these non-obligatory provisions are:[21]

(a) representation to members of the state legislature and parliament on panchayats,

(b) representation of the chairpersons of a lower-level panchayat on the immediate higher level,

(c) method of election of the chairperson at the village-level panchayat,

(d) conferring of powers and responsibilities to panchayats to enable them to function as 'units of self-government',

(e) powers of panchayats to prepare plans for economic development and social justice,

(f) implementation of schemes for economic development and social justice, including the items mentioned in the Eleventh Schedule of the Constitution,

(g) power to impose taxes, and

(h) provisions relating to the maintenance of accounts and their audit.

The above clauses cover three important aspects of the constitution and working of PRIs: (a) representation, (b) planning for economic development and social justice, and (c) implementation. In each of these major aspects the state governments are given the discretion to translate the intended objective of the CSAA into state legislation bearing in mind their own local contingencies. The most noteworthy is the discretion the states have to 'endow the *panchayats* with such powers and authority as may be necessary (emphasis mine) to enable them to function as institutions of self-government.' (243G) The state legislature is given the power to decide what 'may be necessary'. This is such a wide area of discretion, especially on such a crucial aspect of the 'power and authority' of PRIs, that one can immediately see the continued control of the third tier by the second. State governments have taken recourse to this discretion to delay the transfer of powers and functions. In early 1999, *sarpanchas* of Andhra Pradesh had to threaten that they would commit self-immolation if the state government failed to devolve items from the XIth schedule. Sixteen items were devolved. The situation remains unclear with PRIs, especially at the *gram* level, having democracy but not decentralization.

(ii) A second set of legal comments calls for further constitutional amendments to improve the status of PRIs. One issue in particular concerning rotation of reserved seats is deserving of debate.

> Article 243(D) clearly directs that the reserved seats, both for scheduled castes (SCs) and scheduled tribes (STs) as well as women, shall be allotted by rotation to different constituencies in a *panchayat*. This has been interpreted to mean that such rotation should take place at the end of every five years. If this interpretation is given effect to, no SC, ST, or woman member will ever get the opportunity of occupying the same seat for a second term, as it is highly unlikely that these persons would be allowed to contest from the same constituency, when the reservation is removed. If we accept the theory that most of the SC/ST and women members do not have any prior experience and will find it difficult to occupy positions of power in the initial period, it would be very difficult to support the idea that they should not continue in such positions, beyond one term.[22]

It is therefore suggested that a seat be reserved for two terms so that members of these groups would get a chance to play an effective role in representing their group's interest.

In the Administrative *Domain*

Several views have been expressed concerning the making of a more efficient PRI administrative structure. They cover a large spectrum of issues and constitute the body of the debate on PRI. I shall here briefly attempt a listing of some of them.

Jurisdiction

The jurisdictional issue, both inter- and intra-tier, is one area where considerable tightening up is possible. Not only have the extent of powers and responsibilities of each tier to be specified in the state acts, and through executive instructions, which appears to have been done rather perfunctorily, but also the 'functions' that are to be performed by each tier. In addition to specifying the operational responsibility between one level of panchayat and another, with respect to scheme, programme, and activity,[23] the executive instructions should also 'specify the relationship of the PRIs with the district bureaucracy'.[24] This remains a grey area, perhaps deliberately so, since, in the absence of clear jurisdictions specified in law, the administration retains the power.

Transfer of Powers and Functions

Related to the jurisdictional issue is that of transference. One needs to specify which functions, now performed by the departments of the state government, need to be transferred to the PRI level. 'Many states like Andhra, Orissa, or Karnataka have chosen to leave the assignment of functions to local bodies more as a task of delegated legislation rather than principal legislation. ... A debate has however begun in local authority circles about the need to make the list of functions mandatory rather than illustrative and apply it uniformly to the states.'[25]

For example, one needs to specify, (a) which departments are to be brought under the full control of PRIs, (b) how certain committees at the district and sub-district level, should be reconstituted, (c) what the arrangements are for interaction between non-PRI departments with PRIs, (d) what the arrangements are for monitoring by the state governments, (e) what the arrangements are for interaction of members of the state and union legislatures with PRIs.[26] This ambiguity in relation to transference can be best illustrated by the continued existence, in most states, of District Rural Development Agencies (DRDA). The question to be addressed is whether DRDAs continue to be relevant post-CSAA, or whether are they complementary to PRIs, or need to be disbanded because they are administrative rather than participatory agencies, covering the same developmental terrain as PRIs.[27] Another scheme, which runs counter to PRIs, is the newly introduced Members of Parliament Local Area Development (MPLAD) scheme. It creates a parallel development structure based on the largesse of central politicians rather than of local-level participation.

Bureaucracy

These issues of jurisdiction and transference bring into focus the range of issues relating to the PRI bureaucracy. In addition to the issue of whether PRIs should have a separate cadre[28] to protect their promotional avenues, and whether transfer from the state administration to PRI administration would be seen as a decline in status,[29] there is also the major issue of creating a capable bureaucracy committed to the needs of rural society. In the past a punishment posting for incompetent and corrupt bureaucrats was to a remote rural area. In other words, an area that required a competent bureaucrat, instead got one who was being punished for incompetence. This aspect of creating a capable bureaucracy, through training programmes[30] and a more comprehensive policy of producing a group of persons with a 'body of knowledge, skills, attitudes, and values essential for operating effectively a decentralized system of governance,'[31] has been a major area of concern. The relationship between the district bureaucracy and elected PRI members, especially at the block and district levels, has also become a major area of attention. In the early years, in Karnataka there was considerable tension between the two groups, especially as the bureaucracy was loath to report and be accountable to these PRI members. Over time, however, this attitude of suspicion and resistance of the bureaucracy changed and many of them became 'ardent enthusiasts for decentralization'.[32]

Control

The debate on the appropriate administrative structure for PRI highlights the fundamental issue of 'faith' versus 'scepticism' in decentralized democracy. One makes this point because when one, through logical regress, pursues this questioning of the pros and cons of empowering local-level institutions one realizes that one must trust the good sense of PRI personnel, with minimal checks, conceding the case for autonomy and self-government: in other words, one concedes to the PRI personnel the freedom to make mistakes, or one builds up an elaborate system of control on the grounds that those at the higher level know better, are more altruistic, and can better safeguard the public interest. The latter view appears to have prevailed.

For a bureaucratic system that has been accustomed to being the repository of state power, a privilege enjoyed by hiding behind a web of procedures and rules which have regulated the pace and direction of state developmental activity in rural India, ceding power to local administrative structures has not been easy. Indeed, a study of the state acts and the government orders show that the state governments retain enormous control over PRI, belying the argument that the CSAA is a constitutional amendment bringing about 'self-government'. This control is exercised in five ways:[33] (a) through the application of law, i.e. rules and executive instructions passed which abridge the powers of local bodies, or which alter boundaries or which confer wide-ranging powers on executives, etc.; (b) through local functionaries, i.e., threat of removal, dismissal, adverse remarks in confidential reports, etc.; (c) through decisions of local bodies, i.e., cancellation of decisions, withholding of approval etc.; (d) through administrative activities, i.e., inspection of records, institution of inquiries, review of annual reports, etc.; and (e) through panchayati raj finances where grants are withheld, audit reports scrutinized, etc.

While these checks may be justified on the grounds that they constitute routine accountability procedures, the manner in which they are implemented shows that even the limited 'self-government' brought in by CSAA is very vulnerable to the powers of control of the state government. The question of 'routine accountability procedures' needs to be addressed by scholars of decentralization since it is used as a front for centralized power. It is here that the objective of people's empowerment faces its stiffest resistance, not just from ingrained attitudes of distrust of the lower by the higher, the higher being of 'higher integrity', but also by the inability of the system to be reflexive and imaginative.

In the *Fiscal* Domain

The area which has drawn a great deal of attention in the discussion post-CSAA is panchayat finances. Here there has been a widespread debate on issues such as (a) own sources of revenue,[34] (b) the revenue capacity of PRIs in terms of the basis of taxation,[35] the elastic sources of revenue, hesitation to tax because of the proximity problem, dependence on state grants,[36] (c) revenue autonomy of PRIs,[37] (d) internal financing by PRIs to deepen stakeholder participation,[38] etc. I shall not go into details here, but wish merely to state that this discussion has two aspects. The first concerns the 'normative principles' such as autonomy, equity, predictability, efficiency, absorptive capacity, simplicity, and promotion of incentives that should govern fiscal devolution.[39] The second looks at the 'instruments' by which such devolution will be operationalized, i.e., tax-assignments, grants-in-aid, loans, and contributions. Here various issues are raised such as the distinction between the instruments of fiscal policy and of monetary policy. For example, it is argued that fiscal policies of sub-national governments sometimes run counter to those of the central government, the former seeking to try to increase expenditure or raise taxes, while the latter to reduce spending or cut taxes. Three important issues are raised about fiscal decentralization. The first addresses the question of whether a decentralized system is more or less effective in reducing inter-jurisdictional disparities than a centralized system. The second concerns the economic stabilization policies that only the central government has the incentive to introduce. Finally the third engages with the distinction between demand and supply efficiency. Decentralization focuses on the former and ignores the latter.[40]

In the *Planning* Domain

Planning is one aspect of the CSAA where considerable innovation has been attempted. While the meshing of centralized planning with de-centralized planning remains the big problem, there have been some very imaginative exercises of participatory planning such as the People's Campaign for the Ninth Plan in Kerala. Here 'more than a lakh people turned up for the training programmes and 30 lakh people all over Kerala State participated in the special Gram Sabha and Municipal Ward meetings to discuss the planning issue.'[41] The principles of such decentralized planning should be:[42] (i) people's need and local resources, (ii) people directed planning, i.e., they should have a say in identifying need, (iii) on developing backward sub-regions and helping the poor, (iv) cost effective with respect to project implementation and monitoring, and (v) sustainability in terms of the development targeted.

Initiated in 1996, there are six stages of the people's campaign, which go into the making of the state plan. The first is that of *Identification and Prioritization* where the *gram sabha* is convened to identify needs, list priorities, and create awareness. The second stage, the *Development Seminars*, involves a consolidation of *gram sabha* reports, a review of ongoing schemes, the collection of secondary data, a geographical study of the area to establish its resource base, and a brief survey of local history. The third stage, *Task Forces*, involves the constitution of sector-wise task forces to project the recommendations and suggestions that have emerged from the development seminars. The fourth stage, *Annual Plan Finalization*, is where the projects prepared by the task forces are prioritised and incorporated into the five-year plans of the *panchayats*. The fifth stage, *Integration of Plans of Higher Tiers*, is where every block *panchayat* has to prepare its development plan integrating village development reports, as also centrally sponsored poverty alleviation programmes. This has also to be done by the district *panchayats*. The final stage, *Plan Appraisal*, involves an evaluation of the technical soundness and viability of projects prepared by the local bodies before they are approved for implementation. To do this, a Voluntary Technical Experts and Core (VTC) is required to be formed comprising retired technical experts and professionals to help appraise the projects and plans of local bodies. This of course involves extensive training programmes at various levels.[43]

This exercise will not only lead to sustainable development, because of the deeper involvement of people in the planning, implementing, and monitoring process, a more balanced and sustainable use of local resources, and a better maintenance of local assets, but also an increase in self-esteem and knowledge about the development process on the part of hitherto marginalized groups. In this exercise, large numbers of people (see Table 1) got trained in the mechanics of local government with topics such as (a) challenges of development, (b) decentralization philosophy, (c) rules and statutes, (d) *gram sabhas*, (e) PRI techniques, (f) projects, (g) appraisal, (h) micro-development models, (j) integration, (k) SC/ST and gender issues etc. The aim here was to mesh the technocratic approach, i.e., involving planning and coordination mechanisms, budgetary procedures, reporting systems, training schemes, etc., with the political approach, i.e., involving the beneficiaries in the process of planning and implementation.[44]

TABLE 1: PARTICIPANTS IN TRAINING/EMPOWERMENT PROGRAMME[45]

Phase	*State*	*District*	*Block*	*Panch/Municipal*
I	375 (5)	11716 (3)		100000 (1)
II	660 (3)	11808 (2)		100000 (1)
III	300 (4)	1146 (3)	1500000 (2)	
IV	3014 (3)		10000 (2)	
V	1186 (3)			
	304 (2)			
VI	150 (2)	6000 (2)	6000 (1)	
	300 (3)		6000 (1)	
VII	2890 (2)		25000 (2)	
	3360 (2)			

*Numbers in parenthesis represents no of days.

In the *Political* Domain

The concerns expressed at the political level remain the most challenging because, unlike concerns expressed at the legal, administrative, fiscal, or planning levels, which require instrumental responses and can be largely addressed through better designed structures, concerns at the political level, in addition, also raise questions of a normative nature that require us to indicate our preferences rather than engage with an instrumental calculus. Let me list some of them here.

On the Centrality of the Gram Sabha

One of the concerns of the new PRI initiative is how to bring the people into the political system in order to give them a say in decision-making.

The *gram sabha* is seen as the site for such effective political participation. In the past the *gram sabha* was not functioning well, with poor attendance, poor discussion, and no records of proceedings, etc.[46] This needs to be remedied. The *gram sabha* has to be made more vibrant, more central to village self-government. Twenty-one suggestions were made at a conference held in July 1999 to revitalize the *gram sabha*, ranging from a reduction in size, to an expansion of its powers to include police, judiciary, and revenue power, to control of natural resources, etc. The year 1999–2000 was declared by the Government of India as the year of the *gram sabha*.[47]

On Organic Linkages

Another issue of significance is the inter-linkage of the various tiers of government to ensure a smooth functioning. The first issue concerning these linkages is the issue of whether MPs/MLAs should have representation in the PS/ZP that falls within their constituencies and also whether they should have voting rights. Reversing the direction, some have even suggested that the second chamber should be revived in all states and that it should consist of members from the three levels of PRI according to some formula. This would give lower levels a say at higher levels. The second issue concerning linkages refers to the relationship between PRIs and the various district-level bodies such as DRDAs, watersheds, user societies, etc. This is an aspect that has been overlooked in the conformity Acts. Establishing these linkages is important for smooth co-ordination, especially now when watersheds and user societies are also gaining the support of higher-level bodies and international donor agencies. The third issue concerns the composition and function of the District Planning Committee. It remains a neglected aspect in most states, a lapse which is significant, especially as it is the only planning body that has constitutional status and links the rural with the urban localities.

On Growth in Government Bureaucracy

There is the genuine fear that the only beneficiaries of the CSAA will be employed at the third tier. It has been noted that while rural development expenditure is growing at a slow pace, establishment costs (read salaries) have considerably increased.[48] The question being debated is whether government officials from line departments of the state should be transferred to PRI institutions or whether new people should be recruited and the relevant line departments closed. As provision of jobs in the state sector is a major source of political patronage, even at the cost of a decrease in resources available for development, the possibility of growth in the size of government bureaucracy with all its attendant evils, of absenteeism, poor productivity, callousness, etc. appears high.

On Further Fine-tuning of Reservations for SCs/STs

While the general policy of reservations has been widely accepted, there is an anxiety that if this is enforced in an undifferentiated way it may benefit the creamy layer of these groups. The suggestion being made is that within such a policy of reservation there should be further reservations so that representation of the weakest among the backward sections in the PRI is ensured. This is based on the recognition that SCs/STs are not homogeneous groups, some being socially and economically more vulnerable, e.g., bonded labourers, scavengers, sweepers, leather workers among the SCs, and the primitive tribes among the STs. 'The problems of these communities are peculiar to their occupation, and are not comparable to other groups of SCs and STs. Unless there are adequate representatives of the SCs and STs in the PRIs from among these groups, there is a likelihood that the emerging leadership from among the SCs and STs may not be able to bestow proper attention to the problems of these groups. As a result, these groups may be further marginalized.'[49]

On the Issue of Justice for the Rural Population

An argument has been made that 'the present state of judicial administration with its inevitable cost, delay, and technicality has made it unsuitable to the rural public whose disputes are seldom technical and hardly require the luxury of adversarial adjudication of the formal court system.'[50] There are over twenty million cases pending in the courts, some for over a decade. This unsuitability has prompted calls for an alternative (perhaps parallel) system of *nyaya* panchayats while bearing in mind Ambedkar's fear of the oppression in an Indian village. The Law Commission of India in its 114th Report (August 1986) suggested such a system where (i) nomination of judges (ii) method of judgement (iii) procedure to be followed, (iv) power of the *nyayalayas,* and (v) exclusive jurisdiction were discussed.

The Commission recommended a very simple procedure envisaging quick decision, informed by justice, equity, and good conscience. It did not want the *Civil Procedure Code* and the *Indian Evidence Act* to be applied to proceedings before the new version of *Panchayat* courts. The court has to be mobile to visit the place of dispute (village) carrying justice to the doorstep of the people and for this purpose a transport vehicle is to be provided. In all possible cases, on the spot execution of the decree/order was also envisaged by the Law Commission. In respect of jurisdiction, the Commission favoured criminal jurisdiction available to a First Class Magistrate and civil jurisdiction covering boundary disputes, tenancies, use of common property, entries in revenue records, irrigation disputes, minor property disputes, easements, all family disputes, wage disputes, disputes arising out of bonded labour, etc., irrespective of the pecuniary value of the subject matter of the dispute.[51]

On Epistemic versus *Political Community*

One major normative issue, which runs through this extensive literature, especially at the second level of the operationalizing of PRI, is the issue of 'who decides'. While the simple answer has always been 'the people', and that is why an elaborate participatory structure has been envisaged with the *gram sabha* as its cornerstone, this answer does not sufficiently recognize the tension between the epistemic community of policy-makers, e.g., experts, VTC of Kerala, and the political community, i.e. members of the *gram sabha*. In *gram sabha* meetings, for example, to what degree should the experts (officials) prompt the proceedings and how much should they refrain from doing so is a dilemma that is evident right across levels and situations. Whose version of the outcome should prevail: the epistemic or the political community's version? This refers to a tension that remains unresolved at the heart of democratic theory. It is starkest at the level of local rural government where the political community is made up of many illiterate citizens.

Looking at the issues that have emerged consequent to the 73rd Constitutional Amendment, and to the observation that while there may be political decentralization there is insufficient administrative and fiscal decentralization, we now need to attempt an evaluation of the PRI initiative as it has so far developed. Certain general issues will be suggested because they draw attention to the dynamics of the new phase of democratic politics in India, 'the second wind'.

The first important observation that must be made about the new PRIs is that they constitute a new 'opportunity space' for citizens and groups to compete for social resources. This is a political advancement especially as, over the past five decades, there has been a growth in the numbers of citizens who have entered the political system and in the volume and complexity of demands being placed on it. This growth has highlighted the inability of the system to meet these demands, resulting in a demand overload. New institutions were hence required to handle this overload. PRIs can be seen as one package of such institutions.

The features of the 'opportunity space' created by PRIs show how and why many of the impediments to the expansion of democracy in India, especially in terms of its goal of equal citizenship, will be reduced. By creating a third tier of government, which in turn has three tiers, of *gram* panchayat, panchayat *samiti*, and *zilla parishad*, and by giving it constitutional status, and by requiring states to pass their own conformity legislation within a year, by reserving seats for Dalits, Adivasis, and women, by creating an SFC, and an SEC, and by prohibiting supersession and suspension, the CSAA has created new political 'spaces' with potential to impact the system, and in which citizens can make demands. Even in the cynical scenario where these 'spaces' are taken over by local oligarchies, they are considered a political advancement over the pre-CSAA situation even by the victims of these oligarchies.[52] Fortunately, the contrary optimistic scenario has many examples[53] of how the opportunities brought about by PRIs have been used by women,[54] Dalits, and Adivasis to improve their lot, not just to derive some benefits from the state,[55] but also to lay claim to the state. Three aspects of this new 'opportunity space' are worth noting: (a) the *gram sabha*, (b) representation through reservation, and (c) fixed terms.

By making the *gram sabha* the centrepiece of the PRI system the CSAA has sought to derive all the benefits of the system of direct democracy for the larger democratic project.[56] Some of these are:

(i) the small distance between representative and represented, resulting in a flatter power structure,

(ii) the face-to-face exchange which promotes transparent and accountable government and thereby gives it legitimacy,

(iii) the capability-enhancing and empowering experience of participation in the *gram sabha*, especially for vulnerable and oppressed and hitherto excluded sections of the village such as women, Dalits, and Adivasis,[57] and

(iv) the deliberative route adopted by the collective to decide how village resources are to be utilized, leading to better targeted utilization.

The reservation policy for women, Dalits and Adivasis takes empowerment of excluded groups to a qualitatively new plane. This is particularly so in the case of the reservations to the post of the *sarpanch* who in practice, in most cases, leads decision-making in the PRIs. Even though these are vulnerable groups, susceptible to becoming proxies, as has happened in innumerable cases, the fact of reservation at the very least forces dominant groups to negotiate power with them. This is an advance, it now causes these groups to recognize their potential power. This education will, over time, breed resistance to continued domination and exploitation.[58] The tangible experience of having state power, of being able to negotiate with exploiting groups, even if from a position of formal and not substantive equality, of learning about centrally sponsored and state-level schemes, of becoming acquainted with the furniture of government, is one that will change the pattern of social power in rural areas. The potential of this 'opportunity space' cannot be overemphasized. Of course the material conditions for the optimal benefit to be derived from this 'opportunity space' does not exist, given the extent of grinding poverty, but the 'political space' that it has opened up will become the route through which these material conditions will be procured. Signs of this already happening are to be found in Karnataka.[59] By giving PRIs fixed form, and by prohibiting supersession, the CSAA has introduced a new spirit of competition into rural politics. This will ensure better delivery of services.

This article of faith in the potential for empowerment of the post-CSAA PRI must however be tempered by the recognition that the greatest constraint to such empowerment is the rural power structure. The source of this rural power is the pattern of landholdings which gives the landlords not just power over the material lives of those working on their land, but also access to the power of the state. They have been the main beneficiaries of the structure of decentralized administration which characterized the pre-CSAA structure of governance in rural India. The problem of landlessness, rural indebtedness, migration, high malnutrition among women and children, illiteracy, etc. can all be linked to the inability of the rural poor to benefit from even the limited opportunities created by the developmental state. This structure of rural power persists even post-SAA. This has been well documented in the case of UP.

Panchayati Raj, it appears from our case studies, despite honourable exceptions, is the raj of the big people. In the public domain, poor villagers continue to be expected to comply. Some changes have taken place, though, and the factionalism of the dominant castes in at least two cases has been confronted by empowerment from below. These cases demonstrate that panchayats fail to function even in villages where the lower castes have succeeded in securing control over the panchayats. The dominant élite retains sufficient intra-village and supra-village power which allows it to obstruct the development efforts, particularly if they are initiated by and targeted at the poor villages. Access to power, infrastructural facilities and state institutions continue to be mediated through the established land-owning families.[60]

This picture of rural power is poignantly brought out by a remark, made during the elections to the state assembly in Bihar (February 2000). When the landless Dalits of some villages where they had never voted were asked why they did not vote even though the central para-military forces were there to protect them, they replied, 'Sarkar, today we have their protection but who will protect us when they go away if we vote against the upper castes.'

The *India: Rural Development Report 1999* recognizes this link between land, markets, and social institutions like caste. It sees

land and agrarian reforms [as the] unfinished agenda of the last five decades. Even if its scope is severely restricted in the present day due to demographic pressure, access to land, its optimal use, investment and cooperation are possible only if such reforms are put in place. Land reforms is not just distribution of land. Its aims are to break the land–caste based political controls, guarantee access to technology and credit and create conditions for maximum production and marketable surplus, all so necessary for rural transformation.[61]

When this picture of rural power is read through Ambedkar's lens, we find the presence of groups which are doubly disadvantaged. Not only are they landless, i.e., have no material security, but they also have to carry the additional oppressive burden of social and cultural stigmatization. Large spaces of rural society thereby become exclusion zones for Dalits, who not only cannot enter with dignity the localities of the upper caste but also have to remain within their own ghettos. The size of this Dalit segment is put at approximately 170 million 'citizens'. The bulk of the poor 40 per cent of the population are landless agricultural labourers, a majority of whom are Dalits. The extent of their deprivation covers the whole range from land, houses and water to health and education. However, notwithstanding this great deprivation the submissiveness of an earlier era is changing and a new assertiveness is emerging through the language of rights. The journalist P. Sainath, revisiting some of the rural areas he had visited 7–8 years ago, reported at a recent workshop on Dalits and the State,[62] that the 'single biggest battle for human dignity is taking place in India today.' The Dalits are simultaneously fighting on multiple fronts.[63] This is taking place across the country and is expressed in caste violence in Tamil Nadu and caste massacres in Bihar. This aspect of violent reprisal must be recognized here as an important aspect of the upper-caste response to the new language of rights of the Dalits as well as to their increasing political empowerment through panchayati raj.[64] In rural North India there is a privatization of violence through private armies of landowners such as the Ranvir Sena who respond to Dalit demands by torching Dalit houses and raping their women and looting their villages, often in the face of a bystander state controlled by the same landed castes.[65] The story below is illustrative of this struggle.

For the past two months the southern districts of Tamil Nadu have been rocked by caste–related clashes in which 6 persons were shot dead by police while 14 more were killed during the clashes. The main reason behind these clashes was the planned effort by oppressive castes to throw out Dalits from their settlements. It is a sorry state of affairs that even the political and the state power stood beside the oppressive castes. Following this what happened at Melavalavu village on 30 June 1997 was the epitome of intolerance by high caste people. On this day just because Dalits stood for elections to the village Panchayat (Melavalavu being a reserved constituency) the high caste people of the village brutally murdered six persons, including the President and Vice-President of the Panchayat, in broad daylight. They severed the head of the Panchayat president and threw it inside a well ... The post of the Panchayat president in this village was reserved for the Dalits during the recent Panchayat elections. The high caste people, unable to face this encroachment on what they had traditionally considered their domain, protested against it and threatened the Dalits with reprisal if they contested for the post. They burnt even their houses.[66]

The murders were a result of Dalits contesting elections. The failure of the 'rule of law' to protect the vulnerable Dalits can be illustrated by what P. Sainath refers to as the seven stages that a Dalit has to go through before a court can even hear the case. These are, (i) pressure from the caste panchayat, (ii) entry fee to enter the police station, (iii) resisting a brokered compromise, (iv) paying money for filing an FIR, (v) delay in recording the statement of witnesses, (vi) coercion in the village, and (vii) 'feeding' of the judges. The struggle for a new language of rights has however begun and the CSAA has contributed to it.

Another important observation that can be made, with respect to the post-CSAA PRIs, is the entry of new political leaders into the system. The number of new entrants is nearly two and a half million,[67] a number that has revolutionary consequences for politics in India. This is particularly so as these new leaders now have legitimate authority and also since a sizeable number of them are women, Dalits and Adivasis. In addition to their potential for mobilizing citizens, and of making local government more accountable, thereby resulting in better utilization of resources,[68] these new agents in politics exert pressure on state-level leaders to improve service delivery because they represent, for the latter, a threat of replacement. Members of this group, because each represents a small constituency, ensure that the locality, both in terms of its needs and its imagination, gets a hearing in politics. Hence, minorities, in the broadest sense, find a place.

Another important observation that can be made is the enormous potential that the post-CSAA PRIs represent for incorporation of people's needs in development programmes through decentralized planning. The need for such planning has been regularly stated by the Planning Commission in its various reports, most recently in the Ninth Five Year Plan 1997–2002 document. Chapter 5 on 'Implementation, Delivery Mechanism and Institutional Development', lists ten reasons why the development programmes have so far an unsatisfactory performance record. Some of these are (i) inadequate analysis of available information during programme formulation, (ii) top-down and target-oriented rather than a bottom-up approach, (iii) lack of accountability of the implementing agencies either to the government or to the people, (iv) social sector programmes formulated without addressing the question of sustainability of benefits, (v) failure to ensure timely and adequate flow of funds to the implementing agencies, etc. Many of these impediments can be overcome by a structure of decentralized planning where the people are consulted and where they participate in the planning process.

The foregoing should, however, not convey the impression that, with the passage of the CSAA, the millenium of democracy has arrived. There are many obstacles to its arrival, ranging from bureaucratic resistance, to manipulation by rural élites, especially the nexus represented by the local politician, contractor, and criminal. I have written optimistically of its potential because the CSAA represents an institutional watershed which has brought 'the people' back into the political process. People have been given a voice. This voice, even in a situation of pervasive asymmetric power, will result in a flattening of the asymmetry, a process that can have only emancipatory consequences.

One final point needs to be made. The post-CSAA PRI experiment that has been under way for now nearly eight years has already exposed one generation to the system. It has, in these years, gained momentum and legitimacy as a result of which it has changed the agenda of politics in India. Various decentralization routes are being tried out, from Janmabhoomi in Andhra Pradesh, to 'land reform with political reform' in West Bengal, to the 'people's campaign for the ninth plan' in Kerala, to the recent devolution of sixteen subjects to PRIs in Uttar Pradesh, to the more comprehensive functional and financial devolution in Madhya Pradesh. These various initiatives show that the state governments, ruled by different political parties, have begun to compete with one another to design better and more effective mechanisms for the delivery of basic services. In the context of coalition politics at the national level, where states have become powerful actors and hence have to be secured by political parties so that they can forge winning national coalitions, decentralization appears to be the face of the future.

Notes and References

1. The material for this paper was drawn from my recent study for the World Bank entitled 'Multi-State Studyof Panchayati Raj Legislation and Administrative Reform'.
2. H. Tinker, *The Foundations of Local Self-Government in India, Pakistan and Burma*, Lalvani Publishing House, Bombay, 1967, p. 35.
3. Ibid., pp. 44, 45.
4. K.C. Sivaramakrishnan, 'Sub-State Level Governments', in Subhash C. Kashyap, D.D. Khanna and Gert W. Kueck (eds), *Reviewing the Constitution*, Shipra Publications, 2000, p. 321.
5. M. Venkatarangaiya and M. Pattabhiram (eds), *Local Government in India: Select Readings*, Allied Publishers, Bombay, 1967.
6. Peter. R. deSouza, 'Democratic Decentralization of Power in India', in D.D. Khanna and G.W.Kueck (eds), *Principles, Power, and Politics*, Macmillan, New Delhi, 1999.
7. H.D. Malaviya, *Village Panchayats in India*, Economic and Political Research Department, AICC, New Delhi, 1956, p. 247.
8. M.K. Gandhi, *Collected Works*, vol. 85, pp. 32–4.
9. Gandhi wrote a foreword for a book titled *Gandhian Constitution for Free India* by Principal Sriman Narayan Agarwal , in which he appreciated Agarwal's attempt because 'he has done what for want of time I have failed to do.' Ibid., p. 246.
10. *Constitutional Assembly Debates*, 4 Nov. 1948. Ambedkar's scorn for the intellectual Indian's romanticizing the village also says something for the class character of the discourse.
11. C.H. Hanumantha Rao, 'Decentralized Planning: An Overview of Experience and Prospects', *Economic and Political Weekly*, 25 Feb. 1989.
12. S.S. Singh. *Legislative Status of Panchayati Raj in India*, Indian Institute of Public Administration (IIPA), New Delhi, 1997, p. 19.
13. 'Now all these defects—public apathy, the election of interested parties, exaggerated regard for economy or careless extravagance, an inability to think in terms of large expenditure, lack of foresight, prejudice, unregulated recruitment of officials, mediocre quality of staff, inefficiency, delay—are all qualities which are frequently alluded to in official reports from India and Burma, as if they were peculiar to those countries. But local representative bodies almost everywhere suffer similar shortcomings in greater or lesser degree; they are part of the price of democratic government.' H. Tinker, *The Foundation of Local Self Government in India, Pakistan and Burma*, 1967, p. 5.

14. To summarise some of the supportive ideas in the case of India: (i) encourage local participation, (ii) promote equitable growth, (iii) increase accountability of local officials, (iv) increase pressure on government to choose concerns that are of priority to local people, (v) reduce costs and increase efficiency, (vi) introduce locally diverse solutions, (vii) improve maintenance of locally constructed community assets, (viii) deepen the sense of belonging, (ix) strengthen community bonds, and (x) give representation to disadvantaged groups and thereby empower them both politically and psychologically.
15. G.K. Leiten and R. Srivastava, *Unequal Partners: Power Relations and Devolution, in Uttar Pradesh*, Sage Publications, New Delhi, 1999. With respect to Uttar Pradesh they note that 'most studies have concluded that, at least until the early 1990s *Panchayat* leadership and the supporting staff have remained in the hands of the landowning upper castes.'— p. 33.
16. NIRD, *India: Rural Development Report: Regional Disparities in Development and Poverty*, Hyderabad, 1999.
17. S.P. Jain, 'The Gram Sabha: Gateway to Grassroots Democracy', *Journal of Rural Development*, vol. 16 (4) (1997), pp. 557–73.
18. Mahipal, '*Panchayati* Raj in India: Issues and Challenges', *Kurukshetra*, Aug., 1997, pp. 72–9.
19. See n. 47.
20. A point must be made here about the size of the polity. Not only is India large in population and geographical terms but it is also very diverse. Since the goal of 'good governance' is for a common constitutional order to extend and penetrate all spaces of the polity, the adoption by the ruling élite of a constitutional democratic framework has created spaces in the polity where political institutions faithful to the constitutional order have still to reach. There are empty spaces where other (non-constitutional) structures of power still operate. These must be occupied by the impersonal practices of rule-governance that underlie a constitutional democracy.
21. S.P. Ranga Rao, 'The Constitution (73rd Amendment Act) Act: What Next?' *Kurukshetra*, April, 1995, p. 11.
22. S.S. Meenakshisundaram, 'The 73rd Constitution Amendment: A Case for Further Amendment', *Journal of Rural Development*, vol. 61(4), 1997, p. 554.
23. T.R. Satish Chandra, 'Inter-Tier Allocation of Functions' in *The Administrator*, vol. XXXVIII, 1993, pp. 15–30.

24. S. Mitra, 'Inter-Tier Allocations of Responsibilities in *Panchayati* Raj Institutions', in S.P.Jain and T.W. Hochgesang (eds), *Emerging Trends in Panchayati Raj*, NIRD and Konrad Adenauer Stiftung, Hyderabad, 1995, pp. 141–53.
25. K.C. Sivaramakrishnan, 'Sub-State Level Governments', and 'Decentralization: Sub-State Level Governments', in S.C. Kashyap *et al.*, *Reviewing the Constitution*, Shipra, Delhi, 2000, pp. 3–49.
26. S. Krishna, 'Restructuring the Institutional Arrangements to Strengthen the *Panchayati* Raj', *The Administrator*, 1993, vol. XXXVIII, pp. 87–100.
27. V. Ramachandran, '*Panchayati* Raj in the Coming Years', *The Administrator*, 1993, vol. XXXVIII, pp. 1–6.
28. S.S. Meenakshisundaram, 'Personnel Policies for *Panchayats*', *The Administrator*, 1993, vol. XXXVIII, 1993, pp. 101–8.
29. S.S. Krishna, 1993, 'Restructuring ...'.
30. R. Hooja, 'Training of *Panchayati* Raj Functionaries: Some Issues', *Journal of Rural Development*, 1997, vol. 16 (4), pp. 723–37.
31. V.K. Agnihotri, *et al.*, 'Human Resources for Development for *Panchayats*', *The Administrator*, 1993, vol. XXXVIII, pp. 109–32.
32. R.C. Crook, and J. Manor, *Democracy and Decentralization in South Asia and West Africa*, ch. 2, 'Karnataka', Cambridge University Press, Cambridge, 1988, p. 46.
33. S.P. Ranga Rao, 'Autonomy: The Essence of *Panchayati* Raj', *Kurukshetra*, April, 1998, pp. 25–7.
34. Special issue on PRI Finances, *Kurukshetra*, April 1996.
35. S.K. Singh, 'Taxation Powers of *Panchayats*: A Review', in *Kurukshetra*, Dec. 1996, pp. 22–7.
36. M.A. Oomen, '*Panchayat* Finance and Issues Relating to Inter-Governmental Transfers', in S.N. Jha and P.C. Mathur (eds), *Decentralization and Local Politics*, Sage Publications, New Delhi, 1999, pp. 142–72.
37. J.M. Girglani, 'Financial Resources of *Panchayati* Raj Institutions', *The Administrator*, 1993, vol. xxxviii, pp. 39–63.
38. S. Mitra, and A.K. Dubey, 'State Finance Commissions and State PRIs Financial Relations', in *Journal of Rural Development*, vol. 16(4), 1997, pp. 685–95.
39. Remy Prudhomme, 'The Dangers of Decentralization', *The World Bank Research Observer*, 1995, vol. 10, no. 2, pp. 201–20.
40. Ibid., 'These choices are not so much whether to decentralize in general but rather what functions to decentralize, in which sectors and in which regions. In many cases the problem is not so much whether a

certain service should be provided by a central, regional, or local government, but rather how to organize the joint production of the service by the various levels'. Ibid., p. 201.

41. J. George, '*Panchayats* and Participatory Planning in Kerala', *Indian Journal of Public Administration*, 1997, vol. xliii, no. 1, p. 91.
42. A. Aziz, and P.V. Shenoy, 'District Planning: Principles and Their Organization', *Journal of Rural Development*, 1997, 16(4), pp. 575–88; A. Benninger, 'Rural Development and Decentralized Planning: Who Should Participate and How?' *The Administrator*, 1991, vol. 36, pp. 95–111.
43. State Planning Board, Ch. 13: 'Local Self-Government', *Economic Review*, Government of Kerala, 1998.
44. K.V. Sundaram, 'Decentralized Planning in the Context of the New *Panchayati* Raj System', in S.P. Jain and T.W. Hochgesang, *Emerging Trends in Panchayati Raj in India*, NIRD and Konrad Adenaeur Stifting, Hyderabad, 1995, pp. 47, 52–9.
45. See no. 65.
46. See. S.P. Jain, 'The Gram Sabha: Gateway to Grassroots Democracy', *Journal of Rural Development*, vol. 16 (4), pp. 557–73.
47. R.C. Choudhary, and R.C. Jain (eds), *Strengthening Village Democracy*, NIRD, 1999, pp. 77–80.
48. Refer to CMIE publication on *Public Finance*, 1999.
49. R.R. Prasad, and K. Suman Chandra 'Reservations for Scheduled Castes and Scheduled Tribes in *Panchayati* Raj Institutions: Policy Implications', in S.P. Jain and T.W. Hochgesang, *Emerging Trends in Panchayati Raj*, 1995, p. 47.
50. N.R. Madhava Menon, 'Democratisation of the Polity and Restructuring of the Judicial System at the Grass-Roots', *Kurukshetra*, Dec. 1995, p. 5.
51. Ibid., p. 3.
52. G.K. Leiten and R. Srivastava, *Unequal Partners: Power Relations, Devolution and Development in Uttar Pradesh,* IDPAD 23, Sage Publications, New Delhi, 1999.
53. These are reported regularly in *Panchayati Raj Update* over the past five years.
54. One recent study exploring the use of this 'opportunity space' by women is that of Poornima and Vinod Vyasulu, 'Women in Panchayati Raj: Grass Roots Democracy in Malgudi', *Economic and Political Weekly*, 25 Dec. 1999, pp. 3677–86. Six illustrations are given. Commenting on one case of Gangamma Jayeker who used her position as president of the *zilla*

panchayat to start a *mahila mandal*, and access government schemes such as TRYSEM, they see 'Gangamma Jayker as an example of the new politician emerging from the PRI system in Karnataka. Women like her would have found it impossible to make a mark in the system without the reservations. Yet, she argues this is only a first step. Without educational improvements, women will find it difficult to work the system.'

55. G.Matthew, *et al.*, 1997, 'What it Means for the Oppressed'.
56. At a conference held at the National Institute of Rural Development, in July 28/29, 1999, twenty-one recommendations were made to strengthen the *gram sabha*. R.C. Choudhury and R.C.Jain. (eds), *Strengthening Village Democracy*, NIRD, 1999, pp. 77–80.
57. It is true that so far the level of participation in the *gram sabha* has been poor because of various factors such as the time of the meeting, the location, poor publicity, size, etc. Some states are seeking to rectify this, with Madhya Pradesh seeking to introduce a fourth level of PRI, the village level. The *gram sabha* hitherto comprised of a group of villages.
58. R.C. Crook and J. Manor, *Democracy and Decentralization in South Asia and West Africa: Participation, Accountability, and Performance*. In his discussion of the working of the PRI system in Karnataka, Manor records the increased participation of disadvantaged groups since decentralization in 1987.
59. Ibid.
60. G.K. Leiten, and R. Srivastava, *Unequal Partners: Power Relations, Devolution and Development in Uttar Pradesh*, IDPAD no. 23, Sage Publications, New Delhi, 1999, p. 202.
61. NIRD, *India: Rural Development Report 1999*, p. 121.
62. Workshop on *Dalits and the State*, organized by Vikas Adhyayan Kendra, Old Goa, 2–4 Feb. 2000.
63. P. Sainath has recounted this struggle for human dignity in his series of articles on Dalits in *The Hindu*.
64. Discussant Mark Robinson's comment on the paper of Peter R. deSouza, 'Decentralization and Local Government: The "Second Wind" of Democracy in India', at the conference on Constitutional Ideas and Political Practices: Fifty Years of the Republic, 22–5 Jan. 2000.
65. The emergence of the middle castes as a political force as a result of the Green Revolution has introduced one more theatre of struggle for the Dalits who now have to fight against these castes that have benefited from the limited land reforms and are thus resistant to more radical measures of further redistribution.

66. Mohan Larbeer, 'Atrocities in Melavalavu *Panchayat*', *Panchayati Raj Update*, Govt. of Kerala, Kerala, July 1997, no. 43, p. 6.
67. M. Robinson, 'Panchayati Raj: Five Years On', paper prepared on the Regional Tripartite Interface Interactive Workshop on Panchayati Raj for the Eastern Region, Calcutta, 1999, IIMC.
68. R.C. Crook and J. Manor, *Democracy and Decentralization in South Asia and West Africa*, 1998, pp. 42–9.

16

The 'Politics of Presence' and Legislative Reservations for Women[1]

ZOYA HASAN

Although some prominent women are in the forefront of Indian politics—Sonia Gandhi, Jayalalitha Jayaram, Mamata Banerjee and Mayawati are examples—the participation of women in governance is very small, and their presence in the political system is insignificant. This notwithstanding the fact that sex equality and political rights for women are enshrined in the Constitution. Until the reservation of 33 per cent seats for women in local government bodies came into being in 1992, the gender bias pervaded all levels of governance in India. It is against this background of the continued marginalization of women in the Indian polity that the demand to reserve one-third of the seats at various levels, particularly in local governance, marks a turning point in the debate over the political rights of women. From being acclaimed as a 'revolution' of the millions of deprived women, to being dubbed as the token '*biwi* [wife] *beti* [daughter] brigade', women's bid to challenge political monopolies and enter formal political institutions has generated much discussion, interest and opposition.

In this essay I explore the controversy over reserved legislative seats for women. I describe three key moments in the development of this controversy since the 1930s: the negotiations over constitutional reforms during the closing years of British colonial rule; the discussions around a major government report on the status of women in 1974; and the present dispute over the Women's Reservation Bill which seeks to amend the Indian constitution to guarantee 33 per cent reservations for women in parliament and the state legislatures. It will be my concern here to offer a defence of gender quotas in legislative bodies. To do this, I shall at one level engage with the substantive issues raised in the debate surrounding the demand for a caste quota within the women's quota, and the arguments within the women's movement for a gender quota, irrespective of caste or community. At another level, I shall build a minimalist argument for a 'politics of presence' on the ground; argue that the presence of women in decision-making institutions can transform the political agenda.

The Nationalist Response to Quotas

The demand for women's reservation in legislatures has a long history. Legislative reservations for women were discussed in the context of constitutional reforms in the 1930s. The Government of India acts of 1919 and 1935 granted Muslims, Sikhs and Christians separate electorates. Depressed classes were also allotted a few nominated seats in 1919 and 1925, and some elected seats in 1932.[2] The Indian National Congress, opposed to special electoral rights, argued that reserved seats would irreversibly link religious identity and political power. Following its lead, women's organizations like the All India Women's Congress (AIWC), the National Council of Women of India, and the Women's India Association, though in the forefront for female enfranchisement and civil rights for women, opposed legislative reservations for women on the grounds that 'to seek any form of preferential treatment would be to violate the integrity of the universal demand of Indian women for absolute equality of political status.'[3] Nationalists all over India made statements to this effect, arguing that guarantees of women's presence in legislatures were subsidiary to the principal goal of freedom. They demanded the right to be elected to legislatures, but with 'equality and no privileges'.[4] Sarojini Naidu, who participated in the Second Round Table Conference in 1931, opposed reserved seats for women, pointing out that she represented all Indian women, even orthodox Hindu and Muslim women.[5] The key issue was absolute equality versus preferential treatment, not only of women but also of other groups such as Untouchables, Muslims and landholders.[6] Some women even opposed reservation for lower castes, doubting its efficacy. A number of Muslim women associated with the Muslim League, however, disagreed with the outright rejection of quotas. Unlike Congresswomen, they were eager to obtain reserved seats for Muslims. Even as Muslim men were unhappy at their quotas being diluted by women,[7] Begum Shah Nawaz Khan (who represented India at the first Round Table Conference in 1930) believed that women required special representation.

The colonial government disregarded the opposition to reservations from major women's organizations. Taking their commitment to group-based politics further, the Government of India Act of 1935 granted women forty-one reserved seats in the provincial legislatures as well as limited reservations in central legislatures.[8] Yet, as women protested at the communal award which had divided their ranks, the government went ahead and, what is more, subdivided the legislative seats along religious lines. The AIWC, which was in the vanguard of opposition to the constitutional provisions, nevertheless took advantage of the provision for reservations. In the 1937 elections, fifty-six women became legislators, forty-one in reserved seats, only ten in unreserved seats, and five in nominated seats. In the end, as Gail Pearson has argued, the reserved seats laid the ground for women's participation in politics and provided them with a very important foothold in legislatures.[9] Even as a turning point had been reached in their struggle for political participation, nationalist women continued to fight for universalization of participation in electoral politics on equal terms with men. This awareness remained paradigmatic in discussions on the nature of women's participation in politics until the 1970s.

After independence, the Congress government made partial attempts to fulfill the promises of constitutional equality it had made to women. non-discrimination on the basis of sex and the right to equal protection were included in the justiciable list of Fundamental Rights. Especially important was the acceptance of the principle of affirmative action for backward classes, in other words non-discrimination was compatible with programmes of reservations. The constitution through Article 16(4) permits the state to make 'any provision for the reservation of appointments or posts in favour of any backward class of citizens which, in the opinion of the state, is not adequately represented in the services under the state.' Ever since, quotas have been considered the primary instrument for achieving social justice, even though Scheduled Castes and Tribes are the only groups to have legislative seats and government jobs reserved for them. This provision was based on the understanding that disabilities derived from caste were the most conspicuous impediment to equality, and thus state intervention was necessary to break the link between the social structures of inequality and the political reflection in levels of participation and influence.

The provision for the special representation of minorities in legislatures was extensively debated in the Fundamental Rights Advisory Committee and the Minority Rights Sub-Committee of the Constituent Assembly, but the debate was overshadowed by Partition in 1947. Most Muslim representatives supported proportional representation as a mechanism to facilitate the representation of minorities in the legislature, on the ground that as a numerical minority they would therefore become a permanent minority because they would not have sufficient numbers for election to legislatures. Despite initial backing for protected minority representation, all subsequent proposals for special representation of minority groups were opposed on the grounds that it was both inimical to national unity and incompatible with secularism. It was also feared that it would aggravate communal differences.[10] The sub-committee in the main considered the cultural and religious rights of minority groups, which were left largely untouched because of the uncertainty as to whether the will of the people articulated by a parliamentary majority carried an adequate measure of legitimacy for minority communities. In other words, even though the idea of separate representation for minorities was anathema, their religious practices received support.

Changing Attitudes to Reservation

The constitution guaranteed women equal protection under the law and equal opportunity in public employment and prohibited discrimination in public places. The Hindu Code Bill changed Hindu laws of marriage, divorce and adoption to ensure that women had a measure of equal rights. The new state designed several policies to meet the needs and requirements of women. Many women were satisfied with these measures because they shared the customary view of the time that women would gain from economic growth, the principal concern of the nation. However, notwithstanding their initial promise, democracy, equality before law and universal adult franchise failed to eradicate gender inequalities.

The Government of India in 1971 appointed the Committee on the Status of Women in India (CSWI) 'to examine the constitutional, legal and administrative provisions that have a bearing on the social status of women, their education and employment and to assess the impact of these provisions.' The CSWI in its landmark report *Towards Equality* (1974) presented a scathing critique of the political process, the worsening political position of women and the inadequate positive impact of government-sponsored programmes and policies on the status of women:

Every legal measure designed to translate the constitutional norms of equality or special protection into practice has had to face tremendous resistance from the legislative and other elites. We are therefore forced to observe that all the indicators of participation, attitudes and impact come up with the same results—the resolution in social and political status of women for which constitutional equality was to be the only instrument, still remains a very distant objective ... From this point of view, though women do not lack the three recognized dimensions of inequality: Inequality of class (economic situation), status (social position) and political power. The review of the disabilities and constraints on women, which stem from the socio-cultural institutions, indicates that the majority of women are still very far from enjoying the rights and opportunities guaranteed to them by the constitution ... The social laws, that sought to mitigate the problems of women in their family life, have remained unknown to large mass of women in this country, who are as ignorant of their legal rights today as they were before Independence.[11]

This was the first unequivocal indictment of the government's promise of gender equality. The declaration that social change and development in India had adversely affected women and the bleak picture of women's status shocked many Indians.[12] Despite indications of increased women's electoral participation their influence on the political process was negligible. In the course of their interviews and interactions with women the committee found that women's lack of political equality was a matter of foremost concern for women. Consequently, women's groups pressed the committee to recommend reservations for women in the legislatures. The CSWI was however divided, and hence this recommendation was never made.

A majority of the members felt that reservation would be a 'retrograde step from the equality conferred by the constitution'.[13] They argued that 'women do not constitute a community, they are not a category'; and that women's interests should not be separated from the economic, social, and political interests of other groups, strata and classes in society.[14] Separate constituencies for women also ran the risk of narrowing their outlook. Furthermore, they expressed the concern that official policies based on distinctions between groups would harm national disunity because 'such a system of special representation may precipitate similar demands from various other communities and interests that threaten national integration'.[15] The chairperson of the CSWI, Phulrenu Guha, Union Minister for Social Welfare and the only member to have participated in the national movement, epitomized the nationalist position. Disagreeing with the proposal to reserve seats in panchayats and municipalities, she argued in her Note of Dissent that such a step would help élite women and it 'would encourage separatist tendencies and hamper national integration'.[16] In short, the exigencies of national life ruled out looking at politics from a specifically gender perspective. These arguments were reminiscent of the nationalist argument personified by Sarojini Naidu's declaration: 'I am not a feminist.' Much later, Prime Minister Indira Gandhi said much the same thing when she stated: 'I am not a feminist and I do not believe that anybody should get preferential treatment merely because she happens to be a woman.'[17] Paradoxically, at the same time she referred to women as the 'biggest oppressed minority in the world' and said Indian women were handicapped from birth.[18]

On the whole, the report argued persuasively that greater opportunities needed to be given to women to actively promote their participation in the decision-making process and to recognize the social inequities and disabilities that hamper them.[19] It, therefore, recommended the establishment of statutory women's panchayats at the local level to ensure greater participation in the political process.[20] Two members of the committee, Vina Mazumdar and Lotika Sarkar, dissented. They did not want to limit reservations to panchayats; they favoured reservations in parliament as well. Disregarding the category versus community way of thinking they argued that the active participation of women in the political process would help to widen equality.[21]

This signalled a break from the official discourse on women and reservations. Mazumdar explained this shift in the following words:

Over the last twenty-five years, however, the Indian women's movement, as we know it, has done a complete volte-face on this position. We have found our understanding of nation building changing radically as we sought to come closer to the life experiences, the unacknowledged wisdom and knowledge, the priorities and perspectives of the poor peasant and working women in the informal sector across the country, forcing us to raise questions about the meaning of development, of freedom, traditions, modernization, social progress and the dynamics of economic, cultural and demographic changes, that we had never asked before.[22]

The Question of Political Participation

Twenty-five years later the representation of women in India's central and state legislatures continues to be low. The average percentage of women elected to the Lok Sabha comprises between 6 to 7 per cent seats, among the lowest in the world. The percentage of women in the first Lok Sabha, which was 4.4 per cent, rose to 8.20 per cent in 1999. Within this, the number of Muslim women is extremely small. Only 7 Muslim women have ever been elected to the Lok Sabha over the past fifty years. The situation is much worse in the state assemblies. The average percentage of women in state assemblies over the past fifty years was 4 per cent. The pattern is similar in cabinets. In the council of ministers, both at the national and state levels, women are severely under-represented. India has never had more than one female cabinet minister at a time; in 1996, not one woman headed any of the standing committees of parliament.

Political parties have taken no initiative to reduce gender disparity in elected bodies. Two years ago, the Congress party adopted a 33 per cent target for women in the selection of candidates and positions in the party organization but less than 12 per cent tickets were actually allotted to women in the 1999 elections. Sonia Gandhi attributed the deficit to internal party pressures. Most political parties pass on the blame to women themselves (i.e. their low winnability) although it is well known that in comparison to that of men the performance of women candidates is better.[23] This under-representation exists despite rising women's voter turnout, which was 55.64 per cent, only three per cent less than the average. Political parties recognize the importance of increased female voter turnout, yet representative institutions work in ways that do not always ensure sufficient policy concern for women. Eventually, it is this policy neglect and political exclusion that provides a justification for reserved quotas, and a good reason for what Anne Phillips has described as a 'politics of presence', in which excluded groups are guaranteed fair representation, as opposed to a 'politics of ideas', in which choices between policies are made on the basis of the ideologies and programmes of political parties.[24]

Quotas in the 1990s

A gender quota in legislatures is a contentious issue. It excites and annoys the partisan and non-partisan alike. While there are major differences among women's groups on the issue of reservations and more on the question of working closely with the state, a broad cross-section has moved in that direction. There is a growing consensus that representation in decision-making is vital for women's development and an increasing acceptance of quotas as the way to do it.[25] It has been pointed out that quotas are needed to break the social barriers that prevent women from effective participation in politics. A large body of women's opinion endorsed quotas as a necessary means of encouraging women's presence in legislatures. A countrywide survey conducted by the Centre for the Study of Developing Societies in 1996 showed that 79 per cent women supported active women's participation in politics and 75 per cent supported reservations in legislatures. Likewise an all-India survey on the status of Muslim women conducted in 2000 reveals that 78 per cent women endorse reservations. It is significant that a high proportion of women say that they aspire to contest local elections and hold positions in local and state governments.[26] This is undoubtedly an indication of the transformative effect of reservations for women at the third tier of panchayats, because the relatively greater proximity between elected and electors promotes responsiveness and accountability.

This represents an unmistakeable shift from the nationalist position, and also from the early days of the contemporary women's movement, which scoffed at the very idea of reservation and representation on the grounds that 'such representation would lead to deradicalization, and that women engaging in it would put their own political interests before the feminist cause.'[27] There are two important reasons for this shift. The last two decades have seen the growth of the women's movement, with an expanding base in urban India. Questions of gender inequality were at the forefront of these movements. Spurred by the proliferation of women's groups and the socio-economic ferment and wider developments in Indian politics (the rise of communalism and religious revivalism) and society (lower-caste assertions and caste conflicts), the gender question had been raised at different levels, especially the caste and class basis of gender inequalities.[28] Although the women's movement addressed a range of issues, it put less effort into electoral politics and therefore did not make as much impact. Women's representation in parliament actually declined to 3.7 per cent in 1977, the lowest ever. It improved to 5.2 per cent in 1989 but was only slightly better than the 4.2 per cent of women who were elected in 1952. During this period the women's movement began to search for new ways of wielding its influence over the state and began to consider ways of increasing women's representation in politics.

This period witnessed a confluence of two trends: on the one hand, the state's attempts to foster closer links with social movements and non-governmental organizations, and on the other, the attempt by some women's movement activists to exercise power within the state.[29] From the 1980s, quotas in legislative assemblies became a major demand of the women's movement. The National Perspective Plan for Women prepared under Rajiv Gandhi's government in 1988 recommended that 33 per cent of seats in all elected assemblies, from village to union level, be reserved for women, and political parties promote women's electoral representation by alloting at least 33 per cent of their tickets to women. In 1989, the most important effort to involve women in governance was through quotas in panchayats—and this has proved to be extremely significant against the background of increased women's activism and the state-backed effort to provide greater opportunities to women in local governance. Part of the wider move towards political decentralization, the promotion of panchayati raj institutions over the last few years has sought to ensure adequate and active participation of women by providing quotas for various deprived groups. The 73rd and 74th Constitutional Amendments of 1992 provided reserved quotas for women in local-level institutions in India. In consequence, the number of women elected to panchayats increased to one million. At present there are 655,629 women members in *gram panchayats*, 37,523 in the *panchayat samitis*, and 3161 in *zila parishads*.[30] Despite social and institutional constraints, women's participation has had a significant impact both in terms of the subjective dimension (namely, the way in which women see themselves in their new roles), as well as the objective dimension (namely, the actual developmental impact).[31] Several studies have documented, for instance, that women representatives give greater priority to issues such as drinking water supply, installation of pumps, playgrounds, roads, community infrastructure, schooling, etc.[32] Newspaper reports highlight instances of women succeeding as panchayat leaders who have made a strong case for reservation of seats for them in the legislatures.[33] The impressive efforts of women demonstrate that panchayats are beginning to play an important role in the empowerment of women.[34] In light of this experience the basic argument for reserved seats in legislatures is the same: that these measures are historical correctives to the under-representation of women, which is gross, and structurally therefore unlikely to be rectified in the normal course of things.

In a representation submitted to the chairperson and members of the Parliamentary Select Committee, seven women's organizations urged the committee to recommend the passage of the legislation in the Lok Sabha to reserve 33 per cent legislative seats for women. The pressure mounted both by women in panchayats and women within political parties obliged the government to table the Constitution (Eighty-First Amendment) Bill, 1996, to provide not less than one-third of the total number of seats for women in parliament and the state assemblies. Furthermore, one-third seats of the 22 per cent seats reserved for Scheduled Castes and Tribes were to be reserved for women from these groups. Together this adds up to 33 per cent reserved seats for women in national and state legislatures.

This Women's Reservation Bill (WRB) has been listed for debate in every session of parliament since its introduction in 1996, but a handful of leaders have stalled it each time. A slightly modified version, the Constitution (Eighty-Fifth Amendment) Bill, 1999, was introduced in the Lok Sabha on 23 December 1999, but no discussion was allowed, with MPs tearing up the bill each time it was listed for discussion. The result has been that neither of the two bills has ever been discussed or voted upon.

All major political parties had professed support for women's quotas in their election manifestos and to this day many parties still claim to support the WRB.[35] In the event, as one newspaper headline put it, 'it is indeed a curious case of a lot of will, but no Bill.'[36] The most vocal opponents are small but powerful parties like the Rashtriya Janata Dal (RJD), Samata Party, Samajwadi Party (SP), and Bahujan Samaj Party (BSP). They contend that élite upper-caste women will monopolize reserved seats because they are better educated. Phoolan Devi, a lower-caste MP, disparaged the WRB because women with 'short hair and lipstick' would get into parliament while OBC women would not: 'Our (OBC) women are uneducated and cannot understand anything so unless there is reservations for them they cannot come to Parliament.' Similarly, Uma Bharati, a lower-caste leader of the Bhartiya Janata Party, underlined the limitations of backward-class women and their inability to enter legislatures without quotas. These groups and the parties representing them have been most strident in opposing the WRB. Their combined strength in the Lok Sabha is not even a tenth of its total membership and yet they have managed to even prevent a debate on the bill, which means they could not have stalled the legislation without the unspoken support of MPs from other parties. In short, the relentless opposition encountered by the WRB since it was tabled in the Lok Sabha four years ago points to a more substantial and determined opposition that goes beyond the so-called caste parties mentioned above—indeed it cuts across caste, class and party boundaries.

Some political leaders have pushed for a sub-quota for Muslim women as well, but this is scarcely relevant at a time when the legislative representation of Muslims is extremely meagre, perhaps the lowest ever. The percentage of Muslims (who make up 11.7 per cent of the population) in legislative bodies is a mere 4 per cent. Several key states have no Muslim representatives. Muslims have been a socio-economically disadvantaged group since Partition, but there were no particular efforts to improve their representation in legislatures or public employment. The principal 'privilege' they have is immunity for their personal laws, which permits multiple marriages and easy divorce. Successive governments have refused to address the problem of Muslim under-representation or shown willingness to discuss it openly, even as the last two decades are replete with all kinds of group ordering and group recognition by government for the purpose of representation.

State policy towards minorities has taken three principal forms: Federal arrangements in which state and linguistic boundaries coincide, thus providing a degree of autonomy; the right of religious minorities to establish and administer their own schools fully supported by public funds; and separate personal laws concerning marriage, divorce, custody and adoption of children. This has been the preferred way of dealing with the problem of minorities, thus conveniently sidestepping the fact that most Muslims are poor and illiterate, with very little presence either in government or in legislatures. So far the issue has not even been seriously debated, with the result that the largest minority in the country is severely under-represented in decision-making. While ways must be found to remedy this under-representation, they ought not to be tied to reservations for women as the issue of Muslim under-representation cannot be addressed piecemeal. The solution is more generous politics aimed at accommodating a plurality of interests on grounds of gender, caste and community.

The substantive issue is not Muslim under-representation but concerns the demand raised by backward-caste leaders for a caste sub-quota in the women's quota. The backward castes represent a powerful constituency in democratic politics. Caste-based mobilization has always been a marked feature of Indian politics, but it is much stronger today than when India became independent. Adult franchise and democracy have produced radical changes. No longer will caste groups accept Brahminical ordering of caste hierarchy and status, which implies that there is an even greater emphasis on caste identity and strategies of mobilization based on them. The positive discrimination policy culminating in the 1990 central government decision to grant job reservations to Other Backward Castes (OBCs), the rise of lower-caste parties and the realignment of the power structure on the ground have opened up opportunities for them to enter the political system.[37] Through these strategies the lower castes have succeeded in breaking the upper caste political monopoly. Today the Scheduled Castes and Backward Castes constitute over two-fifths of the members of the Lok Sabha in contrast to a negligible presence in the 1950s and 1960s. However, this impressive change has not benefited lower caste women. The political élite and particularly the lower-caste leadership remain stubbornly male. There are hardly any OBC female MPs even as OBC men have greatly increased their numbers in parliament.

The most strident opposition to women's quotas has come from male politicians who fear that their political careers would be put at risk. Some of them worry that women's reservations will dilute the lower-caste challenge to upper-caste domination. According to them, women's quotas are a means to re-establish the monopoly of the upper castes because they will corner the benefits of quotas. There is however no major conflict between gender and caste; indeed, quotas are likely to facilitate the entry of women from all castes and communities into legislatures. Unlike caste quotas, women's quotas will not alter caste equations. They will change male–female equations and give greater opportunity to women to contest elections. That is why parties would have to find suitable candidates from the same castes for seats currently held by OBC members.

Furthermore, while caste prejudice still exists in varying forms, the belief that OBC women are at a particular disadvantage appears to be a trifle misplaced, not only because it treats them as a homogeneous community, but also because it places them outside the prevailing political milieu which favours the numerically large lower castes in constituencies dominated by them. It is the sheer numerical weight of OBCs that enabled the OBC men to gain entry into state legislatures and parliament without legislative reservations. The same logic will be true for women. Moreover, it is highly unlikely that political parties, especially lower-caste parties, would give legislative tickets to upper-caste women in OBC-dominated constituencies. Even without quotas, women from these groups have managed to win more legislative seats than other groups. In Bihar there are only ten women MLAs, but of them, five belong to OBCs, two each to the Scheduled Tribes and Castes, and only one from the upper caste. However, male domination is more striking: male legislators completely outnumbered women within the OBC group, which suggests that the principal reason for the under-representation of OBC women in public life is gender discrimination. Thus, the conflict is not between women of different deprived groups but between men and women of the same group. This issue has become contentious because the emergence of women as a significant political grouping during the last decade has happened simultaneously with another transformation: change in the caste composition of legislatures and the growing presence of backward castes in these institutions. These two concurrent developments—women and lower-caste assertions—have produced a political stalemate on the question of women's reserved seats in legislatures. Women's quotas are aimed at correcting the denial of representation to women in decision-making by virtue of being women and the total failure of political parties to rectify this injustice.[38]

Curiously, lower-caste leaders who have so assiduously emphasized their commitment to the interests of backward-class women were prepared to break the stalemate if the 33 per cent quota were reduced to 10–15 per cent. In other words, the issue was never sub-quotas for OBC women, but a very high women's quota. A number of women leaders have correctly pointed out that reducing the proportion defeats the very purpose of quotas, as it would mean that not more than 7–8 per cent women candidates could emerge as winners, a proportion they have already attained without reservations. However, the OBC leaders rationalize the lowering of the women's quota on the grounds of scarcity of experienced women. They argue that it would be difficult to find so many women contestants for legislative seats.[39] This argument completely ignores the leadership potential of millions of elected women in panchayats. It is even more untenable because it presumes that parties chose existing elected representatives on merit. What's more, it clearly shows that the problem is not the caste sub-quota, but the gender divide over women's quotas. More importantly, the frequent postponement and deferral in the Lok Sabha of the WRB reveal that hostility is not restricted to lower-caste politicians; rather their vociferous opposition has simply made it easier for a more diverse group of male politicians to scuttle women's quotas. Meanwhile, the government has decided to set aside the WRB and find alternative ways of increasing women's representation.

'The Politics of Presence' and Representation

Why is gender singled out as a problematic category in the context of reservation? Is there a basis for a distinction between women as a group and caste and communities as a group? Should the category of women have preference over other group identities? The debate over quotas echoes feminist debates elsewhere about the status of women as a group, given their multiple locations in the polity. In India the picture is complicated by the heterogeneity of society and the existence of numerous social groups demanding preferential treatment. There are at least two pro-women arguments and one pro-woman and identity–ideology based (implicitly quota within quota) position within the women's movement. Recognizing women as a disadvantaged group, a powerful feminist case for women's reservations has justified affirmative action to redress the historical and continued disadvantages suffered by women regardless of caste and class. In short, reservations are necessary to expand equality of opportunity and to make real the formal equality given by the constitution. The most vocal advocates of this position are the Left parties and Left groups, but this position is widely shared by women's groups and women in general. A former Left MP summed up the position in this way: 'Though reservations policy per se is not democratic, it is nevertheless necessary to rectify existing imbalances. It is a partial measure, but one that is unavoidable if women are to participate effectively in politics.'[40]

The second position is pro-woman but against reservations. Madhu Kishwar, the editor of *Manushi* (a journal about women and society) has suggested an alternative proposal. Opposed to reservations, which according to her are unnecessary because 'our country has a well-entrenched tradition whereby any party, politician or public figure who tries to bad mouth women in public or opposes moves in favour of women's equality is strongly disapproved of',[41] she concedes that Indian democracy has failed to include women in its purview because of the Gandhian legacy that saw women's role in politics as one of self-sacrifice rather than as a bid for power, and more recently because of the corruption and criminalization of politics.[42] Concentrating on women's interests, she advocates a scheme under which parties should field at least thirty per cent women candidates.

The former Chief Election Commissioner M.S. Gill favoured the alternative of mandatory quotas of tickets by every recognized party. This requires all recognized parties to field women in one-third seats in every state for parliament and one-third seats in each region of the state (defined as a group of 15–20 contiguous assembly constituencies) for state assemblies. Parties failing to do so should lose the Election Commission's recognition. This requires an amendment of the Representation of People's Act, 1951, to make it mandatory for parties to allot one-third tickets to women. However, given the gendered response to women's participation in politics and the weakness of women's voices within political parties and alliances between party women and the women's movement, it is unlikely that parties will agree to an amendment that would oblige them to give one-third nominations to women. At most they will concede 10–15 per cent seats to women. The new proposal has received the support of many parties and several smaller women's groups, which believe that the original WRB will simply never be passed owing to the powerful opposition against it and partly because it is not clear that reservation of geographical constituencies is the best route, given all the problems of the rotation system. The WRB, which is valid only for 15 years, proposes that every constituency will in the next 15 years, at least for one term, be represented by a woman. A system of lots will decide the rotation of seats and the schedule will be decided in advance to avoid uncertainties. Critics of the WRB argue that a legislator who knows that his seat will be reserved for a woman in the next election will only be interested in making a quick buck and not serve the constituency. In other words the principle of rotation would destabilize and destroy legislative careers.[43] Besides, a rotation system, it is said, will further diminish the accountability of legislators. A mandatory quota of party tickets for women, on the other hand, has the added advantage of setting in motion party reforms that will change the complexion of party politics since it will be in the interest of parties to select politically active women.

However, Left parties and the Congress Party, particularly the Leader of the Opposition, Sonia Gandhi, have opposed this proposal. Left-wing women's organizations, especially the All India Democratic Women's Association (AIDWA), the largest women's organization in the country, have criticized this proposal as a 'compromise formula' that will only ensure tickets but not seats for women. Critics fear that political parties will allot unwinnable seats to women, given the poor track record of parties in nominating women candidates. It is true that most parties in India have uneven influence at the constituency, state, and national levels so that party leaders may well farm out unwinnable seats to women.

The third position derives from a growing body of feminist politics that pays attention to group identity and the politics of competing identities of caste/community and women. There are two identifiable positions here. The first one argues that public policies must be judged in terms of their sensitivity to the identities of people for whom they are designed.[44] Therefore justification for women's quota must move beyond an evaluation of consequences and pay attention to identity concerns, which is a more fruitful way of understanding and ensuring the representation of women in legislative bodies. As against this, there are those who support women's quota as well as a sub-quota, who nevertheless point out that the timing of the WRB and the strong support for it cannot be explained solely in terms of women's rights. Rather, feminist and upper-caste concerns have joined together at this moment to create a general acceptability of women's reservations, which is capable of restoring upper-caste and class control of politics. Therefore the lower-caste demand for sub-quotas for lower-caste women is justified. Moreover, identity is not pre-political, it does not exist independently of ideology, and presence is constituted by a number of identifications, of which gender is only one: it alone does not guarantee representation. If the category of woman is produced by political mobilization, then quotas for women cannot be promoted in isolation from quotas for other marginalized groups in society.[45]

There are however critical questions here, in particular arguments that relate to the wider issue of 'representation' versus 'presence' of women from lower castes and minorities. The answer to these questions must deal with the key issue of competing identities of caste, community, and women. Women are seldom, if ever, defined as a 'cultural group', despite the fact that women do have a shared history and shared experiences.[46] Given the dispersal of identities across class, caste, religion, and other axes, gender cannot be the sole rallying point for women. However, despite their numerous differences, women can be conceived of as a category on the basis of their oppression in a world defined by a sexual division of labour. Besides, notwithstanding all the differences in feminist positions as to whether the concept of woman constitutes a universal category, the fact is that for some purposes and at some levels they continue to act as such and the world continues to treat them as though they represent a category. Thus, at one level, women from a particular group that has shared experiences of social discrimination can be seen as a group. At another level, these experiences cannot be taken to form a permanent cultural group with predetermined identities that necessitate quotas within quotas. As a number of critics of sub-quotas have pointed out, it is difficult to see how any sub-quota is possible without a further sub-quota for those listed as most backward within the sub-quota of OBC women. Though the claim for sub-quotas emanated from an anxiety that élite women should not be allowed to corner the benefits of reservations, it does not differentiate between privileged and less privileged women within the OBCs. It has raised never-ending disputes over which groups of women should be eligible for reservations.[47] The quotas within quotas can distort the practice of representation, because in the course of redressing political imbalance it tends to valorize identity-based representation, which means, for example, that only Muslim women can represent Muslim women or that Tamil Hindus can only represent Tamil Hindus. Given India's stunning social diversity and the high level of polarization in the polity, the logic of such distinction and division can go on ceaselessly. Besides it is difficult to restrict it to excluded groups.

Conclusion

There has clearly been far greater resistance to legislative reservation for women than to reservations in panchayats and municipal bodies. This may be due to the fact that parliamentarians who passed the two constitutional amendments were not likely to be personally affected by their implementation.[48] But legislative quotas affect them directly. As noted earlier, large numbers of women support the active participation of women in politics and reservations for women in legislative bodies might be the only way to guarantee this. A number of doubts have been raised about legislative reservations, ranging from the argument that such a provision would ghettoize women in politics, to the fear that a quota system would only result in women fighting one another in women-only constituencies, which will not give them the confidence or experience to hold their own, no matter who their opponents. In effect, a measure seeking to obliterate gender divisions will end up creating new gender divisions. Then there is the widely shared uneasiness that quotas encourage proxy politics and women representatives will be pawns manipulated by vested interests in family and society. On the whole these arguments have a ring of truth, but they are in the main truer at the local and state levels than at the parliamentary level. Although the power of women MPs is generally limited, and like most MPs they are more likely to support party agendas than women's agendas, yet many women MPs have been influential leaders in their own right. Many of them have risen to power through institutional channels rather than as appendages of men. Of course, the power of these women to influence policy agendas would be improved if they were more closely connected with the women's movement and organizations.[49] This requires women legislators to forge closer ties with women in office. It is probable that women will better represent women's interests as well as focus attention on such issues as poverty, housing, unemployment, and health care.

While it is quite possible that élite women are expected to outnumber poor women in election to legislatures, poor women are anyway unlikely to be elected in the absence of reservations. There is an understandable apprehension that participation and gaining entry into institutions may conservatize women, but participation in political institutions can also provide opportunities of engaging with and being able to influence state policies and agendas.[50] As Amrita Basu has argued:

> One important reason for supporting reservations in parliament, for all its inadequacies, stems from a recognition both of the state's importance to determining women's life chances and yet the dangers of becoming excessively dependent on the state. Reservations provide a way for the women's movement to engage the state while diversifying its focus from the courts and legislature

to the electoral system. Working through several branches of the state simultaneously rather than focusing exclusively on one reveals the advantages and disadvantages of each.[51]

If the purpose of legislative reservations is to alter the distribution of power and resources in elected bodies where decisions are taken which affect everyone, then surely there should be more women in these institutions. This will rectify the skewed character of the current representation in parliament, which does not reflect the characteristics of the total population. Reserved seats for women in legislatures will not improve opportunities for women in public employment, yet representation aimed at providing access to decision-making in elected legislative bodies can bring about a change in the norms and principles that govern the distribution of resources. As such, there is an argument to be made for the greater presence of women in legislatures and decision-making bodies on the grounds that it provides them with a very important political resource through which they can negotiate structural change. In that case, women's quotas may well transform the quality of public life. Political participation in the decision-making processes is one mechanism through which such radical change might take place, and this could undercut the force of gender in politics and alter the nature of power itself.

Notes and References

1. This essay evolved from a draft on *Reservations for Women and Minorities* presented at the conference on Constitutional Ideas and Practice: Fifty Years of the Republic, organized by the University of Pennsylvania Institute for the Advanced Study of India, New Delhi, in January 2000. A revised version of this was paper presented at a panel on Multiculturalism and Indian Women at the American Philosophy Association, New York, in December 2000 and the University of Chicago Law School in January 2001. I am extremely grateful to Gurpreet Mahajan, Ritu Menon, Martha Nussbaum, and Eswaran Sridharan for their comments.
2. Laura Dudley Jenkins, 'Competing Inequalities: The Struggle for Legislative Seats for Women in India', *International Review of Social History* 44,1999, Supplement.
3. Gail Pearson, 'Reserved Seats—Women and the Vote in India', in J. Krishnamurti (ed.), *Women in Colonial India: Essays on Survival, Work and the State*, Oxford University Press, New Delhi, 1989, p. 16.

4. Ibid., p. 7.
5. Geraldine Forbes, *Women in Modern India*, Cambridge University Press, Cambridge, 1996, p. 97.
6. Ibid., p. 200.
7. Ibid.
8. *Towards Equality: Report of the Committee on the Status of Women in India,* Government of India, Ministry of Social Welfare, Government of India, New Delhi, 1974, p. 356.
9. Gail Pearson, 'Reserved Seats', p. 199.
10. Rachna Bajpai, 'Constituent Assembly Debates and Minority Rights', *Economic and Political Weekly*, 27 May 2000, p. 2000.
11. *Toward Equality, Report of the Committee on the Status of Women in India,* 1974, p. 303.
12. Geraldine Forbes, *Women in Modern India*, p. 227.
13. *Towards Equality*, p. 303.
14. Ibid., p. 304.
15. Ibid.
16. Phulrenu Guha's Note of Dissent, *Towards Equality*, p. 354.
17. Indira Gandhi, 'What Does"Modern" Mean?' in an address delivered at Miranda House, Delhi University. Cited in Geraldine Forbes, *Women in Modern India*, p. 233.
18. Ibid., p. 233.
19. Ibid., p. 304.
20. Radha Kumar, 'From Chipko to Sati: The Contemporary Indian Women's Movement', in Amrita Basu (ed.), *The Challenge of Local Feminisms*, Westview Press, Boulder, Colorado, 1995.
21. Lotika Sarkar and Vina Mazumdar, Note of Dissent, *Towards Equality*, p. 357.
22. Vina Mazumdar, 'Historical Soundings', *Seminar*, Sept. 1997, p. 15.
23. *Statesman*, 11 Sept. 1999.
24. Anne Phillips, *Politics of Presence*, Oxford University Press, Oxford, 1995.
25. Shirin Rai and Kumud Sharma, 'Democratizing the Indian Parliament: the Reservation for Women Debate', in Shirin Rai (ed.), *International Perspectives on Gender and Democratization*, Macmillan, London, 2000.
26. This information is drawn from an all-India survey on the status of Muslim women undertaken by the author and Ritu Menon for a project on the Diversity of Muslim Women's Lives in India, Nehru Memorial Museum and Library, New Delhi, 2000.
27. Radha Kumar, *History of Doing: An Illustrated Account of Movements for Women's Rights and Feminism in India, 1800–1900*, Kali for Women, New Delhi,1993.

28. Semanthini Niranjana, 'Transitions and Reorientations: On the Women's Movement in India', in Peter Ronald deSouza (ed.), *Contemporary India: Transitions*, Sage Publications, New Delhi, 2000, pp. 268–9.
29. Amrita Basu, 'Women's Activism, State and Democracy', p. 6.
30. *Human Development in South Asia 2000: The Gender Question,* Mahbub ul Haque Human Development Centre, Oxford University Press, Karachi, p.143.
31. Ibid., p. 42.
32. Niraja Gopal Jayal, 'Gender and Decentralization', mimeo, Delhi, 2000.
33. 'Some Good News', *The Hindu*, 29 July 2001.
34. *Human Development in South Asia 2000: The Gender Question*, p. 143.
35. '"If 500 MPs are supporting the WRB, why is the will of 42 who are opposed to it prevailing. What's more since the relevant party—the women—want it, it is difficult to understand the reason for it not being put to vote", asked Women's Political Watch in a memorandum submitted to the Speaker of the Lok Sabha.' *The Hindu,* 8 Dec. 2000. However the difficulties encountered in the passage of the WRB clearly indicate that more than 42 MPs were opposed to it.
36. Ibid.
37. *The Hindu,* 21 Dec. 1999
38. Ibid., p. 34.
39. A recent study of 2,200 elected representatives of panchayats in Madhya Pradesh, Uttar Pradesh, and Rajasthan, by Nirmala Buch, former Secretary in the Ministry of Rural Development, demolishes the myth of ineffectiveness of women in this role. She argues that the presence of nearly one million women in panchayats and municipalities should set at rest 'the fears of proxyism and control of posts by élite women'. Among the 843 women representatives studied, the largest percentage of chairpersons and panchayat members was from the OBCs. Significantly, Uttar Pradesh had the largest number of OBC chairpersons and members. *Frontline,* 21 Jan. 2000.
40. Malini Bhattacharya, 'Democracy and Reservation', *Seminar,* 457, Sept. 1997, pp. 23–4.
41. Madhu Kishwar, 'Women and Politics: Beyond Quotas', *Economic and Political Weekly,* 26 Oct. 1997.
42. Ibid.
43. Psephologist Yogendra Yadav made this point at a symposium on women's reservation in Lady Shri Ram College, University of Delhi, Jan. 2001.
44. Meena Dhanda, 'Representation for Women: Should Feminists Support Quotas', *Economic and Political Weekly,* 21 Aug. 2000, p. 2972.

45. Nivedita Menon, 'Elusive "Woman": Feminism and Women's Reservation Bill', *Economic and Political Weekly*, 28 October 2000 pp. 3837–41.
46. Uma Narayan, 'Thinking About the "Culture" in "Multiculturalism"', presentation for APA Panel: Multiculturalism and Indian Women, New York, December 2000.
47. Rosalind O'Hanlon and David Washbrook argue that this is precisely the trouble with the principle of self-representation enshrined in the politics of identity: the idea that there can be unitary and centred subjects who are able to speak for themselves and present their experiences in their own authentic voices. 'After Orientalism: Culture, Criticism and Politics in the Third World', *Comparative Studies in History and Society*, vol. 34: 1, Jan. 1992.
48. Stephanie Tawa Lama-Rewal, 'Women in the Calcutta Municipal Corporation: A Study in the Context of the Debate on the Women's Reservation Bill', Centre de Sciences Humaines, Occasional Paper, New Delhi, no. 2, 2001.
49. Amrita Basu, 'Women's Activism, State and Democracy', *Journal of Democracy*, forthcoming, p. 10.
50. Ibid., p. 11.
51. Ibid., p. 14.

Index